Participative Management and Culture

WS 2

11 -2009

Erna Szabo

Participative Management and Culture

A Qualitative and Integrative Study
in Five European Countries

PETER LANG
Frankfurt am Main · Berlin · Bern · Bruxelles · New York · Oxford · Wien

Bibliographic Information published by the Deutsche Nationalbibliothek
The Deutsche Nationalbibliothek lists this publication in the Deutsche Nationalbibliografie; detailed bibliographic data is available in the internet at <http://www.d-nb.de>.

Gedruckt mit finanzieller Unterstützung des
Linzer Hochschulfonds und der Wissenschaftshilfe
der Wirtschaftskammer Oberösterreich.

ISBN-10: 3-631-55619-5
ISBN-13: 978-3-631-55619-1
US-ISBN 0-8204-8709-0

© Peter Lang GmbH
Europäischer Verlag der Wissenschaften
Frankfurt am Main 2007
All rights reserved.

Printed in Germany 1 2 3 4 5   7

www.peterlang.de

To Lea

Contents

Tables

Figures

Chapter 1

Introduction

The term participation describes a specific form of social interaction applied in such diverse areas as family, sports, politics and business organisations, as illustrated by the following examples: Participation takes place whenever children are involved in the family holiday decision-making process. The sharing of parental responsibilities is also a highly debated question of participation for example in Austria, my home country, where the mother is (still) chiefly responsible for childcare. We also use the term participation with respect to various types of social interaction such as in sports teams or the involvement of the general public in political decision-making. In a business context, participation exists when works council members or union representatives take part in the strategic decision-making on their corporation's supervisory board. Other examples include financial participation of employees via stock ownership as well as participation of subordinates in managerial decision-making.

This book looks at participation in a business context, considering in detail participation in managerial decision-making, i.e. how and to what extent subordinates and/or possibly other/additional individuals are involved in the managerial decision-making processes faced by their superiors as part of their managerial role. This type of participation is typically referred to as *direct* and *informal* participation (e.g. Dachler & Wilpert, 1978). Direct participation means immediate involvement as compared to involvement via representatives, such as works council members. Informal participation refers to the extent of actual involvement independent of organisation-wide agreements or even more formalised arrangements such as legislation.

The scope of this research is best illustrated by a simple triangle. The base line of the triangle points to the fact that two sets of research fields are combined: The *participation* focus aims to reach a holistic understanding of what participation means and how it is enacted in various contexts. The *culture* perspective leads to an exploration of potential cultural influences on participation, raising questions of how and why both meaning and enactment of participation vary between cultures.

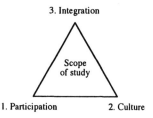

3. Integration

Scope
of study

1. Participation   2. Culture

The *integration* aspect completes the triangle and relates to the research design itself and to the embedding of the current study in existing research and literature.

Ad 1. Participation in managerial decision-making is a complex social phenomenon and it has been a popular research area for many years or even decades. According to Vroom & Jago (1988), two perspectives exist on decision-making. The first perspective concerns the *decision* itself, including defining the problem, generating alternatives and finding a satisfactory solution. The second perspective deals with the *process* of decision-making, which covers both social activities and decisions. It includes deciding whom to consult for solving a given problem, defining which parts of the problem to share with others and determining what kind of setting to choose, e.g. a group meeting or one-on-one conversation. This second perspective on decision-making deals with participation and the issue of managers defining "how to decide" (Vroom & Jago, 1988, p. 6).

Participation is a research area, which has been of great interest to me for a number of years. I have been part of a research group headed by Gerhard Reber at the Johannes Kepler University (JKU) in Linz, which focuses on the cross-cultural variation of participation based on the Vroom/Yetton (1973) decision-making model. As part of the GLOBE project dealing with culture, leadership and organisations (House et al., 2004), I realised that employees in countries belonging to the Germanic Europe cluster have a "voice", i.e. more rights and possibilities for participation, than their counterparts in many other countries (Szabo et al., 2002). Having collected the Austrian data for the Event Management database (Smith et al., 2002), I was intrigued by the country-specific degrees to which managers in different counties rely on their subordinates when handling such organisational events as hiring new employees, designing work processes or replacing office equipment.

This book reviews some of the main theoretical positions concerning participation as well as empirical research in the cross-cultural field and concludes that the results are rather fragmented. My study follows up on this very point by looking at participation in its complexity, e.g. with regard to underlying values, principles guiding managerial behaviour, range of participants in the decision-making process, situational context and cultural embedding.

When beginning the write-up of the study I was faced with the question of how to introduce the very phenomenon studied, not least in the book title. Talking about *participation* did not seem ideal since this term is broad and even possibly misleading. *Participative leadership* was an option, because it highlights the aspect of social interaction. However, I felt that this term concentrates too much on the *person* of the leader/manager as well as on the exclusive interaction with subordinates. It does not sufficiently reflect the participative situation (Vroom, 1993) and the extended context, in other words the holistic phenomenon I set out to study. Furthermore, the term leadership might provide the impression that my study focuses exclusively on top management, which is not the case. *Participative decision-making* was another alternative considered. Although this term indeed points to the very focus of the study, the connotations associated with it are too narrow, similar to the term participative leadership discussed above, and furthermore the term highlights the decision-making aspect more than the participation aspect. Consequently, I decided to use the term *participative management*, because "management" in combination with "participation", in my understanding, refers to the way in which and to what extent managers include their subordinates and/or other people in their own work, without excluding the context in which the interaction takes place. I would like to stress that the use of this term neither limits the concept (1) to a management *initiative* in the sense of subordinate involvement at the discretion of the superior, nor (2) to an interaction taking place *exclusively* between superior and subordinates.

Ad 2. The *culture* perspective of the current study ties in with the culture-specific position (in contrast to a culture-free position) I take with regard to such social phenomena as management and participation. In my understanding, it is impossible to look at participation without also taking culture into account. I agree with researchers such as Hofstede (1980b) and Usunier (1998), who questioned the transferability of management systems across cultural contexts, and with Smith and colleagues, who stated:

> "A behaviour that may be unambiguously defined in one social context may be defined quite differently in other cultures. [...] With more cultures included, it becomes more likely that the meanings of specific behaviours will vary. Although broadly defined behaviours such as leadership, participation, and teamwork are widely assumed to have equivalent meaning in different cultural contexts, individual-level studies cast doubt on this assumption." (Smith et al., 2002, p. 190)

Consequently, my research explores participation as a potentially culture-specific social phenomenon. More specifically, I conducted interviews with managers from five European countries, namely the Czech Republic, Finland, Germany, Poland and Sweden.

It also follows from the culture-specific perspective that the current research is not guided by a single and exact definition of participation or participative management, although numerous definitions exist in the literature (e.g. Marrow, Bowers & Seashore, 1967; Koopman & Wierdsma, 1998; Heller et al., 1998). In contrast, finding out what participation embraces comprises the main part of the study. After all, any definition is an agreed upon convention by a specific group of people. Rather than pre-empting the study with a convention originating from the research community, the goal is in fact to explore culture-specific conventions by the very users of participation.

Ad 3. The *integration* aspect outlined above refers to the following design elements of the current study: (1) a review of earlier participation research as the springboard for the formulation of two research questions, (2) the combined use of qualitative and quantitative methodology, meaning that a qualitative core study is embedded in existing quantitative research, (3) the comparison of the current study's findings with the results of selected large-scale, quantitative research initiatives, (4) the analysis of whether and how the findings of the current study tie in with other forms of participation, most notably with the respective industrial relations systems of the countries under study, (5) the analysis of the findings' fit with the literature on country-specific management practices, and (6) the comparison of the existing participation literature with the theoretical conclusions drawn from the present study.

In summary, this research can be described as a comparative and integrative study with a geographic focus on Europe, exploring variations in participative management across cultural contexts. By looking at situational and cultural context factors influencing participation, the study follows the contingency approach.

As outlined, the concept of culture influences the field of research, and it must be pointed out that it also influences the researcher. Therefore it is crucial to make the researcher's own cultural background explicit and keep it in mind over the course of the study. For this purpose I include some information about myself (more details on my role as a researcher follow in Chapter 5.4.2): I was born and raised in Austria, a country characterised by low power distance, fairly high levels of masculinity, uncertainty avoidance and collectivism (Hofstede, 1980a). Furthermore, Hall (1976) describes German, my mother tongue, as a low context language, meaning that communication is clear and explicit, and not dependent on the person or the situation. Both professionally and personally, I travel internationally on a regular basis. With regard to my professional background as a social scientist and cross-cultural researcher, I am aware that the research projects I was involved in and the methodology I used in the past have influenced the design and conduct of the current study. My first "qualitative experience" was in the field of ethnography, which was introduced to me by the American anthropologist Michael Agar (1996) during the initial stages of the GLOBE study (House et al., 2004). Intrigued by the possibilities of this method, I designed my doctoral dissertation as an ethnographic study into the culture of a Vienna hospital (Szabo, 1998). Later on, and in preparation for the current study, I became increasingly interested in grounded theory (Glaser & Strauss, 1967). The epistemological position I adhere to has remained the same throughout the years, namely interpretative. In the words of Locke (2001), interpretative research focuses "on what events and objects mean to people, on how they perceive what happens to them and around them, and how they adopt their behaviour in light of these meanings and perspectives" (p. 9). It is exactly this focus where the current study is positioned.

The book consists of twelve chapters. The first four chapters set the stage for the qualitative core study. Chapter 2 summarises some of the most commonly cited scientific books, articles, and research projects on participation in managerial decision-making, both in the theoretical and cross-cultural fields. Chapter 3 describes the research questions and study goals as they emerged from the literature review. Chapter 4 summarises three quantitative cross-cultural studies with a participation perspective, which are used for integration purposes in the context of the current study. The remaining eight chapters of the book deal with the qualitative core study itself. Chapter 5 discusses methodological challenges and describes data collection and analysis. Chapters 6 to 10 summarise the within-country analyses and present country-specific findings, while Chapter 11 looks at the findings from a comparative perspective (inter-country analysis). The final Chapter 12 concludes the study by presenting propositions and a contingency model of participative management as well as pointing out areas of future research.

The study described in this book was made possible by a *Charlotte Bühler Habilitationsstipendium*, a post-doctoral stipend for female researchers granted by the Austrian Science Fund (FWF). I am very grateful for this support, without which I would have been unable to realise the research project on such a large scale. I thank Gerhard Reber for his valuable suggestions during the whole course of conducting and writing up the research project. I also wish to express my gratitude to my colleagues Werner Auer-Rizzi, Iris Fischlmayr and Cäcilia Innreiter, who were there for me whenever I wanted to talk about the project. Without Werner's invaluable help, a comparison with the Vroom/Yetton data would not have been possible, and without his willingness to take upon himself many of my administrative responsibilities, the study would still be far from completed. Kurt Matzler and his team at JKU's new Department of International Management, which I joined in 2005, have provided me with much professional and personal sympathy over the last months of writing. Sonja Holm did a marvellous job in raising critical questions regarding content as well as writing style. A number of international colleagues from JKU's partner universities paved the way for data collection in the Czech Republic, Finland, Germany, Poland and Sweden. Some of my international colleagues also served as sources of cultural expertise reflecting upon the initial versions of the emerging country-specific models of participative management. I would particularly like to acknowledge the support and encouragement of Michael Berry, Ingalill Holmberg, Mary Keating, Satu Lähteenmäki, Jerzy Maczynski, Milan Maly, Gillian Martin, Mats Tyrstrup, Jürgen Weibler and Lena Zander. Peter Smith deserves a very special thank you, because his support and information allowed the integration of the qualitative findings with the results of the Event Management study.

Apart from my academic colleagues, I am extremely grateful to the thirty-five managers who volunteered as interviewees and shared their experiences, insights and time with me. Getting to know them and learning about "their world" was a highly enriching experience for me, not merely on the data collection level, but especially on the personal level.

Last but not least, I would like to thank my family. My daughter showed incredible patience and understanding for the long hours her mother had to work. My parents supported me beyond imagination and believed in the success of this project from the very first idea to the very last line of write-up. Likewise, my friends Hannelore Hofer, Gabriele Schneider and Alois Stritzinger provided strength and moral support in moments of doubt, and I do not hesitate to say I had a few over the course of the project.

Chapter 2

Participation from a Conceptual and Cross-Cultural Perspective

2.1 Participation from a Conceptual Perspective

2.1.1 Definitions and Dimensions of Participation

The one pivotal concept of this book is that of participation. The concept of participation is, however, subject to varying interpretation and definition. In the context of business organisations there is no agreed definition of participation. Strauss reviewed various definitions presented in the literature and concluded:

> "Definitions of participation abound. Some authors insist that participation must be a group process, involving groups of employees and their boss; others stress delegation, the process by which the *individual* employee is given greater freedom to make decisions on his or her own. Some restrict the term 'participation' to formal institutions, such as works councils; other definitions embrace 'informal participation', the day-to-day relations between supervisors and subordinates in which subordinates are allowed substantial input into work decisions. Finally, there are those who stress participation as a *process* and those who are concerned with participation as a *result*." (Strauss, 1998a, p. 15, italics in original)

Glew et al. (1995) identified six implicit commonalities in the various definitions of participation: (1) Participation refers to intentional programs or practices developed by the organisation to involve multiple employees. (2) Participation most often refers to extra-role or role-expanding behaviours. (3) Participation requires conscious interaction between at least two individuals. (4) This interaction must be visible to both individuals. (5) Participation actors typically occupy different level positions in a hierarchical, as opposed to a horizontal relationship. (6) Without "voice" there can be no enactment of participation. Voice refers to "any vehicle through which an individual has increased impact on some element of the organisation" (Glew et al., 1995, p. 402).

Theoretical and empirical research into participation began with the pioneering study of Coch and French (1948), and today, the field continues to be characterised by vivid research activity. Black and Gregersen (1997, p. 859) observed that "[f]ew topics have resulted in as much theory, empirical study, controversy and practical application as [participation]." The most frequently researched form of organisational participation is participation in managerial decision-making. Other forms include participation in information processing, goal setting, problem solving and organisational changes (Sashkin, 1984; Wagner, 1994), as well as collective bargaining and financial participation (Gill & Krieger, 2000).

Several new terms, which have in recent years gained popularity in management theory as well as in business practice, are conceptually close to the term participation. Examples of such terms are industrial democracy, worker self-management, power equalisation, autonomous work groups and democratic leadership (Dachler & Wilpert, 1978, p. 1). Hofstede observed:

> "The term *empowerment*, which became fashionable in the 1990s, applies, in fact, to all kinds of formal and informal means of sharing decision-making power and influence between leaders and subordinates: participative management, joint consultation, *Mitbestimmung*, industrial democracy [...], worker directors, worker self-management, shop floor consultation, codetermination." (Hofstede, 2001, p. 389f, italics in original)

Three dimensions representing different ways of looking at participation in decision-making are summarised in the following: formal (*de jure*) versus informal (*de facto*) participation, direct versus indirect (representative) participation and degree of involvement. Most research focuses on these dimensions. However, further dimensions are also topics of research, such as sporadic versus continuous participation (Chisholm & Vansina, 1993), range of people (Dachler & Wilpert, 1978), consultative versus delegative participation (Gill & Krieger, 2000) and participation in different types of decisions. Pusic (1998), for example, explored technical versus interest decisions, and Knudsen (1995) subdivided participation into strategic, tactical, operational and welfare decisions.

Formal (de jure) versus informal (de facto) participation. Most texts on organisational participation (e.g. Dachler & Wilpert, 1978; IDE, 1981; Heller et al., 1998) differentiate between formal and informal participation. *Formal* or *de jure* participation refers to the "written-down, operative rules and regulations for involving various parties in decision-making" (IDE, 1981, p. 5). Participation is legitimised by an "explicitly recorded system of rules and agreements imposed on or granted to the organisation" (Dachler & Wilpert, 1978, p. 10). There exist three bases of legitimisation for formal participation: (1) legislation, such as national laws, (2) contractual bases, such as collective bargaining agreements, and (3) management policies (Dachler & Wilpert, 1978).

In contrast to formal participation, *informal* or *de facto* participation refers to the extent of actual employee involvement in the decision-making process and the ability to influence decisions (Strauss, 1998a). According to Dachler and Wilpert (1978, p. 10) informal participation is defined as a "non-statutory consensus emerging among interacting members", usually in the form of exchange between a manager and one or more subordinates. Informal participation involves few explicit rules concerning the participants, the type of decisions to be taken and the process of participation (Black & Gregersen, 1997). Rather, informal participation is based on a consensus among the involved parties and usually becomes legitimised through practice and emerging norms.

The relationship between formal and informal participation is a much debated topic in the literature. Hofstede (2001) denied a relationship between formal and informal participation. In contrast, Dachler and Wilpert (1978, p. 11) acknowledged that "a formal participatory system is likely to develop some informal participatory social arrangements." Similarly, Reber et al. (2000) and Szabo et al. (2002) assumed that formal structures facilitate changes in actual behaviour. Strauss (1998a) expected some form of relationship between *de jure* and *de facto* participation, although correlations would be difficult to detect. In the same vein, the authors of the Industrial Democracy in Europe project (IDE, 1981) noted with respect to ways of increasing participation:

> "It seems that managers may find it easier to share influence with lower levels when conditions and limits for influence-sharing are sanctioned within the formal rules and procedures laid down by policy. [...] Given the framework of the hierarchy, introducing more rules for employee participation is the most efficient way of increasing employee involvement, particularly that of employee representatives, and of equalising the distribution of power." (IDE, 1981, pp. 289, 328)

Direct versus indirect (representative) participation. Direct participation means the "immediate, personal involvement of organisation members in decision-making" (Dachler & Wilpert, 1978, p. 12). It allows participants "to present personally their information, preferences and opinions to the other members involved in the decision" (Black & Gregersen, 1997, p. 861). Direct participation can take the form of formal as well as informal participation. As formal participation, it usually represents employees participating in specific groups defined by the organisational structure, such as quality circles or semi-autonomous work groups. Most examples of direct and formal participation are initiated by employer decisions, while legal regulations on direct participation are rare (Knudsen, 1995). As informal participation, direct participation usually means the immediate involvement of employees in the decision-making processes of their superiors, such as in the form of consultation.

Indirect or *representative* participation is usually based on formal arrangements and takes place through an intermediary of employee representative bodies (Cabrera, Ortega & Cabrera, 2003). More specifically, employee interests are handled by works councils, union representatives, or other similar organisations. Employees convey their information, preferences and opinions to representatives, who are either elected or appointed. In turn, the representatives interact with management in the interest of their constituencies (Black & Gregersen, 1997).

In organisations in which participation takes place, usually both direct and indirect participation co-exist. However, the two forms may serve different purposes and result from different contextual requirements (Dachler & Wilpert, 1978). For example, work assemblies, i.e. meetings of all employees of an organisation, usually aim at information exchange and consultation, whereas employee representation on the supervisory board constitutes a higher level of authority to influence decisions.

Degree of involvement. Several researchers (e.g. Tannenbaum & Schmidt, 1958; Vroom & Yetton, 1973; IDE, 1981, 1993) conceptualised the degree of employee involvement in decision-making along a continuum. Such continua reflect "the different access that organisation members have to the actual making of a decision, or the amount of influence they can exert toward a given decision outcome" (Dachler & Wilpert, 1978, p. 14). Participation may range from autocratic management on one end of the continuum over consultation and joint decision-making to self-management on the other end of the continuum. For example, Black and Gregersen (1997) identified in their research six categories of degree of involvement: (1) No advance information concerning a decision is given to employees. (2) Employees are given advance information. (3) Employees are allowed to voice their opinion about the decision. (4) Employees' opinions are taken into consideration in making the decision. (5) Employees can veto a decision. (6) The decision is entirely up to the employees.

2.1.2 Theoretical Models Used to Justify Participation

There is agreement in the literature that participation has both advantages and costs. According to Strauss (1998a) three main arguments support participation: the humanistic, the power-sharing and the organisational efficiency arguments.

According to the *humanistic* argument, participation helps satisfy employees' needs for achievement, social approval and creativity. In this view, which is also labelled *human resources model of participation* (Leana & Florkowski, 1992), participation promotes employee involvement as a tool for employee development. Other authors go a step further and consider participative management an ethical imperative (e.g. Sashkin, 1984). Chisholm and Vansina (1993) presented an *overall management philosophy* aimed at designing an organisational system that consists of "structures, processes, values and basic assumptions that pervade the ways an organisation views and relates to employees" (p. 296). In their classical study titled "Management by Participation", Marrow, Bowers and Seashore (1967) similarly considered participation an overall management philosophy, with the aim of creating a climate for personal and organisational development.

According to the *power-sharing* argument, autocratic relationships are "inherently unjust and inconsistent with the values of a democratic society" (Strauss, 1998a, p. 8f). The so-called *workplace democracy model* (Leana & Florkowski, 1992) favours employee involvement as a way of redistributing power within the organisation. However, critics of this view argue that the proposed power redistribution is unrealistic and that participation will remain at a superficial level, because managers fear losing power and legitimate influence (Chisholm & Vansina, 1993).

Finally, the *organisational efficiency* argument focuses on the effects of participation on the organisation. Strauss (1998a, p. 10) lists such statements as the following: Participation may result in higher quality decisions. People are more likely to implement decisions they were part of making themselves than to implement decisions imposed on them. Participation improves communication and co-operation. Participation facilitates organisational learning. Participative subordinates do not need supervision. Employees learn new skills through participation. Leadership potential may be readily identified and developed. All these statements suggest that participation gives employees a voice, which in turn enhances personal dignity, reduces frustration and contributes to higher levels of motivation and stronger degrees of identification with the organisation. Consequently, the urge of employees to demonstrate power through fighting management (Strauss, 1998a) is reduced. As a result of participation, absenteeism and turnover rates may decrease. However, other authors are less optimistic. They accuse the so-called *instrumental management model* of using participation mainly as a vehicle for reaching management goals (Leana & Florkowski, 1992). Another point of criticism is that management might restrict employee involvement to situations in which the sole objective is to positively influence productivity (Chisholm & Vansina, 1993).

2.1.3 Determinants of Participation

This section discusses some of the factors that researchers believe determine the amount and type of participation organisations adopt. Apart from the potential influence of *de jure* participation, which has already been mentioned above, individual, organisational and environment factors play a significant role. The following listing is not exhaustive but tries to capture some of the major factors repeatedly mentioned in the literature.

Organisational members. Both managers' and employees' characteristics seem to moderate the chances for successful implementation of participation programs. Strauss (1998c, p. 211) noted that "trust is almost essential if participation is to lead to more than controversy, deadlock, or apathy." Managers need to trust their employees to be willing and capable of participating, and employees need to trust that participation will not be used to exploit them or stay a mere lip-service. Several authors (e.g. Chisholm & Vansina, 1993; Wilpert, 1998) stressed as key requirements for developing true participation that management is willing to offer participatory opportunities to subordinates and that management is capable of making sure that the change process is sustained over time. Supervisors must believe in participation in order to make it work (Strauss, 1998c).

Studies show that managers who dislike uncertainty and ambiguity use participation less frequently than managers who do not possess these traits (Tett & Jackson, 1990), as do managers who perceive their subordinates as not capable, irresponsible and not trustworthy (Leana, 1986). Pusic supported these arguments by stressing that participation cannot be successfully introduced by rules alone:

> "The behaviour of people as members of organisations, and thus also their participation in decision-making, does not only depend on the rules regulating their organisation roles. In an important part it is predetermined by the mental structures that members carry with them into the organisation." (Pusic, 1998, p. 72)

Empirical studies based on the Vroom/Yetton (1973) model (Section 2.1.5) revealed that managers' demographic characteristics contributed significantly to their tendency to use participation. Country of origin showed the most drastic effect (Jago et al., 1993). Smaller effects were reported for gender and age: Male managers were found to be more participative than females, and older managers more participative than their younger counterparts (Reber et al., 2000). Other demographic factors, such as length of employment with the organisation or functional affiliation, did not produce significant effects (Jago et al., 1993). In contrast to Reber et al. (2000), Steers (1977) and Jago and Vroom (1982) found that female managers demonstrated more participatory behaviour than their male counterparts.

Employee representatives. Gill and Krieger (2000) found that the initiative to introduce direct participation in an organisation is usually taken by management. Yet, employee representatives usually play an active role in ensuring that managers in fact implement participation as agreed upon. In other words, indirect participation via employee representatives has a positive effect on the implementation of direct participation. Based on a recent empirical study in ten European countries, Cabrera, Ortega and Cabrera (2003) reached similar conclusions, yet also described some limitations to the effects of indirect participation on direct participation.

Organisational factors. The characteristics of the organisation, such as size, strategies and structure, also appear to influence the introduction of participation. Precise relationships between the size of an organisation and the use of participation are unclear (Strauss, 1998c), but direct participation seems to be more effective in smaller organisations, whereas representative participation may work better in larger organisations. Cabrera, Ortega and Cabrera (2003) identified the pursuit of a differentiation strategy based on quality (with a positive effect on the amount of participation), and the pursuit of a cost leadership strategy (with a negative effect on the amount of participation) as factors contributing to the introduction of participation. With regard to structure, Chisholm and Vansina (1993) called for a certain degree of formality of the participative system, when they made the point that "structures and processes must be developed to build participation increasingly into the organisation through guaranteeing legitimate power to make key decisions" (p. 306). In addition, they stressed that the implementation of a participative system should be continuously monitored to make sure that the employees have the opportunity to influence the process and the resulting participative system.

Organisational environment. The environment of the organisation also appears to influence the chances for successful implementation of participation. Cabrera, Ortega and Cabrera (2003) found that competition and sector had an impact on the introduction and use of participation. High levels of competition affected the amount of participation positively. Furthermore, service sector organisations showed higher levels of participation than manufacturing organisations.

2.1.4 Outcomes of Participation

The potential effects of participation are of particular interest to researchers. Outcome variables are defined and explored primarily by scholars adhering to the instrumental view of participation (Section 2.1.2). The literature distinguishes between three theoretical approaches of participative effects: cognitive, affective and contingency models (Miller & Monge, 1986; Cabrera, Ortega & Cabrera, 2003). All three models accentuate the potential positive influence of participation on productivity and satisfaction, but suggest different explanatory mechanisms. It should also be noted that the three models are not mutually exclusive in implementation, since "cognitive, affective and contingency variables all play important roles in the participative process" (Miller & Monge, 1986, p. 729).

Cognitive models argue that participation enhances the flow and use of important information in the organisation. Employees often possess more comprehensive knowledge of their work than managers do. Locke, Schweiger and Latham (1986) stressed that subordinate expertise is a key requirement in order for participation to be useful. Consequently, when competent employees are allowed to participate in decision-making, managers gain access to relevant information otherwise not available to them. This information can be used to initiate organisational change, which, in turn, may increase productivity. In other words, productivity is affected directly by way of a better flow of information. Miller and Monge (1986) added that participation has a stronger effect on productivity than on employee satisfaction.

Affective models link participation to productivity and satisfaction through affective mechanisms (Miller & Monge, 1986). These models suggest that participation fulfils employees' needs, such as self-expression, independence and equality, which leads to greater satisfaction, which, in turn, increases motivation. Higher levels of motivation have a positive impact on productivity. In other words, participation affects productivity indirectly. In contrast to cognitive models, affective models predict that participation more highly influences satisfaction than it does productivity (Miller & Monge, 1986).

Contingency models suggest that participation affects satisfaction and productivity differently for different individuals and situations (Miller & Monge, 1986). Therefore, it is important to identify the relevant contingency factors and to consider their impact on participation outcomes. Locke and Schweiger (1979) distinguished between individual factors, such as knowledge and motivation and organisational factors, such as task attributes and group characteristics. According to Glew et al. (1995), situational and organisational factors more substantially influence participation outcomes than do individual differences. Several authors explored the conditions under which participation leads to the best results in terms of satisfaction and productivity. Miller and Monge (1986), for example, considered the contingency factors job type (managers vs. lower-level employees) and organisational type (research, service and manufacturing), but found no moderating effect.

Within the leadership literature, contingency theories stress the relativity of participation outcomes, in particular the Vroom/Yetton (1973) model (Section 2.1.5). These authors speculated that "it appears highly likely that an increase in the participation of subordinates in decision-making may increase productivity under some circumstances but decrease productivity under others" (Vroom & Yetton, 1973, p. 7). In their model, the authors defined outcome not just in broad terms such as productivity and satisfaction, but argued that "[i]t is important to distinguish three classes of outcomes that influence the ultimate effectiveness of decisions. These are: (1) the quality or rationality of the decision, (2) the acceptance of the decision by subordinates and their commitment to execute it effectively, and (3) the amount of time required to make the decision" (Vroom & Yetton, 1973, p. 20).

Black and Gregersen (1997) argued that participation effectiveness is contingent upon the phase in the decision-making process. They separated the decision-making process into five steps: (a) identifying problems or issues, (b) generating alternative solutions to the problem, (c) selecting a specific solution, (d) planning the implementation of the selected solution, and (e) evaluating the results of the implementation. The authors examined the relationship of each step to satisfaction and performance and found that the degree of involvement in the areas of generating alternatives, planning and evaluating results was most likely related to satisfaction, whereas the level of involvement in generating alternatives and implementation planning was inclined to be linked to performance.

Despite the growing amount of knowledge acquired with the help of contingency theories, continuous debate exists in the literature concerning the potential effect of participation on productivity and satisfaction. In the late 1970s, Locke and Schweiger conducted a literature review and concluded:

> "(1) With respect to the productivity criterion, there is no trend in favour of participative leadership as compared to more directive styles; and (2) with respect to satisfaction, the results generally favour participative over directive methods, although nearly 40 percent of the studies did not find participation to be superior." (Locke & Schweiger, 1979, p. 316)

About a decade later, Cotton et al. (1988) concluded after yet another literature review that the effects of participation on satisfaction and performance varied according to the form of participation. Thus, the authors stated, earlier reviews of studies considering participation as a uni-dimensional concept (e.g. Locke & Schweiger, 1979) probably had reached invalid conclusions. Based on their own multi-dimensional view of participation, Cotton et al. (1988) found that informal participation and long-term forms of participation were effective in terms of productivity and satisfaction. Leana, Locke and Schweiger (1990) strongly criticised these findings on two grounds. The categorisation scheme was dismissed as unsystematic and the sampling of studies for inclusion in the review was not considered representative.

Despite this criticism, Cotton et al. (1990) strongly reaffirmed their position that the form of participation leads to different outcomes for satisfaction and performance. Wagner (1994) conducted a meta-analytic reassessment of Cotton et al.'s (1988) data, but was not able to report any significant differences between the various forms of participation.

In the meantime, several other authors (e.g. Miller & Monge, 1986; Spector, 1986; Wagner & Gooding, 1987b; Doucouliagos, 1995) also attempted to answer the question of the effects of participation on satisfaction and productivity by applying meta-analytic reviews, without any consistent results. At about the same time, Ledford and Lawler (1994) equated the on-going debate about the effects of participation on productivity and satisfaction with "beating a dead horse." "Are we headed for the day when we will be reading meta-analyses of the meta-analyses of meta-analyses of research on participation effectiveness?" they asked. If participation was as narrowly defined as in most studies (e.g. excluding studies from the meta-analyses that investigated participation interventions introduced together with other changes such as organisational structure, technology, or reward systems), it was no surprise that the effects were modest at best, Ledford and Lawler (1994) argued. Glew et al. (1995) requested that "it is now time to move on to more interesting, significant and practical elements of the participation question" (p. 397). In a similar vein, Chisholm and Vansina stated:

"Narrow definitions and narrowly conceived research on participation contrast sharply with the growing complexity of work. In general, technologies, organisations and organisational environments are becoming more complex. Consequently, meaningful ways of conceptualising and conducting research on participation must model the growing complexity. [...] In an increasingly complex world, our ways of conceptualising, studying and developing participation also need to become more sophisticated and we must be open to recognise new forms of employee involvement that have vitality for employees, managers and other critical constituents but do not meet our preconceived ideas. [...] Again, there is no single thing as 'participation.' Instead, there is a virtually limitless variety waiting to be discovered, induced and nourished." (Chisholm & Vansina, 1993, pp. 308, 312)

2.1.5 Participation in the Management and Leadership Literature

In the management and leadership literature, participation is usually understood as direct and *de facto* participation. Over time, research interest in participation has shifted parallel to the development of new approaches and theories. Participation is seldom treated as an ultimate value (as the humanistic argument suggests), but rather in an instrumental sense (as the organisational efficiency argument suggests). In other words, research interest concerns the usefulness of participation for the achievement of organisational goals.

The origins of an explicit focus on the manager as a decision-maker can be dated back to the beginning of the twentieth century and, particularly, to the work of Frederick Taylor (1911), whose concept of Scientific Management supported the distinction between decision-making and operational work.

"Scientific management [...] has contributed to this centralisation of decision-making in organisations by focusing on the development of methods by which managers can make more rational decisions, substituting objective measurements and empirically validated methods for casual judgements." (Vroom & Yetton, 1973, p. 10)

Scientific management left its imprint on how researchers and practitioners defined the managerial role for decades to follow. Vroom and Yetton (1973, p. 10) stated that "[t]raditional models of the managerial process have been autocratic in nature. The manager makes decisions on matters within his area of freedom, issues orders or directives to his subordinates and monitors their performance to ensure conformity with these directives."

Parallel to the growing interest in management issues, *leadership research* emerged as a new field of academic inquiry. In the 1930s and 1940s, the *trait approach* marked the beginning of the scientific study of leadership. This approach emphasised the personal attributes of leaders. Research studies looked for stable personality characteristics that distinguished leaders from other persons, and effective from ineffective leaders. These early studies were not concerned with participation.

After World War II, scientists turned to the study of leader behaviour, mainly due to weak support of trait theories in research findings. The *behaviour approach* represents scientific search for behavioural patterns that should guarantee organisational effectiveness. Jago (1995, p. 626) distinguished two lines of research within the behaviour approach: (1) people vs. task orientation, and (2) autocratic vs. democratic leadership. As the labels suggest, researchers began to consider the concept of participation in their theories and models, particularly in the people orientation and democratic leadership areas. The Ohio studies constitute a prominent example of the behaviour approach, and within these studies the two factors *consideration* (people orientation) and *initiating structure* (task orientation) were introduced. Within the factor consideration, defined as "behaviours indicating open communication between leader and followers, mutual trust and respect, follower *participation* in decision-making and interpersonal warmth" (Chemers, 1997, p. 22, italics added), participation was explicitly taken into account.

The introduction of democratic (in contrast to autocratic) leadership in the field dates back to early studies by Kurt Lewin and his group. The observation of Boy Scout troops, led by students trained in different leadership styles, revealed that boys in the democratically led groups showed the highest levels of satisfaction. In addition, these groups displayed high levels of productivity. Boys in the autocratically led groups demonstrated aggressive behaviour, particularly in absence of the leader (Lewin, Lippitt & White, 1939). Productivity was high in these groups, yet only when the leader was present (Lippitt & White, 1943). With regard to degree of involvement, Lewin's and other early studies of leadership styles employed a "bi-polar view of participation" (Zander, 1997), as they differentiated the autocratic-directive from the democratic-participative managerial style. Later studies considered degrees of participation on a continuum. For example, Tannenbaum and Schmidt (1958, p. 96f) presented a taxonomy of leadership patterns with varying degrees of participation: (1) Manager makes decision and announces it. (2) Manager "sells" decision. (3) Manager presents ideas and invites questions. (4) Manager presents tentative decision subject to change. (5) Manager presents problem, gets suggestions and makes decision. (6) Manager defines limits; asks group to make decision. (7) Manager permits the group to make decisions within prescribed limits.

In summary, the behaviour approach introduced the concept of participation into the leadership literature. However, many questions remained unanswered. Major criticism concerned the missing consideration of situational factors (Vroom & Yetton, 1973). This weakness was overcome by the *situational approach*, which "emphasises the importance of contextual factors such as the nature of the work performed by the leader's unit, the nature of the external environment and the characteristics of followers" (Yukl, 1998, p. 10). In other words, these new contingency theories attempted to identify aspects of the situation that moderated the relationship between leader behaviours (or traits) and effectiveness. The new focus brought forth a couple of highly relevant theories. Three of them are discussed below in relation to participation: (1) Fiedler's contingency model of leadership, (2) path-goal theory, and (3) the Vroom/Yetton model of decision-making.

Fiedler's (1967) model, "a situational off shoot of the concept of leadership as a personality trait" (Vroom & Yetton, 1973, p. 207), is based on the assumption that leaders with different characteristics are effective in different situations. Chemers summarised Fiedler's prepositions as follows:

> "Task-motivated leadership with an emphasis on order and direction is seen as most effective under conditions of high clarity or control, while the more *participative* strategies of the relationship-motivated leader are most effective under conditions of greater ambiguity caused by an unstructured task or a less cooperative group." (Chemers, 1993, p. 314, italics added)

In other words, Fiedler preconceived the concept of participation by explicitly including subordinate involvement as part of the relationship-motivated leadership role.

A second contingency theory, path-goal theory of leadership, deals with the question of how a leader's behaviour influences the path-goal perceptions held by subordinates. A leader can motivate subordinates by increasing their perception of performance rewards and by making the path to these rewards easier, for example by specifying performance criteria (Chemers, 1997). Based on the Ohio school consideration/initiating structure distinction, Evans (1968, 1970) suggested that considerate behaviour, such as participation, enhanced subordinates' perceptions of the availability of goals associated with higher order needs, whereas initiating structure provided clarification of the appropriate paths. House (1971) developed path-goal theory further by integrating situational variables as moderators of the effects of leader behaviour, in particular follower and task characteristics. House and Mitchell (1974) distinguished four types of leadership, among them participative leadership. In summary, path-goal theory incorporates participation as an important element, which is not all too surprising given its Ohio school roots (see behaviour approach above).

At about the same time as path-goal theory was developed, Vroom and Yetton (1973) presented an elaborate contingency model of participation in managerial decision-making. This model governs a manager's choice of autocratic versus participative responses to different decision-making situations. It aims at establishing a decision-making process that allows for the best possible fit between the manager, the subordinates and the decision-making situation. Thus, the model stresses the "situational relativity" of leadership styles (Vroom & Yetton, 1973, p. 16). Based on Tannenbaum and Schmidt's (1958) taxonomy of leadership styles, the model takes five degrees of involvement into consideration: (1) Autocratic decision by the manager, using the information available. (2) Autocratic decision, but the manager obtains any necessary information from subordinates; subordinates do not play a role in generating/evaluating possible solutions. (3) One-on-one consultations; decision may or may not reflect subordinates' influence. (4) Group consultation; decision may or may not reflect subordinates' influence. (5) Group discussion and group decision; attempt to reach agreement (consensus).

In addition to specifying five managerial strategies for subordinate involvement, the Vroom/Yetton model defines seven situational influences considered relevant for most participation processes, as well as rules for deciding the optimal level of participation for an effective outcome. These rules concern the quality of decisions as well as their acceptance by subordinates. A decision tree visualises the interplay of the different elements (strategies, situational influences and decision rules).

In summary, the three contingency theories perceive participation in decision-making to be an important aspect of leadership to enhance organisational effectiveness. They specify the conditions under which participation can be used most advantageously. Recent *integrative* approaches to the study of leadership follow the same line of thought in their acknowledgement of participation as a relevant aspect of leadership. For example, Chemers's (1993, 1997) model shows a category labelled "contribution" that encompasses the degree of subordinates' participation in determining group actions. Similarly, Yukl's (1998) leadership model includes the aspect "leader power", which specifies the distribution and sharing of power over decisions.

Smith and Peterson's (1988) conceptualisation of management as the handling of work events is also worth mentioning. Smith and Peterson argue that, when managers deal with work events (e.g. evaluating new work procedures, dealing with conflict in the work team), they make use of alternative sources of guidance (e.g. own experience, consulting with subordinates or the own superior). This approach is particularly interesting as it broadens the view of participation beyond subordinates by including superiors, specialists and managerial colleagues.

It is startling that certain recent trends in leadership research have turned away from participation, as well as from attention to the situation as central element of leader effectiveness. Chemers (1993) is surprised that, whereas a considerable body of research supports the validity of contingency approaches, theorists continue to present arguments in favour of universally effective leadership patterns. Studies into *charismatic leadership* (e.g. House, 1977) and *transformational leadership* (e.g. Bass, 1985) represent such lines of inquiry. Bryman (1993) referred to this class of theories as the "new leadership theories." However, these theories may as well be considered a revival of the traditional trait theories. Participation is, at most, implicitly included in the category of empowerment, which a charismatic or transformational leader must consider when interacting with followers. More specific details are seldom given.

In a similar vein, recently introduced *cognitive approaches* do not deal with the specifics of participation or the situational adequacy of leadership behaviour. Based on implicit leadership theory (Lord & Maher, 1991), these approaches argue that people have a prototype leader in mind and compare real-life leaders and managers with this image. A leader is effective only when s/he shows traits and behaviours that match the prototype. A large-scale research programme, the GLOBE study (House et al., 1999, 2004), has devoted its energy toward the identification of such traits and behaviours in different countries. The study covers broad behavioural patterns, such as autocratic and participative behaviour, but does not go into more situation-specific details.

In summary, the short journey through the history of management and leadership research revealed that participation in decision-making has been given varying levels of importance in the various research streams. The theoretical understanding of participation has been enhanced in particular by the behaviour and situational approaches.

2.2 Participation from a Cross-Cultural Perspective

2.2.1 Does Culture Matter?

Nancy Adler asked the following questions with regard to decision-making:

> "Do managers from different cultures perceive problems in similar ways? Do they gather similar types and amounts of information while investigating a problem? Do they construct similar types of solutions? Do they use similar strategies for choosing between alternatives? Do they implement their decisions in similar ways? The answer to each question is no." (Adler, 1997, p. 168)

The following question could be added to Adler's list: Do managers in different cultures perceive and use *participation* in decision-making in similar ways? Several researchers (e.g. Tannenbaum et al., 1974; Strauss, 1998c; Jago et al., 1993) have raised this or similar types of questions concerning the influence of cultural factors on the process and effectiveness of participation. These researchers argue that participation is more likely to be adapted in a culture that favours participation than in a culture in which values and norms are opposed to employee involvement. In addition, a number of empirical studies emphasise that societal culture characteristics form the context in which participation can or cannot take place.

Research into cross-cultural questions related to participation is a relatively new field that has its roots in the 1970s. According to Wagner and Gooding (1987a), it is not surprising that researchers became interested in the relationship between societal culture and the designs and outcomes of participatory systems at a time when international relations became increasingly central to the conduct of business.

2.2.2 Studies Comparing Participation across Cultures

Several empirical studies have dealt with the cross-cultural comparison of organisational participation. Some of them are briefly reviewed in the following paragraphs. The review includes research programmes that focus exclusively on participation as well as leadership studies that cover participation as one issue among other leadership themes.

Haire, Ghiselli and Porter (1966) presented one of the first large-scale comparative studies in the area of management. The study concerned managers' attitudes toward managerial practices, the managerial role and motivation. With regard to managerial practices, the authors explored "four distinct areas of disagreement between the traditional-directive and the democratic-participative approaches" (p. 19), namely capacity for leadership and initiative, sharing information and objectives, participation and internal control.

Questionnaire data were collected from managers in Argentina, Belgium, Chile, Denmark, England, France, Germany, India, Italy, Japan, Norway, Sweden, Spain and the United States. The authors found similarities as well as differences among managers' attitudes and reported that about thirty percent of the variation was associated with national origin. This finding led the authors to conclude that although "there is a very strong and consistent tendency for managers to express similar beliefs about management", "cultural influence is present and substantial" (p. 9). The study identified five distinguishable country clusters: Anglo-American, Nordic European, Latin European, Japan and a cluster of developing countries.

Tannenbaum et al. (1974) studied actual and ideal participative attitudes and practices in fifty-two plants in Austria, Israel, Italy, the United States and Yugoslavia. These five countries were selected for the study because they represented various models of formally incorporated participation, ranging from the Kibbutz system in Israel to co-determination in Austria. Following the traditional bi-polar view of participation (Zander, 1997), the autocratic-directive managerial style was differentiated from the democratic-participative style. The authors used modified scales from earlier research on participation and hierarchy, and data were sampled from subordinates at all levels of the organisation. The results showed that the hierarchical arrangements in the five countries differed according to the countries' legitimised form of participation.

In the early 1980s, the Industrial Democracy in Europe (IDE) International Research Group, a consortium of sociologists and psychologists from mainly European countries, conducted a large-scale cross-national study (*IDE, 1981*) followed by a replication study some ten years later (*IDE, 1993*). The group studied *de jure* participation structures as well as *de facto* participation behaviour. Twelve countries were involved, namely Belgium, Denmark, Finland, France, Italy, Israel, the Netherlands, Norway, Sweden, the United Kingdom, West Germany and Yugoslavia. Participants, all of them subordinates, were given a series of descriptions of specific decision-making situations and were asked to choose the appropriate decision-making method for each case. In contrast to studies with a bi-polar view of participation, such as Tannenbaum et al. (1974), the IDE study defined participation on a continuum of decision-making behaviour. The study found large between-country differences in *de jure* participation, and the legal framework proved to be the most common and important formal basis for participation in most countries. The intensity of prescribed participation turned out to be the strongest predictor of *de facto* participation. The replication study (IDE, 1993) found that changes had taken place since the original 1981 study, particularly in *de jure* participation, but these changes were not (yet) reflected in *de facto* participation.

McFarlin, Sweeney and Cotton (1992) sampled interview and questionnaire data about managerial attitudes toward employee participation in a U.S. multinational corporation with operations in Britain, the Netherlands, Spain and the United States. The findings revealed significant cross-cultural differences. Spanish and, to a lesser degree, British managers reported lower levels of participation among subordinates than did Dutch and U.S. managers. The study also discovered significant differences regarding managers' perceptions of the ideal level of participation and of subordinates' desire and moral right to participate.

Studies based on the Vroom/Yetton (1973) model (e.g. *Jago et al., 1993; Reber et al., 2000*) have compared habits of participatory managerial behaviour across cultures. This on-going research initiative has sampled data in Austria, the Czech Republic, Finland, Germany, Ireland, Poland, Sweden, Switzerland and the United States, among others. The method consists of a projective test, with managers reacting to thirty hypothetical decision-making cases. Respondents choose their behavioural intent from a continuum of possibilities ranging from autocratic to joint decision-making. The findings suggest a significant difference between country cultures. According to Vroom and Jago, cultural differences represent a stronger influence factor on behaviour than do differences related to hierarchical level, function, or gender:

> "[O]f all the variance that could be explained by these four demographic factors, 82% was attributable to national origin. Within a country, managers differ from each other in some predictable ways. However, this study suggests that culture-sharing managers are far more alike than they are different." (Vroom & Jago, 1995, p. 177)

The normative Vroom/Yetton model prescribes rules to ensure effective decision-making. Managers from Western countries are very similar in terms of *quality rules*, i.e. the way managers take into account the technical and task-related issues of a decision. With regard to *acceptance rules*, i.e. the way managers take subordinate acceptance of the selected decision-making process into account, country clusters emerge. To a great extent, these clusters parallel cultural clusters identified by other researchers (e.g. Ronen & Shenkar, 1985), such as a Germanic Europe and an Anglo cluster.

Smith and Peterson's (1988) Event Management model also triggered a series of cross-cultural studies (e.g. *Smith, 1997; Smith et al., 2002*). Within this model, subordinate participation is one of several choices available to managers to handle organisational events. Data about such handling of events have so far been sampled from middle managers in sixty countries. Using a questionnaire, respondents indicate to which degree different factors influence their way of handling typical work events, such as the hiring of a new subordinate. No matter which country is concerned, managers seem to have a strong preference for vertical sources of guidance, which include own experience and training, subordinates, the managers' superior and formal rules (Smith et al., 2002; analysis based on the data of 47 countries). Despite these similarities, country-specific differences become visible when the data are analysed in more detail. In one of the earlier studies (Smith & Peterson, 1994) managers were not only asked to mark which sources of guidance they had used in the past when dealing with work events, but also to evaluate the typical outcome of their strategies. According to Smith (1996) such a procedure "provides access not just to the manager's description of what usually happens, but also some expression of sentiment as to what courses of action are actually preferred" (p. 99). The analysis revealed diversity in the evaluation of subordinates as source of guidance. Subordinate participation was evaluated positively in Australia, Finland, France, Germany, India, Mexico and Britain, whereas reliance on subordinates was judged negatively in Brazil, Iran, Korea, Nigeria and the Philippines.

Suutari (1996a) compared managers' beliefs in the area of ideal managerial leadership behaviour in five Europe countries, namely Denmark, Finland, Germany, Great Britain and Sweden. Ideal leadership behaviour was conceptualised by proposing fourteen specific aspects of leadership, one of them labelled *decision participation*. This scale consisted of questionnaire items such as "The manager should consult with subordinates before making decisions" and "The manager should get work group approval on matters before going ahead." The findings suggested that decision-participation varied significantly between the five countries represented in the study.

Zander (1997) studied the relationship between managers and their subordinates in eighteen countries. She defined and explored a concept labelled *interpersonal leadership* (IPL), which included empowering, coaching, directing and communicating. The IPL construct is closely linked to participation, as Zander noted:

> "[I]n countries where employees consider that their manager should espouse participation in decision-making, the employees also consider that they should be appreciated for taking initiatives and giving advice. Correspondingly, in countries where the employees want to participate less in decision-making, they also feel that they should be less exposed to interpersonal participation." (Zander, 1997, p. 160)

The countries represented in the study were Australia, Austria, Belgium, Brazil, Canada, Denmark, Finland, France, Germany, Japan, the Netherlands, Norway, the Philippines, Spain, Sweden, Switzerland, United Kingdom and the United States. The results confirmed the author's hypothesis that employees' preferences for IPL varied across countries.

Dorfman et al. (1997) studied types of leadership behaviour across five nations in North America and Asia, namely Mexico, the United States, Japan, South Korea and Taiwan. The aim of the research project was to extend contingency theories of leadership to include national culture as a situational variable. The authors used scales developed by other researchers, one of which was a participation scale, including items such as "asking followers for suggestions, giving consideration to followers' inputs and modifying proposals in light of follower objections" (Dorfman et al, 1997, p. 264). The findings showed cultural specificity of participative behaviour. Furthermore, the data revealed a country-specific positive effect of participative leadership for productivity and subordinate satisfaction: In the U.S. sample, participative leadership was found to be a strong predictor of follower performance. A positive impact of participation on subordinate satisfaction was found in South Korea, whereas participation had no impact on productivity and satisfaction in Japan, Taiwan and Mexico.

The Global Leadership and Organisational Behaviour Effectiveness research program (GLOBE) (*House et al.*, 1999, 2004), a consortium of approximately 170 social scientists from sixty-two countries, studied the impact of societal culture on organisational leadership prototypes, such as autocratic and participative leadership. Data were elicited from middle managers. The results show that participative leadership, a second-order factor revealed through factor analysis, is viewed positively across countries, but varies in the degree to which it is considered a contributor to outstanding leadership.

Gill and Krieger (2000) set out to investigate the nature and extent of participation in ten European countries by analysing the EPOC database. The EPOC (1997) survey, a study commissioned by the European Foundation for the Improvement of Living and Working Conditions, had sampled data from general managers in more than 5.700 organisations based in ten European countries, namely Denmark, France, Germany, Ireland, Italy, the Netherlands, Portugal, Spain, Sweden and the UK. The questionnaire included items pertaining to consultative participation as well as delegative participation. Among other questions, the authors examined the "incidence and scope" of direct participation. Incidence refers to the form of direct participation, such as individual or group consultation or delegation, whereas scope measures the range of issues on which employees are consulted or given rights to make decisions. The authors stated that "[a]t first sight, it seems that direct participation is widely practised by the workplaces in the EPOC survey. [...] No fewer than 82 percent of respondents said that they practised at least one of the forms of direct participation; the proportion was highest in the Netherlands (90 percent) and lowest in Portugal (61 percent)" (p. 116). However, the authors also found: "[T]here appears to be a considerable gap between the rhetoric and reality of direct participation" (p. 118) and "[i]t seems that the adoption of direct participation practices has been piecemeal and patchy in the great majority of European enterprises, and that management has been highly selective in choosing elements of direct participation to suit themselves" (p. 119).

Cabrera, Ortega and Cabrera (2003) also conducted an empirical study based on the EPOC (1997) database. Their primary aim was to identify determinants of direct participation rather than to compare countries. Nonetheless, they also reported upon average consultative and delegative participation scores per country. These data suggest significant differences among the countries for both forms of participation. The Netherlands showed the highest level of both consultative and delegative participation, whereas Portugal, Spain and Italy were found to be the lowest ranked countries for both forms of participation.

2.2.3 Studies Exploring the Culture-Participation Link

Not all studies of participation in the field of cross-cultural management compare participation across cultures. Researchers have also been interested in the question of whether and in which way participation is embedded in societal culture.

2.2.3.1 The Relevance of Culture Dimensions

One way to conceptualise societal culture is by means of culture dimensions. Most prominently, *Hofstede* (1980a) employed the findings of a large-scale survey across forty countries and three regions within the IBM corporation to define four dimensions along which societal culture can be differentiated: power distance, individualism-collectivism, uncertainty avoidance and masculinity. A fifth dimension, long-term versus short-term orientation, was introduced later, after data from Asian cultures became available (Hofstede & Bond, 1988; Hofstede, 2001). Hofstede's dimensional approach became very popular among cross-cultural management scientists and led to several replication studies (e.g. Hoppe, 1990; Lowe, 1994; Søndergaard, 1994). Although criticised on methodological grounds - for example, Sorge (1983) argued that Hofstede's sample originating from just one organisation made the results vulnerable to organisation culture influences - most follow-up studies confirmed the relevance of the five dimensions.

Other cross-cultural researchers have also explored culture dimensions. For example, Triandis (1988, 1993) focused on individualism versus collectivism, and Schwartz (1994) studied such dimensions as hierarchy, conservatism and egalitarian commitment. Nonetheless, Hofstede's framework is still the most commonly used and cited work in the area of culture dimensions and it seems not to have lost relevance, even some twenty-five years later. For example, Smith (1996) reviewed three large post-Hofstede surveys, namely Hoppe (1990), Trompenaars (1993) and Smith, Dugan and Trompenaars (1996). Based on this review he concluded that dimensions similar to Hofstede's individualism-collectivism and power distance emerge from all three studies.

"There are no indications that the cultural diversity mapped by Hofstede is in progress of disappearing. [...] [T]here is substantial evidence that these two dimensions do not simply identify values endorsed by managers. They are reliably linked to the ways in which managers describe their day-to-day behaviour and to the types of difficulties which arise in cross-cultural negotiation, joint venture management and team-work within multinationals." (Smith, 1996, p. 101)

In the following, the culture dimensions of power distance, uncertainty avoidance and collectivism are discussed in more detail, since these dimensions appear to be conceptually connected to participation.

Power distance refers to the degree to which members of a society expect power to be unequally shared among its members (Hofstede, 1980a; House et al., 2004). Table 2.1 lists some work-related differences between cultures with low and high power distance indices.

Table 2.1 Implications of Low and High Power Distance

Low PDI (Power distance index)	High PDI (Power distance index)
Decentralised decision structures; less concentration of authority.	Centralised decision structures; more concentration of authority.
The ideal boss is a resourceful democrat; sees self as practical, orderly and relying on support.	The ideal boss is a well-meaning autocrat or good father; sees self as benevolent decision-maker.
Subordinates expect to be consulted.	Subordinates expect to be told.
Consultative leadership leads to satisfaction, performance and productivity.	Authoritative leadership and close supervision lead to satisfaction, performance and productivity.

Source: Hofstede (2001, pp. 107f)

Two of the three Hofstede power distance scale items measure leadership behaviour or expectations of leadership behaviour. In other words, power distance "deals directly with expectations of and relationships to authority" (Offermann & Hellmann, 1997, p. 343) and is, therefore, the most relevant societal culture dimension to consider in a discussion of participative management from a holistic standpoint. Hofstede (1980a) suggested that decision-making processes are likely to be more participative in low power distance countries than in countries with higher levels of power distance: "Distributing influence comes more naturally to low- than to high-PDI cultures" (Hofstede, 2001, p. 389). The GLOBE study (House et al., 2004) empirically tested the relationship between societal culture values and practices on the one hand and leadership dimensions on the other hand. Analyses showed that both power distance values and practices have a statistically significant and negative relationship with participative leadership ideals (Carl, Gupta & Javidan, 2004). It follows that participation is more likely to be perceived as contributing to effective management in societies with low power distance scores.

Uncertainty avoidance defines a society's reliance on social norms and procedures to alleviate the unpredictability of future events (Hofstede, 1980a; House et al., 2004). Table 2.2 shows some of the work-related differences between cultures with low and high levels of uncertainty avoidance.

Table 2.2 Implications of Low and High Uncertainty Avoidance

Low UAI (Uncertainty avoidance index)	High UAI (Uncertainty avoidance index)
Power of superiors depends on position and relationships.	Power of superiors depends on control of uncertainties.
Appeal of transformational leader role.	Appeal of hierarchical control role.
Superiors optimistic about employees' ambition and leadership capacities.	Superiors pessimistic about employees' ambition and leadership capacities.

Source: Hofstede (2001, pp. 169f)

A country's level of uncertainty avoidance is not predictive of the *level* of participation, but one can assume that participation is more formalised (*de jure* participation) in high uncertainty avoidance countries, and the higher level of formalisation most likely has an impact on *de facto* participation (Szabo, 2004). Hofstede (1980a, 2001) related uncertainty avoidance (together with power distance) to the form of participation adopted in a country. In countries with low UAI combined with low PDI (e.g. Anglo countries, Scandinavian countries), organisations are likely to adopt informal and spontaneous forms of participation. In countries with medium to high UAI combined with low PDI (e.g. German-speaking countries) organisations are characterised by formal, legally determined systems of participation.

Collectivism, as opposed to *individualism*, describes "the relationship between the individual and the collectivity that prevails in a given society" (Hofstede, 2001, p. 209). Societies with high levels of collectivism differ from societies with high levels of individualism on many grounds, some of which are listed in Table 2.3.

According to Hofstede (2001), group processes are more likely to occur naturally in organisational settings of countries with high levels of collectivism. Participation includes such group processes in the form of managers consulting with their subordinates or as joint decision-making. Ceteris paribus, one can expect a higher degree of participation in collectivist countries.

According to the GLOBE study (House et al., 2004), statistically significant relationships exist between collectivist societal culture values and participative leadership ideals. Two value dimensions employed in the study, institutional and in-group collectivism, were shown to be positively related to participation ideals (Gelfand et al., 2004). It follows, similar to Hofstede (2001), that participation is more likely to be perceived as contributing to effective management in societies with high collectivism scores.

Table 2.3 Implications of High Collectivism and High Individualism

High collectivism	High individualism
Belief in collective decisions.	Belief in individual decisions.
Employees and managers report teamwork and personal contacts at work.	Employees and managers report working individually.
Management is management of groups.	Management is management of individuals.
Leadership is inseparable from the context.	Leadership is a property of the leader.

Source: Hofstede (2001, pp. 244f)

2.2.3.2 Studies Employing Culture Dimensions

Several studies have attempted to empirically verify the proposed link between culture dimensions and participation, among them Hofstede (2001), Suutari (1996a), Offermann and Hellmann (1997), Zander (1997) and Gerstner and Day (1994).

Hofstede (2001) correlated the country scores of the power distance index (PDI) with various country-level scores of participation published by other authors, such as Tannenbaum et al. (1974). He found that "where Tannenbaum et al. measured *formal* elements of hierarchy, these did not show any relationship with PDI at all. [...] Where they measured *informal* elements of hierarchy, these followed more or less the PDI order" (Hofstede, 2001, p. 109, emphasis in original). He concluded that formal and informal participation should be clearly distinguished and that *de facto* participation was not reflective of *de jure* participation. Hofstede's conclusion is in contradiction to other researchers who argued in favour of a relationship between *de facto* and *de jure* participation (compare Section 2.1.1).

In *Suutari's (1996a)* comparative study of ideal leadership behaviour in five European countries (compare Section 2.2.2), most of the research questions were based on Hofstede's (1980a) framework of culture dimensions. Except for small deviations, his findings fitted the proposed country rankings as suggested by Hofstede's indices. For example, the country rankings on Suutari's participation decision scale paralleled those for power distance insofar as Germany and Great Britain showed higher scores than Finland

and Denmark. Contrary to what could be expected, Sweden scored lowest on participation decision. Suutari speculated that the divergence might be explained by limitations in the matching of his country samples.

Offermann and Hellmann (1997) examined the relationship between work-related values held by managers (in particular power distance, uncertainty avoidance and individualism-collectivism) and their leadership practices. The sample consisted of thirty-nine countries. Direct reports by subordinates were used to assess perceptions of managerial behaviour in the areas of leader communication, leader control, delegation, approachability and team building. Power distance was found to be significantly and negatively associated with leader communication, delegation, approachability and team building. High levels of uncertainty avoidance were significantly associated with more leader control, but less delegation and approachability. Contrary to the authors' expectation, collectivism was not significantly related to increased team-building behaviour.

Zander (1997) compared the results of her 18-country study on interpersonal leadership (compare Section 2.2.2) with 25 culture dimensions identified by other researchers, namely Hofstede (1980a), Laurent (1983), Trompenaars (1993), Schwartz (1994) and Lane, DiStefano and Maznevski (1997). The comparison confirmed that country-specific preferences for interpersonal leadership (empowering, coaching and directing) were significantly related to national cultural values and beliefs. With regard to Hofstede's dimensions, the "operationalisation of power distance by using behavioural items" (Zander, 1997, p. 224) instead of values and beliefs made her exclude this dimension from her analysis. Contrary to what could be expected, empowering was not significantly related to uncertainty avoidance, whereas coaching showed the predicted negative correlation with uncertainty avoidance. Collectivism correlated significantly and negatively with employees' preferences for coaching. Zander speculated that "[it] is possible that coaching with its component of managerial concern for the employees' careers is of particular interest in countries where value is placed on the individual as the basic unit in society" (p. 249). Directing, operationalised by items related to supervision and review, was expected to correlate positively with uncertainty avoidance and this prediction was confirmed by the data.

Gerstner and Day's (1994) study represents a more general enquiry into the relationship of societal culture dimensions and perceptions of ideal leadership, and deals with participation only indirectly. University students in eight countries (France, Germany, Honduras, India, Taiwan, China, Japan and the United States) evaluated attributes relevant to leadership (e.g. authoritarian, directing, co-operative). The study found significant differences across countries in the ratings provided for particular traits. Multidimensional scaling revealed three dimensions in which the country data varied. These dimensions had rank order correlations with Hofstede's (1980a) measures of power distance, uncertainty avoidance and individualism of 0,81, 1,00 and 0,70, respectively. The authors concluded that their findings provide empirical support for the relevance of Hofstede's dimensions in understanding cultural differences in leadership perceptions.

2.2.3.3 Studies Employing Culture-Related Factors

In addition to the described studies into the relationship between participation and culture dimensions, other researchers have explored potential links of participation with such culture-related factors as a society's political and legally-coded arrangements, patterns of conflict and preferences for the structuring of organisations.

Jacob and Ahn (1978) explored the question of whether the socio-economic and management systems, in which people work, affect their participatory behaviour. The study included six socialist and nine non-socialist countries. Data were sampled from both managers and workers. The authors found statistically significant differences in participation between the fifteen countries, and these differences pertained to level and type of participation, as well as to opportunities for and commitment to participation, but were not related to the differences in the economic systems, i.e. socialist versus capitalist. Jacob and Ahn's study revises assumptions made by other researchers (e.g. Hofstede, 1980a) that the (former) communist countries shared similar levels of power distance.

The *IDE (1981, 1993)* project did not only compare participation between European countries (compare Section 2.2.2). One major aim of the research initiative was the study of the impact of *de jure* upon *de facto* participation. As mentioned above, law was found to be the most important formal basis for participation in most countries and the data revealed a strong relationship between *de jure* and *de facto* participation, in particular for representative participation. This finding indicates that "participation is to a significant extent a result of socio-political will" (Wilpert, 1998, p. 50).

The IDE group also explored the relationship between participation and such culture-related factors as conflict and the degree of formalisation of organisations. With regard to conflict, the findings suggested that "greater involvement in participative decision-making is accompanied by increased levels of conflict, although [...] the conflicts are related to specific decisions and do not correlate with overt behaviour like strikes" (IDE, 1981, p. 287). Formalisation was found to contribute to an increase in influence by employees.

Chapter 3

Research Focus

3.1 Research Questions and Study Goals

The concept of participative management concerns the way in which and to what extent managers include their subordinates and/or other people in their own work, and most notably in their decision-making. As shown in the Chapter 2 review, participative management is extensively covered both in the conceptual and empirical cross-cultural literature. A systematic classification of the publications and their foci provides an understanding of the current status in this field of research. Therefore, Table 3.1 groups the material according to the attributes of participative management dealt with in each publication. The classification scheme follows Strauss and Corbin's (1998) recommendation for a structured perspective on theoretical concepts. Key attributes of participative management, such as "level of participation" or "participation range", are listed in the left-hand column of the table. The middle column summarises the theoretical contributions to the discussion with regard to each attribute, whereas the right-hand column lists empirical cross-cultural studies.

Table 3.1 addresses a couple of important issues. Firstly, certain attributes of participative management such as "assumptions underlying participation", "participation range" or "outcomes of participative management" are discussed in the theoretical literature but have yet to be covered by cross-cultural studies. A probable reason for this lack of coverage lies in the complexity of the research area: Empirical studies into such areas as underlying assumptions would require a more holistic approach into the *meaning* of participative management than is commonly employed.

Secondly, the empirical cross-cultural studies do not lend themselves easily to comparison. For example, quite a few studies focus on the level of participation, yet they measure various intra-personal concepts such as attitudes (e.g. Haire, Ghiselli & Porter, 1966), reflections of own participative behaviour (e.g. Smith et al., 2002), habits of participatory behaviour (e.g. Jago et al., 1993) or perceptions of the ideal level of participation (e.g. House et al., 2004). Furthermore, some researchers (e.g. Cabrera, Ortega & Cabrera, 2003; House et al., 2004) treat participative management as a broad behavioural pattern while other studies such as the studies based on the Vroom/

Table 3.1 Summary Review of the Participative Management Literature

Key attributes of participative management	Theoretical literature	Cross-cultural studies
Level of participation	Bi-polar view of participation: Autocratic-directive vs. democratic-participative (Lewin, Lippitt & White, 1939; Lippitt & White, 1943) Participation as a continuum (Tannenbaum & Schmidt, 1958; Vroom & Yetton, 1973; Black & Gregersen, 1997)	Managerial attitudes toward participation (Haire, Ghiselli & Porter, 1966; McFarlin, Sweeney & Cotton, 1992) Reported degree of participation (Tannenbaum et al., 1974; Dorfman et al., 1997; IDE, 1981, 1993; Gill & Krieger, 2000; studies based on the Event Management model, e.g. Smith et al., 2002; Cabrera, Ortega & Cabrera, 2003) Habits of participatory behaviour (studies based on the Vroom/Yetton model, e.g. Jago et al., 1993) Ideal level of participation (Suutari, 1996a; GLOBE study, e.g. House et al., 2004)
Assumptions underlying participation	Humanistic view, power sharing, organisational efficiency (Strauss, 1998a)	-
Prerequisites and mediating factors at the individual level	Attitude toward participation (Chisholm & Vansina, 1993; Wilpert, 1998; Strauss, 1998c; Pusic, 1998) Trust (Strauss, 1998c; Leana, 1986) Type of leader (Contingency model of leadership: Fiedler, 1967; path-goal theory of leadership: Evans, 1968, 1970; House & Mitchell, 1974) Traits of manager and subordinates (Glew et al., 1995) Subordinates' expectations (Jacob & Ahn, 1978)	Gender and age (Tannenbaum et al., 1974; studies based on the Vroom/Yetton model, e.g. Reber et al., 2000)
Prerequisites and mediating factors at the situational and organisational level	Quality and/or acceptance requirements, information, problem structure, goal congruence, prior probability of acceptance, subordinate conflict (Vroom & Yetton, 1973) Decision type (Content, importance and complexity: Dachler & Wilpert, 1978; technical vs. interest decisions: Pusic, 1998; strategic, tactical, operational and welfare decisions: Knudsen, 1995)	Decisions with quality and/or acceptance requirements, information, problem structure, goal congruence between manager and subordinates, prior probability of acceptance, subordinate conflict (studies based on the Vroom/Yetton model, e.g. Reber et al., 2000) Participation of subordinates in relation to other guidance sources (studies based on the Event Management model, e.g. Smith et al., 2002)

Table 3.1 (continued)

Key attributes of participative management	Theoretical literature	Cross-cultural studies
Prerequisites and mediating factors at the situational and organisational level (continued)	Degree of formality of the participative system (Chisholm & Vansina, 1993); Organisational size (Strauss, 1998c); Differentiation strategy based on quality vs. cost leadership (Cabrera, Ortega & Cabrera, 2003)	Hierarchical level and organisational size (Tannenbaum et al., 1974)
Prerequisites and mediating factors at the macro level	Competition and sector (Cabrera, Ortega & Cabrera, 2003); Societal characteristics (Dachler & Wilpert, 1978; Strauss, 1998c)	Culture dimensions (Hofstede, 1980a, 2001; Suutari, 1996a; Offermann & Hellmann, 1997; Zander, 1997; Gerstner & Day, 1994); Socio-economic system (Tannenbaum et al., 1974; Jacob & Ahn, 1978); De jure participation (IDE, 1981, 1993)
Participation range	Subordinates immediately affected (Dachler & Wilpert, 1978)	-
Managerial behaviour and the decision-making process	Differing access to decision-making by employees (Dachler & Wilpert, 1978); Different strategies by manager, incl. consultative and joint decision-making (Vroom & Yetton, 1973); Participation in different steps of the decision-making process (Black & Gregersen, 1997)	Employees' preferences for empowering, coaching and directing (Zander, 1997); Influence and involvement (IDE, 1981, 1993); Consultative vs. delegative participation, range of issues (Gill & Krieger, 2000); Different strategies, incl. consultative and group decision-making (studies based on the Vroom/Yetton model, e.g. Reber et al., 2000)
Outcomes of participative management	Productivity and satisfaction (Locke & Schweiger, 1979; Cotton et al., 1988; Miller & Monge, 1986; Wagner, 1994); Decision quality and acceptance (Vroom & Yetton, 1973)	-

Yetton model (e.g. Jago et al., 1993) explore participative behaviour on a more specific level and take the context into account. The number of countries represented in the empirical studies ranges from four (McFarlin, Sweeney & Cotton, 1992) to sixty-two (House et al., 2004). Different studies sample data from different countries and only a few countries, such as the United States, Germany or Sweden, are represented in more than five of the reviewed studies. Most of the studies take a purely comparative perspective, while a few go beyond this focus by looking at *de facto* participation in relation to *de jure* participation (IDE, 1981, 1993), societal culture dimensions (Offermann & Hellmann, 1997; Zander, 1997) or the economic system (Jacob & Ahn, 1978).

The fact that the meaning of participative management has been given only little consideration in most of the previous research combined with the lack of integration of the reviewed studies formed the basis for the current research initiative, namely an integrative cross-cultural study with five European countries selected for close exploration: the Czech Republic, Finland, Germany, Sweden and Poland (see Section 3.2.1.1 for a description of the selection criteria). The study explores two core themes of participative management, namely meaning and enactment. Meaning relates to how people in different countries define and understand participative management, while enactment deals with the results of how this meaning is translated into behaviour. In its concentration on the meaning *and* enactment of participation, the current study takes a holistic perspective. In contrast to existing studies that measure only one attribute of participative management, in most cases "level of participation" (compare Table 3.1), the current study aims at a *parallel* exploration of relevant attributes, because they are assumed to be interwoven and interdependent. For example, the attribute "assumptions underlying participation" is likely to be a key attribute relevant for understanding "managerial behaviour and the decision-making process". In addition, certain attributes may vary in relevance from country to country. The meaning of participative management may for instance be guided by internalised values such as equality in some countries, while this might not be the case in other countries.

In addition to an integrated consideration of relevant attributes of participative management, the study also explores contextual factors including country-specific concepts. Contextual factors may influence participative management in unique ways, as Vroom and Jago stressed:

> "Participation cannot be studied without explicit attention to the context in which it is displayed. Leadership measures that try to capture a leader's style by asking a few questions about typical or average behaviour are simply of little value. Certainly, there are those of us who are predisposed to be more autocratic or participative than another. However, the circumstances a person faces often dictate behaviour other than that to which he or she is predisposed. And

those situational forces have the larger effect when pitted against the person's inclinations or desires." (Vroom & Jago, 1995, p. 179)

It follows from the previous discussion that the aim of this study is to explore the social phenomenon of participative management in a holistic sense rather than to test predefined concepts. Qualitative methodology was selected as best suited for the core of the study (for details see Chapter 5.1), and integration of the findings with existing quantitative research subsequently takes place. In each of the five countries, qualitative interviews are conducted with middle managers and the resulting data serve as the basis for the development of country-specific models of participative management as well as for the integration effort. As for methodology, elements of grounded theory (Strauss & Corbin, 1998), in part adapted to fit the cross-cultural nature of the study, help to achieve this goal.

The following two broad research questions summarise the focus of the study.

Research Question 1: What is the meaning and enactment of participative management in the Czech Republic, Finland, Germany, Poland and Sweden?

Research Question 2: What are the main contextual factors in which the meaning and enactment of participative management is embedded?

By exploring the meaning and enactment of participative management within its context, the current study also relates to the following theoretically and practically oriented goals:

Study Goal 1: Integration of the qualitative findings, in particular with earlier quantitative cross-cultural studies of participative management.

This goal emerged from the issues discussed at the beginning of this chapter and addresses the criticism by researchers such as Yukl (1998), who argues that a vast number of (leadership) studies have been carried out and published over time, without at the same time establishing links and building on existing knowledge. In the current study, integration is planned into the following three areas: existing quantitative studies, the country-specific management literature and the countries' industrial relations systems. With regard to the first area, a subset of three studies is selected for closer inspection: the GLOBE study, the Event Management study and the Vroom/Yetton study (see Section 3.2.2.1 for a description of the selection criteria). Concerning the third area of integration in this study, researchers differ in their theoretical positions about the relationship between a country's industrial relation system (mainly *de jure* participation) and *de facto* participative management, and assumed relationships are difficult to support empirically (compare Chapter 2.1.1). In studying participative management in its wider context, the current study may provide new information about the relationship.

Study Goal 2: Enhancement of theoretical knowledge about participative management.

The grounded theory approach (Strauss & Corbin, 1998) employed in the current study explicitly facilitates the building of theory originating in empirical data: Firstly, the study is designed to result in country-specific models of participative management, representing "substantive theories" (Glaser & Strauss, 1967). Secondly, the country findings are compared among themselves, with earlier research and with the literature. This process may lead to new theoretical insights and possibly to modifications and/or additions to existing theoretical positions about participative management. Thirdly, a grounded theory study typically results in theoretical statements of a more general nature, thus continuing theory building toward a more "formal theory" (Glaser & Strauss, 1967).

Study Goal 3: Enhancement of practical knowledge about country-specific versions of participative management within Europe.

The economic integration in Europe implies that managers are increasingly being confronted with colleagues and subordinates from other countries and cultural backgrounds. For fruitful interactions to take place, it is important to know about the dynamics that play a role in shaping managerial behaviour. The current study provides a contribution to this kind of knowledge building.

Study Goal 4: Increased knowledge about areas of convergence and divergence between countries and/or country clusters.

The country-specific models of participative management may be similar in some aspects, while they may differ in others. Particularly awareness about and attention to areas of divergence can influence the success or failure of intercultural interaction.

To answer the two research questions and to address the four study goals, the subsequent parts of this volume are structured as follows: Section 3.2 below sets the stage for the study by zooming in on five European countries and on three quantitative studies, which serve as the basis for integration (Study Goal 1). Chapter 4 describes these three quantitative studies: the GLOBE study, the Event Management study and the Vroom/Yetton study. The chapter also lists areas of consistency and contradiction between the country scores of the three studies, thus further supporting the need for integration that is one of the main aims of the current study. Chapter 5 summarises the methodological approach and focuses particularly on the study's qualitative core including research instruments, procedures and interview partners. The chapter also describes in detail the principles of data analysis originating from the grounded theory approach. Chapters 6 to 11 present the study findings, each of the first five chapters focussing on one country (within-country analyses) and Chapter 11 summarising and comparing between the five countries (inter-country analysis). More specifically, Chapters 6 to 10 present the country-specific models of participative management as they emerged from the qualitative core study. Each country chapter covers the meaning and enactment of participative management (Research Question 1) as well as emerging contextual factors (Research Question 2). Each country chapter also contains a section labelled "integration", in which the fit with the selected quantitative studies, the country's industrial relations system and the country-specific management literature are discussed (Study Goal 1). Each country chapter aims to enhance both theoretical knowledge about country-specific versions of participative management (Study Goal 2) and practical knowledge (Study Goal 3). Chapter 11 describes the inter-country analysis and lists areas of convergence and divergence in participative management between the five countries (Study Goal 4). The chapter further compares the outcomes of the current study with the conceptual positions about participative management summarised in Chapter 2.1 and suggests additions and/or modifications (Study Goal 2). Finally, Chapter 12 concludes the study by formulating theoretical propositions arising from the study's findings, suggesting a general model of participative management in context (Study Goal 2), drawing conclusions and pointing out areas of future research.

3.2 Zooming In On Five Countries and Three Quantitative Studies

3.2.1 Selecting Five European Countries

3.2.1.1 Selection Criteria

It was decided to compare participative management in a number of *European* countries. Being a native of Austria where I also live, it seemed natural to me to explore participation within a European context. Apart from this personal interest, it is a given that most models and theories in management research have been developed by U.S. American scholars on the basis of U.S.

American data. Many of these models and theories have influenced the design of European management education programmes and certainly in part also the way European businesses operate. Yet, management within Europe is different from management "made in the United States" and this difference continues to call for theories and models that adhere to European requirements and acknowledge the diversity that exists within Europe. More than twenty years have passed since Geert Hofstede (1980b) asked the question of whether or not American theories apply abroad. The current study is a contribution to theory building grounded in data collected from European sources.

It was, of course, impossible to include all European countries in the current study. As for the selection of a subset of countries, the following criteria were defined: (1) In order to allow integration (Study Goal 1), country data should be available for the three selected quantitative studies: the Vroom/ Yetton, the Event Management and the GLOBE studies. (2) The countries should represent different cultural clusters within Europe as well as geographic regions with manifold historical and economic backgrounds (Study Goal 4). (3) The institutional context for participative management, in particular the system of industrial relations, should differ among the selected countries in order to allow an exploration of the fit with the emerging country-specific models of participative management (Study Goal 1). (4) On a more pragmatic note, data collection should be feasible in the selected countries, for example through facilitating local partners. (5) The number of selected countries should be large enough to be able to drop a country without jeopardising the overall project, in case data collection in a country was delayed or turned out extremely difficult.

Initially, eight European countries were selected for inclusion in the study, namely Austria, the Czech Republic, Finland, France, Germany, Ireland, Poland and Sweden. These countries are represented in the three selected quantitative studies, thus making integration feasible. The countries represent different clusters within Europe (for details see Section 3.2.1.2 below) and also feature varying systems of industrial relations (for details see Section 3.2.1.3 below). In all eight countries, colleagues at universities or other research institutions agreed to assist in setting up the study by establishing contact with organisations and managers.

During the data collection phase, France had to be dropped from the study. The reason was that the French database was too sparse to allow thorough analysis and interpretation, although three contact persons tried their best to find managers willing to participate in the study. Consequently, data from seven countries were available for analysis. The findings for Austria and Ireland are presented in separate forthcoming publications. Thus, the study, as it is presented in this volume, is based on the data collected in five countries.

3.2.1.2 Cultural Clusters

Following the criteria described in Section 3.2.1.1, the countries to be included in the current study should represent different cultural clusters within Europe. A cultural cluster is a group of cultures sharing relevant similarities, such as geography, common language, history, religion or the ethnicity of its inhabitants (Ronen & Shenkar, 1985; Gupta & Hanges, 2004). Either based on large-scale empirical studies or on in-depth reviews of earlier cross-cultural studies, several researchers tried to identify such clusters. The outcomes of some of these initiatives are summarised in Table 3.2.

Table 3.2 European Country Clusters

Clusters based on the synthesis of earlier research (Ronen & Shenkar, 1985)	Clusters based on GLOBE societal culture data (Gupta, Hanges & Dorfman, 2002; Gupta & Hanges, 2004)	Clusters based on GLOBE leadership data (Brodbeck et al., 2000)
Anglo (United Kingdom, Ireland)	Anglo (England, Ireland)	Anglo/Nordic (England, Ireland, Netherlands, Sweden, Finland, Denmark)
Nordic (Finland, Norway, Denmark, Sweden)	Nordic Europe (Finland, Sweden, Denmark)	
Latin European (France, Belgium, Italy, Spain, Portugal)	Latin Europe (Italy, Portugal, Spain, France, French speaking Switzerland)	Latin Europe (Italy, Spain, Portugal)
Germanic (Austria, Germany, Switzerland)	Germanic Europe (Austria, German speaking Switzerland, Netherlands, former East Germany, former West Germany)	Germanic (Austria, German speaking Switzerland, former East Germany, former West Germany)
-	Eastern Europe (Hungary, Russia, Albania, Poland, Greece, Slovenia)	Central Europe (Poland, Slovenia)
Near Eastern (Greece, Turkey)	Arab Cultures (Turkey)	Near East (Greece, Turkey)

Notes: Some of the clusters, e.g. the Anglo cluster, include European as well as non-European countries. This table shows the European countries only.

Ronen and Shenkar (1985) reviewed eight cross-cultural studies using attitudinal data, including Haire, Ghiselli and Porter (1966), Sirota and Greenwood (1971), Hofstede (1976), Redding (1976), Ronen and Kraut (1977), Badawy (1979), Griffeth et al. (1980) and Hofstede (1980a). Based on their review, Ronen and Shenkar identified eight country clusters, five of which include European countries (see left-hand column in Table 3.2). As part of the GLOBE project, Gupta, Hanges and Dorfman (2002) and Gupta and Hanges (2004) examined whether the societal culture data of sixty-two countries clustered in accordance with classifications identified by earlier research and "found very good support" (Gupta, Hanges & Dorfman, 2002, p. 14). The European GLOBE country clusters are listed in the middle column of Table 3.2. As another part of the GLOBE project, Brodbeck at al. (2000) aimed at identifying clusters of European countries sharing similar leadership concepts. Their study is based on the assumption that clusters of European countries sharing similar cultural values also share similar leadership concepts. The authors reported that their results "strongly support the hypothesis that leadership prototypes vary as a function of cultural differences" (p. 14). The country clusters identified by Brodbeck and his colleagues are listed in the right-hand column of Table 3.2.

In addition to these three studies, other researchers identified dividing lines in Europe between the West and East (Smith, Dugan & Trompenaars, 1996), as well as between the North and South (Smith, 1997).

The clustering studies show that the countries selected for the current study indeed belong to different clusters, as defined in the selection criteria. Sweden and Finland are part of the Nordic Europe cluster, Germany (former West) of the Germanic Europe cluster, and the Czech Republic and Poland of the Eastern Europe cluster. In other words, the current study is comprised of countries belonging to three of the European clusters reported in Table 3.2. With regard to the West vs. East differentiation reported by Smith, Dugan and Trompenaars (1996), three countries selected for the current study are part of the Western Europe cluster (Germany, Sweden, Finland) and two countries (Czech Republic and Poland) belong to the Eastern Europe cluster. In respect of the Northern vs. Southern distinction reported by Smith (1997), three of the selected countries belong to the Northern cluster (Finland, Sweden, Germany).

3.2.1.3 Industrial Relations Systems

Study Goal 1 concerns the evaluation of the relationship between the emerging country-specific models of participative management on the one hand and the country-specific systems of industrial relations on the other hand. In order to be able to explore and compare different approaches, one of the criteria listed in Section 3.2.1.1 states that the countries to be included in the current study should feature different systems of industrial relations.

Before demonstrating that variance exists among the five selected countries, some general remarks must be made: The term "industrial relations" is strongly related to that of "industrial democracy". In this volume, definitions by Hoffmann et al. (2002) and Hammer (1996) provide the basis for the use of these two terms:

"Industrial relations consist of a web of institutionalised relationships between employees and their representatives (trade unions), employers and their representatives (employers' associations) and the state." (Hoffmann et al., 2002, p. 7)

"The term 'industrial democracy' refers to the structures and institutional mechanisms that give workers or their representatives the opportunity to influence organisational decision making in their places of employment. [The four main types are:] (1) co-determination, or supervisory board representation; (2) works councils and similar bodies, such as labour-management committees; (3) trade union representation; and (4) shop-floor programmes." (Hammer, 1996, p. 1921f)

European countries feature a variety of different types of industrial relations (Cabrera, Ortega & Cabrera, 2003) and industrial democracy (Ronen, 1986). Industrial relations may be based on statutory regulation (*de jure* participation), whereas hardly any regulation might be common in others, and yet other countries may adopt a mixture of legal and voluntary elements. Collective bargaining, i.e. the institutionalised process by which employees or their representatives negotiate with employers or their representatives aiming to jointly determine terms and conditions of employment (Strauss, 1996), plays a vital role in the EU15 member states (EU member states before the most recent round of enlargement in 2004), whereas it is a new element in the former communist countries (Thirkell, Scase & Vickerstaff, 1997). Furthermore, collective bargaining can be centralised or de-centralised (Carley, 2002). Works councils and trade union representatives constitute the two main forms of workplace representation. In 2002, the EU adopted a directive, which sets the stage for a general framework for informing and consulting employee representatives and which calls for such mandatory employee representation structures as works councils by 2008. This directive has led to differing reactions among the European countries.

In addition to these general differences between European countries, the five countries selected for the current study show the following patterns: (1) Germany, Finland and Sweden are among the highly regulated European countries, whereas the systems of industrial relations are still under construction in Poland and the Czech Republic. (2) In Finland and Sweden, collective bargaining concerning issues such as wages and working conditions mainly takes place *above* company level, i.e. at the national or sectoral level, whereas most of the bargaining processes occur at company level in countries such as Poland. (3) The coverage of collective bargaining, i.e. the proportion of employees who have their salary and work conditions set by collective agreements, varies greatly between the five countries. The proportion is lowest in the Czech Republic, namely about twenty-five percent, whereas it amounts to almost hundred percent in Sweden. (4) There are substantial differences in union density, ranging from about fifteen percent in Poland to close to eighty percent in Sweden and Finland. (5) Co-determination ranges from extensive employee participation, such as the legal requirement of including a labour director on the management board of German firms in the Coal, Iron and Steel industry, to no representation at all on the supervisory boards of private companies, for example in Poland. (6)

Works councils or union representatives are legally mandated in Finland, Germany and Sweden, whereas such legislation does not exist in the Czech Republic and Poland.

In summary, the selection of the Czech Republic, Finland, Germany, Poland and Sweden for the current study fulfils the requirement of diversity in the systems of industrial relations and industrial democracy, as stated in Section 3.2.1.1 above.

3.2.2 Selecting Three Quantitative Studies

Chapter 2.2 provided a review of a number of cross-cultural studies dealing with participative management. A subset of these studies is selected to serve as the basis for integration with the current study's findings (Study Goal 1).

3.2.2.1 Selection Criteria

The following criteria guided the selection process: (1) Studies to be included in the current study should be based on theoretical models to facilitate the integration and interpretation of their results. (2) To allow comparability, the studies should focus on the same key attribute of participative management (compare Table 3.1), while showing some variation in the measurement of this attribute. (3) The collected data should represent comparable cohorts of a country's society, ideally middle managers. The rationale for focussing on middle management is that such a position unites two organisational roles within one person, namely the managerial role on the one hand and the subordinate role on the other hand. (4) The studies should use different quantitative methods in order to allow triangulation (Jick, 1979).

3.2.2.2 Studies Overview

The empirical studies based on the Vroom/Yetton model, the Event Management model and the GLOBE project focus on the same key attribute of participative management, namely "level of participation", and they also fulfil the other selection criteria defined in Section 3.2.2.1. Table 3.3 summarises the three research initiatives in terms of their theoretical basis, focus and method.

As shown in Table 3.3, the three studies provide a useful basis for comparison with the current study. In particular, they measure the level of participation based on different intra-personal concepts: The GLOBE study covers the degree to which country-specific images of ideal leadership take participation into account. The Event Management study measures managers' assessment of their reliance on the "guidance source subordinates" in the handling of typical work events. The Vroom/Yetton study focuses on managers' habits of participatory decision-making behaviour, measured on the basis of a number of very specific decision-making scenarios. The degree of contextuality differs between the three studies, with the GLOBE study on the low end and the Vroom/Yetton study on the high end of the continuum.

Table 3.3 Characteristics of the Selected Quantitative Studies

	GLOBE study	Event Management study	Vroom/Yetton study
Theoretical basis	House et al. (1999, 2004)	Smith & Peterson (1988)	Vroom & Yetton (1973)
Covered aspects of participation	Leadership ideals (implicit leadership theories), such as participative behaviour, in relation to dimensions of societal culture	Guidance sources (persons/factors, such as subordinates) employed by a manager to attach meaning to work events and to guide behaviour	Habits of participatory behaviour (continuum autocratic/consultative/group decision-making)
Data collection	1990s	1990s	1990s
Sample	Middle managers	Middle managers	Mostly middle managers
Method	Questionnaire	Questionnaire	Projective test (reaction to case descriptions)
Number of countries	62	47	18

The GLOBE study has the additional benefit that it does not only present data concerning participative management, but also relating to such societal culture dimensions as power distance, uncertainty avoidance and collectivism. These factors have repeatedly been cited in the cross-cultural literature as related to the concept of participative management. The GLOBE data were collected in the late 1990s, thus providing a more recently collected database for exploration of the societal culture context of participative management than the original Hofstede (1980a) dimensions.

The Event Management study introduces the participation index "guidance source subordinates", which is directly related to the current study. Additionally, the study also provides such indices as reliance on the manager's superior, on own experience or on formal rules, thus offering a further comparison basis for the evaluation and exploration of the context of participative management.

More details on the three quantitative studies are provided in Chapters 4.1 (GLOBE study), 4.2 (Event Management study) and 4.3 (Vroom/Yetton study) below.

Chapter 4

The Three Quantitative Studies

As outlined in Chapter 3, three quantitative cross-cultural studies serve as the main basis for integration with the qualitative findings of the current study. This chapter describes the conceptual basis, the method and the country results of each of these three quantitative research programmes.

4.1 The GLOBE Study

4.1.1 Conceptual Model

The Global Leadership and Organisational Behaviour Effectiveness Research Programme (GLOBE) is a multi-phase, multi-method research initiative, which includes one hundred and seventy social scientists from sixty-two countries. The aim of the project is to examine the relationship between societal culture, organisational culture and organisational leadership from a cross-cultural perspective. Project initiator was Robert J. House from the Wharton School of the University of Pennsylvania.

The GLOBE project is summarised by House et al. (1999) and House et al. (2002) and is described in detail in House et al. (2004). The GLOBE conceptual model aims at integrating four traditions (House & Javidan, 2004): (1) implicit leadership theory (Lord & Maher, 1991), (2) the value/belief theory of culture (Hofstede, 1980a; Triandis, 1995), (3) implicit motivation theory (McClelland, 1985) and (4) the structural contingency theory of organisational form and effectiveness (Donaldson, 1993; Hickson et al., 1974). Figure 4.1 illustrates the relationship between the various concepts as hypothesised by the research initiative.

The first sections of this chapter pertain to the current study on participative management and focus on how the GLOBE study deals with participative leadership ideals (Section 4.1.1.1) and societal culture values and practices (Section 4.1.1.2) as contextual influence factors on participative management.

Figure 4.1 GLOBE Theoretical Model

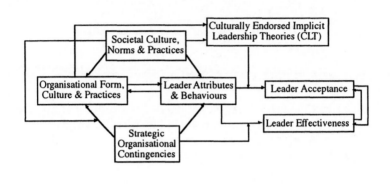

Source: House & Javidan (2004, p. 18)

4.1.1.1 Ideal Leader Attributes and Behaviours

Within the GLOBE project, organisational leadership is defined as "the ability of an individual to influence, motivate and enable others to contribute toward the effectiveness and success of the organisations of which they are members" (House & Javidan, 2004, p. 15).

The GLOBE project suggests high within-culture agreement with respect to the types of leader attributes and behaviours that are considered contributors or impediments to effective leadership. These leader attributes and behaviours constitute "culturally endorsed implicit leadership theories" (CLTs) (House & Javidan, 2004, p. 16). Implicit leadership theory, introduced by Lord and Maher (1991), states that individuals have implicit theories, beliefs or assumptions about the attributes that differentiate leaders from other persons, and that distinguish effective leaders from ineffective ones. The better the fit between a perceived individual and the leadership concept held by the person perceiving, the more likely that the perceived individual is viewed as a leader, and also the more likely that this individual will find followers.

Based on data collected from middle managers in sixty-two countries, the study identified twenty-one first-order scales (dimensions of leadership patterns) that are viewed as contributors or impediments to outstanding leadership. On the basis of factor analysis these twenty-one scales group together in six second-order factors (Table 4.1).

The current study takes a closer look at the second-order factors *participative* and *team-oriented* (see Section 4.1.3.1 below). Country-specific participative leadership ideals are directly linked to the research questions of the current study. Team-oriented leadership is assumed to be conceptually related to participation, because participative processes such as consultation and joint decision-making build on group processes. Analyses in the context of the GLOBE study strengthen the assumption of the proposed link. The data show a statistically significant relationship between participative leadership ideals and collectivist societal culture values (Gelfand et al., 2004), i.e. values that enable and encourage group settings.

Table 4.1 Leader Attributes and Behaviours

Second-order factors	First-order scales	Definition
Charismatic/value-based	Integrity, inspirational, performance-oriented, visionary, decisive, self-sacrifice	Reflects ability to inspire, to motivate and to expect high performance outcomes from others based on firmly held core values.
Participative	Participative, non-autocratic	Reflects the degree to which managers involve others in making and implementing decisions.
Team-oriented	Team integrator, collaborative team orientation, malevolent, diplomatic, administratively competent	Emphasises effective team building and implementation of a common purpose or goal among team members.
Humane-oriented	Humane-oriented, modesty	Reflects supportive and considerate leadership but also includes compassion and generosity.
Autonomous	Autonomous	Refers to independent and individualistic leadership attributes.
Self-protective	Status conscious, conflict inducer, procedural, face saver, self-centred	Focuses on ensuring the safety and security of the individual and group through status enhancement and face saving.

Source: House & Javidan (2004, p. 14)

4.1.1.2 Societal Culture Values and Practices

Within the GLOBE project, culture is defined as "shared motives, values, beliefs, identities, and interpretations or meanings of significant events that result from common experiences of members of collectives that are transmitted across generations" (House & Javidan, 2004, p. 15). Culture is operationalised "by the use of indicators reflecting two distinct kinds of cultural manifestations: (a) the commonality (agreement) among members of collectives with respect to the psychological attributes specified [in the definition of culture], and (b) the commonality of observed and reported practices of entities such as families, schools, work organisations, economic and legal systems and political institutions" (House & Javidan, 2004, p. 16).

GLOBE identified nine dimensions of societal culture (Table 4.2) that show high within-culture agreement and high between-culture differentiation (House et al., 1999, p. 181). Assertiveness, gender egalitarianism, institutional collectivism and power distance build on Hofstede's (1980a) dimensions. Masculinity/femininity became gender egalitarianism. Assertiveness was previously included in Hofstede's masculinity/femininity dimension, but became a separate dimension in the GLOBE study. Institutional collectivism builds on individualism/collectivism, whereas in-group collectivism is derived from Triandis (1995). As for the additional dimensions, future orientation and humane orientation draw on Kluckhohn and Strodtbeck's (1961) temporal focus of human life and man's human nature orientation. Humane orientation also draws on Putnam's (1993) work on the civic society. Performance orientation is based on McClelland's (1961, 1985) work on need for achievement.

Table 4.2 Societal Culture Dimensions

Dimension	Definition
Assertiveness	The degree to which individuals in societies are assertive, confrontational and aggressive in social relationships.
Future orientation	The degree to which individuals in societies engage in future-oriented behaviours such as planning, investing in the future and delaying individual or collective gratification.
Gender egalitarianism	The degree to which a society minimises gender role differences while promoting gender equality.
Humane orientation	The degree to which individuals in societies encourage and reward individuals for being fair, altruistic, friendly, generous, caring and kind to others.
In-group collectivism	The degree to which individuals express pride, loyalty and cohesiveness in their families.
Institutional collectivism	The degree to which societal institutional practices encourage and reward collective distribution of resources and collective action.
Performance orientation	The degree to which a society encourages and rewards group members for performance improvement and excellence.
Power distance	The degree to which members of a society expect and agree that power should be stratified and concentrated at higher levels of an organisation or government.
Uncertainty avoidance	The extent to which members of a society strive to avoid uncertainty by relying on established social norms, rituals and bureaucratic practices.

Source: House & Javidan (2004, pp. 11ff)

A subset of three dimensions was selected for use in the current study, namely *power distance, institutional collectivism* and *uncertainty avoidance*. All three dimensions are assumed to be directly or indirectly linked to the concept of participative management (compare Chapter 2.2.3.1): Managerial decision-making is likely to be more participative in low power distance countries than in high power distance countries. Participation is also more likely to occur in countries with high levels of collectivism. In high uncertainty avoidance countries, participative processes are assumed to be more formalised compared to countries with higher levels of uncertainty tolerance.

4.1.2 Method and Data Collection

Data were sampled from 17.300 middle managers in sixty-two countries. The countries represent all major geographic regions of the world and different types of economic and political systems. The respondents represent three industries, namely food processing, banking and telecommunications. These industries were selected because they exist in all countries and "collectively provide a wide variety of external organisational environments, organisational sizes and dominant organisational technology" (Javidan & House, 2001, p. 293). In countries with more than one "dominant" culture, data were sampled for the subculture with the greatest amount of commercial activity (House et al., 1999, p. 207).

The middle managers filled out questionnaires related to ideal leader attributes and behaviours, societal culture values and practices, and organisational culture values and practices. The sampling strategy controlled for nation, industry, occupation in a broad sense (managers) and organisational level in a broad sense (middle management). Such a sampling strategy "increases the internal validity of the study by ensuring that the units of analysis are well defined and internally homogeneous" (House et al., 1999, p. 191).

Leadership scales. When developing the initial item pool for the leadership questionnaire, the researchers focused on collecting a comprehensive list of characteristics rather than on developing a priori leadership scales (House et al., 1999, p. 195). Researchers from different cultural backgrounds reviewed and evaluated the items. Q sorting, translation/back-translation and pilot testing procedures were employed. The resulting 112 questionnaire items each consisted of a characteristic or behaviour plus an explanatory definition. Items were rated on 7-point Likert-type scales ranging from "this behaviour or characteristic greatly inhibits a person from being an outstanding leader" to "this behaviour or characteristic contributes greatly to a person being an outstanding leader" (House & Javidan, 2004, p. 21). The collected data were standardised, resulting in correlations of r=,90 and above between the raw scores and the standardised country scores (Hanges, 1997; Hanges et al., 1998).

Societal culture scales. A questionnaire measured respondents' values and perceptions of practices on 7-point Likert-type scales. *Practices* were measured by responses to "questionnaire items concerning 'what is,' or 'what are,' common behaviours, institutional practices, proscriptions and prescriptions" (House & Javidan, 2004, p. 16). The following is an example of an "as is" item: "In this society, a person's influence is based primarily on one's ability and contribution to the society, [vs.] the authority of one's position." Respondents' *values* concerning these practices were measured by responses to "questionnaire items concerning judgements of 'what should be'" (House & Javidan, 2004, p. 16). The following represents an example of a "should be" item: "I believe that followers should obey their leader without question, [vs.] question their leader when in disagreement."

Initially generated items were screened for appropriateness by use of Q sorting, item evaluation, translations/back-translation and two pilot tests (House et al., 1999, p. 196). Additionally, the items were analysed by conventional psychometric procedures, such as factor analysis and generalisability analysis, to establish the nine dimensions of societal culture summarised in Table 4.2 above.

4.1.3 Country Results

A detailed analysis of the worldwide data is presented in House et al. (2004), whereas an anthology (Chhokar, Brodbeck & House, in press) contains emic descriptions of societal culture and leadership in twenty-five countries. In earlier publications, House et al. (1999) and Den Hartog et al. (1999) analysed which leadership ideals are universally endorsed and which are culturally contingent. Brodbeck et al. (2000) compared the leadership ideals of twenty-two European countries. A special issue of the Journal of World Business reported findings about the Germanic Europe cluster (Szabo et al., 2002), the Eastern Europe cluster (Bakacsi et al., 2002), the Latin Europe cluster (Jesuino, 2002), the Anglo cluster (Ashkanasy, Trevor-Roberts & Earnshaw, 2002), the Arabic cluster (Kabasakal & Bodur, 2002) and the Southern Asia cluster (Gupta et al., 2002). Further regional analyses within Europe include comparisons between Austria and Ireland (Keating, Martin & Szabo, 2002), Austria, Germany and Switzerland (Weibler et al., 2000; Szabo et al., 2001), Finland and Poland (Maczynski et al., 1997) and the Netherlands and Poland (Den Hartog et al., 1997).

4.1.3.1 Leadership Dimensions

Table 4.3 gives an overview of the results for the six second-order factors related to ideal leader attributes and behaviours. The table shows the range of country means based on the findings in sixty-two countries. Scores range from one to seven. The right-hand column shows which second-order factors were found to be universally endorsed as contributors or impediments to outstanding leadership and which factors emerged as culturally contingent (House et al., 1999).

Table 4.3 Leadership Factors

Second-order factors	Range of country means	Universally endorsed vs. culturally contingent
Charismatic/value-based	4,51 – 6,46	Universally endorsed as contributor to outstanding leadership
Participative	4,50 – 6,09	No clear evaluation possible
Team-oriented	4,74 – 6,21	Universally endorsed as contributor to outstanding leadership
Humane-oriented	3,82 – 5,75	Culturally contingent
Autonomous	2,27 – 4,63	Culturally contingent
Self-protective	2,55 – 4,62	Universally endorsed as impediment to outstanding leadership

Source: House et al. (1999)

With regard to the two factors of interest in the context of the current study, namely participative and team-oriented leadership (compare Section 4.1.1.1), *team-oriented* emerged as universally endorsed as contributor to outstanding leadership. Similarly, the country means for *participative* range between 4,50 and 6,09. In other words, all country means are greater than 4,00 (which represents "neither contributing nor hindering to outstanding leadership"), suggesting that being participative is a positive element of ideal leadership in all countries included in the GLOBE study. However, the data for participative leadership are not as unambiguous as the data for other factors, leading House et al. (1999) to the conclusion that a clear evaluation of whether participative leadership is culturally contingent or universally endorsed as contributor to outstanding leadership is not possible.

Because of the ambiguity concerning the second-order factor *participative*, the current study compares the qualitative findings with the first-order scales instead of using the aggregated second-order factors. Therefore, the focus of the following paragraphs is on the country results of the first-order scales contained in the second-order factors *participative* and *team-oriented*.

Scales participative and non-autocratic. The second-order factor participative leadership is comprised of two first-order scales, *participative* and *non-autocratic*. Figure 4.2 shows the country results for the Czech Republic, Finland, Germany, Poland and Sweden, sorted by the scores for the scale participative in ascending order. In all five countries both scales are contributing to outstanding leadership, reflected by mean scores higher than 4,00.

Interestingly, some countries such as Poland and Germany show quite wide gaps between the two scale results. Poland is also the country with the lowest scores on both scales, suggesting that the two concepts might be less important for outstanding leadership in Poland than in the other countries. Finland scores highest on the participative scale, whereas Germany is the country with the comparatively highest score on the non-autocratic scale. In Poland, being participative is considered comparatively more contributing to outstanding leadership than being non-autocratic, whereas the opposite is true for Sweden, Germany and the Czech Republic. The two scores for Finland are almost identical.

Figure 4.2 Scales Participative and Non-Autocratic

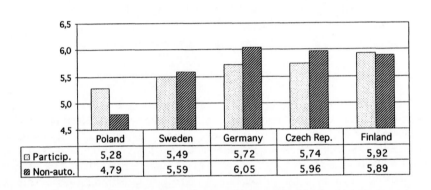

	Poland	Sweden	Germany	Czech Rep.	Finland
☐ Particip.	5,28	5,49	5,72	5,74	5,92
▨ Non-auto.	4,79	5,59	6,05	5,96	5,89

Source: GLOBE (2001)

Scales collaborative team orientation and team integrator. Figure 4.3 displays the country scores for the two scales comprising the second-order factor team-oriented leadership, *collaborative team orientation* and *team integrator*. The results are sorted in ascending order for collaborative team orientation, which scores higher than team integrator in all five countries. The countries are more similar with regard to the team integrator scores (ranging between 5,05 and 5,55) compared to the results for collaborative team orientation (5,48 to 6,35). Germany is the country with the comparatively lowest scores on both scales. Finland scores highest on collaborative team orientation.

Figure 4.3 Scales Collaborative Team Orientation and Team Integrator

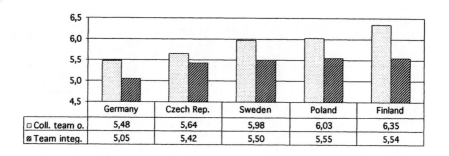

	Germany	Czech Rep.	Sweden	Poland	Finland
▢ Coll. team o.	5,48	5,64	5,98	6,03	6,35
▨ Team integ.	5,05	5,42	5,50	5,55	5,54

Source: GLOBE (2001)

4.1.3.2 Societal Culture Dimensions

The current study makes use of a subset of the nine GLOBE societal culture dimensions (compare Section 4.1.1.2), namely power distance, uncertainty avoidance and institutional collectivism. The displays in Figures 4.4 to 4.6 contain the findings for both the "as is" and "should be" scales. Scores range from one to seven. The letters "a" to "c" indicate that countries with the same letter belong to a group of countries that significantly differs from other country groupings (GLOBE, 2001).

Power distance. Figure 4.4 shows the country findings for the societal culture dimension power distance except for the Czech Republic, for which no power distance data are available. The data are sorted in ascending order of the "as is" scale. Higher scores indicate greater power stratification. The country scores are generally higher for the "as is" scale than for the "should be" scale, indicating that respondents perceive power distance to be higher than they would prefer it to be. The four countries for which data are available form one large subgroup "a" on the "as is" scale, suggesting that the perceived level of power distance is similarly high across countries. In contrast, there is more divergence on the "should be" scale, resulting in three distinct subgroups.

By and large the GLOBE results for the five countries parallel the patterns of power distance identified in earlier research (Table 4.4).

Figure 4.4 Power Distance

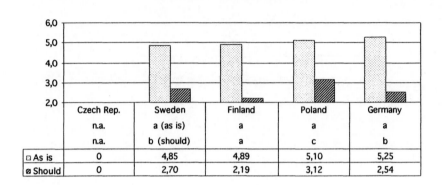

	Czech Rep.	Sweden	Finland	Poland	Germany
	n.a.	a (as is)	a	a	a
	n.a.	b (should)	a	c	b
□ As is	0	4,85	4,89	5,10	5,25
⊠ Should	0	2,70	2,19	3,12	2,54

Source: GLOBE (2001)

Table 4.4 Hofstede's Power Distance Index

Country	Power distance index	Relative position among 50 countries and three regions
Czech Republic [1]	76	Upper third
Finland [2]	33	Lower third
Germany [2]	35	Lower third
Poland [3]	72	Upper third
Sweden [2]	31	Lower third

Sources: [1] Replication by Lang (1998), [2] Hofstede (2001), [3] Replication by Nasierowski & Mikula (1998)

Institutional Collectivism. The GLOBE study distinguishes between two dimensions of collectivism, namely *institutional collectivism*, i.e. the degree to which societal institutional practices encourage and reward collective action, and *in-group collectivism*, i.e. the tendency to identify with family or organisations as in-groups. *Institutional collectivism* was selected for the current study, because it fits well with the concept of participation in its institutional and business context. The country results are presented in Figure 4.5, sorted in ascending order of the "as is" scale. Higher scores indicate more collectivism, while lower scores indicate more individualism. On the "as is" scale, the five countries group together in three significantly different subgroups "a" to "c". The Czech Republic is the most individualistic among the five countries, Sweden the most collectivist. Except for Germany and Sweden, the gaps are rather narrow when comparing the "as is" and "should be" scales. Czech and German respondents reported a preference for more collectivism, whereas the Polish, Finnish and Swedish managers opted for more individualism.

Figure 4.5 Institutional Collectivism

	Czech Rep.	Germany	Poland	Finland	Sweden
	a (as is)	a	b	c	c
	a (should)	c	b	b	b
□ As is	3,60	3,79	4,53	4,63	5,22
▨ Should	3,85	4,82	4,22	4,11	3,94

Source: GLOBE (2001)

In comparison to earlier research, GLOBE's institutional collectivism dimension does not seem to tap the exact same construct as Hofstede's individualism/collectivism dimension, summarised in Table 4.5. For example, Finland and Sweden are comparably high on "as is" institutional collectivism (subgroup "c"), yet they are positioned in the upper third among over fifty countries on Hofstede's individualism index.

Table 4.5　Hofstede's Individualism Index

Country	Individualism index	Relative position among 50 countries and three regions
Czech Republic [1]	58	Upper third
Finland [2]	63	Upper third
Germany [2]	67	Upper third
Poland [3]	56	Upper third
Sweden [2]	71	Upper third

Sources: [1] Estimate reported in Hofstede & Hofstede (2005), [2] Hofstede (2001), [3] Replication by Nasierowski & Mikula (1998)

Uncertainty avoidance. Figure 4.6 gives an overview of the uncertainty avoidance "as is" and "should be" scales. Higher scores indicate a tendency toward higher levels of uncertainty avoidance. The data are sorted in ascending order of the "as is" scale. The five countries form different subgroups on both the "as is" and the "should be" scales. In Poland, the perceived ("as is") level of uncertainty avoidance is lower than the preferred ("should be") one, whereas the opposite is true for the other countries. Wide gaps between "as is" and "should be" show in particular for Finland, Germany and Sweden.

Figure 4.6 Uncertainty Avoidance

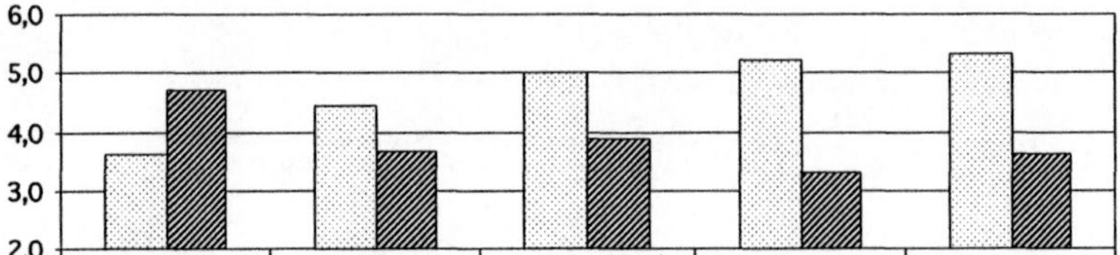

	Poland	Czech Rep.	Finland	Germany	Sweden
	a (as is)	b	c	c	c
	c (should)	a	b	a	a
□ As is	3,62	4,44	5,02	5,22	5,32
▨ Should	4,71	3,64	3,85	3,32	3,60

Source: GLOBE (2001)

Table 4.6 Hofstede's Uncertainty Avoidance Index

Country	Uncertainty avoidance index	Relative position among 50 countries and three regions
Czech Republic [1]	74	Middle third
Finland [2]	59	Middle third
Germany [2]	65	Middle third
Poland [3]	106	Upper third
Sweden [2]	29	Lower third

Sources: [1] Estimate reported in Hofstede & Hofstede (2005), [2] Hofstede (2001), [3] Replication by Nasierowski & Mikula (1998)

The comparison of the GLOBE "as is" data with earlier research into uncertainty avoidance (Table 4.6) shows that the results match for the Czech Republic, Finland and Germany, whereas they do not for Sweden and Poland: The Swedish GLOBE data suggest a comparatively high level of perceived uncertainty avoidance (subgroup "c"), whereas the opposite is true according to the Hofstede study. Furthermore, "as is" uncertainty avoidance is relatively low in Poland according to the GLOBE study (subgroup "a"), but the Hofstede data suggest the opposite. Related to a possible explanation for these differences, Søndergaard (1994) suggested that uncertainty avoidance is the least robust Hofstede dimension in replication studies.

4.2 The Event Management Study

4.2.1 Conceptual Model

The Event Management model, introduced by Peter B. Smith and Mark F. Peterson (1988), looks at management through the lenses of organisational events, such as the hiring of a new subordinate or the evaluation of new work procedures. The reason for this focus is that "organisational life does not present organisation members with discrete problems, but with an unending flow of 'events'" (Smith & Peterson, 1988, p. 79). Event management is the process of a manager dealing with such regular occurrences. In particular, s/he needs to interpret an event before action can be taken. This interpretation does not happen in a vacuum, and the manager uses different sources of guidance to make sense of the occurrence. In the authors' words:

> "All events require interpretation before a manager can determine the best way to handle them. [...] In handling work events, managers operate within a context of alternative sources of guidance, many of which extend beyond the individual." (Smith et al., 2002, p. 191)

Potential sources of guidance can be divided into four main categories (Smith et al., 2002, p. 191): (1) the individual's own expertise, (2) social sources such as superiors, subordinates, specialists and colleagues, (3) impersonal sources such as formal or informal organisational norms, and (4) beliefs that are widespread in the country as to what is right.

Own *expertise* is based on the manager's prior experience and training. In handling an event, a manager may be self-reliant and focus primarily on her or his own "interpretive structures such as memories, thoughts and understandings to which new events can be connected" (Smith et al., 2002, p. 191). However, the manager may also consult other individuals inside or outside the organisation. These *social sources* include downward influence by the manager's superior, upward influence by the manager's subordinates, lateral influence by manager colleagues, and influence by other individuals internal or external of the organisation, such as specialists. The third type of guidance sources is called *impersonal sources*, as they "have a 'reality' apart from any particular individual transmitting them" (Smith & Peterson, 1988, p. 82). Formal rules as well as unwritten rules are covered under this heading. *Widespread beliefs* refer to "viewpoints perceived to prevail in society in general, due to government, a particular religion or traditional value systems" (Smith et al., 2002, p. 191). Such beliefs may influence what a manager considers right or wrong in handling an organisational event.

Individual managers differ in their selection of guidance sources and often the specific context influences their preferences. However, recent cross-cultural research conducted by Peter Smith and his colleagues shows that there are country specific patterns of event management. Of interest to the current study are social sources of guidance, in particular subordinates. In contrast to other quantitative studies into participation, the event management research places the involvement of subordinates in a wider context by simultaneously looking at various actors, including the manager her or himself and the manager's superior. The event management model also takes the situation into account, by focusing on different typical types of work-related events, such as the appointment of a new subordinate, the replacement of office equipment or the introduction and evaluation of new work procedures.

4.2.2 Method and Data Collection

Respondents were presented with a questionnaire containing eight typical organisational events. The questionnaire was designed to elicit managers' self-reports of the sources on which they relied in handling these work events. For each event, respondents were asked to rate on a 5-point scale to what extent the actions taken were affected by the factors and/or persons listed. The questionnaire was originally created in English and later translated into other languages. Back-translation with subsequent correction ensured translation accuracy.

The questionnaire was filled out by middle managers in fifty-three countries, representing all regions of the world. Each country sample includes hundred or more respondents from a variety of industries, organisations (of both private and public ownership) and functional areas. The collected raw data were standardised to account for response bias, which is "likely to vary by nation both as a consequence of norms about responding positively and due to subtle differences in translation of response alternatives" (Smith et al., 2002, p. 197).

A recent analysis of the data from fifty-three countries (Smith et al., 2002) revealed that four sources of guidance are highly correlated, namely own experience, reliance on subordinates, reliance on one's superior and reliance on formal rules. Therefore, a category labelled "vertical sources" was created, combining these four guidance sources. This category was selected for use in the current study.

4.2.3 Country Results

Country results are presented in Smith et al. (1994), Smith, Peterson and Misumi (1994), Smith, Peterson and Wang (1996), Smith (1997), Smith et al. (1997), Smith et al. (2002) and Smith et al. (2005).

4.2.3.1 Sources of Guidance, an Overview

Table 4.7 gives an overview of the different guidance sources reported as most relevant by middle managers in the countries selected for the current study. As described above, the category *vertical sources* combines reliance on own experience, subordinates, superior and formal rules.

Table 4.7 Overview of Different Sources of Guidance

	Vertical sources	Unwritten rules	Specialists	Colleagues	Widespread beliefs
Czech Republic	-17	-33	-28	-40	-68
Finland	-41	7	-39	-20	-68
Germany	-28	-29	-25	-40	-79
Poland	15	-53	-48	-50	-66
Sweden	-7	-24	-38	-44	-39
Range	-41 to +15	-53 to +7	-48 to -25	-50 to -20	-79 to -39

Source: Smith et al. (2002)

The higher a score, the more on average managers in a country rely on a particular source of guidance. It follows that *vertical sources* are on average the most common guidance source among the managers in the displayed countries, with scores ranging from –41 to +15, followed by unwritten rules, ranging from –53 to +7. Vertical sources are the comparably most important source of guidance in the Czech Republic, Poland and Sweden. Unwritten rules are highly preferred among Finns, and German managers tend to rely on vertical sources, unwritten rules and specialists to the approximately same degree.

4.2.3.2 Reliance on Vertical Sources and Rules

The aggregated findings presented in Table 4.7 do not answer the question of how reliance on vertical sources is distributed between reliance on subordinates, on the superior, on own experience and on formal rules. Although the correlations are high and the combined index shows a Cronbach alpha of ,69 (Smith et al., 2002, p. 198), the countries might diverge on individual guidance sources. Therefore, Figure 4.7 presents the guidance sources reliance on subordinates, superior and own experience separately, sorted in ascending order of the subordinate scale. Notably, *own experience* is the most relevant source of guidance in all countries except for Poland, where managers rely on their superior to a slightly higher degree. With regard to *subordinates*, the continuum ranges from Poland (where subordinates are the least important source of guidance compared to other countries) to Germany (where subordinates are the most important guidance source). Reliance on the *superior* shows the comparatively lowest score in Sweden and the highest in Poland. A within-country comparison between reliance on the superior and the subordinates shows an interesting finding. In countries, in which reliance on subordinates is relatively low, reliance on the superior is particularly strong (countries toward the left end of the continuum in Figure 4.7). In contrast, reliance on subordinates is substantially higher and almost equals the level of reliance on the superior toward the right end of the continuum. In other words, the gap between subordinates and superior narrows considerably. The extreme cases are Poland with the widest gap and Finland and Germany with the narrowest gaps.

Figure 4.7 Reliance on Subordinates, Superior and Own Experience

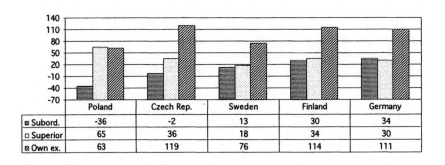

Source: Smith (2003)

Figure 4.8 displays the forth source of guidance represented in the verticality index, reliance on *formal rules*. The display also contains reliance on *unwritten rules*. Generally speaking, formal and unwritten rules seem to be less important sources of guidance compared to own experience, superior and subordinates. Finland is the country with the lowest level of reliance on formal rules in the direct comparison of the displayed countries, whereas Sweden, the second Nordic nation in the display, is the country with the highest reliance on formal rules. Compared to other countries, unwritten rules are particularly unimportant in Poland, whereas they seem to be highly in use in Finland. In Germany, the Czech Republic, Poland and Sweden formal rules are considerably more important than unwritten rules, whereas the opposite is true for Finland.

Figure 4.8 Reliance on Formal and Unwritten Rules

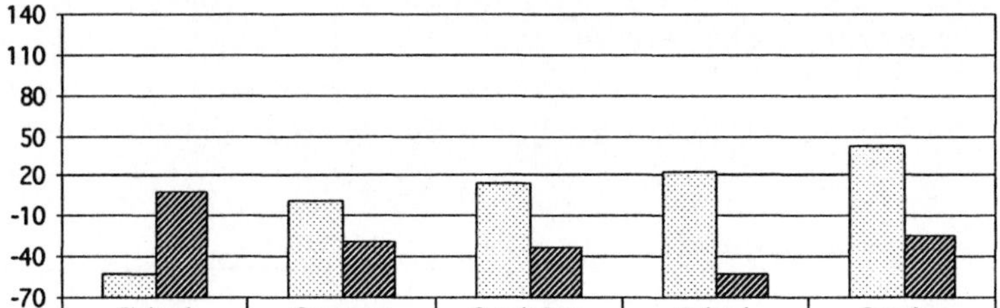

	Finland	Germany	Czech Rep.	Poland	Sweden
☐ Formal	-53	2	14	23	43
▨ Unwritten	7	-29	-33	-53	-24

Source: Smith (2003)

4.3 The Vroom/Yetton Study

4.3.1 Conceptual Model

The Vroom/Yetton (1973) model, designed by management scientists Victor H. Vroom and Philip W. Yetton, is a rational decision-making model proposing the conditions under which a particular leadership style proves most successful. Leadership style may vary on a continuum ranging from autocratic to participative behaviour. With its focus on particular characteristics of the situation, the model is grounded in contingency theory. As Vroom (1993) put it, "the most appropriate degree of participation must depend on the circumstances surrounding the participative act" (p. 24). Vroom and Jago (1995) reported that the situation is three times more powerful in explaining variance in participative behaviour than are individual differences in overall leadership styles. In contrast to other leadership style research, the Vroom/ Yetton model deals with *specific* decision situations and behaviour, not with generalised behavioural tendencies:

> "Other survey measures of leadership style, including measures of autocracy-participativeness, typically pose questions that attempt to measure *amount, attitudinal agreement* or *frequency*. [...] Each of the three formats produces an implicit

aggregation across situations to create a metric of average leadership behaviour or overall leadership style. Within-leader variation in response to different situations is treated as either non-existent or irrelevant." (Vroom & Jago, 1995, p. 175, italics in original)

The model aims at establishing a decision-making process that allows for the best possible fit between the manager, the subordinates and the decision-making situation. Figure 4.9 lists four steps implicit in the Vroom/Yetton model in order to ensure the fit.

Figure 4.9 Steps Implicit in the Vroom/Yetton Model

	What to do	How to do it
Step 1	Analyse the situation and the problem that requires a decision	Ask the diagnostic questions suggested by the model
Step 2	Consider quality and acceptance require-ments in order to en-sure a good decision	Apply the decision rules suggested by the model
Step 3	Decide to which degree to involve the subordi-nates	Chose appropriate decision-making process by selecting one of the strategies sug-gested by the model
Step 4	Start the decision-making process	Let subordinates participate according to Step 3

Source: Szabo (2004)

Step 1. To ensure an appropriate decision-making process that leads to an effective decision, the manager first of all needs to know about the problem that requires a decision and the context in which it takes place. Therefore, the model suggests asking diagnostic questions (Table 4.8) concerning seven situational attributes that are assumed to be the most relevant ones in the majority of decision-making situations.

Table 4.8 Diagnostic Questions

Issue	Question
Quality requirement	Is the technical quality of the decision important?
Leader information	Do you as the manager have the knowledge, or is it readily available in on-hand manuals or documents, to reach a sound decision?
Problem structure	Is the problem well structured?
Acceptance requirement	Is it important that those who report to you commit to the decision?
Goal congruence	Do those who report to you share the organisational goals to be attained in solving this problem?
Prior probability of acceptance	Are you confident that those who report to you would commit themselves to a decision that you would reach alone?
Subordinate conflict	Are those who report to you likely to be in disagreement over the nature of the problem or over the alternatives each might wish or recommend?

Source: Reber et al. (2000)

Step 2. Depending on the analysis of the situation, the manager may handle the decision-making process in different ways, in particular by including the subordinates more or less intensively. The model suggests that participation has an impact on both the quality and acceptance of decisions. Therefore, the model guides the manager in the choice of a particular decision-making process (ranging from autocratic to participative) by establishing seven *quality* and *acceptance* rules. The application of these rules ensures that quality and implementation of the decision are not jeopardised. More specifically, decision *quality* is protected if the decision-making process guarantees the best possible solution in terms of its technical and task-oriented requirements. For instance, if a manager lacks relevant information, the model advises to seek this information by at least listening to the subordinates, since they may possess the necessary information. Under these circumstances an autocratic strategy should be avoided. Decision *acceptance* is guaranteed, if the subordinates, who are usually the ones to implement the decision, commit to the solution. Only when committed will they be willing to implement the solution. Subordinate commitment allows the manager to adjust the decision-making process towards more participation. However, there may also be situations in which a manager cannot count on subordinate commitment and in such cases the model suggests that the manager avoid group decision-making. The model also states decision rules for cases in which the subordinates are in conflict with the leader's aspirations or with the company goals, or for cases in which subordinates presumably cannot reach a consensus about how to tackle the task at hand.

Step 3. The application of the decision rules leads to the next step, the selection of an appropriate decision-making process. The model differentiates between five strategies (Table 4.9), which vary in their degree of subordinate involvement by differentiating between soliciting ideas from subordinates, inviting subordinate suggestions and joint decision-making. Depending on the outcome of Steps 1 and 2, the model suggests one or more appropriate strategies for the manager to choose from.

Step 4. The chosen strategy defines the nature of the decision-making process.

Table 4.9 Decision Strategies

Strategy	Description	Degree of participation in percent
AI	Autocratic decision, using the information available	0
AII	Autocratic decision, but manager obtains any necessary information from subordinates; subordinates do not play a role in generating/evaluating possible solutions	10
CI	One-on-one consultations; decision may or may not reflect subordinates' influence	50
CII	Group consultation; decision may or may not reflect subordinates' influence	80
GII	Group discussion and group decision; attempt to reach agreement (consensus) on a solution	100

Source: Reber et al. (2000)

A newer version of the Vroom/Yetton model, the Vroom/Jago (1988) model also seeks to provide managers with guidance about matching the decision-making process with situational demands. In contrast to the original model, it "is driven by a set of four equations which purport to model what is known about the effects of participation on four conceptually and empirically separable outcomes of the participation process" (Vroom, 1993, p. 25). These outcomes are decision quality, commitment to the decision, time required to make the decision and the subordinates' subsequent learning.

4.3.2 Method and Data Collection

The original Vroom/Yetton model has been widely taught in management training seminars. In the preparatory phase for such seminars and before learning about the theoretical model, managers are invited to analyse their individual leadership style, which is then compared with the recommendations of the model.

The method includes a booklet containing thirty short case descriptions (Vroom, Yetton & Jago, 1976). These cases describe hypothetical decision-making situations, in which the situational attributes covered by the seven diagnostic questions (compare Table 4.8) are systematically manipulated (Jago et al., 1993). Participants are asked to assume the role of the manager portrayed in each case and to mark which decision-making strategy (compare Table 4.9) they would choose for each of the thirty scenarios. It is assumed that, similar to many real life decisions, the decision strategy responses to the thirty cases are unlikely to reflect conscious and active thought processes but habits, which were developed during socialisation and which are grounded in tacit knowledge (Auer-Rizzi, Reber & Szabo, 2005).

Various indices are derived from the managers' data by comparing the responses with behavioural prescriptions suggested by the Vroom/Yetton model. In other words, indices show the degree to which a manager's habits of participatory behaviour conform to the theoretical model. Detailed feedback also tells the participants to what degree and under which conditions they prefer participation and whether they change their participatory behaviour under specific circumstances or not. The feedback serves as a learning instrument for personal decision-making behaviour in the future.

Training seminars have provided data for empirical research over the last fifteen years. To date, data from more than 12.000 managers (most of them at the middle management level) from a variety of organisations in thirteen countries have been sampled. The managers are employed in a wide range of areas, including managerial, functional and technical fields. The different time periods of data collection do not pose a problem for country comparisons. A longitudinal study of the data from six European countries (Reber & Jago, 1997) shows that the leadership styles elicited through the Vroom/Yetton methodology are quite robust and do not easily change: The fall of communism did not result in any short-term changes in the leadership styles of Czech or Polish managers, nor did the reunification of Germany lead to significant changes in the styles of West German managers.

A series of studies provide evidence of the method's reliability and validity. For example, validation studies conducted by Jago and Vroom (1978) for the United States and replicated by Böhnisch et al. (1988) and Böhnisch (1991) for Austria concluded that reported behaviour in response to the thirty scenarios parallels actual behaviour. Critique of the model comes from Field (1979) and House and Aditya (1997). These authors argue, for example, that (1) the theory wrongly assumes that managerial goals are always congruent with organisational goals, (2) extensive training is needed in order to use the theory reliably, (3) managers often do not have the skills necessary to actually solve problems in a group, (4) the manager's or subordinates' stress and intelligence are not considered, and (5) the data based on managers' self-reports may include a strong rationality bias based on social desirability. Furthermore, it has been argued that the theory is more strongly supported in field studies than in laboratory studies (House & Aditya, 1997). Laboratory studies (Heilman et al., 1984; Field & House, 1990) found that the data obtained from managers (or individuals being assigned the role of manager) supported the model, while those obtained from subordinates (or individuals assigned the role of subordinate) did not.

4.3.3 Country Results

The studies based on the Vroom/Yetton model suggest that culture is the factor with the highest predictive power with regard to decision-making style. Other demographic factors, such as age, sex, hierarchical level and functional area have also proven to be influential, yet to a much lesser degree (Jago, 1980; Jago & Vroom, 1982; Jago et al., 1993; Reber, Jago & Böhnisch, 1993). For example, while culture accounts for more than 70 percent of explained variance, the percentage is, while statistically significant, only about three percent for gender and slightly over one percent for age (Reber et al., 2000).

Country-specific results and country comparisons have been described in Böhnisch et al. (1988), Reber, Jago & Böhnisch (1993), Jago et al. (1993), Maczynski et al. (1994), Jago et al. (1995), Jago, Maczynski and Reber (1996), Reber and Jago (1997), Szabo et al. (1997), Maczynski (1998), Reber et al. (2000), Reber (2001), Reber and Auer-Rizzi (2003), Leichtfried (2004), Szabo (2004) and Auer-Rizzi, Reber and Szabo (2005). Data collection in various countries is taking place continuously. The scores presented in this section are based on the contents of the overall Vroom/Yetton database. Therefore some scores may vary slightly from the ones presented in earlier publications.

4.3.3.1 Mean Level of Participation

The mean level of participation (MLP) score shows the averaged behavioural responses across all thirty cases for managers of the same country of origin. The MLP score ranges from zero (autocratic) to ten (consensus decision), indicating the general tendency to be autocratic or participative. In other words, the higher the MLP score the greater the involvement of subordinates in the decision-making process.

Figure 4.10 shows the results of the five countries selected for the current study on participative management. Additionally, this and subsequent displays in Figures 4.11 and 4.12 indicate subgroups of countries, represented by the letters "a" to "d". The lowest and highest country scores within each subgroup do not significantly differ from each other on the Duncan Multiple

Range Test (p=,05 level). It follows that overlapping subgroups are possible and a country may belong to more than one subgroup for a particular index.

Figure 4.10 Mean Level of Participation (MLP)

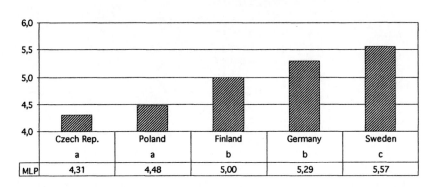

	Czech Rep.	Poland	Finland	Germany	Sweden
	a	a	b	b	c
MLP	4,31	4,48	5,00	5,29	5,57

Source: IIM (2003)

The Czech Republic and Poland form subgroup "a" on the least participative end of the MLP continuum, while Sweden is the most participative country, differing significantly from the other countries. Finland and Germany group together between these two extremes in subgroup „b".

As pointed out above, the MLP is an aggregated score. Detailed calculations of the intra-personal standard deviation of the individual managers' responses to the thirty cases suggest than the country cohorts differ in the degree of intra-personal flexibility with regard to using participation (IIM, 2003): Czech and Polish managers appear to be particularly flexible.

4.3.3.2 Use of Specific Decision Strategies

Table 4.10 presents the percentages of country-specific use of the five decision strategies (compare Table 4.9). The most autocratic strategy AI is used most commonly in the Czech Republic and Poland, whereas group decision-making (GII) shows the highest relative frequency in Germany and Sweden. Consultative strategies (CI and CII) are more common than autocratic strategies (AI and AII) in Finland, Germany and Sweden, whereas the opposite is true for the Czech Republic and Poland. In all five countries, consultation (CI and CII) is more common than joint decision-making (GII).

Table 4.10 Use of Specific Decision Strategies in Percent

Strategy	Czech Rep.	Finland	Germany	Poland	Sweden
AI	26	19	20	25	16
AII	21	18	14	19	14
CI	16	18	16	18	18
CII	23	29	30	22	31
GII	14	16	20	16	21
Autocratic (AI + AII)	47	37	34	44	30
Consultative (CI + CII)	39	47	46	40	49

Source: IIM (2003)

4.3.3.3 Quality and Acceptance Requirements

The two indices presented in Figures 4.11 and 4.12 report whether country cohorts on average diverge from the prescribed rules to protect decision quality and acceptance and, if so, by how much. These indices do not reflect the *level* of participation, but the *appropriate use* of participation according to the Vroom/Yetton model. In the terminology of the model the indices are called quality and acceptance rule violations.

Figure 4.11 Violation of Quality Rules

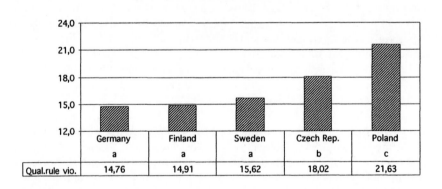

	Germany	Finland	Sweden	Czech Rep.	Poland
	a	a	a	b	c
Qual.rule vio.	14,76	14,91	15,62	18,02	21,63

Source: IIM (2003)

In Figure 4.11, the quality rule violations for the selected five countries range between about 15 and 22 percent. This means that in 78 to 85 percent of problems with task-related requirements, managers choose a decision-making strategy that is also recommended by the Vroom/Yetton model.

This high rate of agreement is not surprising since the model was developed on the basis of expert interviews with a large number of managers (Vroom & Yetton, 1973). Figure 4.11 also shows that Germany, Finland and Sweden cluster together and that the two former communist countries each form a separate subgroup.

Figure 4.12 Violation of Acceptance Rules

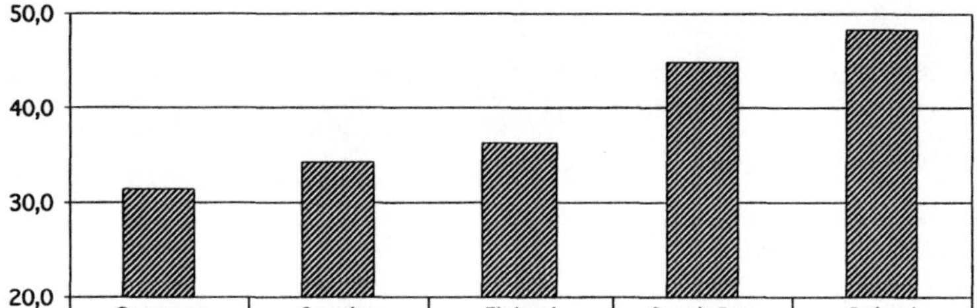

	Germany	Sweden	Finland	Czech Rep.	Poland
	a	a, b	b	c	d
Acc.rule vio.	31,52	34,42	36,42	44,98	48,32

Source: IIM (2003)

Quality rule violations represent the task-related side of decision-making, whereas acceptance rule violations are reflective of the more interpersonal, social side of decision-making. As demonstrated by Figure 4.12, the profile of the five countries with respect to acceptance rule violations looks rather different from the profile for quality rule violations shown in Figure 4.11. The scores are significantly higher, ranging from about 32 to 48 percent. In other words, when subordinate acceptance is an issue in decision-making, managers choose a strategy recommended by the Voom/Yetton model only in 52 to 68 percent of the cases. This means that deviations from the prescriptions of the model are more likely to result from violations of acceptance rules than from violations of quality rules. In explaining this, Jago et al. (1993) noted that "[the] typical manager is more likely to have his or her effectiveness impaired by a lack of appropriate attention to issues of acceptance than by inattention to issues relative to the technical quality of decisions" (p. 453f). Additionally, there is less convergence among the countries compared to the quality rule violations. The five countries form four partly overlapping subgroups, hinting at different cultural orientations reflected in the interpersonal, social side of decision-making.

4.3.3.4 Participation in Specific Situations

Table 4.11 Degree of Participation in Different Situations

Issue	Czech Republic	Finland	Germany	Poland	Sweden
Quality requirement					
Technical quality of decision important	4,52	5,12	5,48	4,44	5,75
Technical quality not important	3,43	4,52	4,55	4,62	4,85
Difference	+1,09	+,60	+,93	-,18	+,90
Leader information					
Manager possesses all information	4,13	4,74	5,20	3,93	5,55
Manager lacks relevant information	4,92	5,51	5,75	4,95	5,96
Difference	-,79	-,77	-,55	-1,02	-,41
Problem structure					
Problem well structured	4,10	4,70	4,84	4,47	5,55
Problem unstructured	5,74	6,31	6,65	5,42	6,36
Difference	-1,64	-1,61	-1,81	-,95	-,81
Acceptance requirement					
Subordinate acceptance necessary	4,60	5,24	5,53	4,61	5,73
Subordinate acceptance not necessary	3,72	4,53	4,81	4,20	5,27
Difference	+,88	+,71	+,72	+,41	+,46
Goal congruence					
Subordinates share goals to be attained	4,93	5,71	5,87	4,69	6,27
Subordinates do not share goals	4,12	4,53	5,08	4,19	5,24
Difference	+,81	+1,18	+,79	+,50	+1,03
Prior probability of acceptance					
Subordinates accept autocratic decision	3,44	3,80	4,09	3,68	4,61
No acceptance of autocratic decision	5,77	6,68	6,97	5,55	6,84
Difference	-2,33	-2,88	-2,88	-1,87	-2,23
Subordinate conflict					
Subordinates in conflict over decision	4,26	4,80	5,29	4,27	5,31
No conflict among subordinates	4,36	5,20	5,29	4,68	5,84
Difference	-,10	-,40	,00	-,41	-,53

Source: IIM (2003)

The Vroom/Yetton method allows verification of how managers react to particular attributes in the decision-making situation. The mean behaviour in situations possessing a specific attribute (e.g. conflict among subordinates) can be compared with the mean behaviour in situations failing to possess that attribute. This comparison allows determining if, on average, a country sample of managers becomes more or less participative in situations that possess particular attributes. As noted above, seven diagnostic questions help analyse the situation (compare Table 4.8). This generates fourteen different types of situations, assuming that the answer to each question can be either Yes or No. Table 4.11 lists these fourteen types of situations and the average scores of the five country samples. Like the MLP score, these scores can theoretically range from zero to ten.

When the quality of a decision is important (*quality requirement*), managers in all but one of the countries display higher scores compared to when decision quality is not an issue. The score labelled "difference" demonstrates by how much and in which direction managers react to this specific situational attribute. Positive scores suggest that managers of the same country on average become more participative when decision quality is important. By contrast, negative scores mean that managers become more participative when facing trivial problems, which is the case for Poland (compare Maczynski et al., 1994; Szabo et al., 1997). The normative Vroom/Yetton model would suggest more participation when decision quality is important.

When the manager possesses all relevant information (*leader information*), there is consistency among the managers of the five countries. The tendency to become more participative when information is missing is present in all country samples, although to different extents. This finding parallels the suggestion of the Vroom/Yetton model. Germany and Sweden display particularly large degrees of participation when all relevant information is available to the manager.

With regard to the next three types of situations, the results for the five country samples parallel the theoretical model. Unstructured problems (*problem structure*), i.e. problems that do not possess a defined set of alternative solutions and are possibly altogether new to the decision-makers, call for more participation than structured problems. *Acceptance requirement* means that the subordinates need to commit to the decision. This is, for example, the case when subordinates have to implement the decision or when the consequences of the decision impact on their work. Such conditions call for a higher degree of participation compared to situations in which the decision has no impact on the subordinates. When *goal congruence* is missing, i.e. when subordinates do not share the organisational goals to be attained in solving the problem, decision quality is threatened and managers should not make use of participation to its full extent, i.e. in the form of joint decision-making.

Decision situations, in which subordinates accept an autocratic decision by their manager (*prior probability of acceptance*), in theory allow a manager to solve such a problem autocratically. The managers in all five countries display this tendency with rather low scores (ranging from 3,44 to 4,61). By contrast, when there is reason to assume that subordinates will not accept an autocratic decision, the scores of all country cohorts are substantially higher (ranging from 5,55 to 6,97).

Finally, the model deals with differences among subordinates regarding preferred solutions (*subordinate conflict*). Managers in the Czech Republic, Finland, Poland and Sweden react to task-based conflict by becoming less participative, whereas the German managers, on average, do not react to this situational attribute at all. Managers in countries not included in Table 4.11, such as Austria, become more participative in the case of conflict. Vroom and Jago (1995) and Reber et al. (2000) assume that this distinction in reacting to conflict represents a conflict-avoiding versus conflict-approaching style.

4.4 Areas of Consistency and Contradiction

The preceding Sections 4.1 to 4.3 described the three quantitative studies along with empirical results for the selected five countries. The next step calls for a direct comparison of the findings *between* the studies. The scale scores are not directly comparable across studies. However, each study was conducted in a large number of countries, thus allowing a comparison of the relative country positions.

Table 4.12 shows the relative positions of the five countries on four quantitative participation indices. The GLOBE study measured the country-specific relevance of *participative* and *non-autocratic* leadership ideals (compare Section 4.1.3.1). The Event Management research studied the degree of reliance on *subordinates* as source of guidance (compare Section 4.2.3.2). The Vroom/Yetton study's *mean level of participation (MLP)* score is reflective of managerial habits to let subordinates participate in decision-making (compare Section 4.3.3.1).

Table 4.12 Relative Country Positions of Quantitative Participation Scores

Scale	Participative (GLOBE)	Non-autocratic (GLOBE)	Guidance source subordinates (Event Management)	Mean level of participation (MLP) (Vroom/Yetton)
Upper third	Finland Czech Republic Germany	Germany Czech Republic Finland Sweden	Germany Finland Sweden Czech Republic	Sweden Germany
Middle third	Sweden Poland			Finland
Lower third		Poland	Poland	Poland Czech Republic

Notes: Sources: GLOBE (2001), Smith (2003), IIM (2003). The GLOBE sample included 61 countries, the Event Management sample 56 and the Vroom/Yetton sample 13.

Table 4.12 suggests that the country positions resulting from the three quantitative studies are partly consistent, partly contradictory. Only Germany ranks in the same third, namely the upper third, on all four indices. Finland

and Sweden are positioned in the upper and middle thirds, respectively, while Poland is located in the middle and lower thirds. The Czech Republic shows an even stronger contradiction between the findings. The Czech scores are located in the upper third for the GLOBE and Event Management data and in the lower third for the Vroom/Yetton data.

Tables 4.13 to 4.15 present additional indices originating from the three quantitative studies. They concern theoretical concepts assumed to possess conceptual closeness to participation.

Hierarchy-related concepts. Table 4.13 contains the GLOBE societal culture dimension *power distance ("as is")* and the Event Management study's measures of reliance on the guidance sources *superior* and *own experience.* Hierarchical relations, autocratic managerial behaviour and reliance on one's superior are assumed to prevail in countries with high levels of power distance (compare Chapter 2.2.3.1). Consequently, reliance on the own experience could have more relevance in low power distance countries. Consistent with this assumption, Table 4.13 suggests that the guidance source *superior* is indeed inversely related to the degree of subordinate participation. There is a tendency for countries with high ranks on subordinate participation (compare Table 4.12) to be positioned low on the guidance source superior. For example, Poland ranks low on subordinate participation and high on the guidance source superior. In contrast, Sweden and Germany rank high on the participation indices, whereas the guidance source superior seems to play a minor role.

Table 4.13 Relative Country Positions of Hierarchy-Related Concepts

Scale	Power distance "as is" (GLOBE)	Guidance source superior (Event Management)	Guidance source own experience (Event Management)
Upper third		Poland	Czech Republic Finland Germany
Middle third	Germany Poland		Sweden Poland
Lower third	Finland Sweden	Czech Republic Finland Germany Sweden	

Notes: Sources: GLOBE (2001), Smith (2003). The GLOBE sample included 61 countries and the Event Management sample 56. No Czech data available for the power distance "as is" scale.

Team-related concepts. Table 4.14 presents the GLOBE leadership indices *collaborative team orientation* and *team integrator*, as well as the societal culture dimension *institutional collectivism ("as is")*. On the one hand, team-related concepts seem related to participative management in such a way that countries with higher levels of collectivism and team-orientation also show higher levels of participation (compare Chapter 2.2.3.1). On the other hand, the GLOBE data indicate that team-related concepts might not directly mirror participation. Some of the countries with high scores on the participation indices (Table 4.12) rank low on the dimensions *collaborative team orientation* and *team integrator*. A similar trend shows for the societal culture dimension *institutional collectivism ("as is")*.

Table 4.14 Relative Country Positions of Team-Related Concepts

Scale	Collaborative team orientation (GLOBE)	Team integrator (GLOBE)	Institutional collectivism "as is" (GLOBE)
Upper third	Finland		Sweden Finland Poland
Middle third	Poland Sweden	Poland Finland Sweden Czech Republic	
Lower third	Czech Republic Germany	Germany	Germany Czech Republic

Notes: Source: GLOBE (2001). The GLOBE sample included 61 countries.

Uncertainty-related concepts. Table 4.15 summarises the results for the GLOBE study's *uncertainty avoidance ("as is")* index and the Event Management study's reliance on the guidance sources *formal* and *unwritten rules*. As pointed out in Chapter 2.2.3.1, high uncertainty avoidance together with a strong focus on rules and regulations seem to be related to a high degree of formalisation of participative arrangements.

In some contrast to this assumption, the empirical data presented in Table 4.15 suggest that the guidance source *formal rules* might not be reflective of societal culture "as is" uncertainty avoidance: Some countries with a high level of "as is" uncertainty avoidance rank low on formal rules, for example Germany.

In summary, the relationship between participation and concepts suggested by the literature as conceptually connected to participation does not seem to be straightforward. If one zooms in on individual countries, the following within-country areas of consistency and contradiction emerge:

The Czech Republic ranks in the upper third for participative and non-autocratic leadership (GLOBE study) as well as for the guidance source subordinates (Event Management study), whereas the country is positioned in the lower third according to the Vroom/Yetton study. Collaborative team orientation and team integrator are of relatively low relevance to the Czech ideal of outstanding leadership, and institutional collectivism ("as is") is also very low. Czech managers attribute more importance to the use of their own experience than do managers from all other countries in the Event Management study (Smith, 2003), whereas the manager's superior as well as formal and unwritten rules play a medium to low role. At the societal level, the Czech Republic ranks relatively high on "as is" uncertainty avoidance.

Table 4.15 Relative Country Positions of Uncertainty-Related Concepts

Scale	Uncertainty avoidance "as is" (GLOBE)	Guidance source formal rules (Event Management)	Guidance source unwritten rules (Event Management)
Upper third	Sweden Germany Finland Czech Republic	Sweden	Finland
Middle third		Poland Czech Republic	
Lower third	Poland	Germany Finland	Sweden Germany Czech Republic Poland

Notes: Sources: GLOBE (2001), Smith (2003). The GLOBE sample included 61 countries and the Event Management sample 56.

Finland ranks high on participative and non-autocratic leadership (GLOBE study) and on subordinates as guidance source (Event Management study). In agreement, societal culture power distance is low in Finland, and collaborative team orientation, team integrator and institutional collectivism ("as is") are relatively high. In some contrast, the Vroom/Yetton study positions Finland in the middle third for participative behaviour. Finnish managers rely heavily on own experience and unwritten rules, whereas the superior and formal rules are used comparatively less strongly than in other countries. In contrast to the low importance of formal rules, uncertainty avoidance ("as is") is higher than in many other countries.

Germany is positioned in the upper third for the ideal leadership indices participative and non-autocratic (GLOBE study), for the guidance source subordinates (Event Management study), as well as for habits of participative behaviour (Vroom/Yetton study). But while the participation indices fit together well, the scores representing concepts related to participation show some inconsistency. Germany ranks in the lower third for collaborative team orientation and team integrator and is also positioned in the lower third for "as is" institutional collectivism. With regard to the perceived level of power distance ("as is"), the country shows a medium position relative to the other sixty-one countries in the GLOBE study. Formal and unwritten rules play a relatively minor role as guidance sources, whereas at the societal culture level uncertainty avoidance ("as is") is very high.

The *Polish* results are quite consistent among the three quantitative studies. Being participative and non-autocratic are relatively unimportant attributes in the Polish understanding of outstanding leadership (GLOBE study), subordinates are of low relevance as guidance source (Event Management study) and habits of leadership behaviour are much less participative than in most other countries (Vroom/Yetton study). Correspondingly, Poland is positioned relatively low on the societal culture dimension power distance ("as is"). In contrast, collaborative team orientation and team integrator are of some relevance to the image of an outstanding leader (middle third) and the level of institutional collectivism ("as is") is high (upper third). Polish managers use the guidance source superior more strongly than managers from many other countries, whereas own experience and formal rules are at a medium level and unwritten rules play a comparatively weak role. In contrast to the medium focus on formal rules, Poland ranks very low on "as is" uncertainty avoidance (GLOBE, 2001). Of the five selected countries, only Polish managers envision a higher level of societal culture uncertainty avoidance ("should be") than they perceive ("as is") (compare Figure 4.6).

The data for *Sweden* suggest a high level of participation, but some inconsistency surfaces as well. The GLOBE study positions Sweden in the upper third for non-autocratic leadership, yet only in the middle third for participative leadership, collaborative team orientation and team integrator. The Event Management Study ranks Sweden in the upper third for the guidance source subordinates, whereas the other guidance sources display varying and quite extreme scores (Smith, 2003): Sweden ranks comparatively low on own experience, very low on superior and unwritten rules, whereas the focus on formal rules is much stronger than in the other countries. Habits related to leadership behaviour, as measured by the Vroom/Yetton study, are very participative in Sweden, indicated by the country's position on top of the upper third (IIM, 2003). Correspondingly, "as is" power distance is very low and "as is" institutional collectivism is very high. Uncertainty avoidance ("as is") is also high, which is consistent with the strong focus on formal rules.

In summary, the within-country comparisons of the three studies' main indices suggest that areas of consistency as well as inconsistency exist between the respective results. This conclusion holds true for the participation scales summarised in Table 4.12, as well as for related concepts in the areas of hierarchy, team-orientation and uncertainty avoidance. In Chapters 6 to 10, the country-specific results of these quantitative indices are further analysed and tested for their fit with the country-specific models of participative management emerging from the current qualitative study.

Chapter 5

Methodological Considerations

5.1 Overview and Rationale

5.1.1 Challenges

The current study aims at answering two research questions: (1) the meaning and enactment of participation from a cross-cultural perspective, and (2) the main contextual factors in which the meaning and enactment of participative management is embedded. Additional goals of the study concern the enhancement of theoretical and practical knowledge of participation and the integration of the findings into earlier research.

Such a research focus entails both a holistic view of the concept of participative management as well as a comparative dimension (Adler, 1983). Selecting the appropriate methodology is a task that gives rise to a number of considerations and challenges for the researcher. The pivotal considerations for this study include the following:

- Conceptualisation and definition of the study unit (Which aspects of participation to focus on, which cohorts to study, what kind of data to collect?).
- Questions related to access to organisations and potential informants.
- Duration of the researcher's presence "in the field" and related financial and time constraints.
- The role of the researcher in a cross-cultural research setting: Necessity to avoid such biases as the ethnocentric bias (Usunier, 1998; see Section 5.1.5) or the courtesy bias (Brislin, 1986; see Section 5.2.1.4).
- Issues pertaining to language and culture during data collection and analysis, such as interview language, first vs. second language or potential cultural misunderstandings (e.g. differing meanings assigned to concepts by the researcher and the interviewees).
- Comparability of the findings across countries/cultures, while simultaneously accounting for culture-specific aspects.
- Issues related to the integration of the study's findings into existing research (e.g. which studies are comparable?).
- Theory advancement as well as practical relevance: How to analyse the data and how to present the findings?

5.1.2 Choice of Methodology

"Choosing a methodology determines what we can study as well as the range of possible results and conclusions." (Adler, Campbell & Laurent, 1989, p. 61)

Considering the challenges pointed out above, it is crucial to find an appropriate method to fit (1) the research questions dealing with the meaning, enactment and context of participative management on the one hand and (2) the potential problems arising from the cross-cultural perspective of the research on the other hand.

Ad 1. Participative decision-making involves human interaction. There are two basic ways to study such interaction: One may want to study the participants' "observable outside" (how they behave) or their "inside" (what they feel and think, and what constitutes the intra-personal motivation for their behaviour). The "inside" is often not easily accessible, especially when habits or unconscious motives are concerned. Both quantitative and qualitative methods can help bring intra-personal factors to the surface, and each method has its strengths in particular areas. The qualitative method is quite successful in the study of cognitive components (such as attaching meaning), for instance in the exploration of behaviour and its explanatory factors. Interviewees may for example be asked to reflect upon their own behaviour, and such reflection may trigger learning and new insights, both by the interviewee and the researcher. This type of reflection constitutes valuable data, although the researcher's theoretical explanations for observed/described behaviour will not necessarily overlap with the interviewee's own explanatory statements.

Because of its strength in the area of studying the meaning of social phenomena, qualitative methodology would qualify well for the current research initiative. Yet, an increasing number of researchers (e.g. Mintzberg, 1983a; Peng, Peterson & Shyi, 1991; Eisenhardt, 1989; Usunier, 1998; Schaffer & Riordan, 2003) suggest the *combined* use of qualitative and quantitative methods, based on the assumption that both approaches are needed for a thorough understanding of a social phenomenon (Miles & Huberman, 1994). Quantitative and qualitative methods may be combined in a number of ways (Rieger & Wong-Rieger, 1995; Parry, 1998; Strauss & Corbin, 1998), seeking to triangulate, strengthen the research basis, confirm findings, elaborate the analysis, initiate new lines of thinking and/or expand the scope and breadth of a study (Jick, 1979; Rossman & Wilson, 1985, 1994; Greene, Caracelli & Graham, 1989; Bryman & Bell, 2003). The triangulation benefits are well summarised by Jick:

"Triangulation [...] can be something other than scaling, reliability and convergent validation. It can also capture a more complete, *holistic* and contextual portrayal of the unit(s) under study. That is, beyond the analysis of overlapping variance, the use of multiple measures may also uncover some unique variance which otherwise may have been neglected by single methods. It is here that qualitative methods, in particular, can play an especially prominent role by eliciting data and suggesting conclusions to which other methods would be blind. Elements of the context are illuminated. In this sense, triangulation may be used not only to examine the same phenomenon from multiple perspectives but also to enrich our understanding by allowing for new or deeper dimensions to emerge." (Jick, 1979, p. 138, italics in original)

Jick's argument that "elements of the context are illuminated" by qualitative methods ties in with the current study's second research question treating main contextual factors of participative management. In summary and considering the mixed-methodology debate, the current integrative study would most likely benefit from triangulation and a research design that is at least partly qualitative. However, the cross-cultural perspective of the study has not been considered so far. The following paragraphs intent to shed some light on this area.

Ad 2. In the cross-cultural field, studies following the objective, quantitatively oriented paradigm are labelled "etic" research (Jahoda, 1995). Phenomena are studied from a position outside the social system, by making use of assumingly universal concepts and pre-determined characteristics that can be compared across countries/cultures in order to identify commonalities and differences (Peng, Peterson & Shyi, 1991; Usunier, 1998; Schaffer & Riordan, 2003). The etic approach provides informative overviews about universal aspects of social behaviour and cross-cultural differences. The results of etic studies are often "central tendencies in the answers from each country" (Hofstede, 1991, p. 253).

In contrast to etic research, "emic" studies (Jahoda, 1995) are positioned within social systems and mainly use qualitative methodology. The emic approach assumes that "attitudinal or behavioural phenomena are expressed in a unique way in each culture" (Usunier, 1998, p. 34). Therefore, such research initiatives are of a more exploratory nature. Phenomena are examined with the aim of understanding the phenomenon "as the people from within that culture understand it" (Schaffer & Riordan, 2003, p. 171). The results of such investigations are rich descriptions of the researched area. However, such research findings do not render themselves easily to comparison. Uniqueness and richness move to the foreground at the expense of cross-cultural comparability and external validity (Usunier, 1998).

In summary and taking the cross-cultural debate into account, the current study should consequently take an approach combing etic and emic research, given its research questions and study goals. However, the challenge to ensure cross-cultural comparison while at the same time staying sensitive to country-specific particularities remains.

Combing the methodological conclusions related to (1) the research topic of participative management and (2) the cross-cultural focus briefly summarised above, the decision was made in favour of the combined quantitative-qualitative approach outlined in Figure 5.1.

Figure 5.1 Design of the Current Study

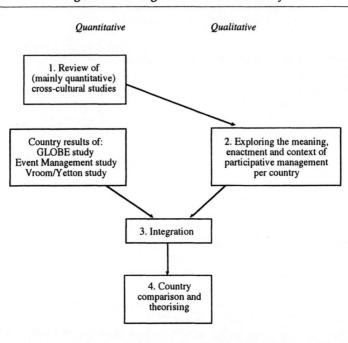

Quantitative   Qualitative

1. Review of
(mainly quantitative)
cross-cultural studies

Country results of:
GLOBE study
Event Management study
Vroom/Yetton study

2. Exploring the meaning,
enactment and context of
participative management
per country

3. Integration

4. Country
comparison and
theorising

As illustrated in Figure 5.1, a review of earlier (mostly quantitative) cross-cultural studies into participative management (see Chapter 3.1) constitutes the outset for a qualitative core study. The decision to build on prior research meets the requirements for the integration of scientific knowledge (e.g. Yukl, 1998; Bryman, 2004). The core of the study is emic in nature and explores the phenomenon holistically by employing qualitative interviews in five countries (within-country analyses). In order to address both the issue of comparability across countries and country-specific particularities, a modified version of the grounded theory method (Glaser & Strauss, 1967) is used to collect and analyse the data. Based on the goal of integration, the results of three large-scale quantitative research programmes (see Chapter 4) are then compared with the findings of the qualitative study. The evaluation of the fit of the qualitative findings with the respective industrial relations systems and a search for supporting/ contradicting accounts in the literature are further steps toward integration. In a final step, an inter-country analysis looks for areas of convergence and divergence among the country samples. Whereas the within-country analyses and the inter-country analysis additionally serve the goal of practical relevance, theory advancement is sought by taking the conclusions to the level of abstraction.

5.1.3 Qualitative Core Study

5.1.3.1 Characteristics

The exploration of the meaning and enactment of participative management in the context of five European countries forms the core of the current study. As indicated above, qualitative methodology was selected for this endeavour. It is a long, yet not very strong tradition to use qualitative methods in the field of management and leadership research: Cyert, Dill and March's (1998/1958) work is an example of an early qualitative study of the role of expectations in decision-making. More recently, Bryman's (2004) review of a large number of leadership studies using qualitative methods indicates an increasing interest in this type of studies.

Qualitative methods are well suited for the exploration of participative management from a holistic perspective. They place an "emphasis on people's lived experience" (Miles & Huberman, 1994, p. 10) and help understand the "meaning, not the frequency, of certain more or less naturally occurring phenomena in the social world" (Van Maanen, 1983, p. 9). Qualitative research masters complexity (Usunier, 1998), leads to new integration (Miles & Huberman, 1994) and can result in the "generation of theory, traditionally 'grounded' in data" (Symon & Cassell, 1998). Strauss and Corbin summarised:

> "Qualitative methods can be used to explore substantive areas about which little is known or about which much is known to gain novel understandings [...] [Q]ualitative methods can be used to obtain the intricate details about phenomena such as feelings, thought processes and emotions that are difficult to extract or learn about through more conventional research methods." (Strauss & Corbin, 1998, p. 11)

Qualitative research requires researchers to be present "in the field" for extended periods of time, which is why this type of research is typically intensive both in terms of time and financial requirements. The "rewards" are naturally occurring data with regard to the studied phenomenon (Silverman, 2001), an understanding of the phenomenon's context (Bryman & Bell, 2003) and the chance to document the world from the viewpoint of the people studied (Hammersley, 1992).

The current study does not merely aim at a holistic exploration of participative management in general terms, it has a cross-cultural component, which adds challenges with regard to (1) studying culture and (2) comparing the findings between countries. As for the first issue, qualitative methodology is commonly known as *the* methodology for studying *culture*: The cultural anthropologists Margaret Mead and Franz Boas were among the first to explore indigenous cultures, thus implicitly providing the foundation for the qualitative research paradigm. Currently, qualitative methodology is employed in a variety of disciplines and on numerous topics, but the study of culture in a broad sense has remained one of its focal strengths. Examples in the area of management research include the study of occupational cultures (e.g. Van Maanen & Barley, 1984), organisational cultures (e.g. Pettigrew, 1979) and organisational life in specific countries (e.g. Kondo, 1990). The second criterion, *comparability*, is more problematic because one of the criticisms faced by qualitative research is exactly the difficulty of comparing qualitative research findings across settings (Berry, 1989). Therefore, in preparation for the current study, established qualitative methods were checked for their fit with the study's requirements. Section 5.1.3.2 below describes the outcome of this search.

5.1.3.2 Grounded Theory Approach

The qualitative method known as "grounded theory" turned out to serve the specific requirements of the current study well, in particular after adapting some of its elements (for more details see Section 5.3.2). The method was first introduced by Barney G. Glaser and Anselm L. Strauss, two sociologists from the University of California at San Francisco. In their 1967 book "The Discovery of Grounded Theory: Strategies for Qualitative Research", they described a method in which theory emerges from and is grounded in data. After its initial introduction, grounded theory developed into two separate strands, each advocated by one of the two original authors. Glaser (1978, 1992, 1998) concentrated more on theoretical coding, i.e. the generation of higher levels of theoretical abstraction (Parry, 1998), while Strauss, together with Juliet Corbin, focused more on the development of a systematic set of coding procedures with a strong emphasis on concepts and their relationships, context factors, conditions and consequences (e.g. Strauss & Corbin, 1998). It is this version of the method that fits well with the current study's requirements.

Today, grounded theory is put to use in many different disciplines such as psychology, nursing and education research. It became visible in management and organisation research in the 1970s (Locke, 2001). Major strengths apply to the following areas:
- *Holistic perspective*. Grounded theory captures action in context: "Grounded theory is particularly useful for examining situated processes such as decision-making" (Locke, 2001, p. 95). Typically, fairly broad research

questions initiate the inquiry and any relevant concepts are allowed and expected to emerge from the data (Strauss & Corbin, 1990).

- *Comparability.* Grounded theory offers structured procedures for coding and developing categories, which supports comparison of findings across country settings.
- *Theory building.* Grounded theory is well suited for the study of meaning and the development of theoretical concepts (Strauss & Corbin, 1998). Furthermore, grounded theory can stimulate new perspectives to established theoretical areas, enlivening and modifying existing theoretical frameworks (Locke, 2001). This advantage fits the current study's aim to enhance theoretical knowledge about participative management.
- *Practical relevance.* Grounded theory links well to practice (Locke, 2001). As Glaser and Strauss (1967) argued, a well-developed grounded theory fits the area of study, is understandable to laypersons affected by the study topic and is sufficiently general to be applicable to a range of different situations within this area.
- *Culture and language.* With regard to the link between culture and language (Section 5.1.5), Gales (2003) argued that grounded theory "provides the advantage of not stripping cultural context from the analysis" (p. 131).
- *Flexibility.* Finally, an important reason in favour of grounded theory is the possibility to customise the method to fit specific research questions:

"Researchers in additional substantive and professional areas and countries will experiment with and use or adapt the methodology. [...] The procedures suggested or used in the current grounded theory literature will become elaborated *and* specific adaptations will be made by researchers for a greater range of phenomena. This elaboration and adaptation will include also multi-site studies in a variety of settings, including cross-cultural work." (Strauss & Corbin, 1994, p. 283, italics in original)

5.1.3.3 Qualitative Interviews

Within the grounded theory framework, the current study employs in-depth interviews for data collection. Additional qualitative methods such as participant observation are not used at this stage, for reasons of feasibility and complexity reduction. The interviews are conducted with middle managers, thus allowing comparability of findings with the three quantitative studies (integration perspective). Additional samples, such as subordinates, are not considered at this stage.

Interviews generally play a prominent role in qualitative management research. In his review of qualitative leadership studies, for example, Bryman (2004) found that 49 of 66 studies made use of qualitative interviews, either stand-alone or in combination with other qualitative methods such as documentary analysis or focus groups. Interviews are also a suitable method for studying people's own views, as is the case in the current study. Other qualitative methods, such as observation, could shed light on participative *behaviour*, yet would not allow eliciting the *meaning* of participative management.

The interviews are theme-focused, in other words semi-structured, thus differentiating them from unstructured qualitative interviews. The focus on pre-defined themes emerged from the clear research objective at the offset of the investigation and the necessity to create some structure in the data to ensure comparability across interviewees and countries.

5.1.4 Defining the Study Unit and the Term Culture

Chapter 3.2.1 described the process of zooming in on five countries to focus the current study. The question arises whether *country* is an appropriate unit for the study of *culture* in general and of cross-cultural similarities and differences in particular. In a discussion of difficulties typically experienced by cross-cultural researchers, Tayeb argued:

> "Culture is a woolly concept, almost impossible to observe and 'measure' all its visible and hidden corners; like the air that we breathe, we cannot see or weigh it, we cannot put our arms around it and feel its strength and power, but we know it is there." (Tayeb, 2001, p. 92)

Different strategies exist for dealing with such difficulties in the study of culture. One common approach is to study social phenomena within the boundaries of national culture, in other words to equate culture and country. Schaffer and Riordan (2003, p. 175) observed that country was used as a proxy for culture in 79 percent of cross-cultural studies reviewed. While such an approach represents a convenient solution to the problem, it does not address the issue of potential incongruity between country and culture possibly arising for the following reasons:
- *Arbitrary borders.* History shows that national borders have frequently been set as a consequence of wars, revolutions or political decisions, often with little respect for cultural areas (Schaffer & Riordan, 2003).
- *Cultural change* within a political entity (Peterson & Smith, 1997).
- *Multiculturalism.* Some countries' cultural identity may support or tolerate more than one relatively distinct subculture (Schaffer & Riordan, 2003; Peterson & Smith, 1997).

Keeping this in mind, using country as a delimiter for culture does, in fact, makes some sense: Country borders typically mark areas within which more social interaction is going on than across borders. Furthermore, laws and institutions are the same for all people living on a country's territory.

Hofstede (1980a) argued that national cultures are characterised by rein-forcement. Peterson and Smith added:

"People form distinguishable (but not entirely), bounded (but not rigidly) communities. The link between nation and culture tends to occur because peo-ple prefer to interact with other people and be guided and politically governed by institutions consistent with values and beliefs with which they identify." (Peterson & Smith, 1997, p. 934)

Country is not the only delimiter for culture. Peterson and Smith (1997) listed a number of additional categories of culture predictors, such as lan-guage, proximity and topography, economic systems, economic and techni-cal development, climate and religion.

Another relevant issue in defining the study unit in cross-cultural re-search concerns the overlap of different cultural contexts. Country culture needs to be disentangled from other forms of culture, such as professional culture, organisational culture, regional and industrial culture (Alvesson & Berg, 1992; Berthoin, Dirkes & Helmers, 1993; Sackmann, 1997). Addition-ally, non-cultural factors also should be regarded:

"It is true that one's behaviours and actions are informed by one's values and taken for granted assumptions, but these values are not purely national culture based. One's education, age, occupation and life experience in general exert powerful influences on one's values and taken for granted assumptions." (Tayeb, 2001, p. 96)

The current study focuses on countries, as outlined in Chapter 3. However, the country samples are not only drawn with regard to national boundaries, but also on the basis of several other determinants. Each country sample is *homogeneous* with regard to the following criteria: (1) The interviewees in each country sample were born and raised in that country and are native speakers of the "main language group". For example, the Finnish sample consists entirely of Finnish speaking Finns, thus representing the majority of the Finnish population (Swedish is spoken as a mother tongue by about six percent of the population; Jarvenpa, 1992). (2) All interviewees are members of the same professional group, namely middle management. Focusing on middle managers allows comparability of the current study's findings with the results of the three quantitative studies (integration perspective). (3) All interviewees live and work in regions with the same level of eco-nomic/technical development. This criterion relates to regional culture dif-ferences and was included mainly because of the German sample, in which all interviewees except for one are from the former West Germany (see Sec-tion 5.2.2.1 for more details on the sample characteristics).

Last but not least, it is necessary to define my own understanding of what culture means. There has been extensive debate in the literature as to the

most appropriate definition for the concept of culture (Geertz, 1973). As
Smith et al. (2002) pointed out, some theorists conceptualise culture as defined by shared meanings assigned by culture members to things and persons around them, while others assert that culture entails not just shared
interpretations but also actual differences in behaviour. The second type of
conceptualisation is more holistic and fits well with the current study's focus
on the meaning and enactment of participative management. Therefore, I
base the present study upon the following working definition of culture:

> "Culture contains the set of enduring meanings assigned to persons, things,
> concepts and behaviours, which is shared by the members of a cultural group
> and guides their behaviour."

5.1.5 Language Issues

> "[Language] is a significant component of culture [...] and conveys meanings
> which may be unique to a cultural community. Moreover, our native language
> frames our way of looking at real world phenomena and interpreting them."
> (Usunier, 1998, p. 31)

The relationship between language and culture has traditionally been the
focus of linguists, originating from Sapir's (1929) description of language as
a guide to social reality and elegantly accentuated by linguist and ethnogra-
pher Michael Agar, who coined the term "languaculture" (Agar, 1994, p. 20).
The language-culture link has also become an increasingly important issue
in the cross-cultural literature, reflected in statements such as, "[a] study of
cultures that approaches the comparative problem through language is immediately trapped in the fact that language itself is part of the culture"
(Haire, Ghiselli & Porter, 1966, p. 4), "language tends simultaneously to
reflect and shape our world views" (Usunier, 1998, p. 53), "language represents and expresses the culture, the value systems behind it" (Tayeb, 2001, p.
103) and "the dramatic increase in cross-cultural management research has
been accompanied by growing concerns about methodology. [...] Language
is an area of particular concern" (Gales, 2003, p. 131).

There is good reason for cross-cultural researchers to be concerned with
language issues. Frequently there is no shared native language between the
researcher and the researched. Misunderstandings might occur, for example,
because the culture-specific meanings of concepts and words used in the
context of a study differ between the two groups. Warning voices include:

> "To whatever extent one disregards the differences in connotation in the inter-
> est of comparability, one may be spuriously removing true cultural differences
> which are germane and important to the study itself." (Haire, Ghiselli & Porter,
> 1966, p. 4)

"[Language] can be seen as influencing the whole research process, including the researcher, the researched field and the ways in which to address issues and to collect data." (Usunier, 1998, p. 18)

"The problem of achieving parity of meaning of concepts and constructs in most cases goes beyond language barriers and mistranslation. Some concepts are more or less universal, some are generated and organically developed in a particular culture and bear the hallmark of that culture to such an extent as to make it incomprehensible to outsiders. Some can be imported but made workable only after conscious or unconscious modifications and adaptations. Some do not even exist in certain cultures and therefore cannot be compared across cultures." (Tayeb, 2001, p. 98)

Quantitative studies typically try to solve upcoming language problems by employing such procedures as translation and back-translation of the research instruments or Q-sorting of questionnaire items (e.g. House et al., 2004). Such approaches ensure translation equivalence, most notably lexical and idiomatic equivalence (Usunier, 1998). *Qualitative* studies face the challenge of dealing with language issues in an even more complex way than quantitative research, because the researcher and the persons under study interact and communicate directly. Both sides bring their own cultural assumptions to the encounter, possibly represented by different languages. The following main questions arise:

- What if there is no shared first language? Conducting research in a second language is a serious challenge for researchers and persons under study alike.
- What if there is no common language at all? The issue of using translators/interpreters arises (Temple & Young, 2004), opening the door to additional culturally-based interpretations of what is said: "The translator makes assumptions about meaning equivalence that make her an analyst and cultural broker as much as a translator" (Temple & Young, 2004, p. 171).
- At which point during the research is it necessary and advisable to switch to *one* language? Is it necessary to have transcripts translated? What are the consequences of an "early domestication" of the data, typically into written English (Temple & Young, 2004, p. 174)?
- What about the cultural bias of the researcher? Usunier (1998) stressed in particular the "ethnocentric bias" and Hofstede and Tayeb observed:

"Not only the people within organisations, but also those writing about organising are children of a culture; they grew up in families, went to schools and worked for employers. Their experiences represent the material on which their thinking and writing has been based. [...] [O]rganisation theorists are perfectly human and as culturally biased as other mortals." (Hofstede, 1994, p. 8)

"The researchers' own cultural values and attitudes could get in the way of understanding their subjects of study. How do you detach yourself from your cultural background and iron out the filter through which everything reaches you from the outside world and is sent out to it? Impossible. The best that one can do is to acknowledge one's cultural bias, which can never be entirely eliminated." (Tayeb, 2001, p. 102)

How are these issues and questions to be dealt with? General advice circles around the notions of raising awareness of the implications of language differences and exploring the meanings and worldviews expressed in different languages in the best possible way:

"A practical solution for investigating world views as they are reflected by language is to interview native speakers, local collaborators and informants, observe, discuss with them, check meaning differentials and, if possible, try to speak their language even modestly." (Usunier, 1998, p. 143)

The current study tries to reply to the language and culture challenges at several levels (more details on the interviews follow in Section 5.2.1.4, on the analysis process in Section 5.3.2):

- The quantitative instruments used in preparation for the interviews (Section 5.2.1.3) were employed in validated language versions.
- The interviews were conducted either in German or English. German is my, the researcher's, mother tongue and I am also fluent in English. The choice between German and English was determined by the language skills and preferences of the interview partners. Whenever possible, the interviews were conducted in the native language of the interviewed person or in the second language they used in their professional environment.
- In a minority of cases, translators were necessary. In these cases, extensive reflection between the translators and myself immediately followed the interviews, concentrating on the process and contents of the interviews and trying to reveal cultural meaning differences.
- Instead of introducing the term "participative management", which is more commonly used in the academic literature, I consistently used the terms "participation" (in English) and "Partizipation" (in German). This decision follows Bryman and Bell's (2003) advise to use language that is "comprehensible and relevant to the people you are interviewing" (p. 349). Earlier research and discussions with local researchers had suggested that the interviewees were familiar with the chosen terminology.
- At the beginning of the interviews, all managers were asked to define the concept of participation in their own words. This was the first of a number of steps intended to bring to light each interviewee's personal, possible culturally defined, meaning of participation.

- Before collecting the data, I thoroughly reflected upon my own understanding of participation, defined participation to myself and examined the definition for theoretical and cultural influences.
- The interviews consisted of several parts, each looking at participative management from a different angle. This procedure allowed checking for intra-personal consistency in the interviewees' statements. In other words, the analysis made several rather than single statements about the same phenomenon by each interviewee available, thus maximising the possibility to let cultural meaning differences emerge.
- During the interviews, I tried to stay alert to cultural meaning differences inherent in language and to ensure common understanding across languages as well as possible: (1) Questions were asked in a simple manner and rephrased whenever it was unclear if the interviewee understood them as intended. (2) I listened carefully to what the interviewee said and, when in doubt, mirrored back the interviewee's statements by summarising and/or rephrasing them. (3) I asked the interviewee to elaborate on issues touched on only briefly but which seemed relevant for common understanding. (4) The interviewee was asked to explain in her or his own words what s/he meant by concepts used, such as conflict or teamwork. (5) I asked the interviewee to illustrate her or his statements with examples from personal experience. (6) Special attention was paid to hesitation and pauses in the interviewee's speech, because such reactions might reflect difficulty in expressing original meaning in the second language, thus hinting at potential meaning differences. (7) Words and concepts described as untranslatable by interviewee or translator were explored further, both in the current and subsequent interviews.
- All interviews were taped in full length, including the interviews conducted with the assistance of translators. In other words, the interaction in its entirety including the statements in both native and foreign languages was tape-recorded. During the analysis process, the original tapes were listened to concurrently with reading the transcripts. As for the interviews conducted with the help of translators, the tapes allowed to double-check the original meaning with native speakers.
- Most interviews were transcribed by myself, the researcher. For part of the Swedish, Finnish and German interviews I used professional transcription services. In these cases, I discussed the transcripts with the person who typed them and I worked through the final transcripts once again, making corrections based on listening to the tape myself.
- Codes and categories originating from the analysis process were given English names and descriptions, except for codes referring to such terms as "lagom" (Swedish), which were described as untranslatable by the interviewees and consequently left in the original language.

5.2 Data Collection

5.2.1 Procedure and Instruments

5.2.1.1 Overview

Data collection for the qualitative core study took place over the course of about a year, from July 2000 to June 2001. Access, sample size and sampling strategy are described in Section 5.2.1.2, whereas the process of interviewing and the contents of and issues surrounding the interviews are summarised in Section 5.2.1.4. The data collection process and all instruments used in this process were pilot-tested (Section 5.2.1.5). In preparation for the interviews, the managers completed the instruments of the Vroom/Yetton, Event Management and GLOBE studies and received written feedback (Section 5.2.1.3). This "feedback package" served as a trigger during one part of the interview. More specifically, it facilitated the elaboration and reflection on individual and country-specific quantitative information.

5.2.1.2 Access and Sampling

Access. Data were collected from middle managers in five different European countries. Such an endeavour is difficult to accomplish by one person alone. Therefore, I sought and found co-operation with international colleagues based in the five countries. These contact persons helped to set up the study in their respective countries and facilitated access to local managers. Based on the sampling criteria (see below), they sent out invitation letters and/or called up potential candidates. All interviewees knew their respective contact person prior to being asked to participate in this study. In some cases, interested managers contacted me directly. In other cases, the contact persons forwarded e-mail addresses to me and I established contact. Table 5.1 lists the institutions and contact persons.

Table 5.1 Contact Institutions and Persons

Country	Institution	Contact persons
Czech Republic	University of Economics Prague	Milan Maly
Finland	Turku School of Economics and Business Administration	Satu Lähteenmäki
Germany	USW (Universitätsseminar der Wirtschaft)	Kirsten Meyer
Poland	University of Wroclaw	Jerzy Maczynski
Sweden	Stockholm School of Economics	Ingalill Holmberg, Mats Tyrstrup, Gunnar Stenvall

Sample size. As this is an exploratory study, it was decided to start out with a small number of middle managers. A pilot test in the Czech Republic (Section 5.2.1.5) showed that data resulting from interviews with no more than five managers were rich enough to detect stable patterns and build a country-specific model of participation. As a conservative estimate for the main study, it was decided to sample data from at least six managers per country. The final sample exceeded this number and totalled thirty-five middle managers, counting seven Czechs, eight Finns, eight Germans, six Poles and six Swedes. The different numbers in the various countries result from a larger number of managers initially approached, assuming that some might withdraw from participating in the study, which only a few did.

Sampling strategy. A small sample size requires an appropriate sampling strategy: The participating managers were selected based on the study's homogeneity criteria with regard to citizenship, language, middle management position and region (Section 5.1.4). Defining the sample in these terms goes beyond a pure equation of country and culture. Within these boundaries, sampling was based on the principle of *maximal differentiation* (Agar, 1996), which requires for the interviewees to be as different as possible in as many respects as possible. Miles and Huberman (1994) suggested that the data from a small number of interviewees selected according to the strategy of maximal variation potentially reveal patterns of common understanding shared by the majority of members of a larger population. In the current study, the country samples are purposely *heterogeneous* with regard to sex, age and education of its members, as well as characteristics of their workplace. This enables some degree of generalisation of the findings to the general cohort of middle managers in the five countries, regardless of their other characteristics (Section 5.4.3).

5.2.1.3 Interview Preparation

In a first step, the managers were provided with the instruments of the three quantitative studies, namely a shortened version of the GLOBE questionnaire, the Event Management questionnaire and the booklet containing the thirty Vroom/Yetton case descriptions, together with a short demographics questionnaire. The shortened GLOBE questionnaire included all items of the first-order scales *participative, non-autocratic, team integrator* and *collaborative team orientation* (Chapter 4.1.1.1) as well as all items of the societal culture dimensions *power distance, institutional collectivism* and *uncertainty avoidance* (Chapter 4.1.1.2). The data collection for these three societal culture dimensions is undertaken with the aim of measuring culture dimensions directly in the specific research context rather than using existing country scores, and thus avoiding ecological fallacy (Hofstede, 1980a; Smith, 1996). Ecological fallacy refers to the potentially wrong assumption that the current research sample reflects the mean country scores reported by earlier studies. The demographics questionnaire contained items related to the personal, educational and professional background of the interviewees. Additionally, it included some items eliciting information about the functional area and organisation the managers worked in.

A letter explaining the study and the data collection process completed the "quantitative package". The managers were ensured absolute confidentiality. The packages were either in German or English, depending on the interviewees' mother tongue and language skills. The thirty Vroom/Yetton case descriptions of decision-making situations were distributed in the German, Polish, Czech, Swedish or Finnish language version, as required. When in doubt, the preferred language version was discussed with the managers either on the phone or by electronic mail prior to sending the package.

After having filled out all instruments the managers returned them for statistical analysis, usually within the next couple of weeks and by mail. In some cases the material was forwarded to and handed back by the contact persons.

The second step of the preparatory phase consisted of the processing of the quantitative data and the printout of individual "feedback packages", which were returned to the managers. The feedback allowed managers to compare their individual results with the mean scores of a larger sample of managers from their home country. In addition, some key results were also presented in a cross-cultural comparison with the other four countries participating in the study. Contrasting the individual managers' responses with the country findings and highlighting country patterns allowed the managers to reflect upon issues related to participative management before the interview took place.

Neither questionnaires nor written feedback directly stressed the concept of participation. Rather, the documents referred to leadership styles, leader attributes and guidance sources. Thus, while setting the stage for the interviews, the risk that the initial quantitative data collection would "contaminate" the qualitative data was minimised. During the interviews this assumption was supported: There was no indication that a preconditioning of the interviewees with regard to the concept of participation had taken place.

5.2.1.4 Qualitative Interviews

General characteristics. In-depth, theme-focused interviews constituted the core element of the data collection process. The interviews were between one and two hours in duration and were recorded on audiotape with the permission of the interviewees. All managers expressed familiarity with the research instrument "tape-recorded interview" and were assured that their responses would remain anonymous. Most interviews took place at the managers' workplace, with no additional people present in the room. In some cases, it was agreed to meet in a different location following the interviewees' suggestions.

Language. Part of the interviewees (German sample) and I shared the same mother tongue. Consequently, these interviews were conducted in German. Other interviewees had a very good level of either English (Finnish and Swedish samples, part of the Czech and Polish samples) or German (part of the Czech sample), due to their background and/or regular use of that language at work. These interviews were conducted in the respective working language of the interviewees. A minority of interviews were dependent on translators. In the Czech Republic, one interview was partly translated into German: The interviewee spoke German fairly well but had brought along her assistant, who translated part of her statements. Three Polish interviews were fully translated: Two local students, both familiar with the concept of participative management, were present during the interviews. One student translated my statements from English into Polish, the other translated the interviewee's statements from Polish into English. For a general discussion of how the language challenge was dealt with see Section 5.1.5.

Interview style. I took the role of a sympathetic and interested outsider and foreigner and refrained from expressing my own opinion on the topics of the study. The interviews were theme-focused in order to structure the data and to ensure a certain level of comparability across interviewees and countries. Interviewees were asked to bring in their own experience in order to obtain rich personal descriptions. Specific attention was paid to the "courtesy bias" (Brislin, 1986, p. 163; Usunier, 1998, p. 121), the risk of shaping answers to please the interviewer. Due to my professional background and the exclusive use of interview-based data, this was a potential concern. To address this issue, each part of the interview looked at participation from a different angle thus allowing me to evaluate each interviewee's data for internal consistency. Furthermore, asking for personal experience rather than abstract statements also helped minimise the bias.

Interview topics. The interviews consisted of six parts, following a broad interview guide (Table 5.2).

The *first part* of the interview consisted of a brief introduction of myself and the research project, reflecting my overt research role (Schwartzman, 1993). To minimise researcher effects on the interviewees (Miles & Huberman, 1994), the managers were informed in a corresponding fashion about the interview and study purposes. Since it was the first face-to-face encounter with the interviewee, this phase also served the purpose of establishing rapport (Agar, 1996; Schaffer & Riordan, 2003). Additionally, it allowed me to stress that the interview would take the format of a "rather normal" conversation rather than being based on a predefined list of questions.

Table 5.2 Interview Guide

---

1. Warm-up (introducing myself and the project, establishing rapport)
2. Defining participation: Personal definition
3. Elaborating on personal experiences
    3a. Areas/problems where participation has been good/helpful?
    3b. Areas/problems where participation has been useless/harmful?
4. Reflections on feedback package incl. examples
5. Discussion of themes conceptually related to participation
6. Wrap-up (questions and comments)

The *second part* of the interview concerned the interviewee's personal definition of participation and represented the first step into the exploration of the meaning and enactment of participative management in its cultural context. More specifically, interviewees were asked to define in their own words what participation meant to them and relate this definition to their own managerial practice.

The focus on personal experience continued in the *third part*. Interviewees were asked to elaborate on areas and problems, for which they had personally found participation to be good and helpful vs. useless or even harmful.

The *fourth part* of the interview was used to let interviewees reflect on the quantitative information provided in the feedback package (Section 5.2.1.3). The managers were asked to comment on the quantitative results, to provide examples from their own experience and to elaborate on emerging country-specific themes. With regard to the GLOBE study, I asked the interviewees to describe their personal image of an outstanding manager/leader. As for the Vroom/Yetton study, the managers were asked to explain and provide background information about their responses to selected case descriptions, such as the decision strategy used to allocate scarce parking space among subordinates. Reflection took place on two levels: (1) individual responses as compared to the country means, and (2) country scores of all five countries.

The *fifth part* of the interview was rather focussed and concentrated on themes conceptually related to participation: team orientation (Chapter 4.1.1.1), power distance, individualism-collectivism and uncertainty avoidance (Chapter 4.1.1.2). Interviewees were asked to define their understanding of these concepts, to evaluate the link of these concepts with participation and to provide examples from their own experience.

The *sixth and last part* of the interview was reserved for questions and comments by the interviewee. Also, as anticipated, some interviewees continued talking "off the record" after the tape was switched off. Such information was not treated as data, but as confidential background information that helped understand emerging themes later on during the analysis process.

5.2.1.5 Pilot Test

A pilot test was conducted with five Czech managers. Three of them preferred English as interview language and two opted for German, which allowed the instruments to be tested and refined in both languages. The main reasons for the pilot test were to test the procedure (initial contact, interview preparation, interview), to check whether the feedback package was clear and understandable and to verify whether the interview guide worked as planned in terms of content, number of themes and length of interview. Furthermore, the analysis of the pilot test data should enable an evaluation of the number of interviews required in each country.

The instruments of the three quantitative studies themselves would not have required a pilot test, since they had been validated and repeatedly used in the past. However, a shortened version of the GLOBE questionnaire was used and the demographics section was in a format not used before. Thus, it seemed useful to test whether the questionnaires contained any formal errors.

The pilot test showed that the data collection procedure worked well. Additionally, the quantitative instruments did not contain any errors and the feedback package was well understood by all five managers. During the qualitative interviews, the managers were explicitly asked about how to improve the procedure and the layout of the feedback package. Only some minor improvements were suggested. Consequently, the procedure remained the same for the main study and there were only minor changes in the feedback package's explanatory text and scale display.

The interview scheme also worked well. The five pilot interviews lasted 95 minutes on average and were thus within the estimated limits. The interviewees seemed to understand the interview questions without any problems, even when the interviews were conducted in a second language. All main interview questions had an open format and caused the interview partners to elaborate on the various themes in great detail, as intended. Furthermore, the interviewees seemed to have no problems talking about their personal opinions and experience. Examples were easily provided and described in detail. The interviewees had no apparent problems reflecting on the results of the quantitative instruments.

With regard to sample size and analysis, the data resulting from the interviews with the five Czech managers turned out to be rich enough to detect stable patterns and build a country-specific model of participation.

5.2.2 Interviewees

5.2.2.1 Demographic Profile

Table 5.3 and the succeeding paragraphs provide a demographic profile overview of the interviewees, which shows the fit with the sampling criteria described above. The five-country sample consists of a total of thirty-five middle managers.

Table 5.3 Demographic Profile of the Current Sample

	Czech Republic	Finland	Germany	Poland	Sweden
Number of interviewees	7	8	8	6	6
Number of organisations represented	7	7	8	5	6
Homogeneity criteria:					
Born and raised in the country	Yes	Yes	Yes [1]	Yes	Yes
Mother tongue	Czech	Finnish	German	Polish	Swedish
Position in middle management	Yes	Yes	Yes	Yes	Yes
Maximal differentiation criteria:					
Age of interview partners	41 (32-51)	41 (33-49)	38 (33-43)	37 (26-46)	41 (34-48)
Male / female split	5 / 2	5 / 3	7 / 1	4 / 2	5 / 1
Years of formal education	18 (16-20)	17 (13-20)	18 (12-26)	17 (14-19)	17 (15-20)
Years of full-time work experience	18 (10-28)	16 (6-25)	13 (7-19)	13 (2-22)	17 (10-29)
Years with current employer	11 (0-25)	10 (1-25)	9 (0-17)	6 (0-12)	8 (0-16)
Years in managerial position	12 (5-25)	9 (2-14)	7 (4-10)	7 (0-18)	10 (4-15)
Number of direct subordinates	6 (4-8)	9 (1-25)	7 (3-10)	6 (3-18)	7 (4-12)

Notes: Numbers before brackets represent mean scores, while the numbers in brackets stand for the minimum and maximum scores, respectively.

[1] One of the German interviewees was born and raised in the former Eastern Germany.

As shown in Table 5.3, all homogeneity criteria were met and there was extensive intra-country variation with regard to the defined areas of maximal differentiation: *age, sex*, years of *formal education*, years of *full-time work experience*, years with *current employer* and in a *managerial position*, as well as *number of subordinates* directly reporting to the manager. Additionally, the *educational background* of the interviewees ranged from compulsory to university education and included such diverse fields as engineering, economics, business administration, information technology, chemistry, pharmacology, medicine, geology and history. The *functional areas* of the interviewees included finance/accounting, sales, marketing, engineering, HR management, production, quality control and research and development. *Organisational characteristics* varied within countries with regard to industry, type of organisation, ownership and size. Part of the interviewees' organisations produced goods as diverse as sports equipment, cigarettes, noodles or faucets. Other organisations were service providers, among them a local energy provider, a trade union, a couple of banks and an insurance company. Ownership structure included private companies, multinationals, government-owned and combined forms. Organisation size ranged from fifteen employees to almost a hundred thousand. The interviewees worked and lived in the following regions: Bohemia in the Czech Republic, the Turku region in Finland, Nordrhein-Westfalia in Germany, the Wroclaw region in Poland and the Stockholm region in Sweden.

5.2.2.2 Fit with the Quantitative Samples

The current study aims at an integration of the qualitative findings with the results of earlier quantitative studies. A basis for doing so is the equivalence of the samples: The sample descriptions of the three quantitative studies (Chapter 4.1.2: GLOBE, Chapter 4.2.2: Event Management and Chapter 4.3.2: Vroom/Yetton) suggest that there is homogeneity in terms of country membership and language affiliation, similar to the current study. Additionally, middle managers are the explicit target group in the Event Management and GLOBE studies. The Vroom/Yetton sample, although sampling different kinds of managers, includes close to sixty-five percent middle managers. Also corresponding with the qualitative sample, the Vroom/Yetton respondents vary in age and functional membership. The male/female split in the current study is roughly the same as in the three quantitative studies.

In addition to comparing the demographic characteristics of the samples to evaluate the fit, empirical comparison of data elicited from these samples provides another viable method. This is possible, because the interviewees of the current qualitative study completed the instruments of all three quantitative studies in preparation for the interviews. By contrasting the current sample's country averages with the country means originating from the three quantitative studies it is possible to test whether the samples show similar response profiles.

Pearson correlations of the country means were conducted for the main quantitative indices in order to compare the original samples of the three quantitative studies with the current sample. Similarity of the samples should result in positive correlation scores. Of course this is a very rough procedure, yet it helps strengthen trust in the current sampling strategy and consequently, in the findings of the qualitative data.

The correlation coefficients presented in Table 5.4 indicate a number of similarities in response characteristics between the samples of the three quantitative studies and the current study, in particular for the Vroom/Yetton study. The MLP score as well as three of the more specific indices (violation of acceptance rules, strategies AI and AII) correlate significantly and positively. With regard to ideal leader attributes (GLOBE study) and guidance sources (Event Management study) the analysis did not reveal any significant relations, although all correlations were positive. It is necessary to keep in mind that the scales of these two studies show less divergence between countries than the Vroom/Yetton data (compare Tables 4.12 to 4.15). As a consequence, even if the current small sample fits the characteristics of its larger counterparts, this similarity is possibly not reflected in significant correlation coefficients. The comparison of the GLOBE societal "as is" culture dimensions also led to positive correlations, all of them larger than ,75. A significant correlation coefficient was reached for uncertainty avoidance.

Table 5.4 Evaluating the Fit of the Current Sample

Variable	P
GLOBE leadership scales	
Participative	,23
Non-autocratic	,67
Team integrator	,21
Collective team orientation	,10
Event Management study	
Guidance source subordinates	,33
Guidance source own experience	,01
Guidance source superior	,75
Guidance source formal rules	,15
Guidance source unwritten rules	,59
Vroom/Yetton study	
Mean level of participation (MLP)	,96 **
Violation of quality rules	,75
Violation of acceptance rules	,98 **
Strategy AI	,89 *
Strategy AII	,88 *
Strategy CI	,02
Strategy CII	,78
Strategy GII	,76
GLOBE societal culture scales	
Power distance "as is"	,81
Institutional collectivism "as is"	,76
Uncertainty avoidance "as is"	,95 *

Notes: n=5 * p<.05 ** p<.01

In summary, all correlation coefficients were positive, giving support to the assumption that the current sample is similar in its response patterns to the managerial samples used in the three quantitative studies. The conducted analysis also helps avoid ecological fallacy (Hofstede, 1980a; Smith, 1996), i.e. the possibly wrong assumption that individuals or subgroups under study "automatically" show the same patterns as country means do.

5.3 Data Analysis

5.3.1 Principles of Grounded Theory

The Strauss and Corbin (1994) version of grounded theory, selected for the current study (compare Section 5.1.3.2 above), is characterised by the following features:

Theory building rather than testing. A grounded theory is "inductively derived from the study of the phenomenon it represents" (Parry, 1998, p. 89). Theory evolves "during actual research, and it does this through continuous interplay between analysis and data collection" (Strauss & Corbin, 1994, p. 273). In other words, grounded theory supports the process of abstracting from data and thinking theoretically, rather than staying at a pure descriptive level (Goulding, 2002). Such theory building from data is linked with "a rejection of *a priori* theorising. This does not mean, however, that researchers should embark on their studies without the general guidance provided by some sort of orienting theoretical perspective" (Locke, 2001, p. 34, italics in original). In other words, it is acknowledged that researchers have their own "disciplinary background, which will provide a perspective from which to investigate the problem. Nobody starts with a totally blank sheet" (Goulding, 2000, p. 262). However, researchers should be cautious not to be unconsciously disposed to testing rather than exploring.

Data may be collected from various sources, including interviews, field observation, life histories, focus groups and documents such as diaries, biographies, historical accounts or media materials (Strauss & Corbin, 1994; Goulding, 2000). "Glaser and Strauss do advocate what is now called 'triangulation', that is collection of data from multiple sources that all are relevant to the studied phenomenon" (Locke, 2001, p. 45). Kan and Parry's (2004) study is a good example of using triangulation within the grounded theory method: Their data include non-participant observation, informal/unstructured and formal/semi-structured interviews, document analysis and questionnaires.

Theoretical sampling. Data collection is based on the principle of *theoretical sampling,* i.e. data sources are chosen for theoretical, not statistical, reasons (Glaser & Strauss, 1967). Theoretical sampling defines the choice of data at the outset of the study as well as data collection during the course of the research, which is "directed by the emerging theory" (Goulding 2002, p.

170). In other words, cases and material are selected against the background of the state of the analysis (Flick, 2002). The goal is to choose data sources, which are likely to support theory development.

Theory building and theoretical saturation. Data collection, data analysis and theory building are closely interwoven (Strauss & Corbin, 1994). Theory building begins with the analysis of the first incoming data, by identifying potentially significant concepts, i.e. abstract representations of events, objects, actions or interactions. As data collection progresses, concepts are refined and relationships between concepts are identified. Data collection continues until *theoretical saturation* is reached, i.e. until new data bring no new insights. The final theory is "an explanatory scheme that systematically integrates various concepts through statements of relationship" (Strauss & Corbin, 1998, p. 25). Data analysis is described as a systematic procedure, which at the same time requires for the researcher to be creative.

> "Creativity manifests itself in the ability of researchers to aptly name categories, ask stimulating questions, make comparisons and extract an innovative, integrated, realistic scheme from masses of unorganised data." (Strauss & Corbin, 1998, p. 13)

Asking questions and constant comparison. These are the two major procedures throughout the whole analysis process that increase the likelihood that "analysts will discover both variation and general patterns" (Strauss & Corbin, 1998, p. 85). Questions and comparisons may relate to (1) systematic inquiries among the different data, with the goal to look for emerging patterns and themes (Goulding, 2000, p. 262), and (2) inquiries between theory and data, with the goal to build theory that closely fits the data (Eisenhardt, 1989). Additionally, the use of a broad range of comparative sources such as secondary data, academic literature and fiction is possible. These sources are not to be treated as direct data, but as triggers for further inquiry and sensitising devices so that the researcher recognises concepts and relationships in the own data.

Coding at three stages. In the grounded theory approach, data coding takes place during the overlapping stages of *open coding* (detailed analysis, e.g. line-by-line coding during the early phases of a project), *axial coding* (aggregating codes to categories, refining and linking categories, generating first theoretical concepts) and *selective coding* (verifying and finalising theoretical concepts, formulating propositions) (Strauss & Corbin, 1994). These stages are related to the strategy of theoretical sampling. While data collection is very broad during the initial stages, only selected data are collected in later phases in order to fully develop categories and answer open questions.

Supporting techniques. Strauss and Corbin (1994) introduced a series of techniques supporting data analysis. Among them are the use of *diagrams*, the *conditional matrix*, "a device for tracking the various levels of influence on the phenomenon studied" (Goulding, 2002, p. 169) and *memos*. Memoing is a reflexive practice that helps researchers to articulate and conserve their thoughts during data analysis (Locke, 2001).

Use of literature. Towards the end of a grounded theory study, in other words, when data collection and analysis are completed, Strauss and Corbin (1998) suggest to turn to the scientific literature about the area under study. The literature can be used to confirm findings as well as to illustrate where existing publications simplify or provide only partial explanations. "Bringing the literature into the writing [...] allows for extending, validating and refining knowledge in the field" (Strauss & Corbin, 1998, p. 51f).

5.3.2 Adaptations for the Current Study

This section demonstrates how some of the features of grounded theory have specifically been adapted to fit the requirements of the current study. Before doing so, a few words on terminology are necessary. In the grounded theory literature, the use of key terms has varied and changed over time and several terms have been used synonymously (Locke, 2001). The current study consistently uses the terminology summarised in Table 5.5.

Table 5.5 Grounded Theory Terminology Used in the Current Study

Key term	Description
Code	Common name or phrase assigned to incidents in the data that are similar. Codes highlight what data segments go together and what data segments are distinct from each other. Codes are not predefined but emerge during the analysis.
Category	Term used for a number of codes that can be logically grouped together under a unifying header. Similarities in the data reinforce existing categories while differences suggest new categories or variations on already identified ones. Descriptive categories are differentiated from more abstract and theoretical categories.
Concept (conceptual category)	Term used for one or more theoretical categories that belong together. Concepts are abstract representations of events, objects, actions or interactions, such as "participation". "Abstract concepts encompass a number of more concrete instances found in the data" (Goulding, 2000, p. 262).
Attribute	Dimension or specific aspect of a concept. "The more [attributes] a particular conceptual category possesses, the more fully described or theoretically dense it is" (Locke, 2001, p. 40). For example, the concept "participation" has attributes such as "degree of involvement" and "frequency".
Attribute variation	For example, the concept "participation's" attribute "degree of involvement" may vary from "providing information" to "consultation" and "joint decision-making", and the attribute "frequency" may show variations such as "occasional" or "regularly".
Proposition	Proposed relationship between concepts. Propositions are the final outcome of grounded theory research.

How grounded theory is used in the current study is illustrated in Figure 5.2 (based on a similar representation by Bryman & Bell, 2003, p. 431). All steps are described in more detail in the paragraphs below.

Figure 5.2 Elements of Grounded Theory in the Current Study

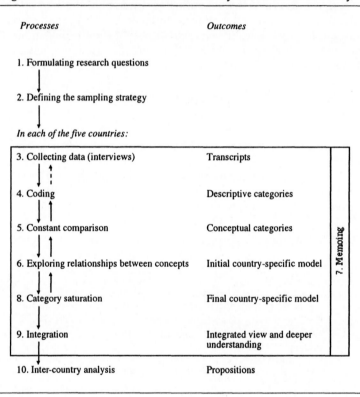

Ad 1. Formulating research questions. The current study was designed following a review of sixteen cross-cultural research programmes and the resulting observation that existing research findings are poorly integrated and some aspects of participative management have not yet been studied from a cross-cultural perspective (Chapter 3.1). This springboard for the current study is no contradiction to grounded theory's advice to refrain from theorising, i.e. specifying hypotheses and setting out to test them. On the contrary, the literature review resulted in *exploratory* research questions.

Ad 2. Defining the sampling strategy. The samples were defined from a theoretical perspective, consistent with grounded theory's intentions. The principle of maximising differences within pre-set parameters (interviewees born and raised in the country, members of the "main" language group, middle managers) clarifies the domain of the findings (Eisenhardt, 1989), satisfies the criterion of "ample variation within cases to enable the researcher to compare concepts for similarities and differences" (Strauss & Corbin, 1998, p. 288) and enables the holistic exploration of key concepts and their attributes:

> "Maximising brings out the widest possible coverage on ranges, continua, degrees, types, uniformities, variations, causes, conditions, consequences, probabilities of relationships, strategies, process, structural mechanisms and so forth, all necessary for elaboration of the theory" (Glaser & Strauss, 1967, p. 57).

A within-country analysis was conducted in each of the five countries separately (Steps 3 to 9).

Table 5.6 Transcription Symbols

Symbol	Explanation	Example
.	Dot indicates a stopping fall in tone.	It depends if the conflict is personal.
,	Comma indicates a continuing intonation.	But the boss said, OK, I understand
_	Underscoring indicates some form of stress, via pitch and/or amplitude.	And there are some formal rules
:	Colon indicates prolongation of the immediately prior sound.	Ye:s, but there is a reason for this.
-	Hyphen followed by a word or part of a word stands for discontinuation.	But the danger- yes, the danger is indeed that you can spend an endless amount of time.
/	Up to three slashes indicate one, two or three seconds of silence.	The sales people are / / involved.
(number)	Numbers in brackets indicate elapsed time of silence longer than three seconds.	Hmm, (4) hard to tell.
(word)	Text in brackets indicates possible hearings.	That's my (understanding)
(...)	Three dots in round brackets indicate inability to hear what was said.	It's not only (...)
[...]	Three dots in square brackets indicate interview passages not transcribed or omitted when presenting interview statements in the country chapters (Statements were shortened only when there was no change in meaning).	[...] But now back to the interview.
[word]	Words in square brackets were inserted by the researcher with the objective of clarifying the meaning of a statement.	They expect us [managers] to solve such problems right away.
(WORD)	Capitals in brackets indicate researcher's comments.	(TELEPHONE RINGS, TAPE STOPPED)

Ad 3. Collecting data (interviews). All interviews were conducted using the same broad interview guide (Table 5.2), which supported the collection of at least partially comparable raw data with regard to concepts and their attributes. The interview structure reflects a combination of openness with regard to the phenomenon participative management (interview parts 2 to 4) and more directed data collection in areas, in which literature and earlier research identified concepts related to participative management (interview part 5). Aiming to narrow and direct the analysis is not very common in grounded theory studies, yet such an intention was employed earlier by researchers such as Harris and Sutton (1986) and Eisenhardt and Bourgeois (1988).

All interviews were transcribed verbatim. Transcription symbols (Table 5.6) that are similar to Silverman's (2001) suggestions, were included in the text. The transcription symbols supported the analysis and facilitated the detection of cultural meaning differences (Section 5.1.5).

Ad 4. Coding. As data collection was restricted to a small number of interviews per country, open coding (line-by-line analysis) was employed during the analysis of *all* interviews, not just during the initial stages of the research. Analysis processes described by Strauss and Corbin (1998) for the phases of axial and selective coding, such as linking categories or developing theoretical concepts, were applied parallel to open coding.

Initially and at the lowest level, data coding resulted in *descriptive* codes (e.g. group meeting, time pressure, teamwork or compromise), which were aggregated to more *general* categories later on during the course of the analysis, which, in turn, served as the basis for the formation of *theoretical* concepts (e.g. meaning of participative management, managerial role). The number of codes and emerging concepts per country is summarised in Table 5.7. The count refers to codes and concepts that repeatedly emerged from the data. The similar number of concepts across countries is related to a series of concepts designed for each country for comparison reasons, such as "meaning of participative management", "enactment of participative management", "outcomes of participative management", "role of the manager" and "role of subordinates". Other concepts, such as "power distance", "uncertainty avoidance" or "individualism/collectivism" were purposely explored for their relationship with participative management (Section 5.2.1.4).

Appendix A lists the descriptive codes emerging from the country sample data. Appendix B gives an overview of the country-specific key categories and provides the main codes related to each category as well as further remarks pertaining to the analysis, e.g. notes concerning detected relationships among concepts or concept attributes.

Table 5.7 Number of Codes and Emerging Concepts

	Czech Republic	Finland	Germany	Poland	Sweden
No. of interviews	7	8	8	6	6
No. of codes	69	84	98	81	92
No. of emerging concepts [1]	16	14	15	15	14

[1] All emerging concepts are fully described in the country chapters (Chapters 6 to 10) and summarised in graphic representations of the country-specific models of participative management at the beginning of each country chapter.

Grounded theory recommends a close relationship between data collection, data analysis and evolving theory. Similarly, Eisenhardt (1989) suggests that an overlap of data collection and analysis can reveal helpful adjustments to data collection and allow probing of emerging themes. In the current study, a full overlap did not take place as an extended stay in each of the five countries was not feasible due to time and financial constraints. However, themes emerging from prior interviews influenced subsequent data collection, in the form of probing questions and requests to elaborate on emerging country-specific themes (illustrated by the dotted arrow between "4. Coding" and "3. Collecting data (interviews)" in Figure 5.2). After each interview I listened to the taped conversation at least once and wrote a memo before the next interview took place.

Ad 5. Constant comparison. The steps "4. Coding", "5. Constant comparison", "6. Exploring relationships between concepts", "7. Memoing" and "8. Category saturation" are closely related and separated in the display primarily for presentational reasons.

In the current study, comparative analysis was employed as suggested by grounded theory and it took place on several levels, including the following: (1) Comparison processes in the data guided the development of codes and categories. (2) Each interview transcript was checked for internal consistency, thus seeking to detect meaning differences based on language or cultural issues and the possible existence of a "courtesy bias" in the data (Section 5.2.1.4). (3) The interview transcripts of one country were compared with the purpose of detecting country-specific patterns.

Ad 6. Exploring relationships between concepts. In this part of the analysis, the categories were analysed to find connections, based on the data. This analysis focused on the meaning and enactment of participative management. Thus, there was no follow-up on relationships between concepts not relevant for the study questions. Defining the nature of relationships also included verifying whether concepts could be labelled as conditions for and/or consequences of other concepts. The result of these relationship-building processes was the development of initial country-specific models of participative management. These models are based on repeated data patterns. Obviously, the interview material also contained person-specific data. Such information was not followed up in order to allow a focus on recurring patterns of managerial thinking and behaviour. In some cases, it was hard to evaluate whether data were person-specific or hinted at contradictory patterns. When in doubt, the data were incorporated into the models.

Ad 7. Memoing. The grounded theory approach suggests the continuous use of memos, i.e. recording interpretations and insights about collected data. In the current study, the writing of memos started with the first interview and continued until the country-specific models of participative management were finalised. Memos were used for storing questions and ideas and for summarising emerging concepts and concept attributes, as well as relationships between them. Additionally, summary statements for each interviewee and per country supported the comparison of raw data and conceptual ideas between managers and countries. The memos guided subsequent coding and data analysis and also helped detect possible blind spots resulting from my own cultural conditioning (Section 5.1.5).

Ad 8. Category saturation. In grounded theory, theoretical sampling is inevitably linked to theoretical saturation. For the reasons pointed out above (financial and time constraints), theoretical sampling was replaced by an *a priori* definition of the sample based on maximising differences and it was not possible to define the point of theoretical saturation *during* data collection and analysis, as the grounded theory approach recommends. How can one verify theoretical saturation in such a case? There is no clear answer. As Eisenhardt stated:

> "In practice, theoretical saturation often combines with pragmatic considerations such as time and money to dictate when cases collection ends. In fact, it is not uncommon for researchers to plan the number of cases in advance. [...] [P]lanning may be necessary because of the availability of resources and because time constraints force researchers to develop cases in parallel [...] [A] number between 4 and 10 cases usually works well. With fewer than 4 cases, it is often difficult to generate theory with much complexity, and its empirical grounding is likely to be unconvincing [...] [W]ith more than 10 cases, it quickly becomes difficult to cope with the complexity and volume of the data." (Eisenhardt, 1989, p. 545)

A possible solution to the saturation question would be to formulate *a priori* criteria to ensure that the analysis reflects a defined standard. Such an approach was taken in the current study: I defined two criteria and checked *ex post* whether saturation was reached. The first criterion concerned the number of new codes per additional interview, whereas the second criterion was related to open questions about the emerging country-specific models. Both criteria, number of new codes and open questions, were expected to decrease considerably as the analysis unfolded and eventually amount to zero after all interviews of a country were analysed. In other words, after the analysis of all available data, there should be no major questions left with regard to the content of concepts, including their attributes and relationships. If this were not the case, additional visits to one or more of the five countries would become necessary in order to conduct additional interviews.

With regard to the first criterion, the steadily decreasing number of new codes (Table 5.8) suggested that the number of conducted interviews was indeed sufficient for a thorough country analysis. This finding confirmed the conclusions drawn from the pilot test with five Czech managers (Section 5.2.1.5). With regard to the second criterion, all emerging concepts relevant for the country-specific models of participative management seemed sufficiently developed and there were no essential questions left after the analysis of the interviews, based on a thorough re-reading of the memos written over the course of the analysis process.

Table 5.8 Number of New Codes per Interview

Interview	1	2	3	4	5	6	7	8	Codes per country
Country									
Czech Republic	39	17	7	5	0	1	0	-	69
Finland	43	14	6	7	4	5	4	1	84
Germany	51	28	6	7	5	0	1	0	98
Poland	46	16	6	7	3	3	-	-	81
Sweden	42	32	13	2	2	1	-	-	92

Ad 9. Integration. After the country-specific models of participative management were developed from the interview data, the patterns originating from the qualitative inquiry were compared with the quantitative scores of the three quantitative studies. Furthermore, the qualitative data were analysed for their fit with the country's *de jure* participation and industrial relations system. Researchers differ in their theoretical positions to making such a connection and assumed relationships are difficult to support empirically. The current study, with its focus on participative management in its wider context, may provide hints for areas of further research.

The emerging patterns of participative management were also compared with the existing country-specific management literature. In some cases, valuable insights were also provided by the general literature. According to Eisenhardt (1989), the existing literature improves and sharpens construct definitions and raises the theoretical level of the findings. Additionally, conflicting literature builds internal validity, while similar literature sharpens generalisability.

Ad 10. Inter-country analysis. This final step in the project compared the main country-specific patterns across the five countries for similarity or uniqueness. In other words, areas of convergence and divergence between the five countries were looked for. One might ponder the question of whether convergence/divergence only exists across countries. Maybe factors apart from country and culture also play a role or even a significant one. It is possible that there is convergence among the members of, for example, one of the gender cohorts. To answer this question, the qualitative data were screened for potential demographic effects. Since the sample is very small, the analysis concentrated on age group and gender, while the number of interviewees available was too low for grouping them according to such factors as functional area. The analysis suggested that no major influences seem to exist with regard to age and gender.

Consistent with grounded theory's advice to generate theory, the current study tried to raise the findings to a higher theoretical level and to formulate (potentially testable) propositions. Additionally, the findings were compared with the theoretical literature on participative management.

5.4 Assessing the Quality of the Study

5.4.1 Quality Criteria

There is an ongoing debate in the literature as to whether criteria such as *validity* and *reliability*, originating from quantitative research, are appropriate to evaluate qualitative studies:

> "There is considerable unease about the simple application of the reliability and validity criteria associated with quantitative research to qualitative research. Indeed, some writers prefer to use alternative criteria that have parallels with reliability and validity." (Bryman & Bell, 2003, p. 311)

The following assessment takes a midway position and discusses some criteria with regard to the current study, based on Bryman and Bell (2003), Miles and Huberman (1994) and Hammersley (1992):

Credibility/internal validity/authenticity. Validity is the "extent to which an account accurately represents the social phenomena to which it refers" (Hammersley, 1990, p. 57). In grounded theory, the logic of asking questions and making constant comparisons ensures that validation of the findings is incorporated into every step of the analysis, as Strauss and Corbin explained:

"We are not talking about testing in a statistical sense of counting. Analysts constantly are comparing the products of their analyses against actual data, making modifications or additions as necessary based on these comparisons and then further validating the modifications and additions against incoming data; therefore, researchers constantly are validating or negating their interpretations. Only the concepts and statements that stand up to this rigorous constant comparison process become part of the theory." (Strauss & Corbin, 1998, p. 212)

In a similar vein, Eisenhardt stated:

"The likelihood of valid theory is high because the theory-building process is so intimately tied with evidence that it is very likely that the resultant theory will be consistent with empirical observation." (Eisenhardt, 1989, p. 547)

In the context of the current study, additional validation was sought by asking local research colleagues, who were familiar with the setting but not with the details of my research, to comment on the initial country-specific models of participative management. I attempted to verify their suggestions based on the data at hand and I incorporated the recommendations, whenever fitting.

Transferability/external validity. With regard to the current study, the characteristics of the sample are fully described to permit adequate comparisons with other samples (Section 5.2.2.1). As for generalisability and limitations, the sampling strategy (maximising differences within homogenising boundaries) is described in Section 5.2.1.2 and limitations of the study are dealt with in Section 5.4.3.

Hunt and Ropo (1995, p. 381) argued that "[w]hereas mainstream approaches tend to generalise across frequencies, grounded theory tends to generalise in the direction of theoretical ideas." In this sense, the present exploratory study of participative management based on interviews with a small number of middle managers in five European countries can inform us about a wide range of possible variations in the meaning and enactment of participative management, which can serve as a potential estimate for other cohorts and other countries. Theoretical inferences made out of the qualitative data are presented as propositions and a contingency model of participative management in Chapter 12.1.2.

Dependability/reliability. Reliability refers to "the degree of consistency with which instances are assigned to the same category by different observers or by the same observer on different occasions" (Hammersley, 1992, p. 67). Some social researchers argue that a concern for reliability arises only within the quantitative research tradition. In contrast, Silverman (2001) considers how reliability can be addressed in qualitative studies, in particular when conducting interviews: He suggests to pre-test an interview schedule, tape-record all face-to-face interviews, carefully transcribe these tapes, compare how at least two researchers analyse the same data and finally, present long extracts of data in the research reports. In the current study, a pilot test including five interviews was conducted (Section 5.2.1.5). All interviews were audio-taped and transcribed verbatim. Involving another researcher in data analysis was not feasible, because the type of research conducted ("Habilitation") called for an individual scientific effort. However, local research colleagues were asked to comment of the initial country-specific models of participative management. Finally, the presentation of the findings (Chapters 6 to 10) includes many interview extracts.

Confirmability/objectivity. A detailed description of the data collection process is provided in Section 5.2.1, the sample is characterised in Section 5.2.2 and a summary of the analysis method is given in Section 5.3. The researcher's role is summarised in Section 5.4.2 and special attention was paid to researcher effects.

Relevance. Qualitative research should result in new insights (Eisenhardt, 1989) and be "practically useful" (Glaser & Strauss, 1967). The current study uses earlier research as the springboard for the formulation of research questions and relates the findings back to prior empirical research as well as to the conceptual and theoretical participation literature. Unlike the results of prior research, the findings of the current study are holistic in nature and take the country-specific and general context of participation into account. Such findings are of relevance to theory and practice alike.

5.4.2 Role of the Researcher

Another aspect that requires attention is my, the researcher's, personal background and role in the study. This is of particular relevance in a qualitative study because "the researcher is pre-eminently the research tool" (Goulding, 2002, p. 18), e.g. when conducting interviews, and "is directly in charge of interpretation" (Usunier, 1998, p. 137). Additionally, the researcher's background and role is particularly crucial in cross-cultural research (Section 5.1.5).

With regard to personal and professional background, I was born and raised in Austria, yet I have extensive experience with working and living in other cultures and languages. In terms of epistemological position, I adhere to the interpretive paradigm.

To minimise researcher effects on the site/interviewees (Miles & Huberman, 1994), (1) I took the role of a sympathetic and interested outsider and foreigner and refrained from expressing my own opinion on the study topic, (2) I informed interviewees about the purpose of the study in a consistent fashion (Section 5.2.1.4), (3) I tried to maintain similar levels of rapport with all interviewees ("procedural equivalence", Schaffer & Riordan, 2003), (4) I paid attention to the "courtesy bias" (Usunier, 1998, p. 121) (Section 5.2.1.4) and (5) I focused on obtaining data based on personal experiences rather than abstract statements.

With regard to effects of the site/interviewees on the researcher (Miles & Huberman, 1994), (1) I tried to minimise the "ethnocentric bias" (Usunier, 1998) by defining participation to myself before data collection started, (2) I discussed potentially different cultural meanings of terms and concepts with the interviewees, (3) I used constant comparison during the analysis phase as a means of keeping a close link between data and emerging concepts, (4) I employed memoing to detect and monitor possible effects, and (5) I discussed preliminary findings with local scholars ("cultural experts").

5.4.3 Limitations of the Study

Ex post comparison of intra-cultural samples. The perspective taken by the current study can only be a first step to be followed up upon. Behavioural patterns detected in intra-cultural settings may not fully overlap with those of inter-cultural settings, as Adler and Graham (1989) were the first to demonstrate empirically in negotiation simulations of Canadian, U.S. American and Japanese businesspeople. In a similar vein, Usunier recommended:

> "[I]t is advisable to be prudent before directly transposing data on the business behaviour or strategies of the people and countries studied in intra-cultural settings, to what may happen when these diverse cultures are interacting (inter-cultural setting). [...] It does not mean that every finding obtained from intra-cultural comparison has no implication for inter-cultural interactions, but one needs to put some caveats when extending intra-cultural findings to inter-cultural settings." (Usunier, 1998, p. 156f)

Sample size. The sample can be criticised for being very small. However, the sample was built based on theoretical considerations, maximising differences among interviewees ensures generalisation across different types of middle managers, and the integration with earlier quantitative studies and existing literature strengthens the validity of the findings for this very cohort.

Generalisability. The patterns detected from middle manager data likely apply to other managerial groups because the issues emerging from the current study reflect deeply ingrained ways of thinking (e.g. with regard to the managerial role or concepts such as conflict) which are likely to converge across hierarchical levels and organisational settings. The integration attempts (fit with the three quantitative studies, the industrial relations system and the existing literature) further strengthen the argument that broader patterns are being detected. Besides, as discussed above, the findings of qualitative research are generalised to theory rather than to populations. In this sense, the current study can inform us about a wide range of *possible variations* in the meaning and enactment of participation and its context factors across countries and cultures.

Managerial data. The exclusive use of managerial data is an additional issue to be addressed. Managers represent a very specific cohort of society since managers world-wide face similar challenges, which may reflect upon their values, attitudes and behaviour. Findings may turn out differently if the interviewees' functions are more diverse, e.g. including subordinates.

Data type. The current study employs interviews in the form of self-reports. Silverman (2001) pointed out that what people say in answer to interview questions may not have a stable relationship to how they behave in naturally occurring situations. The current study tries to deal with this concern as well as with the "courtesy bias" (Section 5.2.1.4) by trying to elicit examples from personal experience rather than abstract statements about the phenomenon. Nonetheless, it is unquestionable that a future study of additional cohorts (e.g. subordinates) and the combination of self-reports with other qualitative methods (e.g. participant observation) could improve the quality of the findings.

Chapter 6

Within-Country Analysis: The Czech Republic

6.1 Overview

This chapter pertains to Research Question 1 and deals with the issue of country-specific meaning and enactment of participative management in the Czech Republic. It describes the qualitative study findings, collected during in-depth interviews with seven Czech managers. Figure 6.1 summarises the country-specific model of participative management as it emerged from these data. The model shows concepts based on *repeated* occurrence in the data. Consequently, only part of all available interview material is represented. Readers interested in the data collection process are referred to Chapter 5.2. A detailed description of the data analysis using elements of grounded theory is given in Chapter 5.3. In Figure 6.1, the two broad aspects of participative management under study, namely meaning and enactment, are shown in the grey boxes. Other concepts related to participative management are depicted in the white boxes. Arrows show relationships between the concepts.

In the upper left corner of Figure 6.1 it is shown that participative management in the Czech Republic is influenced by a number of values including *adaptability, flexibility, creativity* and *diplomacy*. These values are related to two guiding principles for thinking and behaviour, namely *adjustment* and a tendency to *take things as they come*. According to the interviewees, Czechs are easily able to adjust to the forces of a situation, while at the same time not taking things too seriously. The value of adjustment results in positive rhetoric about participative management, while the actual participative practice is more autocratic. Furthermore, managers tend to adjust their behaviour in the direction of participation only when doing so seems beneficial.

A number of other concepts also influence the meaning of participative management, including the former and current *political and economic systems*, which are related to such societal culture factors as *power distance* and *uncertainty avoidance* (compare Chapter 2.2.3.1). Power distance refers to the degree to which members of a society expect power to be unequally shared. Uncertainty avoidance reflects the degree to which a society relies on social norms and procedures to alleviate the unpredictability of future events. The

Figure 6.1 The Czech Model of Participative Management

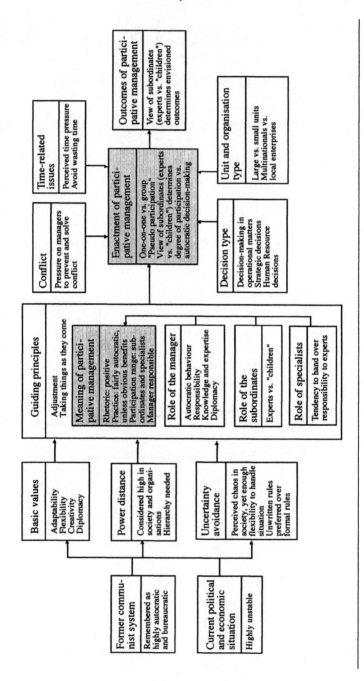

former communist system, for example, still influences Czech organisations, as the preference for hierarchical organisational structures remains. At the same time, the communist system is likely partially responsible for the Czech inclination toward adjustment, flexibility, creativity and diplomacy. Participative management is also shaped by the roles Czechs ascribe to managers, subordinates and specialists. Subordinates are viewed either as experts or as "children", and this differentiation has a major impact on the *enactment* and *outcomes* of participative management. Additionally, the enactment of participative management is affected by such situational factors as *decision type, unit and organisation type, time-related issues and conflict*.

The following sections describe all concepts depicted in Figure 6.1 in more detail, including original quotes by the interview partners.

6.2 The Meaning of Participative Management in Context

6.2.1 Basic Values: Adaptability, Flexibility, Creativity and Diplomacy

In contrast to the data of other countries, the Czech interviews did not reveal one single value that influences the meaning and enactment of participative management most decisively. Rather, a bundle of related values emerged from the interview data, including adaptability, flexibility, creativity and diplomacy.

The interview partners proudly described it as typical Czech to easily master any problem and situation. They further explained that Czechs consider improvisation a way of life and use creativity and diplomacy to solve problems in original ways. The following quotes illustrate these values:

"You probably don't know the Czech mentality. We are very flexible (LAUGHS), within the framework of rules and laws."

"We think we are quite creative. [...] We really want to discover things our own way, even in cases when text book procedures would be simpler, quicker and maybe more efficient."

"We usually don't apply devices and procedures developed by others, we modify them or even develop them from scratch."

"In daily life, being diplomatic is simply important. Non-diplomatic behaviour can lead to unnecessary conflicts. On the other hand one has to recognise the limits of diplomacy. Sometimes, diplomacy and an indirect way of solving problems can complicate things. Or delay the solution."

6.2.2 Guiding Principles: Adjustment and Taking Things as They Come

The above quotes relating to adaptability, flexibility, creativity and diplomacy suggest the desire and skills to adjust to any situation and make the best of life, no matter how complicated things appear to be. The interviewees' descriptions also suggest that Czechs might tend to take things more lightly than people from other cultures. "Life is a game" is probably too strong an expression. However, elements of a generally playful attitude emerged from several interviews. Improvisation, overcoming obstacles and trying to reach one's own goals without investing too much energy were described as being more important than seriousness and hard work. Implicit in some of the interviewees' statements was also the intention to take the path of least resistance whenever possible. One interviewee openly confessed:

"And then there is the Czech mentality to make things easier for oneself."

The emerging bundle of values introduced in Section 6.2.1 and the guiding principles *adjustment* and *taking things as they come* are reflected in various elements of the Czech model of participative management, each of which will be described in more detail (including quotes by the interviewees) in Sections 6.2.3 to 6.2.7 below:

- Participative management is used only when it seems to be the easiest way to find a sound decision to a problem.
- In many cases, autocratic decision-making appears to be the easiest approach, as subordinates seem to expect and accept autocratic managerial behaviour. The data also suggest different patterns of participative management depending on unit and organisation type. This finding may suggest flexibility to adjust to one's work environment.
- According to the interviewees, there is a tendency among some Czech managers to avoid taking responsibility, which can be interpreted as trying to take the path of least resistance. In the interviewed managers' view, part of the Czech employees show a similar tendency, which is reflected in the fact that they avoid getting involved in managerial decision-making.
- Outside experts are highly valued participants in decision-making and their recommendations carry great weight. This preference can be interpreted as some managers' readiness to hand over at least part of their responsibility.
- The data suggest a clear preference for unwritten rules to formal rules. Unwritten rules allow for flexible and creative actions, whereas formal rules are considered too much of a limitation.

- The bundle of values described above seems to be related to people's experiences with the former communist system. This era represents a time when people "officially" adjusted to the system, while at the same time trying to achieve their own goals.
- Adaptability might even have influenced the data collection process. Inconsistencies between the interviewees' responses to the quantitative instruments in preparation for the interview on the one hand and their statements in the face-to-face interview on the other hand might be interpreted as adjusting one's oral responses to what was assumed to be favourable in the eyes of the researcher.

6.2.3 The Meaning of Participative Management

Rhetoric versus practice. The interview data show some discrepancy between what managers described in general and abstract terms as their preferred way of using participative management and what they revealed by giving examples from their own managerial practice. When talking about participative management in abstract terms, most managers described a preference for participation over autocratic managerial behaviour, and they referred to the overall goal of high decision quality:

"I think participation of my subordinates is quite useful."

"I'm convinced that participation is good for most [decision-making] situations."

"Generally, I think it's much better when people themselves can influence what to do and the way how to do it."

In contrast to these abstract statements, the Czech interview partners revealed a much broader spectrum of approaches to decision-making when talking about their personal experience with participative management. Some interviewees described autocratic rather than participative decision-making for most of the situations.

"Those how are supposed to decide have to decide. Pretty fast and pretty reasonable."

Other managers gave examples of participative decision-making, yet limited participation to such situations in which they considered their subordinates to have expert status.

"For this [specific problem], all areas participated in finding a decision, the economist, the lawyer, the physician, people from the information technology department."

Only three interviewees showed consistency between rhetoric and practice, with the examples from their own managerial practice fitting with their more abstract and general talk about participative management. The following quote illustrates this position.

> "It is my personal experience, that even if I think that my opinion is the best one, you can always find somebody whose opinion might be better, or is better. If you are realistic. So, to some extent, I really welcome everybody to participate, to brainstorm, to bring in new ideas."

Range of participation. The interviewees described the involvement of both subordinates and specialists: Subordinates were or were not considered participants based on the role attributed to them by the manager (see Section 6.2.5 below), and specialists were consulted when the manager expected them to provide expertise for the decision-making process (see Section 6.2.6).

Who is responsible for a decision? The majority of the interviewed Czech managers argued that the manager should take the final responsibility for decisions, while only one interviewee was in favour of sharing the responsibility between the manager and the subordinates. Not surprisingly, this one manager held a rather positive view of participative management, while the others showed more autocratic tendencies. The two opposing views are illustrated by the following two quotes.

> "For me it is very important that the subordinates also share part of the responsibility for the decision. Because if it's a direct order, then it's a bit more complicated whether they really feel responsible, and there might be complications."

> "I think that democracy should be locked out of the company. I don't mean it's like in the army, but in the end the manager must decide and it must be his decision."

The limited use of participation and the clear focus on the manager as the responsible decision-maker does not exclude the possibility for subordinates to informally influence a decision if they wish to do so. The interviewees gave examples of subordinates using diplomacy to influence decisions. The previously mentioned tendency to try to influence things to one's own benefit is quite obvious in the following quote.

> "You have to do it in such a way that it looks as if the boss decided himself."

Decisions are considered binding no matter if taken autocratically by the manager or assisted by participative processes, and all decisions are expected to be accepted by the subordinates. As the following quote suggests, decisions reached through participative processes might even help the manager take the path of least resistance: Participation might minimise complaints and prevent confrontation with dissatisfied subordinates.

"The main advantage is that they cannot come to me afterwards and say, 'Boss, it was your bad decision.'"

Assumed change in participation level. The interviewed managers suggested that the management style, as it is currently practised, namely fairly autocratic, is not a question of personal choice. In contrast, it is said to result from external factors related to the economic situation. Once these factors change, the interviewees argued, the level of participation will increase. A repeatedly mentioned factor concerned organisational ownership, in particularly the contrast between state ownership and multinational enterprises.

"A corporate culture changes pretty slowly. But when the influence of foreign companies increases, things will change."

"I hope we are getting closer to the European nations. Foreign managers are coming into the country and they will change the opinion about how to manage in the companies."

A second factor related to the new generation of young Czech managers, most of them educated in Western management practice.

"As soon as today's students become middle managers, things will start moving, I am sure. Because they received completely different education. And not only education but, you know, influence from their environment. They get a chance to go to foreign companies or to foreign countries, they get a completely different background."

"Change will come with the next generation."

In summary, participative management emerged from the interview data as a relatively novel concept for Czech managers. The data suggest individual differences in using participation. Additionally, the meaning of participation seems to be influenced by considerations about trying to make things easier for oneself: The interviewed managers seemed to prefer participative management in particular when it offered obvious advantages over other forms of decision-making, for example when subordinates could provide expert opinions. In most cases, however, autocratic decision-making seemed to represent a somehow "easier" approach.

6.2.4 The Role of the Manager

The managerial role, as it emerged from the interviews with the Czech managers, includes the following main attributes: autocratic behaviour, responsibility, knowledge and expertise, as well as diplomacy.

Autocratic behaviour. The majority of the seven interviewees suggested that the Czech managerial role includes a certain degree of autocratic behaviour.

> "I am of the opinion that our managers lean towards autocracy a bit more than would be necessary."

> "I would say this is O.K., yes! (Czech manager in response to the questionnaire statement "Autocratic behaviour inhibits a person only slightly from being considered an outstanding manager")

What could be the motives behind the preference for an autocratic managerial role? One repeatedly stated reason concerned the subordinates: While not necessarily preferring it, subordinates seemed to expect autocratic management.

> "Czech people need someone who says, 'This way! Not that way, we'll go this way!'"

> "The Czech view autocratic behaviour negatively, but they expect it."

> "In the Czech Republic everyone expects that the boss takes care of everything. And that's indeed the case, isn't it? Just look at our organisation. The employees take no decisions by themselves, they wait and see."

More on the subordinate role follows in Section 6.2.5 below. A second possible reason for the preference for autocratic management concerns the managers' potential fear of losing power. Czech managers were described as figures of authority with a certain degree of role-related power.

> "Like most Czechs, I also lean toward taking the authority of my superiors very seriously."

> "I would say that most Czech managers try to respect their boss more than I do."

The new generation of young managers educated in Western management principles seems to pose a threat to some of the older managers, who are not (yet) familiar with more democratic managerial practices. The two quotes below illustrate this point. In the second quote, one of the interviewees, a young and ambitious Czech manager, described that he even lost his job because of his qualification.

"When someone has become a boss, he thinks he can do everything by himself. [...] Everything has to be done his way. [...] Maybe it's a bit the fear of the bosses that they don't have enough power over their subordinates."

"It was shortly after I finished [the executive education programme] that my boss told me, 'I'm the boss here, not you. I recommend you find a new job, because here, I am the boss.'"

Responsibility. As introduced in Section 6.2.3, it is considered part of the manager's role to take responsibility for decision-making. Furthermore, the managerial role includes far-reaching responsibilities with regard to subordinates' work and well-being. For example, a manager should make sure that subordinates are not overburdened with work and that the working place climate is free of friction and conflict.

Despite the high level of envisioned responsibility, the interviewees provided examples of Czech managers who were not ready to assume such extended responsibility. Two reasons seem plausible for this tendency. The first reason is related to the former political system that did not encourage taking responsibility. On the contrary, it tended to socialise people into passiveness. One interviewee explained how many Czechs felt and behaved during communism.

"There was this unwritten law, 'Why should I decide?' It was easier to wait and see what happened. These things are so deeply in people's heads. It will take one or two generations for them to change. Because the younger generation has adopted exactly the same behaviour as the generation before them."

A second reason for the tendency to avoid responsibility may relate less to the former political system and more to a general tendency among Czechs to follow the path of least resistance. This second reason seems plausible if one considers the dominance of the values adaptability, flexibility, creativity and diplomacy throughout the Czech interview data.

Knowledge and expertise. Another important aspect of the Czech managerial role relates to expertise in technical and task-related matters as well as to competence in administrative issues. Interviewees described both aspects as a remainder of the former communist system. Technical and task-related expertise comprised an integral part of the educational system and had a major impact on work life in general. Administrative skills were not explicitly taught, but many working people acquired them in an attempt to adjust to the system, as the following quote illustrates.

"Administration skills? Maybe that's affected by the past experience that you had to be able to give information to local authorities and the party authorities."

Diplomacy. Being diplomatic was repeatedly mentioned when the interviewees tried to define the managerial role. Diplomacy was described as a helpful aspect in the interaction with others in the organisation, including one's superior and subordinates. These descriptions are consistent with other frequent references to diplomacy throughout the Czech interview data.

> "A good superior might say, 'Well, that's definitely a good idea of yours, but I suggest we do it differently. What do you think about that?' This might be a way to accomplish more."

6.2.5 The Role of the Subordinates

The interviewed managers portrayed subordinates in two different ways: either as trustworthy experts or as unreliable and selfish individuals, whom they even referred to as "children". Three of the seven interviewed managers explicitly were in favour of the second position, while three others held the opinion that subordinates were to be seen as trustworthy experts. One interviewee's statements included aspects of both positions: While he described his own unit as a team of experts which he valued highly, he supported the argument that the majority of Czech subordinates thought and acted like "children".

Trustworthy experts. Managers holding this perspective included their subordinates in decision-making and they described their subordinates' contributions as improving the quality of decisions made.

> "I accept my subordinates as specialists in their positions."

> "I really believe that my subordinates are qualified for the position. They are there, because they are <u>expected</u> to know what they are saying."

Additionally, managers who perceived their subordinates to be reliable experts also expressed trust and a certain degree of readiness to forgive mistakes.

> "Everybody can make a mistake. I've made hundreds of mistakes myself, and I do not view people as computers."

"Children". In contrast to the view of subordinates as trustworthy experts, some interviewees portrayed subordinates much less favourably. In their view subordinates follow their own interests rather than work for organisational goals. Subordinates were described as permanently attempting to take the path of least resistance and to reduce their workload to a minimum. Additionally, they were described as failing to take responsibility and leaving decisions to their superior whenever possible.

"I think Czech people do not want to decide." (Manager in response to my suggestion that subordinates might be able to decide problems among themselves)

"After ten years I am a bit tired now because people just do not think. I mean, if I let them participate, this does not make sense."

"Czech employees would like to have more participation, yes. But not more responsibility. But responsibility and participation have to be at the same level. If you really participate, you have to be willing to take responsibility. But it's nothing but talk, talk, talk, and not be held responsible."

"Subordinates behave the same way as they did fifty years ago. [...] If someone allows them to not work, they will not work. Most of them do not have the commitment, or drive, to work properly. They don't care. The only thing they think about is their salary."

Interviewees reflected upon appropriate methods to deal with such subordinates and consistently voiced the opinion that an autocratic management style was adequate to keep such "children" under control.

The interview data further suggested that at least some the interviewed managers were content with their subordinates' lack of initiative. For these managers, autocratic management of "children" seemed to represent a convenient approach, because exercising strict control was viewed as being less difficult than supervising self-assured subordinates. The following quote relates to this argument.

"I would say that many Czech companies are better off with a strong hierarchy. Because people have a tendency to do what they themselves want to do, not what is important to be done. So:, a hierarchical organisation is easier to manage."

The previously mentioned role of the autocratic manager and the view of subordinates as "children" represent a circle of reinforcement: Managers who have little trust in their subordinates exercise tight control rather than share responsibility. This management style leads subordinates to behave even less responsibly, and managers see themselves "forced" to tighten control, and so on. It is impossible to determine whether the origin of this process comes from the manager or from the subordinates. However, it becomes obvious that such self-reinforcing patterns are extremely difficult to change. This issue will be discussed in more detail in Section 6.6.3.

6.2.6 The Role of Specialists

The data suggest that Czech managers rely heavily on specialists for decision-making. In particular they rely on external experts.

"There is a general tendency in this country to rely on specialists."

"There is a tendency to believe a specialist from the outside more than if
something is recommended from within the company."

Outside experts may serve various purposes. Firstly, they can bring in new
ideas and foster creativity, which is an important aspect considering that
creativity is given high priority and is very highly valued (compare Section
6.2.1). Secondly, consulting with experts may also represent attempts to
delegate at least some of the managerial responsibility, particularly in situations in which neither managers nor subordinates want to be held responsible. In other words, specialists may be used as a 'higher authority', and expert recommendations are accepted and implemented rather uncritically.

"If you have a good specialist as an advisor or subordinate, you say, 'O.K., I
follow the specialist.'"

"It's typical for our mentality to rely on the authority of experts."

The strong reliance on specialists is linked to developments in the history of
the country before and during the communist regime. The educational system has produced specialists rather than generalists throughout the country's past, and thus specialists have traditionally played a vital role.

6.2.7 Individual Differences and Cognitive Dissonance

As indicated above, there was no clear-cut consensus among the interviewees when talking about participative management. The managers were quite
consistent in their abstract statements and spoke favourably about participative management in general terms. However, when they gave examples
from their own experience, only two of the seven interviewees seemed to
prefer participation. Five managers revealed tendencies toward more autocratic approaches, which was different from when they were speaking in
general terms. Furthermore, there were some inconsistencies between the
interviewees' written responses to the questionnaire items of the three
quantitative studies and their oral statements during the interviews.

The data might very well represent the present turbulent times in Czech
society in general and for Czech managers in particular. The data hint at
cognitive dissonance (Festinger, 1957) faced by the managers, mainly between the well-established and accepted autocratic thinking and behavioural
pattern and the recently introduced ways of Western management style. A
typical Czech management strategy to reduce dissonance might lie in the
ability to accept the contradictions and to adjust to the forces of the particular situation. Possibly, this may have happened in the interview situation.

The interviewees may have accommodated their interview responses in favour of participative management, which was the topic in question ("courtesy bias", compare Chapter 5.2.1.4). Also, the visiting researcher might have been regarded an expert on the topic (compare Section 6.2.6 above), whom it would be impolite to contradict.

6.3 The Enactment of Participative Management

6.3.1 Participative vs. Autocratic Decision-Making

Participative decision-making. In some contrast to the Czech interviewees' rhetoric about the benefits of participative management, but in accordance with the emerging overall *meaning* of participative management within the Czech system, descriptions of participative managerial *behaviour* were rare and mainly limited to situations, in which the subordinates had expert standing. The interviewees distinguished between one-on-one conversations and group meetings.

One-on-one conversation was preferred in difficult situations, such as personal conflict (see Section 6.4.4 below). In contrast, a *group meeting* was described as a forum in which experts discussed task-related issues. Group meetings provided managers with the possibility to collect information and opinions and discuss effective ways of solving problems. Interviewees, who held the view that subordinates usually acted like "children", mentioned the difficulty of getting subordinates involved during group discussions: The subordinates would expect the manager to deal with the problem her or himself. Consequently, managers had to face the constant challenge of resisting these expectations.

"I'm involved in the discussions from the very beginning. In fact, they try to come to me and ask me for a decision, but I say, 'This is your job.' So in the end it's an interaction going on until we can say, 'O.K.! That's how we're doing it.'"

The interviewees described that one-on-one and group participation sometimes took a specific form, which can be labelled *pseudo participation*. As described in Section 6.2.3 above, the beneficial use of participative management is talked about to a great extent, whereas the actual practice of the tool is limited. In the context of pseudo participation, interviewees gave details of managerial approaches for the introduction of participation which were not actually serious attempts to get subordinates involved, but stayed a mere lip-service: Managers would hold frequent meetings and encourage discussion, yet the arguments raised by subordinates would never actually be taken into account when making the decision. The following example illustrates the subordinate frustration that can result from such pseudo participation.

> "We have more [customer] orders than we can produce. We could sell much more, but we are not able to produce enough. But every week we hold a meeting and talk about it. It's the same every week. And nothing changes. In this case, participation is equal to zero."

Autocratic decision-making. Consistent with the rather limited enactment of participative management, the interviewees gave many examples of autocratic behaviour, including their own:

> "'It's common that the boss has the final say', I said to them. 'So please, it does not matter whether you have comments or not. You have to follow this decision. Without any discussion.'"

Interviewees, who regarded their subordinates as "children", referred to autocratic decision-making more often than the other group of interviewees, who portrayed their subordinates as experts. However, autocratic decision-making was also mentioned by the latter group of interviewees. The following quote illustrates managerial responsibility for decision-making (compare Section 6.2.4 above), even when consulting with expert subordinates.

> "If they don't agree, I take the decision. But in fact, I don't remember many cases that they were not able to agree among themselves and we found no solution."

6.3.2 Participative Management Outcomes

The envisioned outcomes of participation differed according to how the interviewees perceived their subordinates, as experts or as "children". The interviewees, who regarded their subordinates as "children", did not talk much about the outcomes of participation. When they did, they spoke in rather general terms. This finding is consistent with the theory of positive rhetoric about participative management, although managerial practice shows more autocratic tendencies. Some interviewees related autocratic behaviour to decision quality, as the following example shows.

> "Everyone has his own opinion. If you open up the discussion, you cannot find a solution."

In contrast to managers supervising "children", interviewees, who portrayed their subordinates as experts and active participants in decision-making, repeatedly reflected upon outcomes of participation. In doing so, they mainly focused on decision quality.

"For a good decision it is important to get ideas from all [departments]."

"I was surprised how many fantastic ideas and opinions you can generate from teamwork."

In addition to decision quality, there was also mentioning of such participative management outcomes as decision acceptance, commitment and subordinate self-esteem.

"I think they like to be seen as professionals. If you make decisions the autocratic way, this will not support their self-esteem."

"We have to find a solution that is acceptable for all people who are involved in the [implementation] procedure."

6.4 Main Situational Influence Factors

As described above, the interviewees' perspective on subordinates, experts versus "children", turned out to be a prime factor influencing the enactment of participative management. Decision type also was strongly influential on the interviewees' choice of whether and in which form to use participative management. Additional factors, such unit and organisation type, time-related issues and conflict also showed an impact, although these factors were mentioned less frequently in the interviews.

6.4.1 Decision Type

The interviewees differentiated between a number of decision types. The following list contains the three decision types most frequently referred to.

Decision-making in operational matters. The interviewees who viewed their subordinates as experts mentioned involving subordinates in operational decisions, i.e. decisions directly concerning the subordinates' work environment. Subordinates were described as competent to find an adequate solution. Additionally, their involvement was considered necessary for effective implementation of the decision.

"If we want to make changes on a daily basis or some permanent improvements, the people should be involved. I think they like to be seen as professionals."

Strategic decisions. While participative management was described as favourable for operational decisions, i.e. cases directly involving subordinates, participation was mentioned as being less beneficial for strategic decisions, in particular when "radical or big change" was the issue, or in emergency situations. Not surprisingly, interviewees viewing their subordinates as "children" would predominantly voice this opinion.

> "When you need to do restructuring, or deep change, this should be done autocratically, with only a few people behind you. [...] And then you try to spread the information to the company. If you use a very open approach, you fail."

> "I think that in case of change or in some emergency, it is better for the manager when he is autocratic and does not follow the people too much."

Human Resource (HR) decisions. According to the interviewees, HR questions could best be solved either alone or by consulting with "outsiders", e.g. the personnel department or a consulting firm, but not by asking subordinates. Several interviewees shared this point of view, no matter whether they viewed their subordinates as experts or "children".

> "Let's say I am going to hire somebody, the final decision is up to me. [...] Maybe I can invite someone who is independent, like a consulting company, or someone from the HR department, and / yes, there might be several situations when I am not going to consult with anybody."

6.4.2 Unit and Organisation Type

Small vs. large units and organisations. The use of participative management was primarily described in the context of small departments and organisations. A possible reason for this focus could be the likely closer relationships between managers and subordinates in small units. Examples of small units given by interviewees included start-up companies and in-house teams, whereas large units were usually mentioned in the context of more traditional forms of work, such as production lines.

Interviewees who described large units, either in general terms or in the examples of personal managerial experience, tended to view subordinates as "children". It could be speculated that the reason for managers of large units to tend to perceive subordinates as "children" is related to the fact that large units typically allow for a higher degree of anonymity and diffusion of responsibility. Consequently, managers may want to exercise tight control. Similarly, subordinates wanting to dodge responsibility may get away with it more often in large units.

Multinational enterprises. The data suggest that interviewees working for multinational enterprises already had more exposure to participative management than interviewees working for local Czech enterprises. This experience was described as positive in general and could have influenced the interviewees' positive perspective on participative management.

6.4.3 Time-Related Issues

With regard to time, Czech managers seem to reduce the degree of participation under two conditions. One condition relates to perceived time pressure.

"Depends on how much time you've got. If it's a crisis or something like that, participation just takes too long."

The second condition concerns small decisions that are not considered important for efficient work completion. Similar to conflict (see Section 6.4.4 below), managers do not want to waste time on issues that prevent their subordinates from working. Consequently, they tend to behave autocratically.

"I do not want to keep the brains of my people busy with things like who is parking where. It's nonsense to spend two days or so. Rather keep their brains busy with work."

6.4.4 Conflict

Generally speaking, the interview data did not suggest any tendency among Czech managers to *avoid* conflict.

"I believe I have no problem with talking openly about conflict and problems."

"In the United States there is a tendency to avoid conflict. We [the Czech] tend to fight."

"Conflict is part of work life. One can learn a lot from conflicts."

Despite this stated openness to address conflict, Czech managers obviously perceive some pressure to prevent conflict from taking place. The interviewees argued that it was the manager's responsibility to ensure that subordinates worked productively as opposed to fighting among each other. A decrease in productivity, image loss for the manager, limited managerial career opportunities and even fear of being fired were possible reasons mentioned for Czech managers to feel under pressure. All the described factors are in some way related to the changed situation under market economy conditions.

"Nobody, especially above the level of middle management, wants to have conflict inside the company. They expect people to work. They expect us [manag-
ers] to solve such problems right away and not spend much time on them."

"Managers want to show that they do a good job. If they have to deal with conflict all day long, someone could replace them, especially in middle management. And there is a lot of people out there, just waiting for your job."

"I don't want conflict between the people working for me. I want good work."

Consequently, the data suggested a strong and active involvement on behalf
of the managers to resolve conflicts before they escalate. This tendency is
consistent with the fact that the Czech managerial role includes far-reaching
responsibility for subordinates' behaviour and wellbeing (compare Section
6.2.4). A number of the interviewed managers even seemed to feel that they
had to behave like a parent. The following quotes once again illustrate the
managers' view of subordinates as "children".

"In my experience if there is conflict between two subordinates, there is no
chance to come out with a good result. They will start to cry, [...] really like
small children. [...] I think at least in the first step things should be discussed
with each individual separately. They will tell different stories but hopefully
the manager will know what should be done."

"First of all I have to calm them down."

"If it's a personal conflict it's necessary to keep the two sides apart."

The managerial approaches on how to deal with open conflict included
strategies to initiate group meetings or discuss with subordinates one-on-
one. Some interviewees preferred one-on-one conversations in particular as
a first step in order to be able to understand the situation. Others argued that
a manager should tackle an open conflict right away, even in a group setting. Related to the perceived pressure to end conflicts quickly, there was
little readiness to invest much time in conflict solution. More often than not,
interviewees described autocratic steps.

"There is this pressure on the managers. And that's probably why they want to
avoid any kind of long discussion."

"I would say, 'O.K., the two of you have this problem, go and solve it. Otherwise I will solve it and this will be much more painful for both of you.'"

How does this handling of conflict relate to participative management?
There was consensus among the interviewees that participative management
increased the likelihood of conflict. Therefore, participation was unlikely to

be considered an effective alternative in the decision-making process as soon as conflict seemed possible. One interviewee openly stated:

"When subordinates fight, participation does not make sense."

6.5 Main Society-Related Influence Factors

The possible influences of both planned and market economy on the meaning and enactment of participative management have already been hinted at in the above analysis. The following sections describe the culture dimensions power distance and uncertainty avoidance because they also emerged from the analysis as important factors influencing the use of participation. Both power distance and uncertainty avoidance also seem to be influenced by the *former* communist system. Additionally, uncertainty avoidance turned out to be affected by the *current* political and economic situation. A third culture dimension, collectivism, which is commonly associated with participative management (compare Chapter 2.2.3.1), was not found to have a strong impact on the emerging Czech model of participative management.

6.5.1 Power Distance

In the literature, power distance is defined as the degree to which members of a society expect power to be unequally shared (Hofstede, 1980a; House et al., 2004). The interview data show consistency among the interviewees with regard to the perceived *high* level of societal power distance. There was also agreement that the level of power distance *should* be lower. Examples of the status quo included legislation that did not seem to apply equally to all citizens (privileges for politicians and the financially powerful) and the misuse of power. The interviewees linked the current high level of power distance to the former communist system, which was remembered as being highly autocratic. For example, if a citizen needed something from a government office, "he had to behave like a slave", as one interviewee put it.

With regard to the workplace, there was no consensus among the interviewees as to the best level of power distance. This finding parallels the differing positions concerning the meaning and enactment of participative management (see Sections 6.2 and 6.3 above). Asked about their observations in Czech companies rather than about their personal opinions, the interviewees agreed that the level of power distance was high. In many cases subordinates had to follow the decisions made by their superiors no matter if they agreed or not.

In summary, the findings for societal level power distance parallel the more specific data about participative management.

6.5.2 Uncertainty Avoidance

Uncertainty avoidance reflects the degree to which a society relies on social norms and procedures to alleviate the unpredictability of future events (Hofstede, 1980a; House et al., 2004). The Czech interviewees described the current situation in Czech society as quite unstable, with few social norms and procedures in place to ensure stability. Examples included the bankruptcy of a number of Czech banks, unfulfilled government promises and the missing reinforcement of laws. These examples are likely reflective of the difficulties of the country's transition from planned to market economy. However, there was also a clear understanding among the interviewees that the current problems should not be solved by strict bureaucracy and hard rules, approaches which they related to the former communist system. Rather, the data suggest a tendency among Czechs to find ways to arrange themselves with the current conditions. This finding is consistent with the above-described talent to improvise, be creative, make the best of every situation and try to take things as they come. Based on the interviewees' statements, many Czech may even appreciate the flexibility and chances provided by the current situation.

Interviewees described a preference for unwritten to formal rules, which seems to be related to uncertainty avoidance and the described values of adaptability, flexibility, creativity and diplomacy. "Unfortunately we have to follow formal rules," was a statement by one of the interviewees that clearly reflects this preference. Possible reasons can again be found in the higher degree of flexibility that unwritten rules seem to provide.

The data suggest a direct link between uncertainty avoidance on the one hand and the role of the manager and specialists on the other hand. The managerial role is characterised by far-reaching responsibility, which includes the manager playing a vital role in subordinates' work and wellbeing. The preference of unwritten over formal rules explains why many work-related and subordinate-related aspects are in the personalised responsibility of the manager rather than codified in organisational rules. In this sense, the manager plays the additional role of stability provider, which is further strengthened by the high level of power distance.

The role of specialists is a similar one. Specialists represent the next level of authority, so to speak. Some managers tend to rely on specialists for sound decision-making, thus ensuring increased stability.

6.6 Integration

6.6.1 Fit with the Three Quantitative Studies

The following sections discuss how the emerging Czech model of participative management fits with the results of the three quantitative studies. Four types of quantitative scores are evaluated for their match with the qualitative findings: participation scores, hierarchy-related scores, team-related scores and uncertainty-related scores (compare Chapter 4.4).

Table 6.1 Quantitative Participation Scores for the Czech Republic

Scale	Participative (GLOBE)	Non-autocratic (GLOBE)	Guidance source subordinates (Event Management)	Mean level of participation (MLP) (Vroom/Yetton)
Score	5,74	5,96	-2	4,31
Country position	Upper third	Upper third	Upper third	Lower third
Rank	n.a..	n.a.	13 of 56	12 of 13

Notes: For a detailed description of the scales and country comparisons see Chapter 4. Country ranks not available for the GLOBE scales.

The quantitative *participation scores* (Table 6.1) of the GLOBE and Event Management studies suggest that the level of participative management is high among Czech managers, whereas the Vroom/Yetton study positions the Czech Republic among the countries with a low level of participative management. The MLP score (Vroom/Yetton) fits with the model of participative management as it emerged from the qualitative study, whereas the results of the two other studies do not. What possible reasons could there be for this inconsistency?

The GLOBE study measured *ideal* leadership behaviour and therefore, the data possibly reflect concepts people primarily talk about rather than concepts people act upon. A similar difference was found between the interviewees' abstract talk about participative management and the way they described their own decision-making practice. Further support for the assumption that the GLOBE data represent concepts that do not necessarily shape behaviour comes from a close look at the quantitative data collected from the interviewees. In preparation for the interviews they themselves completed the measures of the three quantitative studies. A comparison of their scores with the qualitative interview data shows that only one of the seven Czech interviewees delivered consistent data. In other words, six interviewees show dissonance between their interview statements and the different sets of quantitative data collected in preparation for the qualitative study. In particular, their scores on the GLOBE questionnaire portray a much more positive attitude toward participative management than what was later described in the interviews. A similar tendency toward positive rhetoric about participative management could have influenced the results of the initial data collection for the GLOBE study.

The Event Management data also suggest a high level of participative management for the Czech Republic. Does the "positive rhetoric hypothesis" suggested for the GLOBE study also hold true for these scores? Probably not, because by having managers evaluate specific work events, the Event Management study measures reflections of own managerial practice in contrast to ideal values elicited by the GLOBE study. However, the work events included in the Event Management questionnaire mainly concern operational matters, such as introducing new work procedures. According to the qualitative interviews, decisions related to operational matters qualify well for participative management, but this does not hold true for other types of decisions. In other words, the Event Management data possibly tell only part of the story. The data lack information about important and strategic decisions that the qualitative inquiry revealed to be handled rather autocratically by Czech managers.

In contrast to the GLOBE and Event Management studies, the Vroom/Yetton study results fit well with the emerging model of participative management. This holds true for the overall mean level of participation (MLP) score, but also for more detailed results (compare Chapter 4.3.3): (1) The intra-personal standard deviation of the individual managers' responses to the thirty cases is higher for the Czechs than for managers from other countries. This finding indicates managerial readiness for flexible and adaptable behaviour, in line with the suggestions of the qualitative study. (2) According to the Vroom/Yetton data, Czech managers show a particularly strong tendency toward autocratic decision-making when assuming that their subordinates are willing to accept such behaviour. This finding is consistent with the qualitative data: Managers expect subordinate acceptance and exhibit autocratic managerial behaviour, particularly if they assume that their subordinates tend to behave like irresponsible "children".

Table 6.2 Scores of Hierarchy-Related Concepts for the Czech Republic

Scale	Power distance "as is" (GLOBE)	Guidance source superior (Event Management)	Guidance source own experience (Event Management)
Score	n.a.	36	119
Country position	n.a.	Lower third	Upper third
Rank	n.a.	38 of 56	1 of 56

Notes: For a detailed description of the scales and country comparisons see Chapter 4. Power distance data not available for the Czech Republic.

It was suggested in Chapter 4.4 that participative management is related to concepts describing the organisational hierarchy, such as the relationship with one's own superior. The Event Management study portrays Czech managers as relying relatively weakly on their *superiors*, whereas the managers' *own experiences* largely influenced their decision-making (Table 6.2). The scores make sense in light of the Event Management study's concentration on operational decision-making. Additionally, the strong focus on own experience plays an important role in particular when managers consider subordinates to be "children" rather than experts to be consulted.

Table 6.3 Scores of Team-Related Concepts for the Czech Republic

Scale	Collaborative team orientation (GLOBE)	Team integrator (GLOBE)	Institutional collectivism "as is" (GLOBE)
Score	5,64	5,42	3,60
Country position	Lower third	Middle third	Lower third
Rank	n.a.	n.a.	n.a.

Notes: For a detailed description of the scales and country comparisons see Chapter 4. Country ranks not available for the GLOBE scales.

Chapter 4.4 hinted at possible overlaps between participative management on the one hand and collectivism and team-related concepts on the other hand. The *team-related scores* of the GLOBE study (Table 6.3) suggest a low to medium team-orientation of Czech managers. Consistent with the quantitative results, the qualitative study did not reveal any particular preference for teams or high levels of collectivism, neither in the workplace nor for the society in general.

Table 6.4 Scores of Uncertainty-Related Concepts for the Czech Republic

Scale	Uncertainty avoidance "as is" (GLOBE)	Guidance source formal rules (Event Management)	Guidance source unwritten rules (Event Management)
Score	4,44	14	-33
Country position	Upper third	Middle third	Lower third
Rank	n.a.	37 of 56	50 of 56

Notes: For a detailed description of the scales and country comparisons see Chapter 4. Country rank not available for the GLOBE scale.

Uncertainty-related concepts provided yet another area of discussion in Chapter 4.4. It was contemplated how the level of uncertainty avoidance related to the enactment of participative management. In contrast to the qualitative findings, the GLOBE data suggest that the Czech Republic is relatively high on perceived *uncertainty avoidance,* and the Event Management study implies that Czechs prefer *formal* over *unwritten rules* (Table 6.4). The inconsistency between the qualitative data and the GLOBE score for uncertainty avoidance may be explained by the time factor. The data collection for the quantitative sample took place in 1993, whereas the qualitative interviews were conducted some seven years later. In 1993, the Czech Republic was in the first phase of the transition to democracy and market economy, and the Czech people likely faced turbulence and uncertainty all around them, in business as well as in private life. This tendency may well be reflected in the GLOBE respondents' answers to the level of uncertainty avoidance they perceived in Czech society. In contrast, the participants in the qualitative study were interviewed in the year 2000 after having gathered experience with the new system. The interviewed managers described the current situation as still being chaotic, however, they also showed confidence in their own ability to manage the situation. Managerial flexibility, adaptability and creativeness are likely qualities, which come to the forefront now that the initial shock of the transition period has been overcome.

The Event Management study suggests a preference of formal over unwritten rules, whereas the qualitative study reached divergent findings, namely a strong preference for unwritten rules. The Event Management study further suggests that neither formal nor unwritten rules play a particularly dominant role in managerial decision-making, compared to such other sources of guidance as own experience. The qualitative study does not hint at such a preference.

In summary, not all inconsistencies between the three quantitative studies and also between the quantitative and qualitative data can be fully explained by the emerging model of participative management. It could be speculated that the inconsistent findings indicate a concept shift: The data may well hint at the possibility that Czech managers experience some insecurity with regard to their own managerial role, struggling between the old, established image of a manager and the newly introduced models of participative management. Assuming that a concept shift is taking place, the point of data collection of the various studies merits closer consideration. The qualitative interviews took place in 2000 and 2001. The GLOBE and Event Management data were also sampled after the fall of the communist regime, whereas Vroom/Yetton data are available from before and after the end of communism. The longitudinal nature of the latter data could best reveal a concept shift. However, no significant changes were found when comparing the yearly data collected since 1989 (Reber & Jago, 1997; Reber, Jago & Maly, 2002).

An alternative hypothesis for explaining the inconsistent findings could come from another source. Based on what the interviewees described as Czech mentality, it is not unrealistic to consider some bias in the data: As described above, adaptability was found to be one of the key values for a better understanding of the meaning and enactment of participative management in the Czech Republic. Adaptability could have played a role in the data collection process (quantitative measures as well as qualitative interviews). Possibly, the discrepancy between what interviewees said about participative management and how they really felt and behaved was a conscious or even unconscious reaction to please the researcher ("courtesy bias", compare Chapter 5.2.1.4). Being invited to take part in a study about participative management might have led the interviewed managers to exaggerate their preference for participation, in particular when describing ideal managerial behaviour (GLOBE questionnaire) or talking about participation in abstract terms (first part of the qualitative interview). In contrast, it is more difficult to hide one's real preferences when asked to provide detailed narratives from one's own experience (qualitative interview) or react to realistic case descriptions (Vroom/Yetton cases).

6.6.2 Fit with the Czech System of Industrial Relations

One of the qualitative study's goals concerns the evaluation of the relationship between the emerging country-specific models of participative management on the one hand and the countries' systems of *de jure* participation and industrial relations on the other hand. *De jure* participation relates to the codified rights of employees and employee representatives to participate in decision-making processes at the country, sectoral and organisational level. The term *industrial relations* summarises the various areas of interaction between employer and employee at these three levels, including collective bargaining, employee representation on supervisory boards and works councils. *De jure* participation and industrial relations overlap in many countries, because usually at least part of the industrial relations processes are codified in law or other written agreements. The Czech model is outlined below, followed by a brief analysis of how the system relates to the findings of the qualitative study.

A discussion of today's Czech system of industrial relations must originate in the communist period. Although unions existed and membership amounted to "almost all economically active citizens" (Dvorakova, 2002, p. 2), their role and function was not comparable to free trade unions. Officially, the unions concentrated on employee care and social policy, such as holidays and recreation, free-time activities and childcare. With regard to the workplace, union rights relating to personnel affairs were only formalities (Koubek & Brewster, 1995). Based on Lenin's ideas, the unions served as "transmission belt" that helped the communist party implement its polities in the companies (Hegewisch, Brewster & Koubek, 1996). It follows that after 1989 the elements of Western-type industrial relations had to be built from scratch. Collective bargaining was introduced and workplace representation was entirely restructured. Free trade unions emerged.

The development of the new system was initially supported by a high degree of tripartism (Carley, 2002): Government consulted and bargained with unions and employer associations on broad economic and social policies. Further roles of the tripartite body were to prevent or regulate conflicts, to deal with the social consequences of the transformation and to maintain social peace (Dvorakova, 2003). However, the role of the newly introduced tripartite body was not clearly defined and changed as the transformation process progressed (Kotíková & Bittnerová, 2003). Today, it is a forum for issues of general interest, while the social partners (unions and employer associations) are supposed to handle most issues among themselves, including wage and social condition bargaining (Dvorakova, 2003). However, both representative bodies' roles are limited. Carley (2002) estimated that only about five percent of all Czech enterprises are members of employer associations. With regard to the employee side, the trade unions face difficult times, since membership decreased considerably and consistently since the beginning of the 1990s. According to Dvorakova (2003), it seems that "political, economic, as well as social factors discouraged manual and administrative staff from setting up trade union organisations or joining them" (p. 427). Obviously, today's Czech employees do not have a high level of trust in unions to protect their rights or negotiate better employment conditions (Dvorakova, 2002).

As a consequence of the weak bargaining position of the unions and employer associations, collective bargaining mainly takes place at the company level. The coverage of collective bargaining, i.e. the proportion of workers who have their pay and conditions set, at least to some extent, by collective agreements, is declining and amounted to only about twenty-five percent in 2002 (Carley, 2002).

With regard to employee representation on company boards, Hegewisch, Brewster and Koubek (1996) reported that Czech employees "have lost the right to co-determination at enterprise level. Trade unions have the right to be consulted about some issues but do not have a veto right" (p. 59).

Works council-type bodies were introduced in the Czech Republic in view of the new EU membership and its requirement to implement such structures. The initial works councils were not yet fully comparable with "typical" Western European works councils (Carley, 2002). However, in 2001 Czech legislation created a framework (Labour Code) for labour relations regulating information and consultation rights that is comparable with EU standards (Dvorakova, 2003).

The development and status quo of the Czech industrial relations system shows that the system is still under construction. It does not show strong elements of employee participation, which is consistent with the managerial and subordinate roles described by the interviewees in the qualitative study. Decentralised collective bargaining likely fits with the Czech desire for flexibility and so does the lack of legislation with regard to co-determination. The qualitative study's finding of a preference for unwritten over formal rules is consistent with these facts.

The quick adaptation of the EU directive concerning works councils hints at an interesting phenomenon. It seems that when formal rules are a given and/or imposed from the outside, such as this EU directive, the Czechs react promptly, at least at the surface level: This piece of legislation was adjusted more quickly than in other former communist countries. This prompt readiness to adapt is in line with the qualitative study's finding of adaptability. Whether the new legislation will be practised as intended remains to be seen. One is reminded of the interviewees' statements referring to laws being in place, yet not being enacted.

6.6.3 Fit with the Existing Literature

Based on the analysis of the qualitative interview data, a bundle of values including adaptability, flexibility, creativity and diplomacy shapes Czech managers' thinking and behaviour. Adjustment and the tendency to take things as they come emerged as the main guiding principles in the context of participative management. The decision-making of Czech managers is characterised by autocratic rather than participative behaviour. The roles that are ascribed to managers and subordinates support this pattern: Managers are expected to behave autocratically, to exercise far-reaching responsibility for the work and wellbeing of their subordinates and to be knowledgeable and diplomatic. Managers frequently view their subordinates as "children", who need to be kept under control in an autocratic manner. Consequently, managers have little trust in their subordinates and do not consider them valuable participants in decision-making. Furthermore, the data suggest that, in contrast to the ascribed managerial role, part of the Czech managers (and subordinates alike) tend to avoid responsibility. Finally, the country's past seems to play a role in the emerging model of Czech participative management. The following paragraphs look at all these aspects from a literature perspective.

Values. The bundle of values emerging from the qualitative analysis were adaptability, flexibility, creativity and diplomacy. These and similar values were also reported by other studies into Czech management: Koubek and Brewster (1995, p. 244) commented on the "Czech tradition of ideas and intellectual curiosity". It is worth noting in this context that the first central European university was established in Prague as early as 1348. Flexibility and improvisation were described by a number of researchers, such as

Schroll-Machl and Novy (2000), Novy and Schroll-Machl (2003) and Reber, Auer-Rizzi and Maly (2004).

Several researchers related the described values to the country's history with its dominance of foreign rule (Novy & Schroll-Machl, 2003). The following historical periods and events are relevant for an understanding of the proposed link.

- The sixteenth century saw the beginning of the reign of the Habsburg dynasty, and the territory of today's Czech and Slovak Republics remained part of the Austro-Hungarian Empire up to 1918. This period marked the beginning of the country's industrial tradition (Koubek & Brewster, 1995). Already during the nineteenth century, Bohemia, the most southern region, was the industrial heart of the Austro-Hungarian Empire. It was known for its heavy industry but also for its ceramic, glass and textile manufacture (Salzmann, 1992).

- 1918 to 1939 marked the time of the First Republic. Czechoslovakia became one of the fifteen most developed nations in the world (Tung & Havlovic, 1997).

- In 1939, the country was annexed by Hitler Germany and remained occupied until the end of World War II in 1945.

- Shortly after, in 1948, the country came under the influence of the Soviet regime. With regard to the economic situation, the strong focus on heavy industry continued (Tung & Havlovic, 1997). In political terms, the 1960s represented a period of attempts to create "socialism with a human face" (Salzmann, 1992, p. 83). However, 1968 marked the end of the so-called "Prague Spring". Warsaw Pact armies invaded the country and reimposed "neo-Stalinist political and economic structures" (Soulsby, 2001, p. 61). The period to follow was characterised by strict centralisation and hierarchical co-ordination mechanisms (Clark & Soulsby, 1995) that brought about socialist state enterprises with hardly any individual decision-making power (Koubek & Brewster, 1995). Nonetheless, resistance against the regime continued. The most prominent example was "Charta 77", a text published by a group of dissidents strongly criticising the government.

- The *Velvet Revolution* in 1989 marked the beginning of the transformation period into a representative democracy. Václav Havel, one of the signers of Charta 77, became the first president of the new republic. Parallel to the political changes, the transition began from planned to market economy. The economy and labour market were freed up (Hegewisch, Brewster & Koubek, 1996). Consequently, foreign organisations and foreign capital began to enter the country and a large part of the former state enterprises were privatised.

- In 2004, the Czech Republic became a member of the European Union.

The relationship between foreign domination in the country's history (most notable by Austria, Germany and the Soviet Union) and the above mentioned values could offer at least part of an explanation of the Czechs' tendency to adjust to the status quo at surface level while at the same time trying to pursue own interests in a diplomatic and creative way. Mills (2000, p. 193) observed a tendency of "dual standards of behaviour" among today's Czech managers. Several researchers commented specifically on the impact of the communist regime on Czech managers' attitudes and behavioural patterns, such as autocratic decision-making (Clark & Soulsby, 1998), administrative skills (Koubek & Brewster, 1995) and improvisation (Schroll-Machl & Novy, 2000). These reports are consistent with the qualitative study's findings. In some contrast to these accounts, Meierewert (2001) found the use of improvisation to decrease in recent years and argued that Czech people today no longer consider improvisation as essential for achieving results as it was during communist times.

Related to foreign rule and its impact on Czech mentality, Czech works of fiction provide some excellent examples of dealing with foreign authorities. *Schwejk*, a simple soldier serving in the Austro-Hungarian army, was an expert in overt obedience, passive resistance, improvisation and taking even tragic things with humour (Hasek, 1960; first published 1921-23). More recently, namely in the communist era, the dissident and Charta 77 signer, Pavel Kohout (1987), wrote the autobiographical book "Kde je zakopán pes" ("Where the dog is buried"). The book impressively illustrates how the author and his wife used humour and creativity to effectively cope with the increasing chicanery imposed by the communist party with the purpose of weakening morale and resistance.

Autocratic decision-making. The qualitative study suggests that many Czech managers reserve the right to taking the decisions. This tendency was also reported by other authors, including Clark and Soulsby (1995), Koubek and Brewster (1995), Nasierowski (1996) and Suutari and Riusala (2001).

Also parallel to the qualitative study's findings, Lang (1998) described Czech subordinates' expectancy of autocratic managerial behaviour. Meierewert (2001) reported a tendency among Czechs to adhere to authority. Subordinates, in expectation of autocratic managers, may implicitly put pressure on their managers to conform to these attributes. An indicator for the correctness of this assumption comes from diploma research by Pibilova (2004), who studied the decision-making patterns of Austrian expatriates in Czech enterprises. She found that Austrian expatriates in the Czech Republic behaved more autocratically than their fellow citizens, who worked in Austrian companies with Austrian subordinates.

The qualitative study also found that managers were the official decision-makers, while subordinates sometimes used diplomatic ways to influence decisions. Schroll-Machl and Novy (2000) portrayed Czech decision-making patterns as relying greatly on informal channels. According to the two authors, decision-making typically involves preparation through informal channels. Parallel to subordinates trying to get their point across in informal settings, managers also use informal channels to get an understanding of employees' opinions and seek support for their own decision preferences.

Consistent with the qualitative study, the literature provides accounts of reluctance to get involved and be held responsible, both on behalf of managers and subordinates. For example, Mills (2000, p. 193) described managerial practices based on "unwillingness to take responsibility for decision-making." Reber, Auer-Rizzi and Maly (2004) stressed reluctance of Czech subordinates to get involved in decision-making. Koubek and Brewster (1995, p. 244) reported on "surviving socialist practices" and observed that the "traditional system of ambiguous responsibilities and unwillingness to decide anything without approval of some superior authority" continues. According to Meierewert (2001), the transition from planned to market economy might have led to additional uncertainty and feelings of not being competent enough to take responsibility for decisions.

Managerial role. According to the qualitative study, the managerial role includes far-reaching responsibility for the work and wellbeing of subordinates. Koubek and Brewster (1995) and Hegewisch, Brewster and Koubek (1996) complemented this finding in their studies examining Czech HRM policies and practices. These authors found a particularly high responsibility of line managers for personnel decisions, including issues of payment and decisions to hire or dismiss personnel.

> "Line managers in Czech organisations have more decision power in the personnel area than the personnel departments, and their power is still increasing." (Koubek & Brewster, 1995, p. 235)

According to the qualitative study, Czech managers act rather autocratically in Human Resource questions. Neither subordinates nor the manager's superior or representatives of the unions seem to have much of a say in such decisions, which suggests that the concentration of power is indeed high among line managers. A potential reason for this tendency may be related to communist times, when there was a strong link between the personnel department and the communist party authorities. Hetrick (2002) portrayed the personnel departments of Czech companies as "an extension of the secret police, their primary function [being] to maintain extensive records on the private and work lives of the employees" (p. 341). Consequently, managers may prefer to take things into their own hands, even more than a decade after the end of communism.

Role of the subordinates. In the qualitative study, part of the interviewees described their subordinates as "children" whom they could not trust with decision-making responsibility. The literature is less explicit on this point.

However, there are some hints that point in the same direction. For example, Suutari and Riusala (2000) analysed the experience of Finnish expatriate managers in the Czech Republic, Hungary and Poland, and reported a "lack of personal initiative and innovativeness among local employees, and thus stronger dependence on managerial initiative" (p. 97). According to Meierewert (2001), Czech subordinates expect to be given orders, while superiors are expected to make decisions and take responsibility.

Relics of the past and envisioned changes. The qualitative data as well as the literature suggest that the autocratic tendency of Czech managers is related to the former communist system. A closer look might help develop a better understanding of this link. Currently, one can differentiate between three types of Czech managers: (1) Experienced managers, who held managerial positions already during communist times. (2) Managers who are new in their managerial roles but were socialised and educated under the communist regime. (3) Managers who are currently educated in Western management practices and/or are experiencing Western type management firsthand, for example in multinational enterprises.

According to Mills (2000), the majority of today's Czech managers still belong to the first type of managers. In some sectors (e.g. banks), many of the current managers are even part of the former *nomenklatura,* a privileged elite with close ties to the communist party. According to a study by Clark and Soulsby (1998) in four Czech companies, 78 percent of the senior managers and 100 percent of the general directors share a *nomenklatura* past. A likely reason why many of these managers kept their position is related to the privatisation approach. In many cases, state-owned companies were transferred to private ownership by distributing vouchers to eligible Czech citizens (Kotíková & Bittnerová, 2003; also see Kost, 1994). Many of these new shareholders assigned their shares to investment companies in the hope of quick profit (Mills, 2000). Consequently, the new ownership of many Czech companies became dispersed, anonymous and unorganised (Hegewisch, Brewster & Koubek, 1996). No one initiated changes in the internal functioning of the organisations. In order to avoid uncertainty, banks and investments companies did not become active either (Reber et al., 2000). In other words, there was little pressure on companies to change their management, also because many of these managers seemed able to ensure a successful future for their organisations: Despite the new challenges that Czech managers had to face under market economy conditions, they were still experts in technical matters and competent professionals. Consequently, their input was vital for successful enterprise transformation and privatisation. The managers themselves were extremely motivated to give their best because their future managerial careers depended on a successful transformation process (Soulsby & Clark, 1998). Despite their importance, it is unlikely that these managers can and want to initiate a shift toward more participative management.

If Czech management is going to change, the initiative must originate with the managers of the second and third type. Although being socialised under the old system, many of these managers are young and ambitious. They are about to experience Western management practice first-hand, for example when working for multinational enterprises. Additionally, part of them is currently receiving management education, thus acquiring a theoretical and cognitive basis that should support an attitude and behavioural shift.

However, one should not be overly optimistic. Some of the interviewees participating in the qualitative study were of the second and third type of managers. Yet, traditional management patterns seem to prevail even among them. In most cases, only the rhetoric has changed so far. The literature is also quite hesitant about drastic changes. Suutari and Riusala (2001) found only a slow increase in decision-making participation. Reber, Jago and Maly (2002) reported a lack of significant changes in managerial decision-making patterns between 1991 and 2001. Similarly, the qualitative study showed a fragmented picture of the current situation, with managers' rhetoric in favour of participative management while behaviour itself was much more autocratic.

According to Soulsby and Clark (1998) and Mills (2000), the current generation of managers possesses good technical skills and has acquired marketing, finance and accounting skills, as well as an increased understanding of business strategy. Thus, Czech managers seem to have learned a lot in terms of *hard skills*, i.e. task and business-related matters. However, there is so far little evidence with regard to a change in *soft skills*, such as participative management. According to the qualitative study, change will be difficult to accomplish, since several factors work together: (1) Responsibility for decision-making is exclusively attributed to the manager, (2) a long tradition of autocratic behaviour with subordinates expecting it, and (3) managers viewing subordinates as "children". However, the Czech interview data and accounts in the literature also attribute a high degree of adaptability, flexibility and creativity to the Czechs. These values might very well enable future Czech managers and subordinates to find democratic ways of interaction and decision-making, which are in line with Czech mentality.

Chapter 7

Within-Country Analysis: Finland

7.1 Overview

This chapter relates to Research Question 1 and the country-specific meaning and enactment of participative management in Finland. It describes the findings emerging from the analysis of the qualitative interviews conducted with eight Finnish managers. Recurring data patterns led to the country-specific model of participative management summarised in Figure 7.1. The model includes concepts stemming from *repeated* occurrence in the interview data. Consequently, only relevant parts of the interview material are represented here. Of course the data showed much more variety than the model can present. However, it was decided to concentrate only on main themes and present patterns of participative management rather than individual preferences. Readers interested in the data collection process are referred to Chapter 5.2. For a detailed description of the data analysis using elements of grounded theory see Chapter 5.3. In Figure 7.1, the two broad aspects of participative management under study, namely meaning and enactment, are shown in the shaded areas. Other concepts related to participative management are depicted in white boxes, and arrows show the relationships between the concepts.

Figure 7.1 illustrates that participative management in Finland is strongly influenced by the basic values of *autonomy* and *concern for quality*. Autonomy leads to a preference for independent thinking and action, while concern for quality guides the understanding that such independent approaches need to be integrated in order for them to be effective and successful. According to the interview data, participative management is considered a *tool* for the integration of independent opinions and actions.

Autonomy is also reflected in the roles attributed to managers and subordinates, as well as in the Finnish communication patterns. Societal culture dimensions such as *power distance, individualism/collectivism* and *uncertainty avoidance* (compare Chapter 2.2.3.1) play an additional role in shaping the meaning of participative management. Power distance refers to the degree to which members of a society expect power to be unequally shared. Individualism relates to the relationship between the individual and the level of collectivism that prevails in a society. Uncertainty avoidance reflects the

Figure 7.1 The Finnish Model of Participative Management

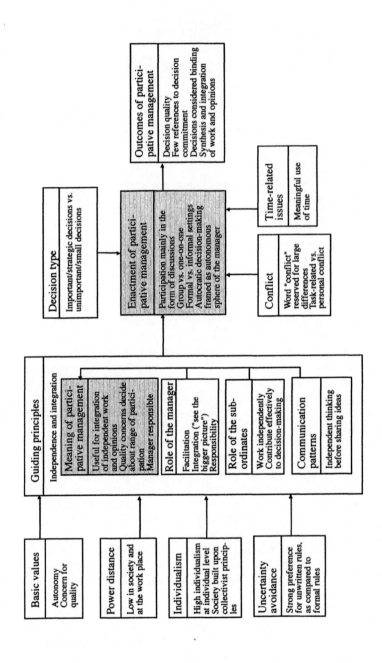

degree to which a society relies on social norms and procedures to alleviate the unpredictability of future events. Autonomy is, for example, represented in low power distance, which enables managers and subordinates to interact on a relatively equal level, which in turn provides the basis for participative management. Autonomy is also reflected by a high level of individualism prevailing among individuals. At the same time, institutional arrangements, such as social security, tend to be more collectivist. Finally, autonomy also shows in a preference for unwritten rules, which, in turn, also influences participation.

The sum of these factors shape the enactment of participative management, which is additionally affected by such situational factors as *decision type, conflict* and *time*. The envisioned outcomes of participative management include the synthesis of opinions and work by individual actors, as well as decision quality. Decision commitment is less of a factor because decisions are considered binding by all participants.

The following sections describe all concepts depicted in Figure 7.1 in more detail, including original quotes by the interview partners.

7.2 The Meaning of Participative Management in Context

7.2.1 Basic Value: Autonomy

The Finnish interviews highlight a strong preference for autonomy. Autonomy was described as the possibility to think things through individually and to follow one's own ideas. Clear responsibility for tasks and a high level of mutual trust emerged as the main preconditions for autonomy. The following list summarises how autonomy influences various areas within the Finnish model of participative management, all of which are presented in more detail (including interviewee quotes) in Sections 7.2.3 to 7.5.3 below.

- The interviewees characterised the relationship between superiors and subordinates with such words as hands-off management and empowerment.
- Consequently, descriptions of the managerial role included integration of differing opinions as a central aspect. Integration becomes necessary because both individual subordinates and teams work rather independently and form their own opinions.
- The data further indicate that autonomy is reflected in the way Finns typically communicate. For example, people develop their opinions before sharing them with others.
- The data also suggest that the Finnish preference for autonomy corresponds with other cultural values, in particular with high individualism and low power distance.

- Autonomy emerged as being related to a preference for unwritten rules compared to formal rules. Formal rules were described as imposing too many limitations, whereas unwritten rules seem to fit better with the preference for autonomous work.

7.2.2 Basic Value: Concern for Quality

Concern for quality turned out to be the second basic value repeatedly appearing in the Finnish interview data. There seems to be a tendency among Finns to strive to do *well* at whatever task they are working on, to finish things they have started, to take their work seriously, to take into account the consequences of their actions and to strive for the best possible solutions to problems. The following quotes illustrate the described patterns.

"[Participation] basically is including those whom you think know best."

"There can be so many social or society consequences that the team, or the subordinates, cannot take that responsibility. I absolutely believe it should be the manager who has to make the decision."

"If you can't give them the same background information, you can't let them decide, because they can't do that in a way."

"In a way you are always required to take into account what is in the best interest of the whole company."

"If there is a problem you have to develop a mutual understanding about what is the best way to proceed."

"I like to take responsibility for my team."

7.2.3 Guiding Principles: Independence and Integration

As mentioned above, autonomy emerged from the Finnish interview data as one of the dominant values. It follows that the Finns seem to share a preference for independent work. However, the data also show that there is a clear and common understanding of the limits of autonomy, which is related to the Finns' concern for quality. Integration is considered necessary to coordinate the autonomous achievements of individuals and teams. This holds true for operational work as well as for decision-making, where integration frequently takes the form of participation. In other words, while autonomy and independent work are highly valued, integration and co-operation are considered important in order to be effective and successful. The following quotes illustrate the parallel consideration of these aspects.

"People from other countries probably think that we are lonely workers and so on. Actually we can work together without speaking very much. But still we think that we need each other."

"In a way Finns are like lone wolves, I would say, but even wolves belong to a pack."

"If you are working autonomously in your area, you may notice, 'Oh, this thing here must be corrected.' And then you tell the others, 'What do you think, what could we do?'"

"The basis is that we work together, but each of us also has areas where they make decisions alone. However, we know how our individual decisions influence the other colleagues' work."

"In some cases it's very good to be very autonomous, but for example if you don't pay attention to subordinates in very difficult problems, if you make a decision alone, then it's not good."

7.2.4 The Meaning of Participative Management

Useful for integration. As mentioned above, participative management, as described by the Finnish interviewees, takes part *within* the context of autonomy. Co-operation is considered necessary for integration purposes. In other words, although participative management does not have the same high status in Finland as for example in Sweden, it is accepted as a useful and important management tool, whenever it can serve the purpose of enabling integration.

The majority of the interviewees equated participation with discussions that helped to "see the bigger picture" and increase knowledge of specific problems.

"Participation for me means working together, taking into account different opinions and things like that."

Other interviewees defined participation as "finding a common understanding about a problem" and "integrating differing views". Thus, the benefit of participation includes "synthesising differing opinions" in addition to making effective decisions, as one interviewee put it. On the one hand, participation reduces managerial autonomy. On the other hand, the data suggest that a reduction in autonomy is accepted if traded in for anticipated benefits, in particular if these benefits include integration, which, in turn, serves to ensure high quality results.

Range of participation. The eight Finnish managers' definitions of participation included explicit foci on superior/subordinate relations as well as holistic descriptions including various organisational members. Again, a strong concern for quality seemed to influence the managers' considerations about whom to include in decision-making.

> "If you buy a new machine, it <u>always</u> means that the men who will be in charge of it will be included."

Usually, it is the manager who decides about the use of participative management as part of her or his managerial role (see below). The interviews did not reveal any examples of *subordinates* themselves asking to be included in decision-making.

Who is responsible for a decision? According to the interviewed managers, the final decision-making and the ultimate responsibility usually lie with the manager. In other words, participative management means a consultative process that usually does not go as far as group decision-making. The data suggest that the subordinates share the assumption of the manager being responsible for decision-making. They accept sole managerial responsibility for the decision and its outcome even after an intensive discussion process.

> "In everyday work the responsibility is on the director's side, so he is ultimately responsible for what is happening. So he must take charge [...] but of course he can communicate and listen."

> "The decision is always yours."

Two factors are related to the managerial responsibility for decision-making and outcome. Firstly, participation means that some participants are likely to have to change their opinion. Finland was the only country, in which this issue was mentioned. It clearly relates to the concept of autonomous thinking and acting. However, the possible decrease in autonomy seems to be accepted in view of the overall goal of integration. Secondly, decisions made by the manager after a process of participation are considered binding to all participants. While this premise clearly includes quality concerns, it also shows that loyalty to the group is expected, even if a participant entered the discussion process with a different opinion.

7.2.5 The Role of the Manager

Consistent with the findings regarding the meaning of participative management, the data also suggest that managerial leadership in Finland is characterised by facilitation, integration and responsibility.

Facilitation. Managers practice what they call hands-off management of empowered subordinates. They act primarily as facilitators and, in turn, expect to be informed about the activities in their unit in *broad* terms, rather than be involved in the details of daily work.

"A good manager is not involved in the small details."

"I think that we have a problem with our boss. Quite often he says, 'I am the boss.' All things must go through his hands and he wants to control all kinds of things."

Integration. It is the role of the manager to integrate autonomous work and independent opinions, which is consistent with what was described as the meaning of participative management in Section 7.2.4 above.

"Good leaders can synthesise different opinions."

"A good leader is responsible for the big picture really."

Some of the interviewees described the role of the manager as a team integrator, and teams and teamwork were frequently mentioned. Yet, the interviewees seemed less focused on operational teamwork than on the integration of opinions. In this sense, teams are no contradiction to individual work. As it turned out, the Finnish definition of teamwork may be broader and more diverse than that in other European cultures. A first hint at this hypothesis was provided by the interviewees' answers to the question of whether Finns were good team players. Answers ranged from "not at all" to "of course", indicating that opinions vary with regard to the concept of team. A second hint came from the interviewees' stories about recent developments in the Finnish business world: In the 1980s the concepts of teams and teamwork started to become popular in Finland, obviously following the trend of an emerging preference for teamwork among American business writers and consultants. As one interviewee put it, "People tried to put teamwork everywhere, even in places where it was clear that it couldn't work." Today, this enthusiasm has somewhat faded. Teams are used when they fit and it is not the manager's job to suggest new areas of teamwork. In contrast, the manager provides support and infrastructure for existing teams.

"If there is a natural team, I give them the job and the freedom to work, but I'm not creating new teams, so I'm not working in the direction that we would have more and more teams."

Responsibility. A final aspect of the managerial role relates to responsibility, which, in turn, reflects the areas of autonomy and quality concerns. The manager is responsible for the activities and outcomes of the unit s/he manages, and s/he acts as a link between the usually quite autonomous unit and its organisational environment. The autonomous character of the unit is also illustrated by the fact that usually little "upward delegation" of problems to the next hierarchical level takes place.

"Normally, when there are different opinions on a matter in my department, the last thing is to get [my] boss involved. It's best to solve the problem over here, in the department."

"There is no need to go and ask things or to tell [your superior] small things."

7.2.6 The Role of the Subordinates

The main characteristics of the subordinate role are consistent with the preference for autonomy, empowerment and independent work. Furthermore, subordinates are expected to work together and contribute effectively to discussions when involved in decision-making processes.

According to the data, participation in managerial decision-making is feasible only when all participants share the same level of background information. Therefore, whenever participation has been decided upon, subordinates can expect to be provided with the information they need in order to be able to provide valid contributions. This procedure ensures high-quality discussions, which ties in with the above-mentioned concern for quality (Section 7.2.2).

7.2.7 Communication Patterns

The data suggest that the accepted Finnish avenues of communication follow distinctive patterns. These include: (1) People think very carefully before speaking up. (2) People prefer to express well thought-out ideas. There is little tolerance for verbalising the thinking process. (3) People consider it impolite to express strong points of view publicly, in particular when the opinions expressed are in opposition to other people's views. Consequently, communication flows more freely in informal settings, in smaller groups and in one-on-one conversations.

It seems that the preferred way of Finnish communication is reflective of the Finns' value orientation toward autonomy and concern for quality: People listen and think things through before sharing their opinions with others. Interviewees also described the fact that they make preliminary decisions before attending group meetings concerning that very problem. This strategy fits their assumptions on autonomous preparation for a meeting. The following quote further illustrates the described communication patterns:

"We have to think very thoroughly before we say something, [...] we don't like to say unfinished ideas [...] People think very hard before they say something. You can even see that it can take five minutes. We may have discussed something and somebody says something related to it five minutes later, because he thought it through and it took five minutes."

7.3 The Enactment of Participative Management

7.3.1 Participative vs. Autocratic Decision-Making

As shown in the analysis of the meaning of participative management, the Finnish interviewees tend to prefer individual work and empowerment. Participation is frequently understood as a means to integrate the work and opinions of autonomous individuals. It follows that participation is not a "must" for all situations. In contrast, there is a high level of tolerance for solutions found by individuals. The following paragraphs provide a short description of the enactment of participative management, followed by an exploration of whether and how the preference for autonomy fits with autocratic managerial behaviour.

Participative decision-making. As suggested in the above section treating the meaning of participative management, the involvement of subordinates mainly takes the form of consultative discussions. One of the main reasons for this preference lies in the integration of autonomous work and individual opinions. Thus, participation is reserved to areas in which integration is considered necessary.

Participation can take the form of a group meeting or one-on-one conversation. In addition, discussions take place either in formal meetings or in rather informal ways. For example, the data revealed a preference for informal discussions when there are differing opinions among the discussants (compare Section 7.4.3).

On the one hand, group meetings are considered fair to the discussants because they indicate that a decision has not been made beforehand. On the other hand, there is consensus on the fact that small groups and one-on-one conversation also have certain advantages. In particular, personal issues tend to be raised in small rather than in large group settings. As suggested by the interview data, a direct link exists between the mode of participation and the Finnish way of communication.

"I don't know, but I think it's not so easy to say all issues in the group. [...] It's very difficult to open up in a group."

"Being polite in Finland means that when you are strongly against something, you don't say it in a very open space. It's much more polite to say it face to face."

"If there are personal issues, I think it's better to discuss individually."

Autocratic decision-making. One could assume that autocratic decision-making by a manager interferes with the autonomous sphere of subordinates. This is indeed the case and leads to a strong rejection of autocratic management. However, there are also areas that could be labelled autocratic from the outside, but which are likely framed as non-autocratic by Finns. Two examples help to illustrate this point. The first case concerns specific organisations and positions, in which autocratic decision-making is typically exercised, such as the military. With regard to such organisations and positions, applicants usually know beforehand what they can expect, and consequently, they can choose. In other words, they can decide for themselves whether to get their autonomy restricted or not. One of the interviewed managers explained:

> "In no-democracy areas, such as a nuclear plant or the army, people have accepted beforehand that they are told things."

A second area of autocratic decision-making being framed as non-autocratic can take place in any organisation and superior/subordinate relation. It concerns decisions for which subordinates do not have enough background information, and providing them with information does not seem feasible either.

> "There are certain things that I can decide without discussing with my people, because I know that they don't have enough background information to discuss it."

The data suggest that the Finnish managers do not frame this area of decision-making as autocratic. Rather, they seem to assume that participation does not make sense under such conditions and they accept it as their managerial duty to take care of such issues. And indeed, the data suggest that the preferred modes of communication (to state thought-out opinions rather than toss out loose ideas and to speak up only when having a strong basis for one's opinion) prevent subordinates from participating effectively. It is likely that such decisions are considered part of the *autonomous* sphere of the manager. The low level of power distance in Finnish society (see Section 7.5.1) further supports this assumption. In other words, such "autocratic" decisions are not considered a manifestation of hierarchical power, but are seen as part of managerial responsibility, in particular when subordinates understand the reasons motivating their manager's behaviour.

7.3.2 Participative Management Outcomes

The data suggest an interesting finding with regard to the envisioned outcomes of participative management. Several interviewee statements related to decision quality, whereas only few references were made to such motivational consequences of participation as decision commitment. The first quote below illustrates decision quality, the second decision commitment:

"In my own work, I've noticed that we always have to listen to different opinions to get a good result."

"When the group makes the decision, they all know that they have the trust from the group and then they are motivated to do [the job]."

In contrast to decision quality and commitment, the synthesis and integration aspects of participation were mentioned frequently, which is consistent with what was described above.

The fact that motivational outcomes of participation were rarely mentioned stands in stark contrast to other countries. When trying to find the reason for this discrepancy, one first of all comes across the fact that decisions are considered binding, no matter whether they are discussion-based or not. Since the binding quality of decisions is usually accepted by all participants, there is little need to ensure commitment for the implementation phase by means of participation, as is common in other countries such as Germany.

However, there could yet be a broader reason, why motivational consequences of participation were hardly raised by the Finnish interviewees. Finns are motivated by an autonomous work setting and prefer to be supported by such measures as empowerment and delegation. These work forms are most likely to represent the type of democracy Finnish employees expect to find in a working place. In contrast, participation does not reflect work democracy to the same degree. Rather, participation represents the manager's responsibility to "see the bigger picture" and to ensure integration. Participation is considered important and good for effective work. However, participation does not have the same connotations and deeply rooted emotional dimension in connection with work democracy as do empowerment and delegation. In sum, whereas empowerment and delegation seem to include a strong motivational component, participation is more of a necessity than a motivating factor.

7.4 Main Situational Influence Factors

The data suggest that the type of problem/decision in question consistently influences the Finnish managers' choice of whether to use participation or not, and if yes, in which format. Other factors, such as time-related issues and conflict also show an impact, yet less strongly.

7.4.1 Decision Type

One Finnish interviewee found participative management preferable in all kinds of situations and for problems of all kinds, whereas his peers found participation useful only for specific decisions and problems.

Important/strategic decisions. According to these managers, participative management was considered particularly useful for decisions having major effects and for strategic decisions, as opposed to operational ones. Also, participation was viewed as a good tool concerning planning (e.g. with regard to products, delivery delays, services offered). These types of decisions all reflect a concern for quality and for the integration aspect of participation discussed above.

"If there are big effects and many people will notice the decision, then I think [participation] is most important."

"Of course, the more operational decision-making is, the less participation you need in a way, I think. But the more vague or uncertain, the more participation you need, just in principle and overall."

Unimportant/small decisions. When asked about problems or situations that did *not* qualify for participation, the Finnish managers mentioned several situations and conditions, but only one theme was dominant. It related to unimportant and small issues. In these cases, participative management was seen as neither needed nor expected by subordinates. This point is consistent with the integration aspect of participative management: Small problems are unlikely to concern a large number of people, while unimportant problems have no major impact that would need to be discussed and integrated.

The detailed analysis of a particular case scenario discussed during the interviews supports the Finnish interviewees' differentiation between important and unimportant problems: As part of a reflection upon the Vroom/Yetton cases, interviewees were asked to share their reaction to a parking space scenario, in which too few parking spaces were available for the members of an organisational unit. The unit manager was expected to address the problem by choosing between different levels of participation in the decision-making process. The interviewees' responses show a clear pattern: Those managers who classified the parking lot problem as important or difficult preferred group processes, as is illustrated by the following quote.

"This was a very difficult problem. [...] I think the discussion should start with a group meeting with all of them, so that they see that they are all in the same position."

In contrast, interviewees who considered the parking lot issue unimportant favoured autocratic decision-making. They felt confident about their strategy, as they were convinced that their subordinates accepted their taking charge.

"In Finland it's totally accepted. It's such a small thing. [...] I think they have better things to do than think what is the right solution for the parking space."

"I must say that I couldn't even imagine working with people who pay much attention to something like a parking place."

The Finnish interviewees' reactions to the parking lot scenario parallel their explicit descriptions of the usefulness of participation for particular types of problems as summarised above: Participative management is not considered useful for small and unimportant problems.

7.4.2 Time-Related Issues

The Finnish managers appeared to be very time-efficient and seemed to be aware of and take into account the fact that participation needs time. More than one interviewee also referred to historic events, in which time was a critical factor for making important decisions:

"I have read and heard that in the Second World War, during the Winter War, there were mainly fast actions and fast decisions. Whatever was the problem, you needed to react fast. If you start discussing, the enemies are coming, and what do you do then? "

Correspondingly, there was consensus among the interviewees that unimportant issues should be solved particularly quickly. Some interviewees even referred to unimportant problems as a total "waste of time". This perspective fits with their overall concern for quality, i.e. spending time on the "useful" parts of work.

"But why should I use [my subordinates'] time for a thing that is not very important? [...] I prefer to give them bigger things to discuss. Usually, I don't like to use time for minor things."

7.4.3 Conflict

The Finnish interviewees differentiated between task-related issues and personal conflicts. *Task-related* conflicts were frequently described as representing differing views of a problem, which is not surprising given the Finnish preference for autonomous work and thinking. It was argued that such differences could best be solved in a group discussion, because this provided an opportunity to attain a better understanding of the topic and the various viewpoints of the discussants.

"If there are really conflicts between substantial issues, then you have to go into
that topic and try to understand which one is correct. I think it's worth doing."

This position fits with the quality concerns and integration aspect of participation described above, where "seeing the bigger picture" was found to be
one of the main arguments in favour of participative management. Informal
discussions and small group meetings are preferred when there is a strong
clash of opinions, which is consistent with the Finnish modes of communication (see Section 7.2.7).

In contrast to task-related conflicts, the manager should limit participation in the case of strong and *personal* conflict among discussants. The following quote illustrates that communication patterns again play a role.

"There are of course some personal things that you have to keep in mind, or
some people are more sensitive and some are more like yourself [...] and normally it's very dangerous to have these discussions in public. [...] When personal matters are concerned, it's always very risky and I don't consider meeting
in the large group. What is the point?"

7.5 Main Society-Related Influence Factors

The qualitative findings suggest that the Finnish meaning and enactment of
participative management is highly influenced by historic and societal culture factors such as power distance, individualism and uncertainty avoidance.

7.5.1 Power Distance

Power distance relates to the degree to which members of a society expect
power to be unequally shared (Hofstede, 1980a; House et al., 2004). One
interviewee described Finland as a young society with no established hierarchy. Consequently, Finns tend to have an egalitarian attitude toward their
fellow citizens, no matter what position they are in. The data show that this
patterns of egalitarian relations is reflected in the work environment, in
particular in the following areas: (1) Work is characterised by the co-
operation of relatively equal organisational members rather than by a steep
hierarchy. (2) According to the data, there are relatively few status symbols
to express hierarchical power. (3) In the description of their own managerial
role, the interviewees stressed responsibility and task completion, in other
words quality aspects, rather than position.

"It's not important for me that people think [that I am the boss]. I just do my
job. [...] But when it's needed to be the boss, I try to be."

The examples indicate that relationships based on egalitarian principles form the foundation for a work environment allowing managers to initiate participative management when considered necessary, and for subordinates to freely offer their contributions.

7.5.2 Individualism

Individualism refers to the relationship between the individual and the level of collectivism that prevails in a society (Hofstede, 1980a; House et al., 2004). The interviewees described high individualism to be characteristic among Finns. Simultaneously, society was portrayed as built upon collectivist principles, exemplified by high taxation in general and progressing income tax rates in particular. While some interviewees argued for more flexibility, for example in the wage system, others concluded that many changes have recently taken place, allocating more responsibility to the individual actors and reducing the harmonising influence of the state.

> "I think we Finns are very individualistic, but then, really, the society is not that individualistic."

> "Finland has much earlier realised [than Sweden] that you should be more responsible as an individual, that the government is not giving everything to you."

The parallel description of individualism and collectivism corresponds to the guiding principles of autonomy and integration that have been a main theme throughout the analysis of the Finnish data. Individualism seems to be the more deeply rooted factor, while collectivism in the form of institutional arrangements is acknowledged and valued for co-ordination and integration purposes.

7.5.3 Uncertainty Avoidance

Uncertainty avoidance reflects the degree to which a society relies on social norms, rules and procedures to alleviate the unpredictability of future events (Hofstede, 1980a; House et al., 2004). The Finnish data revealed an interesting pattern with regard to rules and regulations. On the one hand, the interviewees agreed that, in general, rules should not restrict autonomy. On the other hand, they evaluated stability and co-ordination of autonomy positively. The "Finnish solution" to these possibly conflicting forces seems to be a preference for *unwritten* rules. *Formal* rules are strongly rejected, because they represent restrictions, as illustrated by the following quote:

"We feel that we cannot even write it down because it would limit us too much."

Unwritten rules give people the flexibility they want while providing a certain degree of structure that is not forced upon them from the outside. In this context, one interviewee mentioned a historical novel that illustrated the relationship of Finns to rules in the described way.

"This book about the Second World War, it's really worth reading. There were very good soldiers, but they hated rules. They liked discipline, but the main discipline came from within the group."

Interviewees also offered current examples of unwritten rules. Not surprisingly, their examples related to values that fit in with Finnish cultural assumptions. For example, an unwritten rule in the area of participation says that employees who are directly affected by a decision should always participate in the decision-making process. This rule is in line with the assumption that the autonomous work sphere of subordinates is to be respected. Therefore, the subordinates should be included in any potential instigation of changes within their area.

The interview data further show that the preference for unwritten rules is related to the Finnish communication patterns. In Finnish conversation, words are considered binding. Therefore, one can rely on unwritten rules and does not feel the need for written statements or agreements, as is common in other cultures in which the written word counts more than the spoken one.

7.6 Integration

7.6.1 Fit with the Three Quantitative Studies

The qualitative study explores the meaning and enactment of participative management. The findings allow conclusions with respect to more quantitatively oriented aspects of participative management, such as level of participation. Therefore it is valid to analyse the findings of the qualitative interview data for their fit with the results of the three quantitative studies. Is there a match with the quantitative scores of the GLOBE study, the Event management study and the Vroom/Yetton study? If not, is it possible to explain the differences based on the insights gained from the qualitative inquiry? In order to address these questions, the following paragraphs summarise and integrate the different studies' results.

Table 7.1 Quantitative Participation Scores for Finland

Scale	Participative (GLOBE)	Non-autocratic (GLOBE)	Guidance source subordinates (Event Management)	Mean level of participation (MLP) (Vroom/Yetton)
Score	5,92	5,89	30	5,00
Country position	Upper third	Upper third	Upper third	Middle third
Rank	5 of 61	10 of 61	4 of 56	8 of 13

Note: For a detailed description of the scales and country comparisons see Chapter 4.

With regard to the results of the participation scales (Table 7.1), namely the high scores on *participative* and *non-autocratic* management in the GLOBE study, the high relevance of *subordinates* as a guidance source in the Event Management study, and the medium *MLP* score in the Vroom/Yetton study, the qualitative data fit best with the latter of the three studies. The interview data suggest that participative management in Finland is not used as unconditionally as the GLOBE and Event Management studies would suggest, but that it is rather employed in specific areas, in which the integration of autonomous work and thoughts are concerned. The GLOBE study, with its broad measurement of "participative leadership", does not convey the subtle meanings related to participative management within the context of independence and integration. The same holds true for the Event Management study, although to a lesser extent. The Event Management study explores specific situations yet measures reactions to typical managerial decisions that do not reflect the use of participation as a discussion forum to integrate autonomous efforts. In contrast, the Vroom/Yetton study incorporates a number of contingencies and explores habits of participative managerial behaviour. In doing so, the Vroom/Yetton study likely reflects the actual patterns of Finnish participative management better than do the other two quantitative studies.

Table 7.2 Scores of Hierarchy-Related Concepts for Finland

Scale	Power distance "as is" (GLOBE)	Guidance source superior (Event Management)	Guidance source own experience (Event Management)
Score	4,89	34	114
Country position	Lower third	Lower third	Upper third
Rank	47 of 61	39 of 56	2 of 56

Note: For a detailed description of the scales and country comparisons see Chapter 4.

In Chapter 4.4, participative management was hypothesised to be related to concepts dealing with interactions within the organisational hierarchy. As far as the concept *power distance* is concerned (Table 7.2), the qualitative data are in line with the results of the GLOBE study. However, the qualitative data clearly show that a low level of power distance does not necessarily mean an extremely high level of participation. As the Finnish example suggests, low power distance may well be shown through the implementation of such other democratic work forms as empowerment and autonomous work, whereas participative management is restricted to areas related to the integration of autonomous work and thoughts.

The Event Management study's finding that Finnish managers involve their *superiors* less strongly than their counterparts in many other countries (Table 7.2), finds confirmation and explanation in the qualitative data. Work units are considered quite autonomous and managers typically abstain from getting their bosses involved on a daily basis. These findings also reflect low power distance, as Finnish managers need not report to their superiors in ways known from managers in countries with high power distance. Correspondingly, the Event Management study's finding of a strong use of *own experience* as guidance source (Table 7.2) also reflects the Finnish preference for autonomy.

Table 7.3 Scores of Team-Related Concepts for Finland

Scale	Collaborative team orientation (GLOBE)	Team integrator (GLOBE)	Institutional collectivism "as is" (GLOBE)
Score	6,35	5,54	4,63
Country position	Upper third	Middle third	Upper third
Rank	3 of 61	27 of 61	9 of 61

Note: For a detailed description of the scales and country comparisons see Chapter 4.

Chapter 4.4 also discussed the potential relationship between participative management and team-related concepts. The *team-related* scales of the GLOBE study (Table 7.3) hint at a relatively high level of team orientation of Finnish managers. From a quantitative point of view, the results do not differ much from such other countries as Sweden. In contrast, the qualitative interview data revealed an understanding of teams and teamwork in Finland, which differs somewhat from that of other countries: As is the case for participative management, teams are considered tools for integrating autonomous work.

The interview data provided confirmation with regard to the high level of *institutional collectivism* found in the GLOBE study (Table 7.3). Additionally, the qualitative interviews showed that high collectivism, for example in the social security system, can co-exist with high individualism at the individual level, for example in the form of a strong preference for autonomy.

Table 7.4 Scores of Uncertainty-Related Concepts for Finland

Scale	Uncertainty avoidance "as is" (GLOBE)	Guidance source formal rules (Event Management)	Guidance source unwritten rules (Event Management)
Score	5,02	-53	7
Country position	Upper third	Lower third	Upper third
Rank	8 of 61	56 of 56	12 of 56

Note: For a detailed description of the scales and country comparisons see Chapter 4.

Uncertainty-related concepts provided yet another area of discussion in Chapter 4.4. It was pondered how the level of uncertainty avoidance related to the enactment of participative management. The GLOBE study suggests that perceived *uncertainty avoidance* is high in Finland (Table 7.4), which would hint at a strong preference for *formal* rules, according to how the questionnaire items were phrased. In contrast, the Event Management study portrayed Finnish managers as relying heavily on *unwritten* rules, while at the same time rejecting formal rules (Table 7.4). The qualitative data clearly support the Event Management study's finding of a preference for unwritten rules and do not show any indication in favour of formal rules.

7.6.2 Fit with the Finnish System of Industrial Relations

One of the goals of this qualitative study concerns the evaluation of the relationship between the emerging country-specific models of participative management on the one hand and the country-specific systems of *de jure* participation and industrial relations on the other hand. *De jure* participation refers to the codified rights of employees and their representatives to participate in decision-making processes at the country, sectoral and organisational level. The catchall term industrial relations summarises the various areas of interaction between employer and employee at these three levels, including collective bargaining, employee representation on supervisory boards and works councils. *De jure* participation and industrial relations overlap in many countries, because usually at least some industrial relations processes are codified in law or other written agreements. The Finnish model is briefly outlined below, before it is analysed for its fit with the findings of the qualitative study with regard to participative management.

The Finnish system of industrial relations is characterised by a high degree of centralisation (IDE, 1981), which is enabled by the fact that both Finnish companies and their employees are highly organised (Laurila, 2000). Union density amounts to close to eighty percent, employer representation to about forty percent (Traxler, 2000). On the union side, separate confederations exist for different occupational groups (Carley, 2002), for example the Suomen Ammattiliittojen Keskusjärjestö (Central Organisation of Finnish Trade Unions) or the Toimihenkilökeskusjärjestö (Finnish Confederation of Salaried Employees). However, there has recently been quite a number of mergers among unions (Eironline, 2002a). Since 2004, the employer side is characterised by a singly umbrella organisation, Elinkeinoelämän Keskusliitto, covering industry, services and agriculture.

Consequently, collective bargaining is highly centralised in Finland (IDE, 1981) and centralised agreements cover about ninety percent of the Finnish workforce (Carley, 2002). The dominant level of bargaining is the intersectoral level, at which mainly pay and work conditions are covered.

At the company level, employee representation at the supervisory board level is granted for certain types of companies (Carley, 2002). Employees in companies with 30 or more employees have the legal right to establish works council systems (Luottamusmiesjärjestelmä). The information and consultation rights of these representative bodies are substantial and fully conform with the requirements of a directive by the European Union that calls for mandatory employee representation by 2008 and defines the areas for information and consultation rights.

The high degree of centralisation in the Finnish system of industrial relations can be interpreted as guaranteeing minimum standards and rights to the majority of the workforce, which reflects a *concern for quality* similar to what was found in the qualitative interview data. Accordingly, a strong and centralised system of industrial relations is reflective of an endeavour to *integrate* individuals into a well-represented overall workforce, which is somewhat similar to the integration attempts found in the qualitative study.

Besides concern for quality, autonomy has been the other important value in the findings of the qualitative study. One could argue that the high degree of centralisation of the industrial relations system as well as the binding character of codified employee rights limit the level of autonomy for companies and employees alike. However, these facts may also be interpreted as a chance to provide a guaranteed and shared basis, which is the requirement for autonomy to be able to prosper. This hypothesis would confirm to the finding of the qualitative study that autonomy is not endless but needs to fit with the wellbeing of the larger social system.

7.6.3 Fit with the Existing Literature

The integrative study suggests that in the case of Finland participative management is appreciated for its chance to help integrate autonomous efforts and achievements. Consequently, participation in decision-making focuses on areas in which such integration is required or considered useful for quality reasons. Important problems or problems entailing major consequences, such as strategic decisions, qualify well, whereas small problems are solved preferably within the sphere of autonomous decision-making. The study also revealed that the Finnish meaning of participative management and the distinct Finnish mode of communication go hand in hand. The following paragraphs look at all these aspects from the perspective of the literature.

Autonomy and integration. The dominant value found in the qualitative study is that of *autonomy* which has been intensively discussed in the literature about Finnish management and culture. Berry (1992) commented on the "Finnish cultural preference for respecting and promoting 'competent' or 'self-bossed' individualism'" (p. 6). According to Suutari (1996a) Finnish managers score high on the autonomy-delegation scale, i.e. the degree to which a manager allows subordinates to determine independently how to do their work, make decisions about daily work-related issues and decide about the means by which they try to achieve their goals. In a comparative study among Nordic and Anglo-Saxon countries, Dobbin and Boychuk (1999) found in the case of Finland that job autonomy was high at all organisational levels. Similarly, Smith et al. (2003, p. 499) characterised Finnish management as "autonomy with a bottom-up emphasis."

The qualitative study took place within the context of business organisations and so did the other studies mentioned in the paragraph above. But is the emerging understanding of participation within the parameters of autonomy limited to the business area? Definitely not, as becomes clear in the literature on Finnish culture, which suggests that autonomy is deeply rooted in Finnish society as a whole:

"Gritty perseverance (sisu), personal autonomy and independence, and respect for the autonomy of others are central themes in Finnish child training and the Finnish personality." (Jarvenpa, 1992, p. 103)

Moreover, the preference for autonomy is strongly related to the *history* of the country. Today's Finland was part of Sweden for more than 600 years before the territory was conquered by Russia during the Napoleonic Wars of 1808-1809, when it became an autonomous Russian grand duchy (Laurila, 2000). Finland declared its independence shortly after the Russian Revolution of 1917 (Jarvenpa, 1992). Still today, Finns proudly comment on this achievement and speak highly of the country's sovereignty.

Three famous national epics also illustrate the important value of autonomic thinking and behaviour. The *Kalevala*, Elias Lönnrot's 1835 compilation of Finnish and Karelian rune songs (Jarvenpa, 1992) describes the adventures of such autonomous and strong personalities as the three sons of Kaleva (Finland), Wäinämöinen, Ilmarinen and Lemminkäinen. In the novel *The Seven Brothers*, Aleksis Kivi (1954, first published in 1870) tells the story of autonomous but somewhat rebellious siblings who stand up against authorities and find their own way. More recently, the *Unknown Soldier* by Väinö Linna (1971, first published in 1954) tells the story of the experiences of Finnish soldiers during the Second World War. According to Aaltonen and Berry (1998), this epic illustrates how Finnish military leaders "demonstrated respect for the ability of autonomous subordinates to carry out their responsibilities" (p. 7). According to these authors, individual choice is highly respected, as long as it does not interfere with the need to fulfil obligations to the group and to society.

The need for autonomy and loyalty to the group, as described by Aaltonen and Berry, resembles the qualitative study's finding of the duality of *autonomy* and *integration*. In a similar vein, Parkum and Agersnap (1994), as well as Laine-Sveiby (1987, cited in Lindell, 2002, p. 183) noted that individualism is high at the personal level, while there is a tendency for consensus at the societal level. Furthermore, Berry (1994b) described autonomy as a core Finnish value and defined it as "independence within a framework" (p. 10).

Communication. The literature confirms what was suggested by the qualitative study: Finland is known for its distinct communication patterns that are clearly rooted in cultural values. Nurmi summarised Finnish communication as follows:

> "Finns do not think aloud as much as in Anglo-Saxon cultures, they are less open and slower to communicate, they are relatively more synthetic than analytic in their thinking. What is communicated is meant to be more certain, serious and reliable than in more fluent cultures." (Nurmi, 1989, p. 12)

Taking an ethnographic approach, Michael Berry's work concentrates on eliciting "rules" implicit in the conversation of people with different cultural backgrounds. These rules summarise "guidelines for appropriate ways to talk in order to be a credible and believable person in a speech community" (Aaltonen & Berry, 1998, p. 4). The Finnish conversation rules include observation and reflection before speaking on important and controversial issues (Auer-Rizzi & Berry, 2000). In other words, individuals should think first and only then share the results of the thinking process (Berry, 1992). A common thread in all Finnish conversation is that one should not waste words but add concrete value to the conversation (Nurmikari-Berry & Berry, 1999; Berry & Nurmikari-Berry, 2005). Comfort with quietude is a natural way to be while listening and reflecting before verbalizing an opinion (Berry, Carbaugh & Nurmikari-Berry, 2004). The conversation rules described by Berry and his colleagues are built on a solid empirical foundation, suggesting that they are deeply rooted in Finnish culture. For example, the speech of contemporary Finnish students revealed (among other characteristics) "a coding of 'autonomy' which assumed the legitimacy of societal and institutional limits but 'independence' within those parameters" (Berry, 1997, p. 319). Aaltonen and Berry (1998) found that the Finnish conversation rules could also be detected in such historical national epics as the *Unknown Soldier*.

Participation and management style. Consistent with the findings of the qualitative study, democratic management practices are described to prevail in Finland (Laurila, 2000). Similarly, the Finnish concept of hierarchical relationships is portrayed by Berry, Lähteenmäki and Reber (1998) as including "respect for the boss but considerable leeway for autonomous subordinates who carry primary responsibility for performing the task" (p. 11).

Smith et al. (2003) reported some consistency in management styles among the Nordic countries, and Lindell (2002) observed certain similarities between the Finnish and Swedish approaches to management. However, researchers also acknowledge that Finnish management has its unique features, as is true for any of the Nordic countries (Lindell & Arvonen, 1997; Szabo, 2001). Overall, there is a good fit between the literature and the qualitative study's findings with regard to the Finnish management style.

With more specific regard to *participation*, some features of decision-making that emerged from the qualitative data have also been mentioned in the literature. The Finnish manager acts as the final decision-maker while seeking information and consultation with "self-bossed" (Berry, 1992, p. 6; Berry, 1994a, p. 73) subordinates. The usual outcome of participative decision-making is high commitment to the decision by all involved parties. According to Lindell (2002, p. 183), Finnish managers "are not particularly bureaucratic, autocratic or hierarchical and tend to prefer open and straightforward communication with the aim of conducting business clearly and simply." Simon, Bauer and Kaivola (1996), cited in Lindell (2002, p. 183), reported that "Finnish managers value co-operation, teamwork and participative decision-making." Finally, Reber and Berry (1999) showed that the described participation patterns are not restricted to the cohort of Finnish *managers*, when they found similarities in the approaches to decision-making among Finnish business practitioners, university teachers and business students. This consistency suggests "cultural circles of reinforcement" (p. 318) and also implies that the meaning of participative management is built on a broad cultural foundation.

Chapter 8

Within-Country Analysis: Germany

8.1 Overview

This chapter deals with Research Question 1 pertaining to the country-specific meaning and enactment of participative management in Germany. It describes the qualitative study findings originating from interviews with eight German managers. The model of participative management summarised in Figure 8.1 represents repeated data patterns. The interview material also contained person-specific data, but such information has been excluded from this chapter to allow a focus on recurring patterns of managerial thinking and behaviour. For further information about methodology see the above chapters: Chapter 5.2 describes the process of data collection, while Chapter 5.3 deals with the qualitative data analysis using elements of grounded theory methodology. In Figure 8.1, the two broad aspects of participative management under study, namely meaning and enactment, are represented in the shaded boxes. Other concepts related to participative management are depicted in the white boxes. Arrows show the relationships between concepts as they emerged from the data.

Figure 8.1 shows that the German meaning of participative management is influenced by the value of *effectiveness* and embedded in the broader concept of *optimising work and management*. *Goal orientation* and *learning* are two further core concepts directly related to this guiding principle. The roles ascribed to *managers, subordinates* and external *specialists* also shape the meaning of participative management. Together, these concepts define participative management as a valuable and necessary management tool that helps decision-makers achieve the organisational goals in the best possible way. Societal culture factors, such as *power distance, collectivism* and *uncertainty avoidance* (compare Chapter 2.2.3.1) play an additional role. Power distance refers to the degree to which members of a society expect power to be unequally shared. Collectivism relates to the relationship between the individual and the level of collectivism that prevails in a society. Uncertainty avoidance reflects the degree to which a society relies on social norms and procedures to alleviate the unpredictability of future events. For example, the relatively high level of uncertainty avoidance in Germany is reflected in a preference for structure and order, which influences the characteristics of

Figure 8.1 The German Model of Participative Management

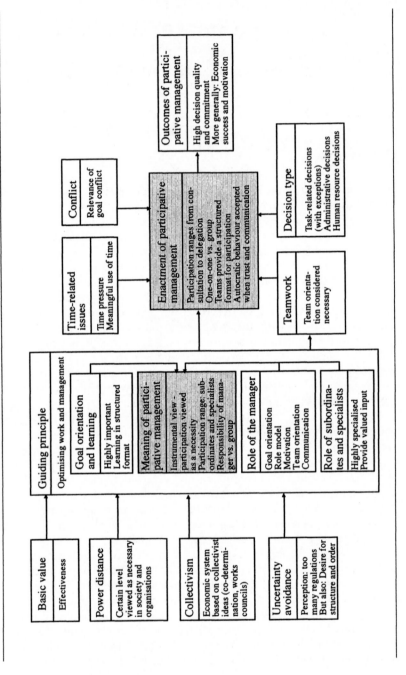

participative management. Additionally, collectivist principles in such institutional arrangements as co-determination on supervisory boards also have an impact on the appreciation German managers have for participative management.

The enactment of participative management is predominantly affected by *decision type, time-related issues*, and goal-related *conflict*. Additionally, participation often takes the form of standardised co-operation, such as *teamwork*. According to the data, the *outcomes* of participative management comprise various aspects, including such decision-specific outcomes as decision quality and decision commitment, as well as more general effects such as economic success and long-term subordinate motivation.

The following sections describe all concepts shown in Figure 8.1 in more detail and include various quotes given by the interviewed German managers.

8.2 The Meaning of Participative Management in Context

8.2.1 Basic Value: Effectiveness

Many of the interviewees' statements suggest that effectiveness guides managerial thinking and behaviour. More specifically, effectiveness seems to form the basis of most concepts included in the German model of participative management. The following summary provides a first impression, while the below Sections 8.2.2 to 8.2.6 cover all mentioned concepts in more detail and include interview quotes.

- Goal orientation and learning are considered effective ways to optimise work and management.
- Participative management is viewed as an effective managerial tool for reaching sound decisions.
- Team orientation contributes to managerial effectiveness, because a functioning team is understood to be one of the prerequisites for ensuring that defined goals can be reached.
- Subordinates are considered valuable human capital that needs to be utilised. An effective way to do so is by way of participative management.

8.2.2 Guiding Principle: Optimising Work and Management

According to the data, German managerial thinking and behaviour is driven by considerations of optimising work at both the operational and managerial level. This does not mean that the German managers are predominantly focused on intra-organisational matters. On the contrary, they aim at improving work and management processes with the goal of economic success in order for the organisation to improve market competitiveness.

Participative management (which is discussed in Section 8.2.3 below), goal orientation and learning are central elements within the context of optimising work and management. *Goal orientation* ensures consistency within the organisation, starting at the top level with the formulation of an overall strategy, and reaching down the hierarchy to the behaviour of individual employees. The interview data suggest that management and decision-making in Germany are guided more strongly by goals than might be the case in other countries.

"[This manager] was characterised by extreme goal orientation, he followed his goals, not at any cost, but for sure strongly. And he worked hard to reach these goals."

"I'm goal focussed, I have to be, because I am given relatively tough goals myself and I have to reach them. And that's what counts for me at the end of the day. Managing my team well is the means to realising these goals."

"I have to be conscious about our strategic orientation. And I have to define goals for my people. And these goals are really hard goals."

Apart from goal orientation, a strong focus on *learning* emerged as a second core concept related to optimising work and management. Learning helps to increase effectiveness. More specifically, learning aims at improving work processes as well as the interaction between organisational members. For example, employees expect to learn from mistakes and from the input of their superiors. The interviewees described learning as essential for all employees, including managers. Learning is considered strongly related to participative management, because skill development is necessary in order to use participation effectively. Frequently, such learning takes place in structured settings, such as workshops, seminars and team development processes. Also, regular subordinate feedback to managers and continuous improvement processes follow set schedules and formats.

"[A good manager] has a strong personality, and you can learn from such a person in every respect, how he handles situations, how he deals with people."

"In our company subordinates give feedback to their managers, once a year. The employees get the chance to communicate to their own boss in a structured way, what an effect he has on them, what they think about him."

"I try to let decisions emerge from among the group of subordinates. And there are teambuilding processes going on, for sure. It's not satisfactory that everyone only defends his own opinion, you have to take a few steps to reach the others."

8.2.3 The Meaning of Participative Management

Instrumental view. The German interview data suggest that participation is an integral part of managerial decision-making. Furthermore, participative management is embedded in the broader concept of optimising work and management. A series of assumptions guide the preference for participative management. Firstly, consensus orientation is considered strength rather than weakness.

"A manager who really strives for consensus is not a softy."

Secondly, participative management is viewed as a necessity rather than a choice. In other words, interviewees assumed that participative management leads to effective decision-making and, in a broader sense, to economic success of the organisation.

"I believe participation is possible everywhere. I mean, you have to do it everywhere."

"If I managed the IT sector of this company without any participation, then that's impossible, I would absolutely fail."

"And I also believe that generally speaking participation is a competitive advantage for a company."

"Non-participative people, whom I've got to know in the twelve years I've worked here, were never successful in the long run."

Thirdly, there is the assumption that increased complexity in the workplace can best be managed by subordinate involvement, in particular in areas in which the subordinates are specialists. Furthermore, the increasingly dynamic business environment frequently forces organisational strategies and goals to be adjusted and redefined, and participative management is seen as a way to master such challenges.

"A very high degree of specialisation. [...] If you want to make correct decisions in here, then you can only do it by asking others their opinion because you do not have all this detailed knowledge yourself."

"One can only limit the risk of wrong decisions if one gathers at least some, or even better, many views."

"Nowadays we follow a totally different approach, we integrate people. We are no longer interested in hundred-percent solutions, which take, let's say, six months or a year, but we want eighty-percent solutions within a couple of weeks. And this is- this only works with a high level of participation."

The last of the above quotes implies that participative decision-making does not necessarily yield perfect solutions, but results in compromises that represent the best solution possible within the context of differing goals. The following quote by another German manager also reflects this readiness for compromise.

"This means that each functional area has to and should bring in their competency, first of all during the first phase, when everyone defines his standpoint. And then you have to look for a compromise that everyone can accept."

Participative management has both effectiveness-related and motivational aspects. Regarding motivation, participative management is perceived to increase the commitment level of subordinates. With regard to the economic aspects, participative management is considered a potential success factor for the organisation, yet only when several conditions are met: (1) The optimal level of participative management depends on the people and on the situation. (2) All participants, managers and subordinates alike, must be trained in areas such as conflict management to be able to successfully contribute to the decision-making process. (3) All participants need to have access to relevant information. (4) Managers should consider the fact that any decision-making process that includes participation is time-consuming and consequently, they should weigh participation against alternative approaches.

In summary, the German data reflect an instrumental view of participative management, meaning that participative management is used as a managerial tool to achieve sound decisions, while at the same time motivational aspects are also taken into account. Despite the perceived benefits of participative management, interviewees agreed that participation should be used wisely and within limits, because an excessive use of meetings and group processes may paralyse the organisation.

Range of participation. The data suggest that subordinates form the primary group that participates in managerial decision-making, mainly because managers consider them valuable human capital that can effectively contribute to good decision making (see Section 8.2.5 below). Specialists such as outside consultants (see Section 8.2.6 below) may play an additional role.

Who is responsible for a decision? The data diverge on the question of who is responsible for the final decision. Some interviewees claimed that assumptions about the manager taking sole responsibility belong to the past and consequently, subordinates ought to share the responsibility whenever they are part of the decision-making process.

"Participation also means that [the subordinates] are not only involved in making a decision, but they also share in the consequences. The positive as well as the negative ones."

"In the past the roles of the management team were such that the production manager, the quality manager and so on had a consulting role and the boss decided. Today, decisions are made unanimously."

Other interviewees took a more traditional stand and argued that the manager had to take responsibility, even if the decision was based on intensive consultation.

"There has to be some sort of a hierarchy in society. And a firm also needs a hierarchy. There always has to be one person who is the final decision-maker."

"Once in a while I experience situations where I say, 'Someone has to take the decision.' And most of the time it's the one in the group who is highest up in the hierarchy. Everyone kind of looks at him, and it's then really up to him."

Despite an overall explicitness found in the German management style, there seems to be no clear and commonly accepted view about final responsibility in managerial decision-making. This lack of shared understanding was also found in connection with a related phenomenon, namely when a manager approaches her or his own superior. Some interviewees argued that approaching one's superior means handing over responsibility to that person, while others assumed that approaching the superior signals trust and a request for consultation, while not necessarily implying giving up responsibility. The following two quotes reflect the two opposing views.

"In Germany, I think, if I get my superior involved in a decision-making situation, then I kind of assume that he will make the decision, or at least it would be all right with me if he did."

"I need him as a sort of sparring partner. Simply to hear his opinion when I come up with new ideas or so. That's what I use my boss for."

8.2.4 The Role of the Manager

According to the interview data, the German managerial role is strongly defined by goal orientation. Furthermore it is expected that the manager serves as a role model and a motivator, as well as provides and supports team orientation and communication within the organisation.

Goal orientation. A manager should pursue the defined goals and make unpopular decisions, if necessary. At the same time, s/he should be flexible enough to make required goal adjustments and must be able to resolve goal conflicts.

Role model. A manager should serve as a role model for subordinates and represent certain moral values, such as integrity and trustworthiness. These values help install subordinates' trust in their manager, which, in turn, increases their readiness to take part in the pursuit of the defined goals.

Intrinsic motivation. The manager is responsible for motivating subordinates, yet not through such extrinsic methods as pay increases. Rather, the manager should focus more on intrinsic motivation, by utilising teamwork and participation. An additional motivational factor seems to be the possibility for subordinates to work independently. In such cases, the manager's role includes receiving and reacting to progress reports and being available for consultation. Interviewees described such an approach as "hands-off management" and "managing on a long leash".

Team orientation. Frequently, participation takes place in existing teams. Teamwork is assumed to ensure a high level of motivation among team members, which in turn, leads to high quality work. In this sense, functioning teams are considered crucial for organisational success. The manager is responsible for team building and should possibly provide opportunities for team development (e.g. in workshops). Generally speaking, the manager should provide a framework that enables the team to work rather independently. For example, the manager could serve as the link to the rest of the organisation and ensure the availability of needed resources, but s/he should not interfere with teamwork on a daily basis.

> "I make sure that you [the team] are on the safe side. [...] I help you to get access to resources and I expect from you that you pursue certain goals, that you finish your projects on time, and that the quality of the products is all right."

Communication. Goals must be communicated and therefore, good communication skills are an important part of the managerial role.

> "It is not only my job to represent the company's interests, but also to communicate the interests, the goals."

Generally speaking, a manager should be in constant dialogue with the subordinates and also exchange ideas with her or his superior. Predefined forums, such as weekly staff meetings, allow communication to take place on a regular basis.

8.2.5 The Role of the Subordinates

Subordinates are important participants in managerial decision-making. According to the interviewees, German managers tend to consider them valuable human capital. In an increasingly complex business world, subordinates are frequently specialists in their field and therefore in an optimal position to contribute their expert opinions. The interviewed managers believe that subordinates want to and expect to provide their opinions, although subordinates' readiness to participate might vary from organisation to organisation, depending on organisational culture and profession.

"The people [here in Germany] are able to accomplish much, much more, if you just let them. You have to make intense use of this."

"For really modern managers, there is no way around [participation]. Because people strive for self-fulfilment, and one way is to be heard and involved."

„There are surely employees who do not want to get involved. They prefer to do their job and not be bothered with decision-making. But those with a higher level of education, those who have attended seminars, they suddenly insist on participation."

8.2.6 The Role of Specialists

In addition to subordinates, the interviewees also mentioned outside consultants as possible participants in decision-making. Traditionally, there has been a high reliance on specialists in the German business world. This preference experienced a particular boom in the 1990s. Today, a common point of view seems to be that consultants should serve primarily in a supporting role, whereas the final decisions should be taken among organisational members themselves.

„I believe that one should try to make progress with one's own people, with their know-how. This does not mean that I do not bring in consultants, for support."

8.3 The Enactment of Participative Management

8.3.1 Participative vs. Autocratic Decision-Making

As described above, the German interviewees have an instrumental view of participative management, looking at it mainly as a highly effective managerial tool. More often than not, participation is either an integral part of teamwork, or it takes place in other rather structured forms, such as weekly unit meetings. Most interviewees equated participative behaviour with consultation, whereas some interviewees went even further and named delegation as a specific form of participative management.

Participative decision-making. The interviewees considered two alternatives of participatory behaviour, namely group discussions with the whole team and one-on-one consultations with individual subordinates. One-on-one consultation was described as a sometimes better way than group discussion, because it represents a somewhat more intimate setting, in which participants are more easily ready to express their honest opinions. Group meetings were described as sometimes bearing the risk of participants hiding in the group.

Autocratic decision-making. An instrumental view of participative management implies that sometimes managers take decisions by themselves. As one interviewee put it, "an ideal compromise is not feasible in all situations." According to the interviewees, autocratic decision-making is possible and accepted by subordinates as long as the relationship with the manager is based on trust, and the autocratic decision is accompanied by *a priori* information or *ex post* explanation to the subordinates. Managers prefer autocratic decision-making, for example, if conflicting goals exist between the subordinates and their manager/organisation, if employee safety is concerned or if the functioning of the team is in danger. All three aspects are illustrated in the following quotes.

> "In certain goal conflicts the manager has to act decisively and say, 'We refrain from B, but we take good care of A.' Any hesitation would mean that self-contained subordinates decide for themselves what serves <u>them</u> best. And those who lack self-sufficiency would not know at all what to do."

> „I believe in such security questions I still decide very hierarchically. Because I have experienced subordinates to sometimes be more careless in such questions. And take a higher risk."

> "I may have top specialists, but they cannot co-operate. Then I have to take out one or two of them. And that's a management decision."

8.3.2 Participative Management Outcomes

The outcomes of participative management envisioned by the German interviewees included task-related as well as people-related aspects: High decision quality and overall economic success were mentioned together with decision commitment and increase in overall motivation.

> "I experienced situations, in which participation led to a clearly better solution in terms of quality, or in which participation helped avoid hasty and not-thought-through approaches."

> "When the others also hear the arguments, they are better able to understand the decision and they are better able to explain it to others. This is quite different from when the decision is a given and the only thing they are supposed to do is live with it."

> "I believe that people feel better when they have fought and finally reached a decision, instead of just translating into deeds what the boss has decided."

8.4 Main Situational Influence Factors

Similar to other countries, decision type and time-related issues emerged as the two main situational factors influencing the enactment of participative management. In contrast to other countries, potential or open conflict did not seriously influence the German interviewees' choice to use participation or not.

8.4.1 Decision Type

The German interviewees referred to a number of different decision types. The ones most commonly mentioned are summarised in the following paragraphs.

Task-related decisions. According to the interviewees, task-related decisions qualify well for participative management, in particular when the degree of complexity is high and subordinates are specialists and able to provide valuable input to the solution. *Unstructured and difficult* task-related problems were viewed as particularly good areas for participative management. Similarly, decisions concerning the direct *work environment* of the employees, such as organising the office space, should also be made by using participative management, or even better, by leaving the decision up to the subordinates themselves.

Exceptions. The following two types of decisions are also task-related, yet additional considerations limit the use of participative management: (1) With regard to *safety at the workplace,* some interviewees expressed the opinion that subordinates often tend to take too many risks. Therefore, it should be the responsibility of the manager to make safety decisions by her or himself. (2) In case of an obvious *conflict of interests or goals* between the manager and the subordinates, it was considered necessary for the manager to be decisive and take the decision by her or himself.

Administrative decisions. Participative management was not considered necessary for administrative decisions of a more general nature, such as buying office equipment, in particular when the problems were trivial or when formal rules left little room for flexibility anyway.

Human Resource (HR) decisions. These decisions were considered problematic for participative management. Interviewees described that it was not common in German society to discuss such issues as pay openly and in large groups. Whenever employees seek managerial consultation on personnel matters, they prefer the one-on-one discussion.

In summary, participative management seems to be mainly used in the task-related area, although with some limitations. Keeping in mind that participative management is generally viewed as a necessity in an increasingly complex world, it is understandable that unstructured and difficult task-related problems qualify particularly well for participative management. In contrast, decisions with goal conflict represent an area in which "being tough on the issue" seems to dominate managerial behaviour, in particular as goal attainment is an integral part of the managerial role. Safety decisions, also suggested to be within the discretion of the manager, might reflect managerial responsibility for the team as well as a tendency to avoid risk (compare Section 8.5.3 below).

8.4.2 Time-Related Issues

Time-related factors seem to influence the decision-making process (participative vs. autocratic) in a similarly strong way as decision type. Generally speaking, there was consensus among the interviewees that participative decision-making requires more time than decisions taken by the manager alone. Consequently, a certain amount of time for the process seems to be tolerated in view of the assumed benefits of participative management, such as better decision quality and commitment.

> "One has to know that participation takes time. The processes take so much longer compared to when you sit down by yourself and say, 'That's how I'm going to do it.' But the quality of the decision is much better, in my experience."

> "But the danger- yes, the danger is indeed that you can spend an endless amount of time."

The second quote implies that situations may occur, in which group processes drag on beyond a tolerated time frame. Other decisions may have to be taken under time pressure. For such cases, the interviewees described two alternative strategies. One strategy is to decrease the level of participation, make the decision alone and hope that the subordinates will understand the necessity of this step. An alternative strategy would be to keep the level of participation high, but to try to find a solution quickly in a final group meeting.

8.4.3 Conflict

The German interviewees described conflict as natural, in particular in connection with teamwork, and even saw it as a learning opportunity. Potential or open conflict did not seem to influence the decision-making processes they described. This finding suggests that German managers may not become more (or less) autocratic in case of conflict.

"In times when individuals are highly educated, it is only normal that people have different views and opinions. That's not necessarily negative. I even think that's useful, because you get to know other viewpoints."

Goal conflict is an exception to the tendency of German managers to not react to conflict (also compare Sections 8.2.2 and 8.4.1 above). In case of differing goals between manager and subordinates, the managerial role prescribes that the manager should ensure continual pursuit of the defined goals. In other words, the manager is ultimately responsible for goal fulfilment. If required, s/he ought to take the decisions necessary for goal pursuit autocratically.

Some of the interviewed German managers described a tendency among subordinates to expect their manager to solve conflicts for them. In such cases, the interviewees argued, the manager should decide by her or himself under which conditions it was *really* necessary to get involved in subordinate conflict. In many cases, subordinates would be capable of finding a solution among themselves. Thus, the manager should make sure that they at least try to face the conflict and find a viable solution themselves.

"The subordinates have to find their own solution. I am not their nanny."

However, in some cases such as escalating conflict, the manager must get involved and should deal with the situation openly and also try to limit the conflict to factual matters.

"I believe the readiness to deal with conflict is increasing nowadays. In the sense of, 'I recognise that there is conflict and I will get it over with.' Instead of covering it up, and either delay the decision or in the worst case not take a decision at all."

„I don't know of any manager in here who avoids conflict."

8.5 Main Society-Related Influence Factors

Among the societal and historical factors explored within the context of the qualitative study, concepts used in cross-cultural management such as power distance, uncertainty avoidance and collectivism proved to be relevant for the meaning and enactment of participative management.

8.5.1 Power Distance

Power distance relates to the degree to which members of a society expect power to be unequally shared (Hofstede, 1980a; House et al., 2004). Interviewees argued that power distance in German society is too high. Examples included concentration of power in the media and inequality between the treatment of celebrities and "normal" people. At the same time there was consensus that a certain level of power distance was necessary. The interviewees equated a total lack of power distance with communism, which they described with terms such as "wrong approach" and "failed experiment". They argued that a certain degree of power distance is good and normal and that it reflects human nature to strive for power.

> "I don't like pseudo democracy according to the motto, "We are all equal but some are more equal than others". Then I will rather accept some power distance."

> "I am not a fan of the argument that everyone is to have the same power. For the simple reason that I believe people to have differing capabilities to deal with power in a responsible way. The communist argument of equality is not realistic, in my opinion. After all I experienced it myself, and it does not work in practice. I grew up in East Germany and the only thing I can say is, these were mere ideals that are really impossible to translate into deeds."

With regard to the workplace, the interviewees seemed satisfied with the existing level of power distance. According to the interview data, this level seems to be fairly low and is best exemplified by narratives about the relationship between managers and their subordinates. For example, one interviewee described how subordinates in his organisation gave regular feedback to their managers. This process had been initiated by management and became part of a structured way of communication and learning.

8.5.2 Collectivism

Collectivism refers to the relationship between the individual and the level of collectivism that prevails in a society (Hofstede, 1980a; House et al., 2004). There was consensus among the German interviewees that the economic system in their country is based on collectivist ideas, which manifest themselves in such areas as co-determination and influential works councils:

> "Well, we have an economic system that is adjusted to the masses. Social security, everyone is equally covered. And also corporate governance, co-determination rights, especially in the mining industry, and all these things. That's quite collectivist to me."

In addition to this perception, some interviewees also argued that collectivism in the traditional form of co-determination and works council system has reached its limits, in particular in the emerging industrial sectors such as the IT sector. It was argued that some of the "old rules" aimed at protecting the workforce can even be a hindrance to the need for more flexibility and innovation in running a business.

With regard to collectivism in the workplace, the interview data suggested teamwork to be highly important. In the early stages of the data analysis, it was not entirely clear where this strong focus originated. Two possible solutions came to mind: (1) Teams represent a "natural ingredient" of a strong collectivist orientation, or (2) teams are an "instrument" supporting the focus on optimising work and management. When all data are viewed in combination, the second alternative seems to prevail. In other words, German managers likely view teams predominantly as an instrument considered useful in optimising work and management. Furthermore, teamwork provides a structured environment for participative management, which in turn provides the basis for high employee motivation.

8.5.3 Uncertainty Avoidance

Uncertainty avoidance reflects the degree to which a society relies on social norms, rules and procedures to alleviate the unpredictability of future events (Hofstede, 1980a; House et al., 2004). The data show some discrepancy in the interviewees' perceptions of the existing level of uncertainty avoidance. On the one hand, there were recurring remarks that uncertainty avoidance in German society is too high. Frequently, the interviewees referred to the vast amount of regulations and bureaucratic restrictions.

"And another rule and yet another rule and- I believe that Germans are fanatic regulators."

"We are over-regulated, and business is nothing but rules from beginning to end. I believe we would need more leeway."

On the other hand and despite these overt complaints, the data also imply that a certain degree of structure and order is valued, in society as well as in the workplace. The interviewees' examples dealt with the desire to improve work in structured ways as well as with high goal orientation. Goals can be interpreted as assuring accorded action, which in turn minimises uncertainty.

There was no reference in the data as to an abundance of formal rules in German business organisations. However, it may be concluded from the characteristics of the German industrial relations system (Section 8.6.2) that organisations do face many rules and regulations, in particular with regard to the required works council involvement. It seems possible that most of the interviewees took these rules for granted and/or did not consider them worth mentioning in the interviews. One interviewee explicitly referred to this phenomenon:

"Well, the only thing is, I need to forward the material [for example a job application] to the works council for them to look at it. That's the same in any German company that you have a works council. But I did not view this as formal rules."

With regard to participative management, it seems that the structured format of many participation initiatives (teamwork, regular staff meetings, team development training) is at least partly related to uncertainty avoidance. In other words, the enactment of participative management is characterised by an attempt to keep the level of uncertainty low.

8.6 Integration

8.6.1 Fit with the Three Quantitative Studies

The qualitative study explores the meaning and enactment of participative management. The findings allow conclusions to be drawn with respect to quantitatively oriented aspects of participative management, such as level of participation. Therefore it is valid to analyse the findings of the qualitative interview data for their fit with the results of the three quantitative studies. Is there a match with the quantitative scores of the GLOBE study, the Event management study and the Vroom/Yetton study? If not, is it possible to explain the differences based on the insights gained from the qualitative inquiry? In order to address these questions, the following paragraphs summarise and integrate the different studies' results.

Table 8.1 Quantitative Participation Scores for Germany

Scale	Participative (GLOBE)	Non-autocratic (GLOBE)	Guidance source subordinates (Event Management)	Mean level of participation (MLP) (Vroom/Yetton)
Score	5,72	6,05	34	5,29
Country position	Upper third	Upper third	Upper third	Upper third
Rank	11 of 61	5 of 61	3 of 56	3 of 13

Note: For a detailed description of the scales and country comparisons see Chapter 4.

The quantitative participation scores (Table 8.1) originate from the scales *participative* and *non-autocratic* in the GLOBE study, guidance source *subordinates* in the Event Management study and the *MLP* score in the Vroom/ Yetton study. Overall, the high level of participation found in the three quantitative studies is in line with the qualitative findings. Examples from the interview data include the frequent mentioning of task-related decision types described as qualifying for participation, statements about the important role of participation in order to succeed in an increasingly complex business environment and narratives about manager-subordinate relations. Moreover, the qualitative data illustrate some areas in which quantitative participation scores must be supplemented by additional qualitative information in order for the meaning of these data to be better understood. For example, some of the German interviewees had marked AI (autocratic strategy) in response to one of the Vroom/Yetton cases that called for the distribution of limited parking spaces to subordinates. Taken at face value, an AI response means autocratic managerial behaviour. During the interviews it turned out that most of these AI responses represented managerial suggestions for a rotating system of the scarce parking spaces. In other words, while the decision-making strategy was indeed "autocratic", i.e. made by the manager alone, it represented a fair and likely accepted approach. This assumption is supported by the qualitative finding that German subordinates tend to accept managerial decisions when the relationship with their manager is based on trust and/or when the decision is accompanied by information and explanation (compare Section 8.3.1).

Table 8.2 Scores of Hierarchy-Related Concepts for Germany

Scale	Power distance "as is"(GLOBE)	Guidance source superior (Event Management)	Guidance source own experience (Event Management)
Score	5,25	30	111
Country position	Middle third	Lower third	Upper third
Rank	29 of 61	43 of 56	4 of 56

Note: For a detailed description of the scales and country comparisons see Chapter 4.

In Chapter 4.4 it was speculated that participative management be related to concepts dealing with interactions within the organisational hierarchy, such as consultations of a manager with her or his superior. With regard to *power distance*, i.e. the (un)equal distribution of power (Table 8.2), the GLOBE data attribute Germany a medium level relative to the other sixty countries. This score is clarified by the qualitative study, as interviewees consistently argued for the necessity of a certain level of power distance. The interview data further showed that such argumentation can only be understood when the context is known. In this particular case the answer must be seen in the light of the most recent political history in Germany, namely the failure of the communist system in the former East Germany. The interviewees did not equate low power distance with equality (as common among interviewees from other countries), but with communism. Their rejection of communist ideas explains why they perceived and accepted the presence of a certain level of power distance even if it seems to contrast a half-century-long tradition of industrial democracy and participation in the workplace.

The involvement of the manager's *superior* in managerial decision-making (Table 8.2) is an example of the quantitative results providing an incomplete picture. The Event Management study suggests a rather low level of involvement by the manager's superior in Germany. In contrast, the qualitative data show that a wide range of approaches exist, ranging from "logical upward delegation" once the superior has been approached, and consultation among "equal partners", to receiving progress reports from independently working subordinates as part of regular feedback procedures.

Table 8.3 Scores of Team-Related Concepts for Germany

Scale	Collaborative team orientation (GLOBE)	Team integrator (GLOBE)	Institutional collectivism "as is" (GLOBE)
Score	5,48	5,05	3,79
Country position	Lower third	Lower third	Lower third
Rank	53 of 61	57 of 61	54 of 61

Note: For a detailed description of the scales and country comparisons see Chapter 4.

Chapter 4.4 also discussed the potential relationship between participative management and team-related concepts. Table 8.3 shows that Germany ranks low on the team-related scales of the GLOBE study, notably *collaborative team orientation* and *team integrator*. In contrast, the qualitative interview data suggest that German managers value teams highly. In most cases, teams are "natural" groupings of work colleagues, whereas cross-functional teams are seldom in use. The teams' degree of specialisation is high, allowing them to function without extensive managerial intervention. Consequently, a manager playing the active role of team integrator may not be necessary. In contrast, the manager sets the stage and only intervenes when needed, for example when the functioning of the team is in danger. A closer look at the questionnaire items comprising the quantitative scales collaborative team orientation and team integrator supports this assumption: German respondents are unlikely to respond very positively to attributes that recommend a high amount of task-related managerial involvement. Furthermore, a focus on loyalty and fraternity, as measured by some GLOBE questionnaire items, may also not fit with the instrumental view of teamwork prevailing among German managers.

Another quantitative result depicted in Table 8.3 also requires further explanation: The German GLOBE score for *institutional collectivism* is very low compared to many other countries and it seemingly contradicts the high level of industrial democracy described in Section 8.6.2 and stressed by the German interviewees. A closer look at the quantitative instruments reveals that the GLOBE questionnaire contains very general items, such as "the economic system in this country is designed to maximise individual interests vs. collective interests." Such items might be difficult to respond to. Furthermore, the questionnaire items do not directly relate to business practice. It seems at least possible that different respondents had different aspects of collectivism in mind when answering the GLOBE questionnaire. The qualitative interviews, in contrast, focused on examples and personal experiences within the context of participative management. Thus, while the questionnaire looks at quite abstract concepts, the interviewed managers expanded on rather concrete phenomena. This divergence in methodological focus might account for the difference between the quantitative GLOBE results and the qualitative interview data.

Table 8.4 Scores of Uncertainty-Related Concepts for Germany

Scale	Uncertainty avoidance "as is" (GLOBE)	Guidance source formal rules (Event Management)	Guidance source unwritten rules (Event Management)
Score	5,22	2	-29
Country position	Upper third	Lower third	Lower third
Rank	4 of 61	47 of 56	48 of 56

Note: For a detailed description of the scales and country comparisons see Chapter 4.

Uncertainty avoidance and dealing with rules provided yet another area of discussion in Chapter 4.4. It was speculated that these factors likely have an impact on the format of participative management. The quantitative results of the GLOBE study indicate a high level of societal *uncertainty avoidance* (Table 8.4), implying that many social norms and regulations are in place to reduce the unpredictability of future events. In contrast to the GLOBE study, the Event Management study reports a weak role of *formal rules* as well as *unwritten rules* as guidance sources for German managers (Table 8.4). The qualitative findings suggest that the results of the two quantitative studies may not contradict each other. Firstly, similar to the GLOBE study, the qualitative study also found a rather high level of uncertainty avoidance, which seems to be related to a general preference for order by way of goal orientation and structured formats for participation and learning initiatives. Secondly, the German industrial relations system is undoubtedly responsible for a number of organisational rules, for example with regard to the information, consultation and co-determination rights of the works councils. However, it is possible that the managers, when filling out the Event Management questionnaire and also when giving the interviews, did not explicitly refer to these regulations. They might have become a given fact of daily life. As one interviewee stated, "That's the same in any German company that you have a works council. But I did not view that as formal rules" (see

Section 8.5.3 above). Consequently, the Event Management data may suggest a weaker reliance on organisational rules in Germany than a neutral outsider would observe.

8.6.2 Fit with the German System of Industrial Relations

One of the qualitative study's goals concerns the evaluation of the relationship between the emerging country-specific models of participative management on the one hand and the country-specific systems of *de jure* participation and industrial relations on the other hand. *De jure* participation means the codified rights of employees and their representatives to participate in decision-making processes at the country, sectoral and organisational level. The term industrial relations covers the various areas of interaction between employer and employee at these three levels, including collective bargaining, employee representation on supervisory boards and works councils. In most countries, *de jure* participation and industrial relations overlap because at least some parts of the processes of industrial relations are codified in law or in other written agreements. The following paragraphs outline the German model, followed by an analysis of its fit with the findings of the qualitative study.

The degree of industrial democracy in Germany is high (Ronen, 1986). Two factors have contributed to this development. Firstly, collective bargaining takes place between well-organised unions and employers' associations. Secondly, there is a long tradition of worker participation at the company level by way of statutory regulations (IDE, 1981, p. 13). A similar evaluation comes from Jacobi, Keller and Müller-Jentsch (1992). These authors list four distinguishing principles of the German system of industrial relations. It is (1) legally binding and extensively juridified, (2) is highly centralised, (3) has a dual structure of interest representation, and (4) the institutions of collective representation encompass their constituents to a high degree. Consequently, wage levels and employment rights are relatively equal among companies of even very differing size (Lane, 1997).

German employees are represented by sector-based unions. Union density amounts to close to thirty percent (Carley, 2002), and about seventy percent of companies are represented by employers' organisations (Traxler, 2000). The latter figure refers to the western part of Germany. Unions and employer organisations have close co-operative relations (Carley (2002). As a consequence, collective bargaining is notably strong (Mills, 1978). The dominant level of bargaining is the sectoral level. Historically, the number of companies and employees covered by sectoral agreements was very high. However, there has been a shift toward company agreements in recent years. In 2001, the proportion of employees covered by sectoral agreements was 63 percent in the western part of the country and 44 percent in the eastern part. Moreover, a considerably large number of companies with no collective agreement use existing sectoral agreements as a point of reference for determining pay and working conditions (Eironline, 2002b). In 2002, the German Ministry of Economics and Labour registered more than 32.000 collective agreements between unions and employers' associations and about 24.500 company agreements between unions and individual employers (Eironline, 2002b).

Co-determination in German enterprises is characterised by a two-tiered board structure: The supervisory board determines corporate policies and initiates major strategic decisions, such as mergers or plant closures, whereas the management board actually runs the enterprise. Co-determination in Germany is based on three statutes for different sectors and company sizes. Firstly, the 1951 Coal, Iron and Steel Industry Co-Determination Act (Montan-Mitbestimmungsgesetz) governs board representation in the coal, iron and steel sector. This most extensive form of co-determination is called "parity co-determination", as half of the members of the supervisory board are employee representatives, while the employer side forms the other half. There is one additional board member, who is needed to act as a casting vote. This person must be elected by the shareholders, following a proposal of the majority of both parties on the supervisory board. In addition to the supervisory board, there is also employee representation on the management board. The so-called labour director, who is responsible for personnel matters, may not be elected against the majority vote of the employee side on the supervisory board (Emire, 2003). Secondly, the Works Constitution Act of 1952 (Betriebsverfassungsgesetz) covers companies with between 500 and 1.999 employees. Employee representatives occupy one third of seats on the supervisory board (Emire, 2003). Thirdly, the 1976 Co-Determination Act (Mitbestimmungsgesetz) covers companies employing 2.000 or more employees. The supervisory board of these large companies has to consist of 50 percent employee representatives. However, there is an option for the employer side to overrule the representatives of the workforce in cases of deadlock (Emire, 2003).

Germany has a statutory and legally binding works council system that dates back as far as the 1920 Works Councils Act (Betriebsrätegesetz). Historically, works council type bodies have existed in Germany for more than a century, established initially by Bismarck as part of his program of paternalistic social welfare (Müller-Jentsch, 1995). Today's works councils, which can be established by the employees of companies with a workforce of five or more, are directly elected by the employees and have information, consultation and co-determination rights. Works councils exist in close to sixty percent of German workplaces (Gill & Krieger, 2000) and are considered highly valuable institutions:

"German works councils [...] are supported by all industrial relations parties and are generally regarded as institutions promoting social integration, productive efficiency and employee influence."(Knudsen, 1995, p. 17)

The findings of the qualitative study fit well with the democratic and formalised structure of the German industrial relations system. The above description of the system reflects the necessity to enable effective co-operation between employers and employees, while at the same time keeping uncertainty at a minimum level. Similarly, a study by Eberwein and Tholen (1993) confirmed that German managers share a positive attitude toward unions and works councils and view them as a stabilising factor for the German economy.

8.6.3 Fit with the Existing Literature

The qualitative study suggests that German managers consider participation to be an integral part of managerial decision-making. Participative management is viewed from an instrumental perspective and in combination with aims of optimising work and management. The preference for participative management found in the qualitative data corresponds with the results of the three quantitative studies and the high level of industrial democracy. Other studies also confirmed that participative management prevails in Germany (e.g. Hampden-Turner & Trompenaars, 1993; Gannon et al., 1994; Lawrence, 1994; Calori, Steele & Yoneyama, 1995).

It is likely that the combination of relatively low power distance and the pervasive nature of the institutional frameworks for participation accounts for this tendency (Szabo, 2004). Values and norms that fit with relatively low power distance seem to provide the reason for German managers to include their subordinates in decision-making. Without such an "implicit cultural agreement" between managers and subordinates, participative management would not be feasible at all. However, the power distance level alone does not seem to fully explain the strong preference for participative management. Some additional factors would appear to be instrumental. History might provide a good starting point for a possible explanation. After World War II, laws governing co-determination were introduced to ensure peaceful future relations between "capital" and "labour" (Szabo et al., 2001). As a result, today's German managers and subordinates alike might be in favour of high participation because they have learned to appreciate its value throughout decades of organisational practice.

This hypothesis may help explain why earlier cross-cultural studies into managerial behaviour found German managers to be less participative than more recent inquiries suggest. For example, Haire, Ghiselli and Porter (1966) reported that the attitudes of German managers toward participation were slightly negative, in contrast to the attitudes of managers from countries such as Denmark, Belgium, the USA or Japan. Similarly, a comparison of British and West German managerial roles by Child and Kieser (1979) showed organisational decision-making in Germany to be more centralised at the top than in Britain. One might hypothesise that the low level of participation found in the two earlier studies and the higher level of participation presented by more recent research represents a progression toward an increased use of participation. This view would fit with the assumption that German managers have gone through a decade-long "participation training" prescribed by institutional arrangements.

However, the explanation does not seem to be so straightforward. In a recent study, Suutari (1996b) reported that Finnish managers perceived their German counterparts as comparatively lower on decision participation and delegation than Finnish managers. This finding is surprising, as it contradicts the findings of the qualitative study and also the participation scores of the three quantitative studies. A possible explanation for the difference can be found in the methodology: The qualitative study as well as in the three quantitative studies are based on managerial self descriptions, whereas the study presented by Suutari builds on perceptions by Finnish managers of their international counterparts. These outside images are likely to differ from how people in a culture see themselves. There were similar accounts of this kind in the data of the qualitative study itself: Confronted with the quantitative results of all five countries, a number of non-German interviewees expressed surprise and disbelief about the German results, as the following quotes illustrate:

"I thought the Germans would be much lower [on the mean level of participation score]. I thought the distance between Sweden and Germany was going to be much larger." (Quote by a Swedish manager)

"The [mean level of participation] score for Germany does not make sense at all. I always thought that it is very, very hierarchical and [that German managers] always make decisions by themselves." (Quote by a Finnish manager)

It is likely that the formality of interpersonal relations and the degree of formalisation with regard to instructions, tasks and rights (Glunk, Wilderom & Ogilvie, 1996), the preference for rules (Hampden-Turner & Trompenaars, 1993; Trompenaars, 1993) and the lack of spontaneity (Hunt, 2002) account at least in part for this stereotype. In other words, formality might have been mistaken for autocratic managerial behaviour.

However, there is yet another perspective on the level of participation of German managers. In a longitudinal study incorporating recent Vroom/ Yetton data, Reber and his colleagues speculated about the possible dawn of a "social ice-age" in the behaviour of German (and Austrian) managers (Reber, Auer-Rizzi & Szabo, 2004; Auer-Rizzi, Reber & Szabo, 2005). These authors noticed a decrease in the mean level of participation starting with the year 2000. Such a drop could either be linked to the overall economic situation, but could also indicate the starting point of a change in attitude toward less participation.

What can we conclude from these diverging findings? It becomes obvious that there is not such a clear and stable pattern of participative management in Germany as it can be found in countries like Sweden, where participation is rooted in the core values of equality and fairness (Chapter 10). In contrast, participative management in Germany seems to be contingent on external factors, including practice over time, institutional embeddedness and the general economic situation. These factors fit with the instrumental view on participative management presented by the qualitative study. However, it should also be noted that there were no hints at all in the qualitative data suggesting that participative management could be a mere fad. In contrast, participative management emerged as an important managerial instrument that has proven useful over time and will not be dropped easily.

Apart from the level of participation, the qualitative study reported a number of quite specific findings, which have also been discussed in other literature. The following paragraphs present some of the concepts that emerged from the qualitative study as important elements of the German model of participative management.

Optimising work and management. In the qualitative study this concept emerged as the guiding principle relevant for understanding the meaning of participative management in Germany. It is paralleled in the management literature by descriptions of the legitimacy of feedback (Avery et al., 1999), the striving for performance improvement (Glunk, Wilderom & Ogilvie, 1996) and perceptions of the importance of continuous learning (Wächter & Stengelhofen, 1992).

Technical and professional competence. The qualitative data repeatedly stressed the high skills of German employees. This finding is in line with the literature's consensus about the high level of knowledge and expertise in Germany (e.g. Warner & Campbell, 1993; Lawrence, 1994; Glunk, Wilderom & Ogilvie, 1996; Liberman Yaconi, 2001). The German focus on knowledge and expertise seemingly dates back to the "Handwerk tradition of the autonomous craft worker" (Warner & Campbell, 1993, p. 90; see also Kieser, 1988). Today's *apprenticeship system* is still rooted in this craft tradition and comprises "all officially recognised professions in industry, commerce and the crafts" (Blum, 1994, p. 50). The apprenticeship system represents a dual education model that combines practical training on the job and theoretical education (Wächter & Stengelhofen, 1992; Marr, 2000) and is "regarded as being among the best in Europe" (Schneider & Littrell, 2003, p. 132). Pupils are taught skillsets (Randlesome, 2000) which can be easily transferred to the actual work situation. Such an approach parallels Mintzberg's (1983b) standardisation of skills. About seventy percent of all German industrial workers have received this type of education (Glunk, Wilderom & Ogilivie, 1996). Additional factors also account for the high level of competence among German managers and workers. For example, there is a strong traditional link between academia and practice. As early as 1899, Germany's technical universities attained equal status with the traditional universities, which led to a strong focus on application of science and engineering (Lane, 1997). Furthermore, German businesses tend to heavily invest in HRM, mainly in the form of continuous education (Glunk, Wilderom & Ogilvie, 1996). This focus on education includes workers and management alike (Heller & Wilpert, 1997), and employee and employer associations play a particularly vital role in assuring training programs.

The consequences of the high competence level of the German workforce are observable in several areas: Firstly, empowerment is possible and practised (Zander, 1997). Warner and Campbell (1993, p. 99) characterised the German mode of working and managing as "independence within agreed parameters". These statements fit with the findings of the qualitative study, in which hands-off management emerged as a way to motivate subordinates. Secondly and with regard to the managerial role, explicit motivation of subordinates may have limited importance (Hunt, 2002). As Schneider and Littrell (2003, p. 135) put it, German workers "do not necessarily need a manager to 'motivate' them". Again, these statements are in line with the findings of the qualitative study, which mentioned motivation predominantly in the context of providing the appropriate task environment (independent work and possibility for participation), and not so much in the context of direct managerial activities such as praise or performance-related incentives. Thirdly, it follows for the macro-economic level that the German workforce is characterised by comparatively high labour costs, and the German industry is competitive on quality rather than price (Warner & Campbell, 1993).

Goal orientation. With regard to the strong goal orientation emerging from the qualitative data, Kakabadse and Myers (1996) attested German management a "goal attainment philosophy" (p. 194) with a specific emphasis on clarity, consistency and discipline. Goal orientation is also an important aspect of managerial leadership definitions formulated by German academics (e.g. Wunderer & Grunwald, 1980). Similarly, role clarity was discussed by a number of researchers as a factor particularly preferred in the German business world (e.g. Avery et al., 1999).

Uncertainty avoidance. The qualitative study suggests that clarity and consistency might offer ways to reduce uncertainty. Risk aversion, explicitness and rule-driven behaviour of the Germans were also discussed by several other authors (e.g. Trompenaars, 1993; Child & Kieser, 1979; Martin, 2001; Hunt, 2002; Schneider & Littrell, 2003). The characterisation of Germany as a low-context society (Hall, 1976; Hall & Hall, 1990) is linked to these observations. Gannon and his colleagues used the metaphor of the symphonic orchestra to explain German culture:

> "There is a clear parallel between the German passion for order and the predictability and regularity of the symphony. In both societal rules and musical expression, there is a demand for regular beat and predictable form, coupled with a creative but somewhat bridled spirit. There is formality to German society that is eloquently expressed in the symphony. Chronometer-like timing, precision, conformity and an understanding of the individual's contribution to the greater score underlie both music and organisational activities." (Gannon et al., 1994, p. 78)

Conflict. The qualitative study found a specific attitude toward conflict, namely taking it as a normal aspect of work life. Decades of practice in participative behaviour could explain this finding. Additionally, the German model of co-determination has likely provided a stage to practice conflict resolution in a constructive way. Thus, role models for participation and conflict management „made in Germany" exist for managers and subordinates alike (Szabo, 2004). Similarly, Marr (2000, p. 230) attested German managers a strength in the area of conflict resolution within a "democratic culture of discussion". Finally, Brodbeck and his colleagues concluded:

> "[I]nterpersonal relations are straightforward and stern. It seems that conflict and controversy are built into the German societal culture." (Brodbeck, Frese & Javidan, 2002, p. 16)

Chapter 9

Within-Country Analysis: Poland

9.1 Overview

This chapter deals with Research Question 1 and the country-specific meaning and enactment of participative management in Poland. It describes the findings emerging from the analysis of the qualitative interviews conducted with six Polish managers. The model of participative management summarised in Figure 9.1 pertains to repeated data patterns. The interview material also contained person-specific data, which have been excluded from this chapter to allow a focus on recurring patterns of managerial thinking and behaviour. For further information about methodology see the above chapters: Chapter 5.2 describes the process of data collection, whereas Chapter 5.3 treats the qualitative data analysis using elements of grounded theory methodology. In Figure 9.1, the two broad aspects of participative management under study, namely meaning and enactment, are depicted in the shaded boxes. Other concepts related to participative management are represented in the white boxes. Arrows show relationships between the concepts, as they emerged from the data.

Figure 9.1 shows that the Polish meaning of participative management is influenced by the value of *economic efficiency* and embedded in the broader concept of *organisational survival and prosperity*. According to the interview data, Polish managers share an instrumental view of participative management. They consider using participation only in situations, in which it clearly entails economic benefits. In many cases participation is reduced to the manager collecting necessary information from subordinates. Rarely does participation include consultation or joint decision-making. The roles ascribed to *managers* and *subordinates* support this interpretation of participative management. Societal culture dimensions such as power distance and uncertainty avoidance (compare Chapter 2.2.3.1) play an additional role in shaping the meaning of participative management. *Power distance* refers to the degree to which members of a society expect power to be unequally shared. In this context, the former communist system is remembered as being highly autocratic and it seems to have left its imprint on today's management. Consequently, autocratic decision-making is no rarity among Polish managers. *Uncertainty avoidance* reflects the degree to which a society

Figure 9.1 The Polish Model of Participative Management

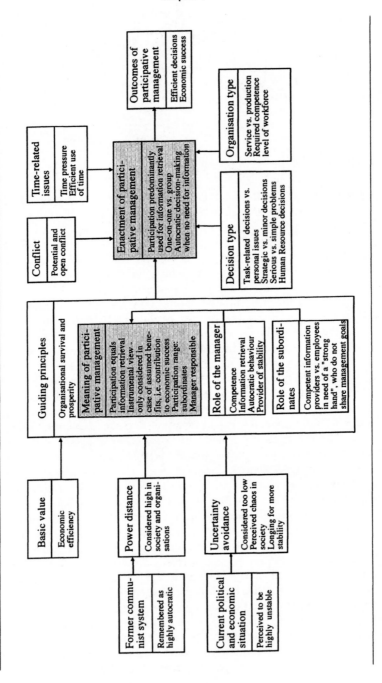

relies on social norms and procedures to alleviate the unpredictability of future events. According to the data, the current political and economic situation is not supportive of the preferred high level of stability. In this regard, Polish managers are ascribed the role of stability providers ensuring the economic success of their organisation.

The enactment of participative management is predominantly affected by *decision type, organisation type, time-related issues* and *conflict*. The *outcomes* of participative management envisioned by the Polish interviewees focus on criteria related to economic efficiency. Motivational effects of participation do not play a major role.

The following sections describe all concepts depicted in Figure 9.1 in more detail, including original quotes by the interview partners.

9.2 The Meaning of Participative Management in Context

9.2.1 Basic Value: Economic Efficiency

Within the context of participative management, economic efficiency emerged from the interviews as the one most frequently occurring value. The following three quotes represent a small selection from a number of similar statements.

"First of all a manager should focus on results."

"There are two things that count the most when there is competition: management of time and finances. In previous times, the [people here in the company] never worried about work, they always had some work to do. But nowadays there are more firms like us. This means more competition. [The people here] are not used to compete, so I am here to teach them how to compete, and to teach them time and financial management."

"The boss can allow himself to be more autocratic sometimes, just to achieve more."

The Polish management style, as it emerged from the data, is driven by an extreme focus on organisational survival and prosperity, which in turn directly influences the meaning and enactment of participative management. The sections below present further efficiency-related quotes pertaining to such specific concepts as the role of the manager, conflict or time-related issues.

9.2.2 Guiding Principles: Organisational Survival and Prosperity

Polish society and organisations have undergone major changes since the fall of the communist system at the end of the 1980s. The country and its population have faced the introduction of capitalism, which means vast new opportunities, but also drastic changes in the legal and business environment. These developments are reflected in the interview sample since a number of the interviewees work for organisations that have changed radically in recent years. At the time of the interviews, some of these organisations had recently been privatised, others were in the midst of a privatisation process and yet others were scheduled for privatisation in the near future. Both start-up companies and organisations that are faced with competition for the first time are represented in the study.

According to the interviewees, many of the changes in the legal and business environment are hard to understand and follow. In order to ensure organisational survival and prosperity Polish managers focus on economic efficiency. In the interviews, frequent references were made to the desire or need to be successful in economic terms. These references were made *explicitly*, for example when the interviewees talked about the pressure to succeed, or judged outstanding business leaders by the economic standing of their firms (see Section 9.2.4). However, they also made *implicit* references to organisational success, for example when they showed a high level of concern for a necessary increase in the effectiveness of internal processes.

"The main goal is to succeed, to achieve a success. With that in mind, we should be able to overcome all troubles."

"A good integration of the team is one of the important things to achieve success. If someone can integrate a team, they will be more successful."

9.2.3 The Meaning of Participative Management

Information retrieval. The interview data suggest an instrumental view of participative management, which implies that participative management is utilised as a result of rational considerations as opposed to occurring "naturally". Participation seems to be restricted to decision-making processes in which the outcome can be evaluated in economic terms.

Information is the key factor in the managerial decision of whether to use participation or not. If a manager has all relevant information in order to make the decision alone, s/he will usually decide to do so. A participatory decision-making process is likely to be initiated only if the manager lacks relevant information and if s/he assumes that the subordinates can provide the required information. In other words, participative management is strongly linked to the concept of information retrieval, as is illustrated by the following quotes:

> "If we have to implement a new plan, step by step, it is always good to get some information from the subordinates."

> "Participation is a possibility to take part in a decision, according to the situation, when there is a need of information, to provide information, and then to find a solution."

> "If a technical problem appears, I certainly need the knowledge of my specialists. And this is a good field for participation."

Range of participation. In the majority of the examples described by the interviewees, participation concerns the subordinates (see Section 9.2.5 below). However, in the context of gathering information some interviewees also mentioned specialists outside the unit or organisation, as well as the manager's superior (see Section 9.2.4 below).

Who is responsible for a decision? The emerging picture of participative management essentially being equal to information retrieval entails the fact that subordinate involvement is limited to the initial stages of the decision-making process, whereas the final decision is usually made by the manager alone. One interviewee described the process as follows:

> "Subordinates give their conclusions, they give their arguments, […] but the manager makes the decision."

9.2.4 The Role of the Manager

Competence. The interview data suggest that Polish managers are expected be experts in their fields. The interviewees described themselves as trying to be up-to-date with recent developments (see first quote below). At the same time, the interviewees also seemed to value their own superiors for their factual competence. Repeated references were made to consultations by managers with their own superiors to discuss work-specific problems (see second quote below).

> "I'm trying to be on top- I mean I want to know what is going on in the industry, so that's why I participate in different kinds of conferences, and I also read a lot of magazines and newspapers. I think I know what is going on."

> "In a small company like ours, my boss' knowledge is of course large about every aspect of the firm."

The manager's high level of expertise is coupled with a wide range of managerial responsibility. The interviewees described subordinates as being rather dependent on their superiors, and in this description they included themselves in their relation to their own superior or to the committee/board they reported to. In other words, the influence organisational members can exercise on decisions seems to be directly related to their rank in the hierarchy.

"My 'boss' is a committee. They have a big influence."

"Often, I have to inform my boss and to discuss my decision with him because he likes to know everything. I think this is neither good nor necessary."

"Every month I have a kind of presentation to the board. [...] Every month I must present something new."

Information. As suggested in Section 9.2.3, participation plays a role when managers lack information relevant for decision-making. In such cases, participative management is used as a tool to extend the knowledge base of the manager. One interviewee explained that he could theoretically look up the missing information personally, but that this option would be too time-consuming and thus highly inefficient.

Autocratic behaviour. Given the instrumental view of participative management, the expert role of the manager as well as the strong reference to efficiency and economic success, it is not surprising that subordinates expect and tolerate a certain degree of autocratic managerial behaviour.

"A boss may just <u>tell</u> what people must do, and this can also bring success."

"I think a boss should be a bit autocratic. I think that people must feel that he always has his own opinions, and being autocratic helps a little. He must go his own way and he must be himself all the time."

Provider of Stability. Subordinates do not necessarily prefer autocratic behaviour, but they accept it, at least as long as it leads to success. A successful manager is one who contributes to an economically successful organisation, which in turn minimises the risk of unemployment and thus provides the individual employee with at least some degree of stability in a highly unstable world. The reference to economic success and stability is illustrated by the following quotes.

"He was an awful man, an awful person, but as a boss I could not say a word. [...] He was respected, oh yes, because he succeeded. I think it works like this."

"Sometimes, if [a manager] is autocratic, [the workforce] might let him be autocratic, as long as he takes care of the safety needs or the basis needs of the workers."

Whether the acceptance of autocratic managerial behaviour mainly stems from subordinates' considerations with regard to success and stability or if it has deeper roots in the country's culture and history is discussed in Section 9.6.3 below. At this point of the analysis, it can be concluded from the data that Polish managers are expected to be more autocratic than their counterparts in many other European countries and that they are inclined to act in accordance with these expectations. However, this does not mean that subordinates' tolerance of autocratic managerial behaviour is unlimited. When a manager fails to be successful for an extended period of time, subordinates will no longer tolerate her or his autocratic management style.

In summary, the Polish managerial role is defined by the characteristics of competence, information retrieval, autocratic behaviour and providing stability. These characteristics also emerged to a certain degree when the interviewees were specifically asked about their personal image of an outstanding manager. In addition to characteristics such as charisma, expertise, innovation, diplomacy and good interpersonal skills, the interviewees also envisioned outstanding managers to be highly competent, efficient and successful in economic terms.

"A very good manager has to have experience, and he has to be in contact with the subordinates. He himself has the general knowledge, but his people could bring him the more detailed information."

"The basis [for outstanding management] is the ability to use the knowledge of other people. The ability to notice the knowledge of others."

(Researcher: "What would be the most important features of an outstanding manager?") "I must see what the company looks like. Everything, how it looks, what he created in other words. [...] So, then I know that he is a good boss. Competence is the other thing, because in lots of situations people are talking about things they have no idea of. [...] I think a boss should know every field of the company's activity."

9.2.5 The Role of the Subordinates

The increasingly complex business environment faced by Polish organisations leads to a demand for employees who are experts in such areas as marketing, finance or computer science. Increasingly, competent employees serve as information sources for managerial decision-making. In the following quote an interviewee refers to his two expert subordinates, one with an economic and the other with a technical background.

"So, the guy who is a technician, he prepares a technical overview, he explains what this technology can do. And the other guy, he goes and looks for information on the market. His responsibility is to answer to me and to my boss, if there is a market for our products and services."

The data suggest that the interviewed managers respect their competent subordinates and also that they are dependent on them to a certain degree. However, this finding does not fully reflect the managers' general attitude toward subordinates: The interviewees agreed that subordinates need a "strong hand". This assumption fits with the above-described role of the manager and with the tendency to exercise autocratic behaviour (Section 9.2.4). To explain the "strong-hand approach", the interviewees argued that subordinates often do not share managerial goals and that they pursue private rather than organisational interests.

"It is important to be a bit autocratic, because in my experience, if a boss is absolutely non-autocratic, subordinates do what they want, and there is kind of a chaos."

Parallel to the "strong hand" approach and the focus on information retrieval and economic efficiency, the data suggest that at least part of the Polish managers show little concern for the emotional wellbeing of their subordinates. In other words, by focussing strongly on economic issues managers seem to disregard the fact that subordinates are human beings with needs, wishes and lives outside the organisation. The following two transcript segments illustrate the two contrasting positions: The first quote represents a managerial view dominated by economic thinking and neglecting the human side of management. The second quote is an example that shows a manager who considers subordinates to be more than "a number of cogs in the machine."

"I don't like the unions. [...] I had a quite bad experience with the court, not using some formal rules toward subordinates about how to pay money. Everything's got rules nowadays and that is why I got in conflict with these trade unions."

"Sometimes it is important to hold back emotions, but in a situation when someone got human problems, I don't just think about the job. Then the solution is to treat them as human beings."

In accordance with the differences in their general attitude toward subordinates, the interviewees did not place equal levels of importance on maintaining good relations with their subordinates: Some interviewees did not mention the relevance of good relations at all. However, one interviewee argued that good relations with his subordinates allowed him to receive "honest information" and to become a better judge in case of conflict among them. Also, maintaining good relations seems to improve motivation among the subordinates, which, in turn, serves the overall goal of achieving economic survival and success.

"When the team is satisfied it means that they do more efficient work and produce more efficient results."

9.3 The Enactment of Participative Management

9.3.1 Participative vs. Autocratic Decision-Making

Participative decision-making. The above description of the meaning of participative management suggests that participation is mainly used as a managerial tool for information retrieval. It follows that subordinates usually take part in the process leading up to the decision rather than in the final decision itself.

"So, we make the decision together. O.K., in the end, when I have all information sampled, I make the decision alone. But with the help of my people, so that I have enough good information to make the decision."

The interviewees talked little about what the decision-making processes actually look like. Also, there were only few references in the transcripts as to the use of group settings versus one-on-one conversations. As it seems, the main factor determining the enactment of participative management is the type of problem/decision (see Section 9.4.1 below). One interviewee raised an additional point. He stated that in his experience subordinates do not give their opinions openly and honestly in a group discussion. This statement was the only one that related to communication issues and problems.

Autocratic decision-making. Consistent with the emerging meaning of participative management (Section 9.2), the interviewees agreed that Polish managers often tend to exercise autocratic behaviour, in particular when they assume that they have all the relevant information.

"There are these situations, when I am sure of something and I have a very strong feeling. It might come from my own experience or from other people's opinion, so I just say, 'We don't do it that way, we do it this way.'"

Some interviewees argued that group consultation *would* theoretically be their favourite way of decision-making. However, in reality they preferred to make decisions themselves, mainly because they perceived too many obstacles complicating the use of participation. Such obstacles include conflict among participants, time pressure and assumed inefficiency of group decision-making.

9.3.2 Participative Management Outcomes

When the interviewees talked about the outcomes of participative management, they referred predominantly to factors related to efficiency criteria.
They were hopeful that a maximum level of shared information would lead
to efficient decisions and consequently to economic success.

With regard to decision acceptance, the interviewees did not refer to a
need to *explain* an autocratic decision. As described in Section 9.2.4 above,
subordinates seem to expect and tolerate a certain degree of autocratic
managerial behaviour, in particular when they benefit from a decision. One
manager was certain of his subordinates' trust in his decisions, which he
attested to their conviction of his expertise. Another interviewee argued that
it was to his subordinates' advantage that he made certain decisions without
consulting with them. He was referring to problems causing fights among
the subordinates. An autocratic decision would solve the problem permanently and at the same time, the manager would help avoid conflict or otherwise hard feelings. He was sure that the subordinates understood and
respected his initiative even without an explicit explanation.

9.4 Main Situational Influence Factors

Apart from the perceived need for information retrieval, decision type emerged as the factor with the strongest and most consistent influence on the
interviewees' choice of whether to use participative management or not.
According to the interview data, further factors such as (potential) conflict in
the group, time-related issues or organisation type also tend to be of importance.

9.4.1 Decision Type

The interviewed Polish managers described a number of different types of
problems/decisions. The ones most commonly mentioned are summarised
in the following paragraphs.

Task-related vs. personal problems. The majority of decisions mentioned by
the interviewees concerned task-related problems. These decisions are well
suited for participation, however, only in principle. Additional attributes of
the decision (see below) specify whether a particular task-related problem
really qualifies for participative management or not. The Polish interviewees
referred to personal issues less frequently than to task-related problems.
Whenever mentioned, however, all found that personal matters should be
handled by way of one-on-one conversation.

Strategic vs. minor problems. There is a general trend in the data that relatively small problems qualify better for participation than do strategic decisions. Four interviewees explicitly mentioned strategic decisions as good examples for autocratic decision-making. With regard to minor problems, interviewees argued in favour of a group meeting in response to the parking lot scenario included in the Vroom/Yetton case set (limited parking space is to be distributed among a large number of subordinates). As one interviewee put it, "[this decision is] not so important for the whole firm." He added that he did not want to damage the good relations with his subordinate by deciding autocratically.

Serious vs. simple problems. These two categories partly overlap with strategic vs. minor problems. Similarly, interviewees argued in favour of participation in the case of simple rather than serious problems.

"It is just a simple case, it's not very serious for the company's field in general, and that's why I think they can take care of it on their own."

In contrast to simple problems, serious cases, such as decisions entailing a potential risk of high loss to the firm, should be solved by the manager her or himself, possibly in co-operation with the manager's own superior. As one manager put it:

"I think we want to make decisions for serious problems on our own. I don't know why, but I think it happens like that."

Human Resource (HR) decisions. One interviewee stated that "these are strictly autocratic decisions." This statement is consistent with other interviewees' opinions. There was not a single reference to consulting HR-related problems with subordinates in the interview transcripts. In contrast, managers repeatedly mentioned their superior as an important guidance source for decision-making. Moreover, the manager's superior was described as the person who had a major say in the final decision.

In summary, the list of decision types suggests that subordinate participation is indeed rather restricted. Generally speaking, important and risky problems as well as HR decisions are within the discretion of the manager, whereas minor and simple problems tend to be left for the subordinates to discuss.

9.4.2 Organisation Type

According to the data, organisation type also serves as a factor influencing the use of participative management. Participatory elements such as team structures are more likely to exist in service organisations than in traditional production firms. The following quote illustrates teamwork in a bank:

"It is the structure of this organisation, that there is a specific range of activities for every department, and there are teams in every department. It is important to work in teams. I am responsible for preparing offers and I am not doing this on my own, we are working as a team."

Additionally, the data suggest that participation is more likely to develop in organisations in which skilled and competent subordinates are employed.

"It depends on the type of the company. There are companies where lots of workers just do simple work, and where some very strict structures have been developed. And then there are companies with more complex management and with more qualified workers, experts in their field. In these companies participation might increase in the future."

This position is consistent with the emerging picture of participative management being used as a tool for information retrieval. The categorisation of organisations according to the competence level of their workforce seems to influence whether managers take participative management into account or not. For example, organisations with complex technology production, such as high-tech firms, or service organisations such as marketing or consulting firms depend on highly competent employees. Consequently, managers in such organisations are probably more likely to make use of participative decision-making than managers in traditional production firms or in service organisations, such as call centres, employing mainly unskilled employees.

9.4.3 Time-Related Issues

Time is another factor that somewhat influences the decision-making strategies chosen by the interviewees. According to the data, autocratic approaches are favoured when the manager is faced with time constraints, particularly when s/he possesses enough information to make the decision alone. Additionally, the interviewed managers referred to an efficient use of time, particularly when conflict is involved (compare Section 9.4.4 below).

"If a company wants to waste time to work on solutions for a longer period, well, then it's O.K. But if there is no consensus, I really prefer to make the decision fast."

The data suggest little managerial consideration for subordinates' emotional wellbeing. Whereas time-related issues are an important factor, it is quite obvious that it is not the primary role of the manager to ensure good interpersonal relations. Managers are more concerned about efficiency criteria than about their subordinates. At this point of the analysis, it seems that the likely reason for this focus is closely related to the emphasis on the manager as an expert and as a provider of economic stability.

9.4.4 Conflict

The data suggest that Polish managers view potential and open conflict through the lenses of efficiency criteria. The interviewees considered conflict an obstacle to good and fast problem solving, which calls for autocratic behaviour in response.

> "Sometimes it is necessary to be autocratic, especially when there is no chance for consensus."

The interviewed managers equated autocratic behaviour with efficient problem solving and seem to share the assumption that their subordinates *expect* them to solve conflicts in an autocratic manner.

> "They do not like to have an argument. They will instinctively think, 'Well, there is a problem, the manager must take care of it, he must tell us that we should do this or that.'"

In contrast to the autocratic approach to conflict resolution, two interviewees considered group meetings to be a good strategy for dealing with conflict. A group meeting could serve discussion purposes, with all participants being allowed to give their opinions. In this way, the manager might be able to obtain additional information, and the opponents could "let off steam." Apart from allowing subordinates to "let off steam", the interviewees did not refer to any managerial activities that aimed at taking the emotional side of a conflict into account. For example, they did not mention attempting to reduce subordinates' hard feelings or frustration. The two interviewees agreed that after such meetings the final decision about how to solve the conflict should be made by the manager alone. There was also consensus that the group size determined whether conflict meetings could be effective or not. The group approach was described as fitting for small groups, whereas an autocratic conflict solution seemed more appropriate for larger groups.

9.5 Main Society-Related Influence Factors

As analysed above, the interviewees' portrayal of Polish managers shows them as rather autocratic and restricted to playing a specific role, which incorporates the provision of economic stability. Both autocratic behaviour and stability provision seem to be grounded in Polish societal and historic factors, and are also reflected in the concepts of power distance and uncertainty avoidance known from cross-cultural management literature.

9.5.1 Power Distance

Power distance relates to the degree to which members of a society expect power to be unequally shared (Hofstede, 1980a; House et al., 2004). The interview data suggest a high level of power distance in Polish society. According to the interviewees, the former communist system has left its imprint on the relationship between superiors and subordinates. Autocratic managerial behaviour prevailed in the communist era, and it still dominates manager-subordinate relations in today's Polish organisations.

> "Maybe it is the influence of the previous communist system. We need some time to develop democracy. In many Polish institutions, many positions are still held by people who were managers in the previous communist system. We need time to change."

> "The Polish mentality is like that, we are accustomed to centralised decision-making, and well, it is not changing so fast."

One of the interviewed managers argued that it would be easier for managers to initiate participation if the country's overall economic situation were better. Another manager reasoned that today, most of the knowledge and expertise lies with the managers, while in the future, employees would be more knowledgeable themselves. Consequently, autocratic managerial behaviour would no longer be required in the future.

Some interviewees questioned whether the current high level of power distance relates exclusively to the former political system. One interviewee referred to the image of Polish managers, which she judged very unlikely to change:

> "A person who is a boss or a manager is a big person. Not a normal person, but some kind of god."

9.5.2 Uncertainty Avoidance

Uncertainty avoidance reflects the degree to which a society relies on social norms and procedures to alleviate the unpredictability of future events (Hofstede, 1980a; House et al., 2004). The interviewees agreed in their perception of high instability in Polish society at the present time. Their examples included the high level of unemployment, difficulties in finding employment even for university graduates, confusing legislation and too many reforms undertaken simultaneously and without sufficient preparation. These circumstances have caused the Polish to wish for more stability in society, business and private life.

"The situation in Poland, the political and the financial situation, is really unstable and this leads to great uncertainty. I am concerned myself, even a bit fearful."

"We don't even know the level of taxes we have to pay."

"We do not have stability and we are longing for it."

A successful manager can provide at least some level of stability by contributing to the economic success of the company, which directly influences the degree of stability experienced by employees. However, although stability is considered a valuable goal it also has its downside, as was recognised by one interviewee: He told the story of a newly appointed manager who had good and innovative ideas, but his colleagues were scared of possible changes and did not appreciate his input.

9.6 Integration

9.6.1 Fit with the Three Quantitative Studies

Despite the qualitative study's holistic exploration of the meaning and enactment of participative management, conclusions can also be drawn with respect to more quantitatively oriented aspects of participative management, such as level of participation. Therefore, it is valid to ask the question of whether the qualitative interview data match the results of the three quantitative studies used as the starting point for this qualitative inquiry. Is there a fit with the results of the GLOBE study, the Event management study and the Vroom/Yetton study? If not, can the detected differences be explained using the insights gained from the qualitative inquiry? Can the qualitative data provide answers to the inconsistencies found among the three quantitative studies (Chapter 4.4)? In order to address these questions, the following paragraphs summarise and integrate the various results.

With regard to the participation scores depicted in Table 9.1, namely the medium to low values on *participative* and *non-autocratic* in the GLOBE study, the low relevance of *subordinates* as guidance source in the Event Management study and the low *MLP* score in the Vroom/Yetton study, all four results fit with the picture of the meaning and enactment of participation as it emerged from the qualitative study: The use of participation is rather limited and autocratic managerial behaviour is exercised and tolerated by subordinates, at least to a certain extent.

Table 9.1 Quantitative Participation Scores for Poland

Scale	Participative (GLOBE)	Non-autocratic (GLOBE)	Guidance source subordinates (Event Management)	Mean level of participation (MLP) (Vroom/Yetton)
Score	5,28	4,79	-36	4,48
Country position	Middle third	Lower third	Lower third	Lower third
Rank	36 of 61	53 of 61	47 of 56	11 of 13

Note: For a detailed description of the scales and country comparisons see Chapter 4.

The Polish managers comprising the Vroom/Yetton sample reported the use of the AII strategy (autocratic decision-making with information retrieval) in nineteen percent of decision-making situations (compare Table 4.10). Furthermore, the CI strategy (one-on-one consultation) was used in eighteen percent and CII (group consultation) in twenty-two percent. The Polish interview data suggest that such consultation strategies as CI and CII might be motivated more by information retrieval than by consultation. In other words, "consultation" aims at providing the manager with information and not so much at discussing a problem in order to find a common solution. The interview data show that the interviewees with the highest individual CII scores talked about information retrieval more frequently and in more varying contexts than was the case for the other Polish managers in the qualitative study.

One specific finding of the Vroom/Yetton study is that Polish managers are more participative when faced with trivial problems, in contrast to high quality problems (compare "quality requirement" in Table 4.11). The interview data back up this finding: The interviewees differentiated between strategic and minor decisions and between serious and simple problems. Minor and simple problems were referred to as being suitable for participation in contrast to strategic and serious decisions.

The interview data hint at the background of such differentiation. Firstly, the Polish business and societal environment puts pressure on managers to ensure economic success. Since Poland is an individualistic rather than collectivist society, the individual manager is made responsible for decisions, and not so much the team as a whole. In conclusion, Polish managers need to be successful as individuals. This may lead to a tendency to avoid sharing decision-making and its successful outcomes with subordinates. Secondly and in addition to a high level of individualism, power distance is also fairly high in Polish society. This tendency shows in the quantitative GLOBE data (compare Table 9.2 below), in a study by Nasierowski and Mikula (1998) and also in the qualitative interview data. It follows that autocratic behaviour is not uncommon in the Polish business context. According to the interviewees, a certain degree of autocratic managerial behaviour represents competence and will power. However, Polish managers do not want to be seen as extremely autocratic, possibly because this type of behaviour is associated with the former communist system. Consequently, Polish managers face a dilemma. Their expected role can best be fulfilled using autocratic behaviour, while at the same time it is important for them to demonstrate that their decision-making style is not associated with the communist system. Varying patterns of decision-making in different contexts are the likely consequence: Managers prefer autocratic behaviour for decisions that promise success and establish a good reputation, and they are likely to base such decisions on information from subordinates. In contrast, they show participatory tendencies when dealing with comparatively unimportant internal decisions. Such decisions are less risky for the image of the successful manager. As one interviewee stated:

"If there is a trivial problem, these are the best circumstances to promote the boss as a non-autocratic person."

Table 9.2 Scores of Hierarchy-Related Concepts for Poland

Scale	Power distance "as is" (GLOBE)	Guidance source superior (Event Management)	Guidance source own experience (Event Management)
Score	5,10	65	63
Country position	Middle third	Upper third	Middle third
Rank	40 of 61	6 of 56	27 of 56

Note: For a detailed description of the scales and country comparisons see Chapter 4.

In Chapter 4.4 it was speculated that participative management be related to concepts dealing with interaction within the organisational hierarchy, such as consultation of a manager with her or his superior. The Event management data suggest that Polish managers use their *superior* (Table 9.2) as a guidance source more often than do managers from many other countries. In a study among Central and Eastern European managers, Smith et al. (2000) collected Event Management data including effectiveness ratings, i.e. they sampled whether respondents considered the guidance sources in question effective or not. With regard to the guidance source own superior, the authors found that Polish managers relied strongly on their superiors, but at the same time thought that this was not the most effective way to handle work events. The interview data confirm the strong involvement of the superior in managerial decision-making and provide possible explanations for the imbalance between reliance on the superior and the perception of this behaviour as being ineffective: The high level of *power distance* leads to a high dependency of employees, including middle managers, on their superiors. In addition to being dependent on their superiors, Polish managers also tend to consult with them, when the superiors are experts for the problem to be solved. However, in most cases the relationship is likely to be dominated by power rather than by expert relations. This power differential may dissatisfy the lower-level manager and may have resulted in the low effectiveness ratings of the Event Management study.

The Event management data further suggest that Polish managers use their *own experience* (Table 9.2) only to a moderate degree compared with their international counterparts. In contrast, the qualitative study indicates that Polish managers consider their own experience highly important for decision-making. A plausible explanation for this divergence is that the quantitative data were collected at the beginning of the transition period after the fall of communism. Possibly, the Polish respondents in the earlier research felt more insecure about the relevance of their own knowledge compared to the interviewees in the qualitative study. For the earlier respondents, the context of managerial activity was completely new, while the interviewees of the qualitative study had already gained some years of experience with the new economic reality.

Table 9.3 Scores of Team-Related Concepts for Poland

Scale	Collaborative team orientation (GLOBE)	Team integrator (GLOBE)	Institutional collectivism "as is" (GLOBE)
Score	6,03	5,55	4,53
Country position	Middle third	Middle third	Upper third
Rank	26 of 61	26 of 61	16 of 61

Note: For a detailed description of the scales and country comparisons see Chapter 4.

Chapter 4.4 also discussed the potential relationship between participative management and team-related concepts. With regard to team orientation, the GLOBE study shows that the concepts of *collaborative team orientation* and *team integrator* (Table 9.3) are of some, but not extremely high, relevance to the image of a Polish manager. The qualitative study suggests that there is no commonly shared understanding of teams and teamwork. Generally speaking, the interviewees appreciated a functioning team for its contribution to economic success. However, there were differences in the individual preferences for teamwork.

Uncertainty avoidance and dealing with rules (Table 9.4) provided yet another area of discussion in Chapter 4.4. It was speculated that these factors likely have an impact on the format of participative management. With regard to *uncertainty avoidance*, the GLOBE indices show an interesting pattern: Poland ranks low on perceived uncertainty avoidance ("as is"), while the level of preferred uncertainty avoidance ("should be") is much higher. The qualitative study provides strong support for this pattern in the two GLOBE uncertainty avoidance scores. All interviewees described the current situation as highly unstable and articulated a desire for more stability in society, business and personal life.

Table 9.4 Scores of Uncertainty-Related Concepts for Poland

Scale	Uncertainty avoidance "as is" (GLOBE)	Uncertainty avoidance "should be" (GLOBE)	Guidance source formal rules (Event Management)	Guidance source unwritten rules (Event Management)
Score	3,62	4,71	23	-53
Country position	Lower third	Middle third	Middle third	Lower third
Rank	50 of 61	30 of 61	30 of 56	55 of 56

Note: For a detailed description of the scales and country comparisons see Chapter 4.

The Event management study lists the guidance source *formal rules* at a medium level in Poland, whereas *unwritten rules* seem to play a comparatively small role. These scores are understandable given the interviewees' perceptions of instability and thus they do not contradict the findings of the qualitative study.

9.6.2 Fit with the Polish System of Industrial Relations

One of the qualitative study's goals concerns the evaluation of the relationship between the emerging country-specific models of participative management on the one hand and the country-specific systems of *de jure* participation and industrial relations on the other hand. *De jure* participation means the codified rights of employees and their representatives to participate in decision-making processes at the country, sectoral and organisational level. Industrial relations cover the various areas of interaction between employer and employee at these three levels, including collective bargaining, employee representation on supervisory boards and works councils. In most countries, *de jure* participation and industrial relations overlap because at least some parts of the processes of industrial relations are codified in law or other written agreements. The following paragraphs outline the Polish model, followed by an analysis of its fit with the findings of the qualitative study.

After the fall of communism in Poland, first steps toward a tripartite system took place in the form of agreements between the government, unions and employer representatives. This early form of a dialogue was not codified in law. In 1994, the Tripartite Commission for Social and Economic Issues was established, mainly as a forum for national social dialogue. In the beginning, the commission was not very successful mainly due to the weakness of employer representation and internal conflicts between the two main unions Solidarnosc and OPZZ (Fichter & Zeuner, 2000). In 2001, the left-wing coalition government introduced new legal regulations and revitalised the Tripartite Commission. Despite some problems, the body is at present functioning relatively well (Eironline, 2003), and additional Tripartite Commissions have been introduced at the regional level.

The union movement has played a significant role in Poland's development over the last decades:

> "In Poland, the issue of workers' rights was subject to public debate and political conflict since the revolts of 1980 and the founding of Solidarnosc. The lifting of the ban on Solidarnosc shortly before the fall of the Berlin wall was a decisive step in the breakdown of communist rule. Solidarnosc became a key actor in the process of institution building which began in the field of labour relations." (Fichter & Zeuner, 2000, p. 25)

However, once market economy was introduced, union density dropped to about fifteen percent (Carley, 2002). Likely reasons for this drastic decline are deteriorating living standards during the 1990s, high levels of unemployment, privatisation, a growing number of small and medium-sized enterprises as well as sectoral shifts (Carley, 2002). Today, the unions are still the main representative body of the Polish workforce at the national level, but at the company level their influence has weakened considerably. Except for recruiting practices, there seems to be little difference in Human Resource activities between unionised and non-unionised firms (Tung & Havlovic, 1997).

On the employer side, there are two main central organisations, which are involved in negotiations and/or consultation processes with unions and government as members of the Tripartite Commission at the national level. Sectoral employer organisations play a weak role (Carley, 2002).

Generally speaking, collective bargaining has a limited impact on Polish industrial relations. Substantial issues are regulated either by the Tripartite Commissions at the national and regional levels or directly by law (Eironline, 2002c). The proportion of Polish employees, who are covered by collective agreements, amounts to about 40 percent. This figure is quite low compared to other European countries and reflects the low level of union membership (Carley, 2002).

At the company level, board-level employee representation exists in the former state enterprises, but not in private companies (Carley, 2002). The same is true for works councils: In some types of state-owned or formerly state-owned enterprises non-union representation is in place, yet its role is limited. A high proportion of Polish employees have neither union nor non-union representation of their interests (Eironline, 2002c). An institutional framework granting the right to establish works councils, as requested by the EU Directive on workplace participation, is opposed by both unions and employers (Carley, 2002).

This short summary of the development and status quo of the Polish industrial relations system shows that the system is still under construction. Until now, the system does not show substantial elements of employee participation. This finding is consistent with the qualitative study, in particular with the autocratic tendencies of Polish managers and their preference not to include subordinates in strategic and important questions. Furthermore, there is a link to the Polish managers' perception that their subordinates need a strong hand because they otherwise follow personal interests rather than organisational goals.

It is interesting to note that the unions' significant role in Poland's recent history has left little imprint on managerial decision-making: Management styles were autocratic in the communist past and the situation is still about the same more than fifteen years after introducing market economy. There are few participatory structures at the company level and few role models for managers, which could support a change toward more participative decision-making.

9.6.3 Fit with the Existing Literature

The qualitative study suggests that managerial decision-making in Poland is characterised by a relatively strong reliance on autocratic behaviour. A complex web of concepts, such as the relevance of the former and current political and economic systems and the specific role of the manager are responsible for the country-specific meaning and enactment of participative management.

The general preference for autocratic managerial behaviour found in the qualitative data is in line with the results of the three quantitative studies, which, in turn, mirror the results of a series of studies reported in the management literature. Examples include Trompenaars (1993), Sood and Mroczkowski (1994), Maczynski (1998), Nasierowski and Mikula (1998), Liberman and Torbiörn (2000), Obloj (2000) and Suutari and Riusala (2001).

Is it possible to formulate hypotheses with regard to the future development of participative management in Poland? Before trying to do so, it is necessary to have another look at the past. The interview data indicate that the autocratic tendency of the Polish managers is influenced at least in part by the communist past. What does the literature tell us about this influence factor? The following paragraphs discuss the management context within the communist system and the managerial role, respectively. A short discussion of the current situation (context and managerial role) is provided next, followed by an outlook on the potential role of participation in the future.

The communist context of management. The transition period in Poland
started long before 1989. Sood and Mroczkowski (1994) summarised some of
the major developments: Already in the 1970s the restrictions on the estab-
lishment of private enterprises were somewhat eased, which led to the es-
tablishment of about 350.000 private, mostly small firms employing about
600.000 people. In 1982, new legislation allowed the founding of co-
operatives independently of state authorities. These new companies mainly
provided services to the state-owned enterprises. The 1986 Law on Foreign
Investment made it possible to establish incorporated firms using foreign
capital. Finally, the 1989 Law on Economic Activity brought about a rapid
increase in the number of incorporated enterprises.

It follows that Polish managers had some experience with managing private companies, although in a highly regulated environment. However, the
communist ideology continued to dominate the activities of business organisations despite the liberalisation trend, and it probably shaped managers
and subordinates alike. Sood and Mroczkowski (1994) concluded that "[t]he
years of indifference toward work during socialist times have conditioned
employees to not be concerned with productivity, quality products, cus-
tomer service, or reliability and performance" (p. 61).

The managerial role during communism. The literature provides varying
information about the managerial role in communist times. While the descriptions of some authors (e.g. Obloj, 2000) imply that managers were predominantly administrators, Kennington et al. (1996) concluded that "Polish
managers' roles were not completely different from their western counterparts and that both groups needed to use many of the same skills in order to
be evaluated positively" (p. 469). Examples cited by Kennington and his
colleagues include leading and decision-making skills, interpersonal skills
and a certain degree of autonomy due to inefficient infrastructure. In summary, although content and context only partly overlapped with current
management, the communist managerial role did include decision-making.
Consequently, it would theoretically have been possible for managers to use
participation. However, there is little indication for a widespread participatory practice.

Today's context of management. The interviewees referred to the instability
of the legal and economic system that prevails in Poland more than fifteen
years after the introduction of market economy. There is a desire for more
stability, expressed for example by higher uncertainty avoidance "should
be" scores compared to "as is" scores. This tendency is not an isolated Polish
characteristic, but symptomatic for many of the countries in the former
communist Eastern Europe. Bakacsi et al. (2002) reported that the Eastern
Europe cluster (in the context of the GLOBE study comprised of Albania,
Georgia, Hungary, Kazakhstan, Poland, Russia and Slovenia) shows the
same tendency. All these countries have undergone drastic changes during

the last decade. In comparison to other countries, Poland mastered the transition relatively well, as Obloj (2000, p. 302) observed: "Poland's economy became a success story among Eastern European countries, growing, on average, at the rate of six percent." Moreover, Poland was successful in meeting the requirements for entry into the European Union by May 2004.

Yet, many problems remain to be solved. Instability, as expressed by the interviewees, can be related to many factors. Some of them were raised in the interviews, such as misleading legislation and unclear reforms. The literature provides additional factors. For example, Nasierowski and Wright (1993) and Nasierowski and Mikula (1998) characterised the post-communist situation in Poland as follows: high power distance, low work ethic, desire to make money quickly, limited experience with Western concepts and unclear perceptions of business needs. Sood and Mroczkowski (1994) concluded from a series of case studies that the lack of work ethics and employee motivation are the major challenges Polish managers have to face. Finally, Obloj (2000) warned that continuing economic growth depends on further reforms and privatisations, the development of a fair pension system and improvement of management skills and ethics. By now, the Poles seem to have mastered initial fears associated with the transition process (Balawajder & Popiolek, 1996). At present, unemployment and the fear thereof is the cause of a high anxiety level in the population. Unemployment was an unknown phenomenon during communist times, but it has steadily risen during the 1990s and has remained at a level of close to twenty percent since 2000, according to OECD figures.

Based on the qualitative interview data, it can be assumed that the high level of preferred uncertainty avoidance will decrease as soon as the environment provides for more stability. Nasierowski and Mikula (1998) reached a similar conclusion when they suggested that the high level of uncertainty avoidance was a reaction to the recent changes in the country. However, they also provided an additional argument:

"[I]n the past, uncertainty was externalised. An individual had limited opportunities to control his/her destiny. Regardless of what had been done in the workplace, assessment was often conducted on the whim of the 'party', and frequently could not be explained on economic or logical grounds. There is still both a social support network and an economic grey zone enabling one to live quite well, despite unfavourable employment conditions. These conditions are unlikely to continue into the future: Hence, again a preference toward avoiding uncertainty." (Nasierowski & Mikula, 1998, p. 503)

These statements are in some contrast to arguments in the cross-cultural management literature, which attribute culture dimensions a high degree of stability (e.g. Hofstede, 1980a). However, one may argue that the concept of uncertainty avoidance is related to safety needs. This group of needs represents the second-lowest level in Maslow's (1943) hierarchy of needs. Therefore, it is understandable that individual anxiety rises when safety needs are not fulfilled.

The emerging role of management in the market economy. The interviewees painted a clear picture of their envisioned managerial role. These descriptions are likely influenced by the former and current political and economic situation, as well as by factors specific to Polish culture and independent of the political and economic context. The interviewees' descriptions of the managerial role are similar to the image of the Polish manager reported in the management and cross-cultural literature. Two main features, namely expertise and efficiency, are shortly discussed in the following two paragraphs.

Expertise. Polish managers are expected to be strong figures possessing factual expertise. Liberman and Torbiörn (2000, p. 46) described the image of the Polish manager as a "strong, expert, self-confident and analytical figure." According to Liberman Yaconi (2001), the Polish managerial role includes being a foreseer (prognosticates, sees a level ahead, plans and acts in advance), being directive (guides, commands, drives people, sets standards, decides, gives directives and sets strategy) and being professional (rational, realistic, based on facts, objective, executes the tasks and does the job, does not allow personal bias to alter decisions and actions).

Efficiency. The qualitative interview data indicate that Polish managerial thinking is dominated by efficiency considerations. The literature on Polish management suggests that this is a fairly new phenomenon. Traditionally, Poles have been characterised as valuing humanism over materialism, and low efficiency orientation was considered related to the former communist system (Boski, 2003). In contrast, recent studies detected efficiency thinking among Polish managers. For example, Suutari and Riusala summarised Finnish expatriates' perceptions of Polish managers as follows:

> "The importance of productivity has become increasingly recognised: Managers are trying to achieve results and make money, not simply to produce products. [...] [M]anagers are trying to increase efficiency." (Suutari & Riusala, 2001, p. 272)

Parallel to the strong focus on economic efficiency, the literature describes the lack of concern for the employees' emotional wellbeing similarly to the qualitative study. Kozminski (1993) observed that managers in the ex-socialist block tend to focus more strongly on the technical side of management than on its human dimension. More recently, Suutari and Riusala (2001) found that Polish managers show little consideration toward their subordinates, i.e. behave in a less friendly, supportive and considerate way than managers from other countries do. How do Polish employees evaluate the way in which they are treated? According to a study by Liberman Yaconi

(2001), they would indeed prefer their managers to be more considerate and accessible.

In summary, managing in today's Poland is clearly not an easy task. The transition is not fully completed yet, and many Polish managers still seem to be in search of their role. Currently, the tendency goes in the direction of economic efficiency (hard facts) and away from an orientation toward people (soft facts). However, as Nasierowski and Mikula put it:

> "[Poles] need time to realise that the soul is worth more than a wallet filled up with 'green bills with a picture of an old man'." (Nasierowski & Mikula, 1998, p. 506)

The future of participation. With regard to potential changes in Polish managerial behaviour, the interviewees were convinced that changes toward more participation take place in the near future. They attributed the autocratic tendency of Polish managers to external forces, mainly to the imprint of the communist past with its high degree of centralisation and the current instability calling for strong managers and efficient decision-making. Whether the interviewees are right or wrong when expecting an increase in participation can only be speculated on at this point in time. Certain indicators speak for an increase in participation and others speak against it. Some of the main arguments on both sides are summarised in the following paragraphs.

Empirical data consistently suggest a high inertia in the autocratic tendency of Polish managers. The quantitative studies providing the start-off point for this qualitative study all show the same patterns, although part of the Vroom/Yetton data were collected before the change to market economy. A longitudinal analysis of the Polish Vroom/Yetton samples dating back as far as 1988 revealed no significant changes in decision-making behaviour over time (Reber & Jago, 1997). Along the same lines, Maczynski (1998) observed that the "radical political transformation between 1988 and 1994 produced few differences in managerial styles" (p. 124). Booth, Maczynski and Poniewierski (2002) even found in a comparative study between British and Polish students that the Polish students considered "a dictatorial approach as strongly contributing to outstanding leadership" (p. 26). Finally, the interviews for the integrative study took place no earlier than 2001 and still, the same autocratic patterns of decision-making emerged.

The reports about autocratic managerial behaviour are paralleled by the image of Polish employees showing little interest in having their level of involvement increased. As Piske observed:

> "Polish employees, especially those on middle and lower hierarchy levels, who have been socialised to accept centralised decision-making, perceive taking responsibility as a threat and thus refrain from showing initiative and taking decisions." (Piske, 2002, p. 308)

Up to this point, autocratic behaviour was discussed within the context of business organisations. However, there are also some broader societal indicators, which are most likely related to managerial behaviour. A look at these indicators may provide hints as to the future development of participative management. Firstly, Poland is a country with a strong catholic tradition (Skreija, 1992). This fact suggests the acceptance of authority, in this case the authority of the Catholic Church. Secondly, Polish families have traditionally been characterised by a strongly authoritarian father figure, a fact that Skreija summarised as follows:

"The father should be respected and obeyed. Ideally, the mother is kind and often mediates between the father, who is the stern disciplinarian, and the children." (Skreija, 1992, p. 203)

Reliance on the Catholic Church as an authority and acceptance of a strong authoritarian father figure are factors, which are independent of the political and economic situation. On the contrary, they suggest deference to authority being a part of the very core of Polish culture. This finding is supported by the fact that the Poles tend to be conservative: According to Schwartz (1994), Poland ranks high on the culture-level value dimension "conservatism", namely in position nine of thirty-eight country samples.

"Cultures that emphasise Conservatism values are primarily concerned with security, conformity and tradition." (Schwartz, 1994, p. 101)

Schwartz's conservatism scale and Hofstede's (1980a) power distance dimension are significantly and positively correlated (Schwartz, 1994). Consequently, it is questionable whether major changes in participative management take place in the near future. However, there are also reports in the literature relating to successful change initiatives. Suutari and Riusala (2001) gave account of Finnish expatriate managers in Poland, who observed that "teamwork and participation in decision-making have increased, at least at the management-group level" (p. 272). Balawajder and Popiolek's (1996) study of Polish firms in Upper Silesia provides another example. Although workers declared a low *de facto* influence on decisions relating to their plants, they also expressed a *preference* for more influence. The data show a clear increase in the workers' desire to gain influence between 1991 and 1995. The authors of the study concluded:

"In many spheres, despite observed rises, a satisfactory level [of participation] is not reached. The worst results are seen in the feelings of the respondents about the influence they exert in very important areas such as: influence on the future of the plant and the changes taking place in it, and also on the level of their own wages and the privileges associated with work. [...] The most favourable situation is found in the area of influence exerted in those spheres, which are largely within the scope of the respondents themselves. [...] [P]eople want to participate in the life of the workplace, they want to exert an influence on what happens to them, and want to be, as far as possible, human beings shaping their own situations, not treated as just 'cogs in the machine'." (Balawajder & Popiolek, 1996, pp. 134-135)

In the above quote, Balawajder and Popiolek described the differentiation between specific types of decisions and their adequacy for more or less participation. This finding parallels the decision types found in the current qualitative study as well as the results of the Vroom/Yetton study: Polish managers use participation in small decisions and trivial problems rather than in strategic decisions and high quality problems. The consistency in the findings across different research programs indicates that this pattern is deeply ingrained and will be hard to break in the future.

In summary, various arguments speak either for or against potential shifts in the degree of participation. In any case, serious barriers must be overcome, and these barriers are not restricted to the economic development, as the interviewees suggested. Firstly, managerial thinking needs to change. As the qualitative study shows, managers have deeply ingrained assumptions about the appropriate roles of the manager and the subordinates as well as about how different types of problems be best solved. Secondly, participatory structures need to be introduced. In this regard, there is some evidence that the future will bring change: (1) In 2008 at the latest, Poland needs to implement the EU Directive on workplace participation. The new legislation will put more pressure on management and workforce alike to start a cooperative dialogue. (2) Many foreign and multinational firms have already established subsidiaries in Poland and the trend is continuing. This new type of Polish workplace is likely to allow "forward diffusion" of Western HRM policies and practices from the international headquarters to the Polish subsidiaries (Hetrick, 2002, p. 349). Finally, there are training needs for both managers and subordinates. As the Polish management researcher Jerzy Maczynski demonstrated, the "autocratic leadership syndrome can be broken through intensive training in participative management" (Maczynski, 1998, p. 125). Based on a series of own studies and managerial training seminars, Maczynski concluded that the main reason for behavioural change of Polish managers may lie in their growing appreciation of the value of participation for management efficiency and effectiveness (Maczynski, 2002). And efficiency is high on the Polish managers' agenda, as the qualitative study shows.

Chapter 10

Within-Country Analysis: Sweden

10.1 Overview

The topic of this chapter is the country-specific meaning and enactment of participative management in Sweden, as raised in Research Question 1. The chapter describes the findings of the analysis of six qualitative interviews with Swedish managers. Recurring patterns in the data led to the country-specific model of participative management portrayed in Figure 10.1. The model includes concepts that emerged from *repeated* occurrence in the interview data. Consequently, only part of the interview material is presented here, although the interview transcripts obviously contained more variability. However, it was decided to concentrate on main aspects and present *patterns* of participative management rather than on individual preferences. Readers interested in the data collection process are referred to Chapter 5.2. For a detailed description of the analysis process using elements of grounded theory see Chapter 5.3. In Figure 10.1, the two broad aspects of participative management under study, namely meaning and enactment, are shown in the shaded boxes. Other concepts related to participative management are depicted in the white boxes. Arrows show the relationships between concepts as they emerged from the data.

The Swedish model of participative management is strongly influenced by the values *equality* and *fairness*. These values tie in with the importance of *smooth interpersonal relations* as the main guiding principle in the context of participative management. However, the preference for smooth interpersonal relations not only defines the meaning of participative management, but also characterises the roles of the various participants involved in decision-making. Furthermore, there is a clear link between the preference for smooth interpersonal relations and the Swedish *communication* patterns. Societal culture factors, such as *power distance, individualism/collectivism* and *uncertainty avoidance* (compare Chapter 2.2.3.1) were also found to play a role in shaping the meaning of participative management. Power distance refers to the degree to which members of a society expect power to be unequally shared. Individualism/collectivism relates to the relationship between the individual and the level of collectivism that prevails in a society. Uncertainty avoidance reflects the degree to which a society relies on social norms and

Figure 10.1 The Swedish Model of Participative Management

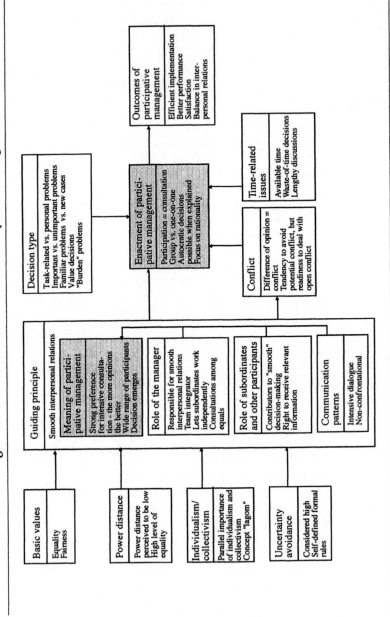

procedures to alleviate the unpredictability of future events. For example, in Sweden the value of equality is reflected in low power distance, which enables egalitarian interactions between organisational members of different hierarchical levels. Egalitarian interactions, in turn, are the pre-condition for participative management to work well.

The enactment of participative management is influenced by the following factors: *decision type, time-related issues* and assumptions about *conflict* and differing opinions within the group. There is a strong overall tendency to avoid open conflict and consequently, Swedish managers and subordinates generally prefer to reduce participation if differences of opinion exist among the participants. The data from other countries also reveal a certain tendency to limit participation in case of assumed conflict, but nowhere is the tendency as strong and predominant as in the Swedish data.

According to the interviewees, the *outcomes* of participative management comprise various aspects related to efficiency and subordinate satisfaction. A further important outcome factor refers to a strengthened balance in interpersonal relations.

The following sections describe the concepts pertinent to the Swedish model of participative management in more detail and include a number of illustrative quotes from the interviews with the Swedish managers.

10.2 The Meaning of Participative Management in Context

10.2.1 Basic Values: Equality and Fairness

Equality and fairness were found to be the two most influential basic values for the meaning and enactment of participative management in Sweden. Moreover, these two values have an impact not merely on participative management. They also emerged as the guiding principles behind interpersonal relations in a broader sense. The interview transcripts included statements referring to equality and fairness in the following manner:

"If you expect your people to fly economic class, you cannot fly first class yourself all the time."

"It's nice to have formal rules in a way, to refer to. Things are de-personalised and it's the same for everyone."

"All guys except for two, who park in front of the building, park in the remote parking lot. And then you can rotate the system every year or you can have a lottery or whatever."

10.2.2 Guiding Principle: Smooth Interpersonal Relations

The term "smooth" was repeatedly used by the Swedish interviewees and it consequently lent its name to one of the central explanatory concepts emerging from the Swedish data, namely that of *smooth interpersonal relations*. According to the Swedish interviewees, the term "smooth relations" refers to a friendly, supportive, non-confrontational way of interacting, which greatly influences problem solving and decision-making. As illustrated in Figure 10.1, the concept of smooth interpersonal relations relates to a number of more specific concepts, such as the meaning of participative management, the role of the manager, the roles of subordinates and other participants in decision-making, as well as to communication patterns. The following list provides an overview of areas, in which smooth interpersonal relations play a role, and the subsequent Sections 10.2.3 to 10.2.6 present more details and include quotes by Swedish managers.

- It is the manager's task to ensure smooth interpersonal relations within the managed unit. S/he is expected to integrate the team and to make sure that the team members work together with as little friction as possible.
- Similarly, employees involved in participative decision-making are also expected to contribute to the smooth handling of problems, for example by providing valid input and avoiding conflict.
- Swedish subordinates expect to be treated as equals. Business practices that are based on equality are considered fair treatment. Such fair treatment limits potential tension between subordinates and management and thus contributes to smooth relations.
- Swedish communication patterns are non-confrontational and emphasise intensive dialogue.

Participation in managerial decision-making is one of the main methods used to achieve smooth interpersonal relations, but it is not the only one. A non-confrontational communication style has already been indicated as another viable solution. Further methods are the use of formal rules, the general tendency to avoid conflict and the use of arguments based on reasoning. These themes will be discussed in detail in the following sections.

10.2.3 The Meaning of Participative Management

Strong preference for participation. The benefits of participative management were more or less unquestioned by the Swedish interviewees taking part in the qualitative study. Their statements imply that Swedish superiors and subordinates alike prefer participation to more autocratic forms of decision-making. This unquestioned preference suggests that participation might be a core principle among Swedes. In other words, it appears that Swedes prefer participative management intuitively and not as a result of a conscious process of reasoning.

A closer look at the interview data revealed that the interviewed managers not only favoured participation in their current managerial positions, but already had experienced participative management as subordinates during earlier phases of their work life. This wide experience with participation is reflected in their personal definitions of participation given during the interviews. The majority of the interviewees let their definition originate in a subordinate's point of view, which was broadened to include the manager's perspective only afterwards, if such a point of view was brought in at all.

"Participation is to be able to affect something, to be within the decision process and to be a part of the decision. [...] From the manager's standpoint it is basically to collect, to get input and to get help in the decision process."

"For me, participation would be to be involved, to have some kind of influence. So when I think about participation, it means, how much influence do I have?"

Range of participation. According to the interviewees, typical decision-making consists of a number of consultations with various parties, not just the subordinates. There seems to be a desire to include as many people in the decision-making process as possible. The manager's superior, colleagues at the same hierarchical level, as well as in-house and external experts are considered relevant participants in decision-making. Knowledge, expertise and the exchange of ideas seem to be more important than the position in the organisational hierarchy.

Who is responsible for a decision? There was consensus among the interviewees that ideally "the decision emerges" from the consultation process. The final decision is often officially made by the manager, but it should reflect the opinions of the participants in the process.

10.2.4 The Role of the Manager

Responsible for smooth interpersonal relations. According to the interview data, the Swedish managerial role is strongly determined by the responsibility to ensure smooth interpersonal relations. This requirement is not limited to decision-making processes, but concerns the overall "climate" in the manager's unit.

Team integrator. In more general terms, a manager is expected to serve as a team integrator. According to the interviewees, a team integrator gets people "to work together in the same direction". Ideally s/he works "more with the *people* in the organisation than with the *things* happening in the organisation", as one interviewee defined it. Moreover, a team integrator also tries to understand and respect individual group members' opinions and mediates in case of conflict. In summary, a manager "need not be glamorous", as one interviewee put it, but should be able to hold the group together and be approachable.

Lets subordinates work independently. At the same time, a manager should not directly interfere with the daily work of the subordinates, but rather "lay out the carpet for them to walk on", as one manager stated. This means that subordinates, individual employees as well as teams, work rather independently of managerial "command and control". The same principle applies between the manager and her or his superior.

Consultations among equals. Nonetheless, consultation and discussion between managers and subordinates take place frequently and intensively. Ideally, a manager should be a colleague rather than a boss in the traditional hierarchical sense. In other words, intensive dialogue works best in an atmosphere of equality.

> "And also, I mean, the sort of relation you have to your own boss plays quite a big role. If your boss is supportive and more like a colleague you can go to and discuss a problem, you probably go to your boss more often than if you are only reporting things."

The data suggest that there are implicit rules involved in the consultation process. A dialogue seems more acceptable to both sides when initiated by the partner who is officially responsible for the decision. Typically, this is the case when managers are faced with decision-making: They tend to get their subordinates intensively involved. At the same time, subordinates typically do their own work rather independently. In case they need or want to consult their superior about problems within their work-sphere, it is accepted to do so, as long as the superior is not expected to solve the problem for the subordinate. This pattern also implies that *upward influence* (subordinates influencing managerial decisions) plays a more important role and is more highly regarded than either *upward delegation* (subordinates expecting superiors to solve problems for them) or *downward influence* (superiors telling subordinates what to do).

10.2.5 The Role of Subordinates and Other Participants

In the understanding of the interviewed Swedish managers, participation in decision-making is not limited to subordinates, but involves a wider range of participants. Among them are the manager's superior (see Section 10.2.4 above), colleagues at the same hierarchical level and experts from other organisational units, as illustrated by the following part of one of the interview transcripts.

Manager: For me participation is that you listen to other people's opinion and listen to their suggestions and experiences. [...].
Researcher: You didn't explicitly say participation is listening to your <u>subordinates</u>.
Manager: No.
Researcher: Is participation a broader concept?
Manager: Yes, broader. I think it can be the people in my organisation, it can be colleagues, can be experts or my boss. I rather listen to people who have experience in their area than to people who have a specific position. I think experience is more important.

The interviewees shared the assumption that interaction on a broad and regular basis is highly important. Structural arrangements tend to exist for consultations between manager and subordinates, such as regular group meetings. Participation within other contexts happens on a more voluntary basis. However, some interviewees suggested that colleagues at the same hierarchical level tend to expect to be consulted.

Participants in the decision-making process are expected to contribute to the smooth running of the process, for example by avoiding open conflict and by providing valid input. In order for the participants to be able to contribute effectively, they must receive all relevant background information.

"Of course it's necessary that you get the facts, I mean that you are presented with the facts. That way you can participate. Otherwise you ask questions just out of the blue. It's hard, if you don't know the facts."

10.2.6 Communication Patterns

According to the interview data, communication often takes the form of intensive dialogue. Communication is expected by all participants and it is considered efficient, as it guarantees as much exchange of information and ideas as possible. Moreover, intensity and frequency of communication can be maximised when discussants have a relatively equal status, as is the case in the egalitarian Swedish society.

The desire for intensive communication also relates to the preference for a wide range of participants in decision-making. Communicating intensively with as many different parties as possible is assumed to be an efficient way of finding good solutions.

Another general characteristic of communication is its non-confrontational nature, as the following part of an interview transcript demonstrates.

Manager: We had a meeting and the French were so accustomed to smoking in the meeting rooms. Then this guy from the UK came in and said, "You folks, you always smoke in the conference room." Quite a conflict!
Researcher: So, a Swede would never say anything like that?
Manager: <u>No</u>! (LAUGHS)

As will be shown in subsequent sections, the non-confrontational communication style is related to a specific handling of conflict and differing opinions. According to the interviewees, non-confrontational means that emotions are under control. However, it does not mean that there are no emotions involved at all, as one interviewee explained:

> "We don't yell or rush away [...] or something like that. We keep sitting and talking, but we can still say mean things."

In such cases it is considered the manager's responsibility in her or his role as a team integrator to mediate and help the participants return to normal interaction.

Another downside of intensive communication is that it can develop into discussions that "drag on for a long time", as one interviewee called it. These lengthy discussions are the negative extreme of otherwise fruitful dialogs that enable information and ideas to surface. According to the interviewees, it is the manager's responsibility to end such discussions by making a decision.

10.3 The Enactment of Participative Management

10.3.1 Participative vs. Autocratic Decision-Making

Participation in the decision-making process usually takes one of two forms: one-on-one conversation or meeting as a group. However, not all decision-making processes involve participation. Autocratic decision-making is also used, depending on factors discussed below. The following paragraphs describe general aspects of the decision-making process. Sections 10.4 and 10.5 continue with a detailed analysis of the main situational and society-related (cultural) influence factors.

Group meetings either take the form of regular meetings, in most cases between a manager and her or his subordinates, or sporadic come-togethers specifically aimed at solving particular problems. These sporadic meetings may involve various parties. The interviewees explained that group meetings are fair. One reason is that group settings allow all involved persons to access the same information simultaneously:

> "I think it's fair in a way to bring them together as a group and to put the problem to everyone at the same time, so they all hear the same thing. If I take one and one, there's always someone who has a different interpretation of what I said, and there's always someone who has the information before the others get it."

Another related reason is that there will be no misunderstandings in the implementation phase, because the involved persons were already part of the decision-making process. This aspect implies efficiency, but it can also be interpreted as a contribution to smooth interpersonal relations by means of a potentially friction-free implementation of the decision.

One interviewee mentioned yet another reason for the implicit fairness of group meetings. In his view, group meetings ensure that all involved parties gain better understanding of each other's point of view. Once again, there seems to be an underlying tendency to ensure smooth interpersonal relations.

Group meetings can also have negative effects. Guided by non-confrontational communication patterns, problems might not be discussed openly. One interviewee argued that subordinates never talk about the real problems in meetings, but give hints at best. One interviewee considered group meetings to be "more complicated" than one-on-one conversations, since they required more organisation and could lead to problems for the manager, if s/he had already made up her or his mind about how to solve the problem.

> "If I consult the people in a group and everybody else thinks one thing, then it's hard for me to go against it, because I already consulted with them."

Another negative aspect of group meetings is that some decision-makers may tend to "hide behind the group", i.e. make the group take an unpopular decision they should have taken themselves. This kind of behaviour is the negative extreme of what is otherwise considered positive, namely to involve subordinates and other parties as much as possible.

One-on-one conversations. Similar to group meetings, one-on-one conversations were described as containing an aspect of fairness. Personal discussions between the manager and a subordinate are especially well suited for personal problems, such as alcohol problems. Discussing this sort of problems in front of the group is considered unfair to the person whom it concerns. As one interviewee put it: "You don't hang someone in front of the group."

Some of the interviewed managers considered one-on-one conversation a generally more efficient form of participative management than group meetings. One-on-one conversation was described as avoiding the downsides of group interaction, such as managers hiding behind the group, participants not openly expressing their opinions or excessively lengthy discussions.

Autocratic decision-making. Depending on situational (see Section 10.4 below) and individual preferences, managers may take certain decisions without consulting with the group. This does not mean, however, that there is no communication involved. According to the interviewees, subordinates are likely to accept autocratic decision-making as long as the motivation behind the autocratic action is clear to them. It seems that autocratic behaviour is most easily accepted if the presented reasons are based on rationality. As one interviewee put it: "I always think that they accept if they understand."

Problems to which rational reasons do not apply were described as hard to solve, in particular when the manager had a personal preference. One of the interviewees explained his usual strategy to convince the group of his personal preference as follows: Hand the problem over to the group and listen to the group discussion. The group will most likely not find a solution based on rational arguments either and will return the problem to the manager. A second round of discussion starts, this time with the manager taking part. After the initial experience of failing at finding a rational solution, the group is now likely to go along with the manager's preferred solution.

10.3.2 Participative Management Outcomes

According to the interviewees, participative management leads to better performance and to a generally higher level of work satisfaction.

> "I think there are a lot of good examples where you can increase quality in decision-making through participation."

> "I like to participate because then I do better work. So as a manager I also try to get people involved. Then I know they perform better."

A participative decision-making process makes all parties involved feel that they are taken seriously and helps them understand the reasons underlying the decision. Both aspects satisfy their expectations of equality and fairness. Additionally, a better understanding of the reasons can facilitate smooth interpersonal relations. More generally speaking, participative management in Sweden is a tool to keep interpersonal relations intact.

10.4 Main Situational Influence Factors

Three situational factors were found to be most influential, namely decision type, time-related issues, and conflict and expected differences of opinion in the group. These factors influence the decision-making process and determine whether subordinate participation is relevant or if the manager should take the decision alone.

10.4.1 Decision Type

When asked about problems that qualified well for participation, the majority of the interviewees initially responded that any kind of problem was suitable. However, more detailed probing and an analysis of the interviewee narratives revealed that decision type does make a difference. The following types of problems and decisions were found to most strongly influence a manager's choice of decision strategy.

Task-related vs. personal problems. Task-related problems were described as being well suited for participative decision-making. This preference applies in particular to intra-unit decisions of which subordinates are directly concerned. Intra-unit problems are to be solved within the manager's sphere of influence, whereas problems that affect other organisational units should be solved in co-operation with people from these units. The interviewees concurrently indicated that such co-operation need not necessarily involve higher managerial levels. In contrast to task-related problems, decisions associated with personal problems of an individual employee, such as alcohol problems, were described as not qualifying for participative decision-making. The manager should solve this type of problem personally, but s/he should talk with the person concerned or at least explain the decision.

Important vs. unimportant problems. Group meetings involving intensive consultation were considered the most constructive setting for solving important problems, although the final and official decision usually stays with the manager. In the case of unimportant problems, the interviewees differed in their preferences. "It does not really matter who decides", one interviewed manager stated. Equality and fairness might call for a group meeting, whereas the danger of drawn-out discussions may suggest one-on-one conversation.

Familiar problems vs. new cases. The interviewees considered familiar problems as easy cases for the manager to decide her or himself. Routine decisions, such as the periodic evaluation of on-track projects, also fall into this category. These decisions were described as a formality without any need for participation. In contrast, new cases seem to call for participative decision-making. Here, all the attributed benefits of participation play a role, in particular intensive dialogue that ensures maximum input of opinions and ideas.

Value decisions. These decisions concern problems that are important to the manager and that s/he wants solved according to her or his own principles. Examples were given for such values as "customers first" or "help people with disabilities." According to the interviewees, value decisions do not qualify for participative decision-making, as participation may result in different solutions from what the manager wants. Value decisions tend to be taken autocratically even if the outcome affects subordinates directly, which would otherwise call for participation.

"Burden" problems. Decision-making concerning certain problems was described as being a burden to the subordinates. Examples include high-risk and health-related decisions. Consequently, it is the responsibility of the manager to take such a decision personally.

> "I should be the responsible person, not put the responsibility on the other people in the group. If something goes wrong they would feel very, very bad, and in that situation it's only me as the boss, who can be responsible."

10.4.2 Time-Related Issues

When interviewees argued in favour of a limited use of participation, they frequently referred to time arguments. Time arguments concerned the facts that, objectively or subjectively, there would not be enough time for an extended decision-making process, that for certain problems participation was considered a waste of time or that consultations would take too long.

Available time. When faced with time pressure, the interviewed Swedish managers seem to prefer autocratic decision-making. "The decision had to be made quickly" was a frequently mentioned statement. In contrast, without such time constraint managers agreed that the time available should be used as effectively as possibly, i.e. by involving as many parties as possible, thus allowing all available knowledge and opinions to be given consideration.

Waste of time. Some problems were labelled as "waste-of-time decisions". These problems were not necessarily described as unimportant, but as problems that presented no need for discussion, for example decisions based on fixed figures. Such decisions ought to be taken by the manager her or himself.

Lengthy discussions. Irrespective of the problem type, a manager's willingness to use autocratic decision-making seems influenced by the fact that some discussions drag on. According to some interviewees, it is the manager's responsibility to end such discussions and "just decide." It must be noted that this step relates to the negative extreme of an otherwise preferred communication style, rather than to a general unwillingness to engage in dialogue.

10.4.3 Conflict

As described above, participative management is related to the principle of smooth interpersonal relations. However, sometimes participation may be seen as hindering to smooth relations. This is, for example, the case when differing opinions in the decision-making group could cause a conflict.

What is considered a conflict is relative. Based on some interview statements it seems that what the Swedish managers labelled a conflict might be considered just a difference of opinion in other countries. An example of this is the Swedish manager who was quoted in Section 10.2.6, and who describes a conflict involving a person accusing others of smoking in a meeting room. Interestingly, he saw a conflict in the mere accusation and not so much in the potentially resulting fight between the two parties.

"We had a meeting and the French were so accustomed to smoking in the meeting rooms. Then this guy from the UK came in and said, 'You folks, you always smoke in the conference room.' Quite a conflict!"

The Swedish interviewees differentiated between potential and open conflict. In case of *potential* conflict, decision-making processes often seem to take other forms than group meetings. The main goal is to keep interpersonal relations intact. Group meetings would create a difficult situation for people holding different opinions. Things could get out of hand and be difficult to repair afterwards. A group setting could not provide a win-win situation because the competitive situation requires for one party to be the prestigious winner. These and similar reasons given by the interviewees suggest that managers take their role as team integrator seriously. They try to be fair and consider the wellbeing of the group members and potential consequences of decisions made.

Similarly, potential conflict resulting from problems related to *one* individual should not be the subject for group discussion either, as one interviewee argued. Exposing weaknesses or problems would not help anyone and would limit the person's chances in the organisation. Thus, a manager should try to solve such issues in private. Again, this argumentation is based on the value of fairness and it highlights the central role of the manager as a team integrator. The following quote further illustrates this point:

"If there is a problem between two persons I talk to them and they have to solve it among themselves. I might say, 'You have to go and excuse yourself for what you did.'"

The interviewees' preferred approaches in case of potential conflict differed widely. Most managers argued that they favoured one-on-one conversation when they felt that differences of opinion could take a confrontational turn. However, not all interviewees avoided group settings. One manager argued that he preferred group meetings to one-on-one discussions because the group was able to prevent the conflict from escalating. In his understanding, the participants themselves would make sure that their interpersonal relations stayed intact. Another manager suggested that the problem be left to the group, thus allowing the conflicting parties to interact directly and in this way learn to appreciate each other's opinions. The latter arguments build on the non-confrontational communication style and the assumption that increased understanding will limit the risk of conflict.

The variation of strategies in dealing with potential conflict shows that there is not *one* commonly accepted approach. It also shows that the preference for participative management is not "untouchable": Participation may be sacrificed with the implicit agreement of all involved parties when the fundamental principle of smooth interpersonal relations is in danger.

The above statements described the strategies of Swedish managers who thought that there *could* be conflict in their group. But what if a conflict already exists? How do the Swedish managers handle *open* conflict? They seem to recognise that they must deal with the problem and there were no hints in the data that existing problems would be "swept under the rug".

"The conflict is already there, it's on the table. It can't be handled in a smooth way, you have to sit down and talk about it."

This active approach fits the principle of smooth interpersonal relations because it reflects a strong desire to return to normal interactions as quickly as possible. Different strategies assist the desired return to "normality". These strategies include attempts to control emotions ("get away from the feelings"), look at the problem from a new and different angle or try to find a logical approach to solving the problem ("Often there is a best answer to it, a logical answer, and then hopefully that's it").

10.5 Main Society-Related Influence Factors

As described above, equality and fairness are the two core values that constitute the basis for the meaning and enactment of participative management and interpersonal relations in general. These two values also seem to influence participative management indirectly through societal culture values and norms related to power distance, individualism/collectivism and uncertainty avoidance. These three societal culture dimensions are repeatedly mentioned in the cross-cultural literature as influence factors on the degree and enactment of participative management. Therefore, questions related to the three dimensions were explicitly asked during the interviews. As it turned out, all three dimensions emerged as directly or indirectly relevant for the understanding of participative management in a Swedish context.

10.5.1 Power Distance

Power distance reflects the degree to which members of a society expect power to be unequally shared (Hofstede, 1980a; House et al., 2004). The interviews revealed a clear relationship between the low level of power distance in Swedish society and the large degree of subordinate involvement in managerial decision-making. Relationships are egalitarian and communication patterns allow discussions between managers and subordinates to take place on an equal level. Furthermore, participative management emerged from the interview data as not limited to subordinates. On the contrary, Swedish managers typically include as many parties as possible in order to enable intensive consultation and exchange of opinions and experience. The manager's superior, colleagues at the same hierarchical level and specialists inside and outside the organisation are considered relevant for consulting before making a decision. According to the interviewees, the position in the organisational hierarchy counts little compared to knowledge and expertise.

10.5.2 Individualism/Collectivism

In cross-cultural management literature, the dimension individualism/collectivism refers to the relationship between the individual and the level of collectivism that predominates in a society (Hofstede, 1980a; House et al., 2004). According to the interviewees, collectivism is high in Swedish society. A concept repeatedly mentioned in the interviews was the Swedish term "lagom", which one of the managers described as follows:

> "Everyone is supposed to have more or less basic standards. And also, you shouldn't stand out much."

Parallel to the high level of collectivism, individualism also seems to be highly valued, although it depends very much upon whether society in general or work life is concerned. With regard to society in general, the interviewees agreed that there should be more individualism. Examples included the school system, which should take better care of the individual needs of pupils, and the role of the unions, which some interviewees described as too influential.

In contrast to society in general, the interviewees' opinions were split when it came to work life. Some interviewees referred to such examples as the pay system and argued that there should be more individual recognition. Other interviewees expressed concern that more individualism would mean less participation and group work.

"Collectivism should be much, much less for the country but not for the company."

On the whole, the data hint at a balance between the individual and the group, at least when it comes to decision-making. Both individualism and collectivism are highly valued, the individual for her or his unique contributions and the group for its possibility to discuss, to integrate the various contributions and to allow the best possible solution to emerge.

The parallel importance of collectivism and individualism is also incorporated in how the Swedish managerial role is defined. On the one hand, a manager should not attract too much attention to her or himself ("lagom") and should include subordinates as much as possible in decision-making (collectivism). On the other hand, the manager is usually considered the official decision-maker, i.e. the responsible person for a decision and its outcome (individualism). These two role expectations are not always tension-free and may at times even be contradictory. To unite the two poles of collectivism and individualism, the manager should give credit to the group members for their contributions and ensure that group members experience a high level of identification with the group.

10.5.3 Uncertainty Avoidance

Uncertainty avoidance was the third culture dimension explored during the interviews. It reflects the degree to which a society relies on social norms and procedures to alleviate the unpredictability of future events (Hofstede, 1980a; House et al., 2004). The Swedish managers perceived uncertainty avoidance to be high in Swedish society and gave examples of low risk-taking and little flexibility. They argued that they would prefer a lower level of uncertainty avoidance, but also assumed that things would be slowly changing in that direction anyway.

Formal rules are a typical expression of high uncertainty avoidance. The interviewees agreed that formal rules play an important role particularly in large Swedish organisations. Such rules are typically not imposed from higher hierarchical levels, but are designed and put in place by the people who actually work with them. Therefore it would be "unfair to fellow employees not to follow the rules", as one interviewee put it. Such self-defined rules make sense because they are grounded in reality. They differ in their degree of detail. Many of them are broad guidelines that allow for some flexibility.

"I think when we have implemented a rule we also have implemented a way to follow it. And then it's important to follow it because everyone knows about it."

"Rules have to make sense, then there is no problem."

The data suggest that the advantages of such formal rules balance out their disadvantages, such as low flexibility: They facilitate interaction, as they provide guidelines on behaviour for everyone to refer to. They are fair because everyone is treated equally. For the manager, rules are a means to de-personalising difficult issues ("I mean it's nice to have formal rules in a way, to refer to."). In summary, formal rules seem to be another piece of the puzzle that ensures smooth interpersonal relations.

10.6 Integration

10.6.1 Fit with the Three Quantitative Studies

This qualitative study explores the meaning and enactment of participative management. The following paragraphs analyse the fit of the qualitative findings with the results of the three quantitative studies building the initial starting point for the qualitative inquiry. Is there a match with the quantitative scores of the GLOBE study, the Event management study and the Vroom/Yetton study? If not, is it possible to explain existing differences with the insights gained from the qualitative study? In order to address these questions, the following paragraphs summarise and integrate the different studies' results.

Table 10.1 Quantitative Participation Scores for Sweden

Scale	Participative (GLOBE)	Non-autocratic (GLOBE)	Guidance source subordinates (Event Management)	Mean level of participation (MLP) (Vroom/Yetton)
Score	5,49	5,59	13	5,57
Country position	Middle third	Upper third	Upper third	Upper third
Rank	25 of 61	19 of 61	7 of 56	1 of 13

Note: For a detailed description of the scales and country comparisons see Chapter 4.

The quantitative participation scores in Table 10.1 originate from the GLOBE scales *participative* and *non-autocratic*, the Event Management study's guidance source *subordinates* and the Vroom/Yetton study's *MLP* score. On three of the four scales Sweden is positioned in the upper third among the countries under study. These results are in line with the country-specific model of participative management that emerged from the qualitative interviews. A closer look at additional Vroom/Yetton results confirms the good fit. For example, the use of group strategies (CII and GII, compare Chapter 4.3.3.2) is higher in Sweden than in the other countries. Decision-making processes in which the manager is responsible for making the final decision (CII; 30,9 percent) are more commonly used than joint decision-making (GII; 20,6 percent). This finding also emerged as a central theme from the qualitative data: Intensive dialogue and consultation during the decision-making process is followed by the official decision made by the manager her or himself. However, the manager is not free in her or his choice, because subordinates and other parties involved in the process expect that their opinions become part of the decision. Therefore, in a number of cases it is probably more fair to say that the solution *emerges* from the process, than to say that it constitutes a conscious decision made by the individual manager. For the Vroom/Yetton results this interpretation suggests that basically only a small difference in quality exists between CII and GII solutions, because both represent consensus decisions based on consultation.

The medium score on the GLOBE scale *participative* does not fully reflect the qualitative findings and the high participation scores of the other quantitative scales. Two possible explanations come to mind: (1) Participation was so self-evident to the Swedish respondents that they, either consciously or unconsciously, did not refer to it explicitly, when filling out the questionnaire. There is some evidence in the qualitative data that this was indeed the case. (2) The GLOBE questionnaire includes items that are not fully consistent with the Swedish model of participative management. Such inconsistent items might lower the aggregated scale score. A closer look at the items comprising the scale *participative* reveals that the item *group-oriented* might indeed be the reason for the lower than expected scale score. In the questionnaire, the item *group-oriented* is defined as "[a manager who is] concerned with and places high value on preserving group rather than individual needs". Such a statement might be interpreted by a Swede as managerial attempts at setting limits to the individual freedom of subordinates and their desire to work independently. In contrast, the qualitative analysis showed that a good Swedish manager "lays out the carpet for subordinates" and respects their independence in doing their work.

Table 10.2 Scores of Hierarchy-Related Concepts for Sweden

Scale	Power distance "as is" (GLOBE)	Guidance source superior (Event Management)	Guidance source own experience (Event Management)
Score	4,85	18	76
Country position	Lower third	Lower third	Middle third
Rank	51 of 61	49 of 56	19 of 56

Note: For a detailed description of the scales and country comparisons see Chapter 4.

In Chapter 4.4, participative management was hypothesised to be related to concepts associated with organisational hierarchy, such as *power distance* or the Event Management study's guidance source *own superior*.

The low score for Sweden on the societal culture dimension *power distance* (Table 10.2) is in line with the qualitative findings and the high relevance of the value equality.

The qualitative data suggest that Swedish managers consider the people-related guidance sources, including subordinates, colleagues and experts, to be particularly important. This tendency is based on the assumption that only intensive dialogue leads to a good solution. The relatively low score on *own experience* (Table 10.2) is consistent with this intensive reliance on other people's opinion.

The rather low Event Management score for the manager's *superior* (Table 10.2) can also be explained by the qualitative findings. Generally speaking, a low score suggests little dependence on the superior and little use of the next-higher organisational level in decision-making. However, this is only one side of the coin. The qualitative data revealed that in Sweden the superior is ideally like a colleague, with whom a dialogue on an equal level is possible. In this sense, the superior may well serve as a source of guidance for a Swedish manager, similar to other people whom the manager trusts to make important contributions to problem solving.

Table 10.3 Scores of Team-Related Concepts for Sweden

Scale	Collaborative team orientation (GLOBE)	Team integrator (GLOBE)	Institutional collectivism "as is" (GLOBE)
Score	5,98	5,50	5,22
Country position	Middle third	Middle third	Upper third
Rank	32 of 61	32 of 61	1 of 61

Note: For a detailed description of the scales and country comparisons see Chapter 4.

Chapter 4.4 also discussed the potential relationship between participative management and team-related concepts. Table 10.3 shows that Sweden ranks at a medium level on the team-related scales of the GLOBE study, notably *collaborative team orientation* and *team integrator*. In contrast, the Swedish score for institutional collectivism was the highest among the sixty-one countries in the GLOBE study.

The high score for Sweden on the scale *institutional collectivism* is in line with the qualitative findings. Additionally, the qualitative data provide insights that go well beyond the quantitative results. The interviewed Swedish managers distinguished between society in general and the workplace. They regarded collectivism in Swedish society as being somewhat too high ("downsides of the welfare state") and expressed a desire for more societal individualism. At the workplace, however, individualism within a collective spirit seems to prevail. In this climate, participative decision-making offers a forum for intensive dialogue ensuring unique contributions of individual organisation members.

The medium scores on the two team-related GLOBE scales, namely *collaborative team orientation* and *team integrator* (Table 10.3) do not fully concur with the Swedish model of participative management as it emerged from the qualitative inquiry. In contrast to the quantitative measures, the qualitative study found that the role of the manager is closely associated with the concept of team integrator and thus with the responsibility to motivate people to work together in the same direction and to ensure smooth interpersonal relations. A closer look at the items comprising the two team-related GLOBE scales suggests that some items might not be fully consistent with the emerging image of a team integrator: (1) The GLOBE items *loyal* and *fraternal* possibly contradict the Swedish values of fairness and equality. (2) The description of the item *mediator* assumes an open approach to dealing with potential conflict, which, according to the qualitative study, is unlikely in a Swedish context. Both factors may contribute to lower than expected aggregated scores on the two team-related GLOBE scales. In this sense, the GLOBE scores fail to capture the strong focus on team integration that the qualitative inquiry revealed as part of the managerial role.

Table 10.4 Scores of Uncertainty-Related Concepts for Sweden

Scale	Uncertainty avoidance "as is" (GLOBE)	Guidance source formal rules (Event Management)	Guidance source unwritten rules (Event Management)
Score	5,32	43	-24
Country position	Upper third	Upper third	Lower third
Rank	2 of 61	12 of 56	46 of 56

Note: For a detailed description of the scales and country comparisons see Chapter 4.

Uncertainty-related concepts provided yet another area of discussion in Chapter 4.4. It was pondered how uncertainty avoidance and reliance on rules related to the enactment of participative management.

Table 10.4 suggests a high level of societal *uncertainty avoidance* for Sweden, implying that manifold social norms and regulations ease the unpredictability of future events. This result is consistent with the qualitative findings. Furthermore, the Event Management study suggests that Swedes rely more on *formal rules and procedures* and less on *unwritten rules* than managers from other countries do. This result is also in line with the qualitative findings. Additionally, the qualitative interview data indicate that formal rules are considered a means to ensure smooth interpersonal relations. Formal rules also fit with the dominant values of equality and fairness, as they ensure de-personalised and equal treatment. It is worth noting, however, that the rules and regulations in Swedish organisations are typically not imposed from higher hierarchical levels, but are decided upon among the actors themselves.

10.6.2 Fit with the Swedish System of Industrial Relations

One of the goals of this qualitative study concerns the evaluation of the relationship between the emerging country-specific models of participative management on the one hand and the country-specific systems of *de jure* participation and industrial relations on the other hand. *De jure* participation means the codified rights of employees and their representatives to participate in decision-making processes at the country, sectoral and organisational level. The term industrial relations refers to the various areas of interaction between employer and employee at these three levels, including collective bargaining, employee representation on supervisory boards and works councils. *De jure* participation and industrial relations overlap in many countries, because at least some industrial relations processes are codified in law or other written agreements. The following paragraphs outline the Swedish model, followed by an analysis of its fit with the findings of the qualitative study.

The degree of industrial democracy is high in Sweden (Ronen, 1986) due to strong and centralised representative bodies. Both unions and employer associations look back at a history of more than a hundred years (Grant, 1996). Currently, union density amounts to close to eighty percent and there are separate confederations for different occupational groups (Carley, 2002). Recently, some mergers took place among unions. For example, the two unions Kommunal (Swedish Municipal Workers Union) and Lantarbetareförbundet (Agricultural Workers Union) announced a merger in 2002 (Eironline, 2002d).

Employer organisations are united under a single umbrella organisation that covers about fifty-four percent of the Swedish employers (Traxler, 2000). Similar to the unions, the employer associations also show a tendency to centralise. For example, Svenska Kommunförbundet (Swedish Association of Local Authorities) merged with Landstingsförbundet (Federation of Swedish County Councils) in 2002 (Eironline, 2002d). Sectoral employer organisations are key components of the industrial relations system (Carley, 2002).

Collective bargaining plays a notably strong role in Sweden (Mills, 1978). Until 1976, there was very little state interference (IDE, 1981). In 1976, the Democracy at Work Act "radically [opened] collective bargaining to matters traditionally considered management prerogative" (Mills, 1978, p. 149). During the 1990s, a shift took place that moved the main collective bargaining activities from the national to the sectoral level. Hoffmann et al. (2002) interpreted this move not as a trend toward uncoordinated bargaining, but as a step toward "organised decentralisation" (p. 29). Sectoral agreements are usually concluded for a period of three years (Eironline, 2001). Collective agreements cover more than ninety percent of the Swedish workforce (Carley, 2002). Only two percent of all Swedish workplaces are not covered by a collective agreement for some or all employees (Gill & Krieger, 2000).

At the organisational level, the Board Representatives Act (Styrelserepresentationslagen) rules that one third of the members on the supervisory boards of private companies must be employee representatives (Mills, 1978). Fackklubbar (local trade unions) act on behalf of the employees at the workplace level. Representation of this kind has been mandatory since 1946 and is possible in organisations with any number of employees, even in very small businesses. As reported by Gill and Krieger (2000), over ninety percent of the Swedish employees work in companies with representative bodies in place. Trade union representation is preferred over works councils. Traditionally, Swedish unions have always been sceptical of separate works councils, probably for fear that "they would compete with unions and threaten union solidarity" (Strauss, 1998b, p. 112). Information and consultation rights of the Fackklubbar are based on the provisions of the Co-Determination Act, complemented by collective agreements (Eironline, 2002d). Employee representatives also take an active role in spreading participative management in their respective organisations: Gill and Krieger (2000) reported that in about seventy-five percent of Swedish workplaces with direct participation (consultation and delegation) union representatives are involved in consultation and joint decision-making on this matter. The authors added that direct participation is exercised in sixty-two percent of Swedish workplaces, making Sweden the leader with regard to participative management among the ten European countries in their study.

The findings of the qualitative study are in line with the democratic and formalised structure of the Swedish industrial relations system. The above description clearly reflects the desire for smooth relations. In particular, the described "organised decentralisation" of collective bargaining and the reluctance of unions to accept works councils indicate awareness of the importance of smooth and non-confrontational interactions. The high level of unionisation and the fact that more than ninety percent of the Swedish workforce are covered by collective agreements seem to indicate a tendency to reduce uncertainty and ensure equal and fair treatment of the Swedish workforce. Finally, co-determination on supervisory boards and union representation in the vast majority of Swedish organisations fit with the general preference for participative arrangements as it also emerged from the qualitative study.

10.6.3 Fit with the Existing Literature

The qualitative study provides a coherent picture of Swedish managerial decision-making strongly dominated by participation. By and large, the qualitative findings are in agreement with the results of the three quantitative studies. Moreover, the qualitative interview data help enrich the quantitative scores, explain contradictions between the three quantitative studies and point out the relevance of situational and cultural factors. The Swedish model of participative management also fits with the Swedish model of industrial relations.

The strong focus on participation as part of Swedish managerial decision-making is not a new finding. It has been observed by a number of researchers, such as Lawrence and Spybey (1986), Guillet de Monthoux (1991), Czarniawska-Joerges (1993), Suutari (1996b), Holmberg and Åkerblom (1998), Gill and Krieger (2000) and Zander (2000). In contrast to most studies, the qualitative study also shows that participation in Sweden has a particular quality: It includes a wider range of participants than just subordinates, and all involved parties *expect* for participation to be an integral part of decision-making. In agreement with these specific findings of the qualitative study, Hofstede (2001, p. 389) suggested that in countries with *extremely* low power distance, such as Sweden, participation is often initiated by the subordinates, which is in contrast to models developed in countries with *moderately* low levels of power distance, where the initiative for participation is usually taken by the manager.

Several of the specific concepts and themes that emerged from the qualitative study were also discussed by others authors in the management, cross-cultural management and communication literature, as the following overview shows.

Equality and fairness. According to the qualitative study, equality and fairness are the two main values defining the meaning and enactment of participative management in Sweden. In a like manner, Zander (2000, p. 345) demonstrated that both egalitarianism and fairness are among the most distinctive characteristics of Swedish management. Similarly, Smith et al. (2003) concluded after a detailed analysis of the Event Management data of the Nordic countries that the Swedish results reflect "formality in a culture of equality" (p. 499). Auer-Rizzi and Berry (2000) explored cultural frames of reference in the group decision-making of international students. They found that Swedish students shared assumptions of extensive boss-subordinate equality, considering competence more important than power status. With regard to fairness, Zander (2000) noted that Swedish management is "based on the logic of order and the principle of fairness" (p. 350), and Holmberg and Åkerblom (1998) discussed examples of individual rights ensuring fair treatment to Swedish citizens, such as the ombudsman system.

Smooth interpersonal relations, consensus orientation and conflict avoidance. Holmberg and Åkerblom (1998) described the Swedes' preference for *consensus*, which overlaps with the qualitative study's concept of *smooth interpersonal relations*:

> "Rather than seeing conflict avoidance as an end in itself, we believe that it is intimately connected to the concept of consensus. Conflicts are clearly threatening to the strong norms of upholding good conditions for dialogue, and therefore one is expected to be kind to others and not to quarrel in Sweden." (Holmberg & Åkerblom, 1998, p. 20)

Several other authors, including Parkum and Agersnap (1994) and Zander (2000), also discussed the Swedish consensus orientation in connection with the desire to *avoid conflict*. The qualitative study found the tendency to avoid conflict as one means among others to ensure smooth interpersonal relations. Zander (2000) added that "[t]here is also a rational aspect to conflict avoidance in that there is a strong belief that conflict is ineffective" (p. 348). This aspect relates to the concept of rationality (discussed below) that was also found in the qualitative study.

Rationality. Holmberg and Åkerblom (1998) observed an emphasis on reason, objectiveness and order in Swedish society and concluded that "[o]nly rational-pragmatic arguments that stick to the point are legitimate during discussions" (p. 19). In a similar vein, Czarniawska-Joerges (1993) witnessed a high of level of pragmatism and Zander (2000) attributed a strong tendency for rationality to the Swedes. Holmberg and Åkerblom (1998) assumed that "[r]ationalism and pragmatism are 'solutions' to the problem of coping with uncertainty" (p. 19). Correspondingly, the qualitative study suggests that rational behaviour is one of the vehicles to ensure smooth interpersonal relations.

Communication. The qualitative study found intensive dialogue and a non-confrontational communication style to be among the building blocks for the meaning and enactment of participative management. Auer-Rizzi and Berry (2000) reached similar conclusions in their synthesis of the communication rules prevailing among Swedes. With regard to intensive dialogue, Zander (1997) noted a preference of Swedish employees for frequent communication with their managers, both about general and personal matters. The non-confrontational communication style was also found in Suutari's (1996b) study into country-specific management styles: Finnish expatriates considered Swedish managers to be low on criticism, i.e. seldom criticising subordinates for showing poor performance or violating rules. In a like manner, Zander cited a statement common among Swedes:

> "A typical Swedish reaction when differing opinions are expressed is that 'there is no use in discussing this since we disagree'." (Zander, 2000, p. 348)

Individualism/collectivism. This culture dimension is the focus of research and topic of debate among researchers such as Hofstede (1980a), Triandis (1988, 1993), Schwartz (1990, 1994), Kagitcibasi (1994) and Kim et al. (1994). With regard to Sweden, opinions differ on the question of where on the continuum to position the country. While Hofstede (1980a) labelled Sweden a highly individualist country and Gannon et al. (1994, p. 115) noted that "[t]here is a common misconception that Sweden is a collectivist society because it is a welfare state", the GLOBE project (House et al., 2004) found Sweden's scores very high on institutional collectivism. In contrast to both positions, Hampden-Turner and Trompenaars (1993) observed that Sweden balanced both extremes of the individualism-collectivism dimension. Holmberg and Åkerblom (1998) reached a similar conclusion after they conducted a detailed analysis of the Swedish GLOBE sample with its seven culture dimensions: Sweden scored very high on *institutional collectivism* while at the same time, the scores were very low for another, partly related dimension, labelled *family collectivism*. Holmberg and Åkerblom (1998, p. 18) used the metaphor "socially concerned individualism" to explain the contradictory results for institutional collectivism and family collectivism. They argued that there seemed to exist a strict border between public and private life and that "Swedes are fundamentally individualists in the private sphere, and collectivists in the public sphere" (p. 18). Finally, Zander observed:

"[P]aradoxically, independence and self-reliance co-exist with dependence and reliance in Sweden. Independent self-reliance is valued in the family and at work, while dependence on social caring and security is a characteristic of Swedish society." (Zander, 2000, p. 350)

The findings of the qualitative study that collectivism is high in Sweden correspond with the positions of Hampden-Turner and Trompenaars (1993), Holmberg and Åkerblom (1998) and Zander (2000). With regard to the workplace, the qualitative findings suggest a simultaneous appreciation of the group and the individual, with participative decision-making going hand in hand with an appreciation of individual contributions and independent work.

With regard to the concept *lagom*, Holmberg and Åkerblom (1998) confirmed the concept's importance for an understanding of individualism and collectivism in the Swedish context. They described the concept's origin as follows:

"The untranslatable term *lagom* [...] expresses the delicate balance and optimisation of individual and collective interests. Its originals are found in *viking* times, when a bowl of a beer-like drink was shared among those seated around the table. Doubts arouse about how much to sip: not too much (which would upset the others by not leaving enough drink left), not too little (as one also wanted to enjoy the drink). A *lagom* sip is 'just right' for fulfilling the two conflicting interests." (Holmberg & Åkerblom, 1998, p. 20, footnote, italics in original)

The role of the manager and autonomous subordinates. Holmberg and Åkerblom (1998) defined *team leadership* as a central element of the managerial role, similar to the concept team integrator in the qualitative study. Likewise, Zander (2000) stressed that a Swedish manager should act as a coach. Even broader, Stymne (1995) viewed the Swedish manager as a mediator between conflicting interests, including those of labour and capital at the top level of the organisation.

With regard to the relationship between Swedish managers and their subordinates, there is support in the literature for high autonomy of subordinates as suggested by the qualitative study. Based on a comparative study between Swedish and French managers, d'Iribarne (1998) concluded that Swedish employees are used to arranging things among themselves. Zander (1997) stated in her comparative study into "interpersonal leadership" that Swedish employees prefer their managers to empower and coach them, whereas they show a very weak preference for supervision. Finally, Suutari (1996b) reported that Finns consider Swedish managers high on autonomy and delegation.

In summary, a large number of publications dealing with management and participation in Sweden confirm the overall findings of the qualitative study or selected parts of it, such as equality and fairness, smooth interpersonal relations, conflict avoidance, rationality, communication patterns, individualism/collectivism, the role of the manager and autonomous subordinates. The contribution of the qualitative study to the literature consists of making explicit the relationships among these concepts within the context of participative management.

Chapter 11

Inter-Country Analysis

11.1 Introduction and Country Summaries

The country-specific models presented in Chapters 6 to 10 are based on concepts that emerged from the interview data with middle managers in the five countries selected for the current study. Tables 11.1 to 11.5 below provide per country summary overviews. The subsequent inter-country analysis compares the country-specific models and looks for areas of convergence and divergence. The analysis also relates back to the conceptual participation literature presented in Chapter 2.1 and assesses the fit of the current qualitative findings with the various theories and models.

In line with the country chapters' focus on *repeated* occurrences in the interview data, the inter-country analysis discusses main *patterns* of participative management. Several of the described concepts, such as the meaning of participation or the role of the manager concern the very core of participative management. Some of the concepts also parallel the *key* attributes of participative management presented in Table 3.1, e.g. participation range or outcomes of participative management. In addition, the analysis presents concepts *related* to participation such as situational and society-level influence factors. Some of these related concepts, for instance the societal culture dimensions power distance, uncertainty avoidance and collectivism, were explicitly inquired into during the interviews. Other concepts such as decision type emerged from the data.

Table 11.1 Qualitative Findings Summary for the Czech Republic

Aspects	Findings
Meaning of pm in context	
Basic values	Adaptability, flexibility, creativity and diplomacy
Guiding principles	Adjustment and taking things as they come
Meaning of pm	Highly positive rhetoric about participation (goal: good decision quality) is contrasted by descriptions of autocratic managerial practice
Responsible for dm	The manager
Range of participants	Subordinates and, when needed, specialists
Role of the manager	Autocratic decision-maker with far-reaching responsibility for subordinates' work and wellbeing, who is a knowledgeable and diplomatic expert
Role of subordinates	Considered either trustworthy experts (involved in decision-making) or irresponsible "children" (excluded from decision-making)
Other participants	Specialists (outside experts) are highly regarded contributors to decision-making
Enactment of pm	
Setting	One-on-one conversation vs. group meeting, pseudo participation
Process	Subordinates, when viewed as experts: consultation
Autocratic behaviour	Autocratic decision-making is common
Outcomes of pm	Subordinates, when viewed as "children": only autocratic behaviour can ensure high decision quality; subordinates, when viewed as experts: high decision quality and motivation of subordinates
Situational influences	
Decision type	Operational matters (+), strategic decisions (-), HR decisions (-)
Time-related issues	Time pressure (-), small decisions are considered a waste of time (-)
Potential conflict	No conflict avoidance per se, but managers are under pressure to prevent conflict (unproductive use of time), participation assumed to increase the likelihood of conflict
Open conflict	Strong and active manager involvement in quick conflict resolution, strategies vary
Organisation type	Small (+) vs. large (-) units and organisations, multinational enterprises (+)
Society-related influences	
Historic factors	Foreign rule in the country's history and former communist system
Economic factors	Transition to market economy
Power distance	Considered high in society and organisations, shared viewpoint that hierarchy is needed
Uncertainty avoidance	Perceived chaos in society, yet enough flexibility to handle situation

Notes: pm = participative management, dm = decision-making, (+) = participation considered positive, (-) = participation considered negative

Table 11.2 Qualitative Findings Summary for Finland

Aspects	Findings
Meaning of pm in context	
Basic values	Autonomy and concern for quality
Guiding principles	Independence and integration
Meaning of pm	Participative management is a tool for the integration of independent work and opinions
Responsible for dm	The manager
Range of participants	Mainly subordinates
Role of the manager	Facilitator and integrator, who is the contact person to other (also rather autonomous) organisational units
Role of subordinates	Autonomous and empowered, are provided all relevant information to ensure effective decision-making
Enactment of pm	
Setting	One-on-one conversation vs. group meeting, formal vs. informal settings
Process	Information exchange and consultation
Autocratic behaviour	Some issues considered autonomous sphere of the manager
Outcomes of pm	Synthesis and integration of autonomous work and opinions, high decision quality, some mention of subordinate motivation
Situational influences	
Decision type	Important/strategic decisions (+), unimportant/small decisions (-)
Time-related issues	Unimportant problems are considered a waste of time (-)
Potential conflict	Task-related conflict expected, assumption that the autonomous approach to work may lead to differing views of a problem
Open conflict	Managers tend to prefer informal and small group meetings (fit with the Finnish mode of communication), participation is limited in cases of strong and personal conflict
Society-related influences	
Historic factors	Foreign rule in the country's history
Power distance	Considered low in society and organisations
Individualism/ collectivism	High individualism at the individual level, society is built upon collectivist principles

Notes: pm = participative management, dm = decision-making, (+) = participation considered positive, (-) = participation considered negative

Table 11.3 Qualitative Findings Summary for Germany

Aspects	Findings
Meaning of pm in context	
Basic values	Effectiveness
Guiding principles	Optimising work and management
Meaning of pm	Participation is an integral part of managerial decision-making, used as a tool to achieve sound decisions and to ensure employee motivation
Responsible for dm	The manager vs. shared responsibility of all decision participants
Range of participants	Subordinates and, when needed, specialists
Role of the manager	Goal-oriented, role model, provides the basis for intrinsic motivation of subordinates, team-oriented, has good communication skills
Role of subordinates	Considered to be "valuable human capital" contributing effectively to decision-making
Other participants	Specialists (external consultants) are used for consultation (final decisions made within the organisation)
Enactment of pm	
Setting	One-on-one conversation vs. group meeting
Process	Consultation and joint decision-making
Autocratic behaviour	Accepted by subordinates for certain issues and when accompanied by trust and a priori information/ex post explanation
Outcomes of pm	Task-related outcomes: high decision quality, overall economic success; people-related outcomes: decision commitment, subordinate motivation
Situational influences	
Decision type	Task-related decisions (+), administrative decisions (-) (participation often not considered necessary, since formal rules apply), HR decisions (-) (problematic for participation, since such issues as pay are a taboo)
Time-related issues	Awareness that participation takes time; when the process exceeds tolerated time frame, managers try to reach quick decision
Potential conflict	Conflict is viewed as natural and as a learning opportunity, usually conflict does not influence choice of decision-making process (exception: more autocratic, when goal conflict)
Open conflict	Managers expect subordinates to try to solve conflict among themselves before approaching the manager (exception: escalating conflict)
Society-related influences	
Historic factors	Country's role in the Second World War
Power distance	A certain level of power distance is considered necessary in society and organisations
Individualism/ collectivism	The economic system is based on collectivist ideas (co-determination, works councils)
Uncertainty avoidance	Perception: too many regulations; but also: desire for structure and order

Notes: pm = participative management, dm = decision-making, (+) = participation considered positive, (-) = participation considered negative

Table 11.4 Qualitative Findings Summary for Poland

Aspects	Findings
Meaning of pm in context	
Basic values	Economic efficiency
Guiding principles	Organisational survival and prosperity
Meaning of pm	Participation equals information retrieval
Responsible for dm	The manager
Range of participants	Mainly subordinates, who possess information relevant for decision-making
Role of the manager	Autocratic decision-maker, possesses knowledge and expertise, seeks information actively, provides stability
Role of subordinates	Some subordinates are highly valued as experts (involved in decision-making), subordinates in general are assumed to need a "strong hand", metaphor: "organisational cogs"
Enactment of pm	
Setting	Meetings (unspecified)
Process	Information delivery
Autocratic behaviour	Autocratic decision-making is common, in particular when the manager has all relevant information to make a decision; no need to explain an autocratic decision to the subordinates
Outcomes of pm	Efficiency and economic success
Situational influences	
Decision type	Task-related (in principle +) vs. personal problems (-), strategic (-) vs. minor (+) decisions, serious (-) vs. simple (+) problems, HR decisions (-)
Time-related issues	Time constraints (-), efficient use of time is important
Potential conflict	Conflict is viewed as an obstacle to efficient and fast decision-making
Open conflict	Managers tend to react to open conflict with autocratic behaviour
Organisation type	Service organisations (+) vs. traditional productions firms (-), organisations that require competent subordinates (+)
Society-related influences	
Historic factors	Former communist system
Economic factors	Transition to market economy
Power distance	Considered high in society and organisations
Uncertainty avoidance	Considered too low, perceived chaos in society; longing for more stability

Notes: pm = participative management, dm = decision-making, (+) = participation considered positive, (-) = participation considered negative

Table 11.5 Qualitative Findings Summary for Sweden

Aspects	Findings
Meaning of pm in context	
Basic values	Equality and fairness
Guiding principles	Smooth interpersonal relations
Meaning of pm	Participation is a "natural" ingredient of decision-making
Responsible for dm	Officially the manager, but decisions emerge from the consultation process
Range of participants	Various parties, including subordinates
Role of the manager	Responsible for smooth interpersonal relations, team integrator, lets subordinates work independently, is an equal partner in consultations with subordinates
Role of subordinates	Expected to contribute to a smooth decision-making process, are provided with all relevant information to ensure effective decision-making
Other participants	Decision-makers ask various parties for their opinions
Enactment of pm	
Setting	One-on-one conversation vs. group meeting
Process	Consultations from which decisions emerge, maintaining good relations
Autocratic behaviour	Autocratic decision-making is seldom, but is likely accepted in case of conflict or when the manager can provide rational reasons for such behaviour
Outcomes of pm	Increased level of performance and work satisfaction, involvement ensures smooth interpersonal relations
Situational influences	
Decision type	Task-related (+) vs. personal (-) problems, important (+) vs. unimportant (-) problems, familiar problems (-) vs. new cases (+), value decisions (-), "burden" problems (-)
Time-related issues	Time pressure (-), problems with no need for discussion are considered a waste of time (-)
Potential conflict	Conflict is considered a threat to smooth interpersonal relations
Open conflict	Managers actively involved in conflict resolution, the goal is to return to normal interactions as quickly as possible
Society-related influences	
Power distance	Considered very low in society and organisations, reflecting a high level of equality
Individualism/ collectivism	Parallel importance of individualism and collectivism
Uncertainty avoidance	Considered high

Notes: pm = participative management, dm = decision-making, (+) = participation considered positive, (-) = participation considered negative

11.2 The Meaning of Participative Management in Context

The first research question of the current study concentrates on the country-specific meaning and enactment of participative management. Meaning relates to how people in different countries define and understand the concept of participative management. Enactment deals with the results of how this meaning is translated into behaviour. This section (11.2) compares the main findings of the country analyses with regard to the *meaning* aspect of participative management. Section 11.3 below deals with *enactment*.

The study of meaning requires exploring the concept of participative management in context: The country analyses presented in Chapters 6 to 10 show that the emerging models of participative management are attributable to a small number of influencing *values*. These values tie in with the *guiding principles* that at least partly define the specific meaning of participative management as well as the respective *roles* of the manager, the subordinates and other parties possibly involved in the participatory decision-making process. In some of the countries, accepted and country-typical *communication patterns* also emerged from the data as being closely related to the meaning of participative management.

11.2.1 Basic Values and Guiding Principles

This section summarises and compares country-specific basic values and guiding principles relevant for participative management.

Table 11.6 Basic Values and Guiding Principles

Country	Basic values	Guiding principles	Chapters
Czech Republic	Adaptability, flexibility, creativity and diplomacy	Adjustment and taking things as they come	6.2.1 - 6.2.2
Finland	Autonomy and concern for quality	Independence and integration	7.2.1 - 7.2.3
Germany	Effectiveness	Optimising work and management	8.2.1 - 8.2.2
Poland	Economic efficiency	Organisational survival and prosperity	9.2.1 - 9.2.2
Sweden	Equality and fairness	Smooth interpersonal relations	10.2.1 - 10.2.2

Table 11.6 shows vast differences between the five countries. Values and guiding principles concern either the individual level (e.g. creativity), the interpersonal/group level (e.g. smooth interpersonal relations) or the macro/organisational level (e.g. economic efficiency). Table 11.7 lists the level(s) at which the emerging values and guiding principles tend to be lo-

cated, thus illustrating the difference between the five countries even more
clearly.

Table 11.7 Levels of Basic Values and Guiding Principles

Country	Basic values	Guiding principles
Czech Republic	Individual	Individual
Finland	Individual and organisational	Individual and organisational
Germany	Organisational	Organisational
Poland	Organisational	Organisational
Sweden	Group	Group

The differentiation between individual/group on the one hand and organisation on the other hand resembles the dichotomy of person/relationship vs.
task orientation in cross-cultural management (Adler, 2002). With regard to
this differentiation, the results of the current and rather specific study (with
its exclusive focus on participative management) have some equivalence in
earlier research of a broader orientation: Laurent (1983) as well as Schroll-
Machl and Wiskoski (2003) attributed high task-orientation to the Germans,
which is in line with the organisational-level values and guiding principles
found in the present study. Schroll-Machl and Novy (2000) described the
Czechs as highly focused on person orientation, which is consistent with the
individual level values and guiding principles emerging from the present
study. As for the Polish managers, the qualitative study suggests a strong
focus on the organisation, which would be consistent with high task orientation. This finding is in contrast to Schroll-Machl and Wiskoski (2003), but
consistent with Hofstede (2001), who observed a certain predominance of
the efficiency paradigm in today's Poland. In exact agreement with the latter
finding, economic efficiency was also the one basic value emerging from the
current Polish data.

11.2.2 The Meaning of Participative Management

The data analysis found distinct country differences concerning the specific
meaning of participative management (Table 11.8)
    The meaning of participative management ranges from the understand-
ing of Swedish interviewees that participation is a "natural" ingredient of
decision-making to the view of Polish managers that participation means
information retrieval from subordinates. In between these two extremes are
the views of the German and Finnish managers, who view participation as a
valuable managerial tool. Finally, the data suggest a specific pattern for the
Czech managers, namely attributing positive connotations to participative

management, which are, however, not reflected in their descriptions of managerial decision-making practice.

Table 11.8   The Meaning of Participative Management

Country	Summary findings	Chapter
Czech Republic	Highly positive rhetoric about participation (goal: good decision quality) is contrasted by descriptions of autocratic managerial practice	6.2.3
Finland	Participative management is a tool for the integration of independent work and opinions	7.2.4
Germany	Participation is an integral part of managerial decision-making, used as a tool to achieve sound decisions and to ensure employee motivation	8.2.3
Poland	Participation equals information retrieval	9.2.3
Sweden	Participation is a "natural" ingredient of decision-making	10.2.3

The German and Swedish models of participative management clearly resemble what Chisholm and Vansina (1993) labelled an *overall management philosophy* (Chapter 2.1.2). In the case of Sweden, managers and subordinates alike seem to share and expect this philosophy implicitly, while the German managers seem to make a conscious effort to employ participation as a highly effective managerial tool. Similarly, the Finnish interviews suggest that participation is considered an important managerial tool. However, participation in the Finnish context is just *one* tool among others, and in terms of relevance it seems to be third to empowerment and delegation.

Glew et al.'s (1995) synthesis of various definitions of participation and conclusion that participation refers to intentional programs or practices developed by the organisation to involve numerous employees (Chapter 2.1.1) seems to represent a view too limited to fit the findings of all five countries included in the present study. Particularly the Swedish data suggest that participation is much more than an intentionally implemented organisational tool. Rather, participation in Sweden seems to be deeply embedded in the culture and is consequently "almost automatically" employed in organisational settings.

Strauss (1998a) differentiated three theoretical arguments supporting participation: organisation efficiency, power sharing and humanism (Chapter 2.1.2). The current study suggests that the country-specific models of participative management rest on partly differing pillars:

Participation from the organisational efficiency perspective concerns such areas as higher quality decisions, better communication and co-operation, facilitation of organisational learning, a minimised need for supervision and new skills development. The efficiency argument fits, at least to some degree, with the Czech, Finnish, German, Polish and Swedish models of participation. High quality decisions are an issue in all five countries (compare Section 11.3.2 below), whereas the focus on economic success is most articulate in the Polish data. With regard to communication, however, arguments such as "participation improves communication" were of little concern to both Czech and Polish interviewees. In contrast, communication and cooperation seemed to be an important matter for the German, Finnish and Swedish managers: In Finland, participation in fact represents an ideal chance to communicate autonomous perspectives and work. From a Swedish perspective, improving communication by way of participation is not needed, since Swedes share a preference for communication and dialogue anyway. Consequently, participation in Sweden is not used as a *means* to increase communication, it rather serves as an *expression* of the desire for intensive dialogue. Among the German managers, the efficiency argument is additionally addressed by a strong focus on learning.

With regard to the power sharing view, i.e. the assumption that autocratic relationships are inconsistent with the values of a democratic society, Germany's past and particularly its role in World War II were pivotal reasons for the post-war implementation of participatory structures (Chapter 8.6.2) that reflect upon today's participatory management practices. The power sharing view may have played a role in Sweden's past as well. However, in contemporary Swedish society and organisations power is perceived to be relatively equally distributed anyway. In this sense, participation is an expression of rather than a tool for equality.

In contrast to the other countries, the German and Swedish models of participation also build on the humanistic view, i.e. the assumption that participation satisfies employees' needs for achievement, social approval and creativity.

Black and Gregersen (1997) described five steps in a typical decision-making process and Adler (2002) discussed cultural contingencies during different stages of decision-making: identifying the problem, generating possible solutions (including information search and construction of alternatives), selecting one solution, implementation and evaluating the results (Chapter 2.2.1). The current study allows explicit statements predominately for the stages ranging from generating possible solutions to selecting one solution. Problem identification was not an explicit topic in the current study. Implementation and evaluation were also not central areas of inquiry, although in some cases interviewees referred to these processes. The findings of the current study suggest that there are country-specific preferences as to which stages to consider relevant for participative management:

The Polish data clearly stress *information search*, more than the other four countries. In fact, the Polish interviewees described participation as limited to this stage. The interviewees of the other four countries did not differentiate information search from the *construction of alternatives*. Rather, they described the whole decision-making process in a rather unspecified way and did not separate information exchange from consultation.

The stage *selecting one solution* parallels the current study's step "final decision", as described in the country chapters. Table 11.9 summarises who, according to the interviewees, tends to make the final decision and to assume responsibility for it.

Table 11.9 Who is Responsible for a Decision?

Country	Person/group	Chapter
Czech Republic	The manager	6.2.3
Finland	The manager	7.2.4
Germany	The manager vs. shared responsibility of all decision participants	8.2.3
Poland	The manager	9.2.3
Sweden	Officially the manager, but decisions emerge from the consultation process	10.2.3

It seems that the managers in the Czech Republic, Finland and Poland reserve the right to make the final decision themselves, whereas the Swedish managers stressed the manager's *official* responsibility, which includes the possibility of joint decision-making *internally*. In Germany, interviewees mentioned the possibility of *explicitly* agreeing upon shared decision-making responsibility in addition to the typical sole responsibility of the manager.

The different meaning of participative management across the five country samples is also expressed in the varying descriptions as to *who* participates in the decision-making process. Of course, the range of participants also varies within each country, this variation depending on individual and organisational preferences as well as on such factors as decision type (Section 11.4.1), time-related issues (Section 11.4.2) and conflict (Section 11.4.3). However, some general country-specific patterns emerged from the data and these patterns are summarised in Table 11.10.

Table 11.10 Range of Participants

Country	Summary findings	Chapter
Czech Republic	Subordinates and, when needed, specialists	6.2.3
Finland	Mainly subordinates	7.2.4
Germany	Subordinates and, when needed, specialists	8.2.3
Poland	Mainly subordinates, who possess information relevant for decision-making	9.2.3
Sweden	Various parties, including subordinates	10.2.3

Irrespective of the country, subordinates are the "obvious" participants in managerial decision-making, whereas other parties, such as specialists, play a vital role in only some of the countries. The Swedish data suggest the widest range of participants. More details on the parties involved in participatory decision-making follow below in the description of the roles ascribed to subordinates and other participants (Section 11.2.4).

The current finding of country differences with regard to the range of participants highlights the relevance of Dachler and Wilpert's (1978) mention of the range of people involved in participation (Chapter 2.1.1). As the current qualitative data suggest, the participation range differs not merely depending on such factors as decision type, it is additionally contingent on country and culture.

11.2.3 The Role of the Manager

The country analyses show that the role ascribed to managers is a factor, which greatly influences the meaning of participative management. Country-specific managerial roles emerged for all five countries (Table 11.11).

Table 11.11 The Role of the Manager

Country	Summary findings	Chapter
Czech Republic	Autocratic decision-maker with far-reaching responsibility for subordinates' work and wellbeing, who is a knowledgeable and diplomatic expert	6.2.4
Finland	Facilitator and integrator, who is the contact person to other (also rather autonomous) organisational units	7.2.5
Germany	Goal-oriented, role model, provides the basis for intrinsic motivation of subordinates, team-oriented, has good communication skills	8.2.4
Poland	Autocratic decision-maker, possesses knowledge and expertise, seeks information actively, provides stability	9.2.4
Sweden	Responsible for smooth interpersonal relations, team integrator, lets subordinates work independently, is an equal partner in consultations with subordinates	10.2.4

Table 11.11 implies divergence in the managerial role in line with Adler's (2002) suggestion that managers in different countries tend to be considered either experts or problem solvers (coaches). Also in agreement with the findings of the current study, the literature suggests the following relationship between the managerial role and culture dimensions: In cultures combining high power distance with high uncertainty avoidance, the preference for experts dominates. In contrast, the combination of low power distance and low uncertainty avoidance implies a preference for a coaching role (Hof-

stede, 2001). The Hofstede data parallel the findings of the current study: Poland (high power distance and high uncertainty avoidance) emerged from both types of research as a country in which a preference for expert managers is prevalent, whereas the Swedish data (low power distance and low uncertainty avoidance) suggest a preference for the manager in a coaching role.

Adler and Hofstede's differentiation between the expert and coaching roles mirrors Laurent's (1983) findings. In this study, respondents in a large number of countries were asked whether they found it important for managers to be able to provide precise answers to most of their subordinates' work-related questions. In agreement with Laurent, who included Sweden and Germany in his sample, the current interviewees' preference for the coaching role was stronger in Sweden (Laurent found only ten percent agreement with the statement requesting precise answers by the manager) than in Germany (forty-six percent agreement).

The qualitative data suggest a link between the role of the manager and the range of participants in the decision-making process summarised in Table 11.10 above. Neither Swedish nor German or Finnish managers seem to be expected to be uncontested experts in the area of their decision-making competencies and consequently, the inclusion of advice and counselling in managerial decision-making is acceptable. The Polish data represent the opposite case: Polish managers are portrayed as experts and consequently, there is likely to be little acceptance of additional participants in the decision-making process.

11.2.4 The Role of Subordinates and Other Participants

Subordinates are the most important participants in managerial decision-making, as shown in the analysis of the range of participants above (Table 11.10). However, the role ascribed to subordinates by the interviewees differs according to country (Table 11.12).

In the Czech Republic, two different subordinate roles emerged from the data: subordinates viewed as trustworthy experts vs. subordinates considered to be "children". The first group of subordinates is involved in decision-making, whereas the second group is typically excluded. A similar pattern emerged from the Polish data, where expert subordinates tend to be involved in decision-making more frequently than other subordinates.

In Finland, Sweden and Germany subordinates are highly valued for their contributions. However, managers in these three countries also differ from one another when ascribing specific roles to subordinates, these roles being consistent with the respective country-specific values and guiding principles: Finnish subordinates are considered autonomous and are expected to participate in decision-making in order to help the manager integrate and synthesise information and ideas. Swedish subordinates are expected to contribute to a smooth decision-making process, and efforts are made to allow them to do so, for instance by making sure they are provided with all relevant information. The German subordinate role includes the image of "valuable human capital", implying that subordinates are assumed to be able to contribute effectively to decision-making.

Table 11.12 The Role of Subordinates

Country	Summary findings	Chapter
Czech Republic	Considered either trustworthy experts (involved in decision-making) or irresponsible "children" (excluded from decision-making)	6.2.5
Finland	Autonomous and empowered, are provided all relevant information to ensure effective decision-making	7.2.6
Germany	Considered to be "valuable human capital" contributing effectively to decision-making	8.2.5
Poland	Some subordinates are highly valued as experts (involved in decision-making), subordinates in general are assumed to need a "strong hand", metaphor: "organisational cogs"	9.2.5
Sweden	Expected to contribute to a smooth decision-making process, are provided all relevant information to ensure effective decision-making	10.2.5

Parties other than subordinates also play a role in managerial decision-making, as the explicit references by the Czech, German and Swedish inter-viewees suggest (Table 11.13). In the Czech Republic and Germany, the focus is on specialists, whereas in Sweden specialists *and* other parties tend to be included in decision-making.

Table 11.13 The Role of Other Participants

Country	Summary findings	Chapter
Czech Republic	Specialists (outside experts) are highly regarded contributors to decision-making	6.2.6
Germany	Specialists (external consultants) are used for consultation (final decisions made within the organisation)	8.2.6
Sweden	Decision-makers ask various parties for their opinions	10.2.5

11.3 The Enactment of Participative Management

Following the above country comparison of the *meaning* of participative management, this section summarises and compares the main findings of the country analyses with regard to the *enactment* aspect of participative management.

11.3.1 Participative vs. Autocratic Decision-Making

Table 11.14 refers to general tendencies in the data independent of situational influence factors (Section 11.4). As a general finding, the data show for all five countries that the patterns of participative managerial behaviour fit well with the emerging overall meaning of participation: The Czech managers in the sample consult with their subordinates only when they consider them to be experts. The Finnish managers exchange information with subordinates and consult with them in a manner consistent with the Finnish preference for integration. The German managers rely on consultation and joint decision-making corresponding to their view of participation as a tool to achieve sound decisions and to ensure employee motivation. The Polish managers seek information in order to be able to make better decisions themselves. Finally, the Swedish managers use consultation in ways consistent with their values and communication patterns and above all they try to maintain good interpersonal relations.

Table 11.14 Enactment of Participative Decision-Making

Country	Process	Setting	Chapter
Czech Republic	Subordinates, when viewed as experts: consultation	One-on-one conversation vs. group meeting, pseudo participation	6.3.1
Finland	Information exchange and consultation	One-on-one conversation vs. group meeting, formal vs. informal settings	7.3.1
Germany	Consultation and joint decision-making	One-on-one conversation vs. group meeting	8.3.1
Poland	Information delivery	Meetings (unspecified)	9.3.1
Sweden	Consultations from which decisions emerge, maintaining good relations	One-on-one conversation vs. group meeting	10.3.1

With regard to setting, there was a general tendency among the interviewees in all five countries to differentiate between one-on-one conversation and group meetings.

In all five countries, the interviewees also described situations in which they made the decision by themselves. In most cases specific influence factors made them choose this option (Sections 11.4 and 11.5). However, there are also some general patterns with regard to autocratic decision-making, which are summarised in Table 11.15. I would like to stress that the term "autocratic" is not meant to be negative, but simply refers to the specific behaviour of a manager making a decision by her or himself without involving others in the decision-making process. The interviewees themselves used the term autocratic to a varying degree. For example, the Swedish and Finnish managers hardly ever mentioned it, but rather referred to the "autonomous sphere" of the manager. The situation was similar in Germany, where expressions such as "I did it by myself" or "I made the decision alone" were common. German interviewees also suggested that the German term "autokratisch" had a quite negative connotation. In the Polish and Czech context, the interviewees used the term autocratic more frequently, but also referred to negative connotations, mainly in the context of decision-making in the former communist system.

Table 11.15 Autocratic Decision-Making

Country	Summary findings	Chapter
Czech Republic	Autocratic decision-making is common	6.3.1
Finland	Some issues considered autonomous sphere of the manager	7.3.1
Germany	Accepted by subordinates for certain issues and when accompanied by trust and a priori information/ex post explanation	8.3.1
Poland	Autocratic decision-making is common, in particular when the manager has all relevant information to make a decision; no need to explain an autocratic decision to the subordinates	9.3.1
Sweden	Autocratic decision-making is seldom, but is likely accepted in case of conflict or when the manager can provide rational reasons for such behaviour	10.3.1

The use of autocratic managerial behaviour complements the use of participation: Autocratic decision-making was described as rather common by the Czech and Polish interviewees, consistent with the finding of rather limited use of participative management. The opposite is true for the Swedish and German samples. In these two countries, the use of autocratic behaviour seems to require a specific context (e.g. conflict in Sweden) and/or accompanying managerial behaviour (e.g. *ex post* explanation) in order to be accepted by the subordinates. Finally, the Finnish interviewees classified autocratic decision-making as "normal" behaviour within the autonomous sphere of the manager in specific organisations and positions as well as in situations in which employees had little or no background information.

11.3.2 Participative Management Outcomes

This section summarises the outcomes that the interviewees described in relation to the use of participative management (Table 11.16). The findings are reflective of the managers' experience and expectations and do not represent actual and measured outcome factors.

Table 11.16 Outcomes of Participative Management

Country	Summary findings	Chapter
Czech Republic	Subordinates, when viewed as "children": only autocratic behaviour can ensure high decision quality; subordinates, when viewed as experts: high decision quality and motivation of subordinates	6.3.2
Finland	Synthesis and integration of autonomous work and opinions, high decision quality, some mention of subordinate motivation	7.3.2
Germany	Task-related outcomes: high decision quality, overall economic success; people-related outcomes: decision commitment, subordinate motivation	8.3.2
Poland	Efficiency and economic success	9.3.2
Sweden	Increased level of performance and work satisfaction, involvement ensures smooth interpersonal relations	10.3.2

The interviewees mentioned various outcomes of participative management. Most of their references fit the categories "decision quality", "decision commitment and motivation" and "additional outcomes" (Table 11.17).

Table 11.17 Types of Outcomes of Participative Management

Czech Republic (Expert view)	Finland	Germany	Poland	Sweden
Decision quality	Decision quality	Decision quality	Decision quality	Decision quality
Decision commitment and motivation	Decision commitment and motivation	Decision commitment and motivation		Decision commitment and motivation
	Additional outcome: Integration			Additional outcome: Good interpersonal relations

Decision quality seems to be a shared concern among the managers from all five countries. In contrast to the managers of the other countries, the Polish managers did not refer to *decision commitment and motivation*. This lack of subordinate focus fits with the strong preference for organisational values and guiding principles in the Polish data, as described in Table 11.7 above. As for *additional outcomes*, the Finnish interviewees mentioned integration, which is consistent with the Finnish meaning of participative management (Section 11.2.2). Good interpersonal relations emerged as envisioned participation outcome from the Swedish data, which fits with the detected Swedish values and guiding principles related to participative management (Section 11.2.1).

As for the Czech managers, only those who described their subordinates as experts mentioned outcome factors. In contrast, when subordinates were described as "children", the Czech interviewees did not consider participation at all and consequently did not refer to any participation outcomes.

The two main groups of outcomes discussed in the participation literature concern the factors productivity and satisfaction (Chapter 2.1.4). Despite differences in the meaning and enactment of participative management, the interviewees from all five countries seem to assume that participative management is beneficial in the area of decision quality, which is in line with the literature's focus on *productivity* as a major participation outcome. The interview data further suggest that decision commitment and motivation, which parallel the literature's participation outcome *satisfaction*, are important to the Finnish, German and Swedish managers, but do not (yet) seem to be a major issue for the managers in the two former communist countries.

Chapter 2.1.4 presented three explanatory models of participative effects: cognitive models (arguing that participation enhances the flow and use of important information in the organisation, which increases productivity), affective models (suggesting that participation fulfils employees' needs leading to higher satisfaction and increased motivation and, in turn, to higher productivity) and contingency models (arguing that participation affects satisfaction and productivity in varying ways for different individuals and situations). The interviewees in all five countries implicitly comply with the *contingency* model: Situational differences were clearly articulated with regard to decision type (Section 11.4.1 below) and conflict (Section 11.4.3 below). The Czechs and Poles further considered organisational factors (Section 11.4.4 below), and the Czechs also differentiated between different groups of subordinates (Section 11.2.4 above). The *cognitive* model is present in the perspectives of the Finnish (co-ordination of and exchange among autonomous actors) and Polish managers (emphasis on information collection). The *affective* model is most clearly represented in the Swedish data (interpersonal relations dominate all elements of the Swedish model of participative management) and the German model has both cognitive and affective perspectives (focus on efficiency including learning and motivation).

11.4 Main Situational Influence Factors

The second research question deals with the main situational factors that constitute the meaning and enactment of participation. As suggested in Sections 11.2 and 11.3, there are many country-specific particularities. However, three situational influence factors emerged from the data in all five countries, namely decision type, time-related issues and conflict. Additional country-specific factors, such as type of work unit and type of organisation, are also described below.

11.4.1 Decision Type

Decision type was discovered to strongly influence whether or not managers make use of participation and to what extent (Table 11.18). The three categories most frequently mentioned relate to major (strategic/large/important) versus minor (operational/small/unimportant) decisions, as well as to Human Resource (HR) decisions (Table 11.19).

Table 11.18 Decision Types

Country	Summary findings	Chapter
Czech Republic	Operational matters (+), strategic decisions (-), HR decisions (-)	6.4.1
Finland	Important/strategic decisions (+), unimportant/small decisions (-)	7.4.1
Germany	Task-related decisions (+), administrative decisions (-) (participation often not considered necessary, since formal rules apply), HR decisions (-) (problematic for participation, since such issues as pay are a taboo)	8.4.1
Poland	Task-related (in principle +) vs. personal problems (-), strategic (-) vs. minor (+) decisions, serious (-) vs. simple (+) problems, HR decisions (-)	9.4.1
Sweden	Task-related (+) vs. personal (-) problems, important (+) vs. unimportant (-) problems, familiar problems (-) vs. new cases (+), value decisions (-), "burden" problems (-)	10.4.1

Notes: (+) = participation considered positive, (-) = participation considered negative

Table 11.19 Groups of Decision Types

Group	Czech Republic	Finland	Germany	Poland	Sweden
Major decisions (strategic/large/important)	(-)	(+)	(+)	(-)	(+)
Minor decisions (operational/small/unimportant)	(+)	(-)	(+)	(+)	Operational/small: + Unimportant: -
HR decisions	(-)	n.r.	(-)	(-)	n.r.

Notes: (+) = participation considered positive, (-) = participation considered negative, n.r. = no reference in the data

Whether a decision-making situation is difficult or easy, important or unimportant is partly based on the manager's subjective evaluation. If and how participation is utilised depends on the framing of the situation, a process during which both cultural influences and person-related factors such as experience are relevant. How a manager reacts to such a perceived/framed situation is, in turn, partially influenced by cultural standards:

In Germany, both major and minor decisions qualify equally well for subordinate involvement in decision-making, this view being based mainly on the assumption that participation can improve decision quality *and* commitment (Table 11.17) irrespective of the decision's level of importance. In contrast to Germany, participatory decision-making is preferred for major decisions by managers in Finland and Sweden, whereas minor decisions are solved with less subordinate involvement in Sweden and with a preference for delegation in Finland. The main argument for the Swedish solution is that managers should not bother subordinates with unimportant problems, whereas all other issues deserve as many opinions as possible. In Finland, empowerment and delegation are highly valued and practised and consequently, only decisions requiring integration (mainly major decisions) call for participation. The Czech and Polish data suggest a reversed pattern. Participation is "tolerated" for minor issues, whereas major decisions are solved at the managerial level. In the Polish case, this pattern likely originates from the image of managers being authoritarian figures, who are under pressure to achieve economic success, and from the assumption that participation should be allowed at least on some occasions. Consequently, allowing Polish subordinates to participate on minor decisions is a compromise to satisfy the divergent forces. In the case of the Czech Republic, mental and organisational structures in the workplace seem to serve as barriers that prevent a more extensive use of participation: Many subordinates and some of the managers still seem to hold the opinion that participation reflects managerial weakness and indecisiveness.

The Czech, German and Polish data show a tendency of managers to restrict participation for HR decisions: According to the Czech managers, HR questions can best be solved either alone or by consulting with outside experts. The German managers described it as unusual to discuss such issues as pay openly and in large groups. The Polish managers considered HR issues to be best dealt with autocratically, possibly involving their own superior.

Knudsen's (1995) observation that direct employee participation is most relevant in operational issues compared to strategic, tactical and welfare decisions is only partly supported by the current study: In three of the five countries represented, managers opted for participatory management in the context of strategic decisions, and only the Czech managers expressed a marked preference for participative management in operational decisions

(Chapter 6.4.1). The fact that the data show a preference for participation in strategic matters in Finland, Germany and Sweden is noteworthy since these particular countries are also characterised by participatory structures of the corporations' advisory boards (compare Chapters 7.6.2, 8.6.2 and 10.6.2).

11.4.2 Time-Related Issues

Time-related issues constitute the second main factor influencing the use of participation across country samples (Table 11.20). Time-related issues mainly concern time pressure and the efficient use of time. The data suggest that managers in all five countries tend to behave in a less participatory manner when facing time constraints, compared with cases of little time pressure.

Table 11.20 Time-Related Issues

Country	Summary findings	Chapter
Czech Republic	Time pressure (-), small decisions are considered a waste of time (-)	6.4.3
Finland	Unimportant problems are considered a waste of time (-)	7.4.2
Germany	Awareness that participation takes time; when the process exceeds tolerated time frame, managers try to reach quick decision	8.4.2
Poland	Time constraints (-), efficient use of time is important	9.4.3
Sweden	Time pressure (-), problems with no need for discussion are considered a waste of time (-)	10.4.2

Notes: (+) = participation considered positive, (-) = participation considered negative

Sometimes, regardless of country origin, participation is considered a "waste of time". However, the issues and time spans that the interviewees described as a waste of time vary across country samples. For example, the tolerated time span is fairly short for the Polish managers, resulting in quick autocratic decisions. In contrast, the German data suggest the shared perspective that participation needs time. However, when a decision-making process exceeds the tolerated time frame, German managers also try to reach a quick decision, yet not necessarily by autocratic means.

The country-specific interpretation of tolerated time spans calls to mind the two differing time concepts described by the anthropologist Edward T. Hall (Hall, 1976; Hall & Hall, 1990), namely monochronic vs. polychronic:

> "In monochronic cultures, time is experienced and used in a linear way - comparable to a road extending from the past into the future. Monochronic time is divided quite naturally into segments; it is scheduled and compartmentalised,

making it possible for a person to concentrate on one thing at a time." (Hall &
Hall, 1990, p. 13)

"Polychronic time is characterised by the simultaneous occurrence of many
things and by a *great involvement with people*. There is more emphasis on com-
pleting human transactions than on holding to schedules. [...] Polychronic time
is experienced as much less tangible than monochronic time and can better be
compared to a single point than to a road." (Hall & Hall, 1990, p. 14, italics in
original)

Germany, Sweden and Finland are described as monochronic cultures (Hall
& Hall, 1990) and the Polish culture is interpreted as polychronic (Schroll-
Machl & Wiskoski, 2003). In contrast to this classification, the current study
found no major time orientation related differences in participative management between the country samples. According to the current data,
monochronic time orientation seems to prevail, particularly among the Polish managers.

11.4.3 Conflict

Conflict is the third main situational factor influencing managerial use of
participation. The data suggest differences between the five countries. The
following paragraphs distinguish between the way managers in the five
countries deal with potential conflict (Table 11.21) and already existing
(open) conflict (Table 11.22).

Table 11.21 Potential Conflict

Country	Summary findings	Chapter
Czech Republic	No conflict avoidance per se, but managers are under pressure to prevent conflict (unproductive use of time), participation assumed to increase the likelihood of conflict	6.4.4
Finland	Task-related conflict expected, assumption that the autonomous approach to work may lead to differing views of a problem	7.4.3
Germany	Conflict is viewed as natural and as a learning opportunity, usually conflict does not influence choice of decision-making process (exception: more autocratic, when goal conflict)	8.4.3
Poland	Conflict is viewed as an obstacle to efficient and fast decision-making	9.4.4
Sweden	Conflict is considered a threat to smooth interpersonal relations	10.4.3

The data on conflict suggest that the word "conflict" carries a unique meaning in each of the five countries. For example, what is considered a "terrible

conflict" in a Swedish setting is likely to be seen as a "lively discussion" in Finland, as the following two quotes illustrate:

> "When it's really a big issue we call it a conflict. So, maybe just an argument or some kind of different opinions, these are no conflicts at all." (Finnish manager)

> "There was a meeting and the French were so accustomed to smoking in the meeting room and this guy from the UK came in and said, 'You folks, you always smoke in the conference room.' Quite a conflict!" (Swedish manager)

Taking the Swedish preference for smooth interpersonal relations into account, conflict might threaten intact relations and must be avoided at all costs, even if this means less participation. In contrast to the Swedes, the Finnish managers' preference for independent work within an integrative framework seems to lead to the expectation that conflicting opinions will and should be voiced in decision-making processes. The German managers similarly view conflict as natural and even as a learning opportunity. They only worry about conflict when it seems to get out of hand. Consequently, participatory behaviour in a German context does not seem to be influenced by potential conflict. As for the Czech Republic, the data suggest no conflict avoidance per se, but it is indicated that a certain pressure on managers to prevent conflict exists, since dealing with conflict represents an unproductive waste of time. Consequently, when a participatory setting seems to breed conflict, the Czech data suggest a tendency to switch to more autocratic forms of decision-making. In a similar vein, the Polish managers view conflict as an obstacle to efficient and fast decision-making and thus also change to more autocratic ways of decision-making.

In summary, the managers in some countries consider conflict a threat (Poland, Czech Republic, Sweden), however based on differing underlying rationales: The Poles and Czechs view conflict as a threat for economic reasons and the Swedes do so for relationship-related motives. In contrast to viewing conflict as a threat, the Finnish and German interviewees describe conflict as natural, but again for different underlying reasons: The Finns refer to the fact that autonomy and independent work naturally lead to differing opinions, whereas the Germans consider conflict an integral part of learning.

Not surprisingly, methods of conflict resolution also differ among the interviewees of the five countries (Table 11.22). Except for Germany, managers tend to get actively involved, but employing differing strategies. The analysis also sugests that actions taken by the manager are partly defined by the managerial role (Table 11.11). For example, Swedish managers are characterised as team integrators and as responsible for smooth interpersonal relations. Consequently, they bring the subordinates together and mediate. In sharp contrast, Czech managers, viewing their subordinates as "children", act in an almost parental manner and more or less try to solve the conflict for them.

Table 11.22 Open Conflict

Country	Summary findings	Chapter
Czech Republic	Strong and active manager involvement in quick conflict resolution, strategies vary	6.4.4
Finland	Managers tend to prefer informal and small group meetings (fit with the Finnish mode of communication), participation is limited in cases of strong and personal conflict	7.4.3
Germany	Managers expect subordinates to try to solve conflict among themselves before approaching the manager (exception: escalating conflict)	8.4.3
Poland	Managers tend to react to open conflict with autocratic behaviour	9.4.4
Sweden	Managers actively involved in conflict resolution, the goal is to return to normal interactions as quickly as possible	10.4.3

The found variance between conflict as a threat and conflict as a natural organisational occurrence corresponds with the literature: Conflict avoidance is described by Novy and Schroll-Machl (2003) for the Czech Republic, by Schroll-Machl and Wiskoski (2003) for Poland and by Zander (2000) for Sweden. Conflict-confronting tendencies of the Germans are described in Schroll-Machl and Wiskoski (2003) in a manner corresponding with the findings of the current study. As for the Czech Republic, the findings of the current study provide additional information: What may look like internalised conflict avoidance of Czech managers is more likely to be a reaction to external pressure.

Studies based on the Vroom/Yetton model also examined managerial reaction to conflict (compare Chapter 4.3.3.4) and measured whether managers in several countries tended to increase or decrease participation when faced with conflict. The findings of the Vroom/Yetton and the current study concur for the selected countries, except for Finland. In contrast to the Vroom/Yetton study, the qualitative research found that Finnish managers in fact expect task-related conflict, and instead of limiting participation they try to solve conflict in informal and small group meetings. This finding ties in well with Finnish communication patterns and also with the suggestion by the management and communication researcher Michael Berry, who argued (in personal conversation) that the Finnish conflict-related Vroom/Yetton results should be interpreted as a change in setting (from group to one-on-one consultation) and not as Finnish managers becoming more autocratic.

11.4.4 Other Situational Factors

Decision type, time-related issues and conflict emerged from the data of all five countries as main influence factors on participatory managerial behaviour. In Poland and the Czech Republic, type of work unit/department and type of organisation turned out to be additional influential factors (Table 11.23).

Table 11.23 Unit and Organisation Type

Country	Summary findings	Chapter
Czech Republic	Small (+) vs. large (-) units and organisations, multinational enterprises (+)	6.4.2
Poland	Service organisations (+) vs. traditional productions firms (-), organisations that require competent subordinates (+)	9.4.2

Notes: (+) = participation considered positive, (-) = participation considered negative

Only the Czech and Polish interviewees mentioned the classification of work units and organisations and their respective suitability for participative management. This point could reflect the organisational changes these countries are still undergoing after the change to market economy, and it may further refer to the fact that participation is a rather newly introduced concept and is therefore more likely attributed to the units and organisations in which it is assumed to be implemented, such as in multinational enterprises.

11.5 Main Society-Related Influence Factors

The data suggest that history as well as past and present economic environment of a given country may influence the degree and format of participative management, as do the societal culture dimensions power distance, uncertainty avoidance and individualism/collectivism. These dimensions have been repeatedly mentioned in the cross-cultural literature as influencing factors on the meaning and enactment of participative management. Consequently, questions related to these three dimensions were asked during the qualitative interviews of the current study (compare Chapter 5.2.1.4). As it turned out during the data analysis, all three dimensions are directly or indirectly relevant for a better understanding of participative management, although not all three dimensions emerged as equally relevant in each of the five countries.

11.5.1 Historic and Economic Factors

The data suggest that both history and recent economic changes influence the meaning and enactment of participative management (Table 11.24). Germany, Finland and Sweden have been stable democracies for decades, whereas a change to a democratic political system and a switch to market economy took place in the Czech Republic and Poland as late as the beginning of the 1990s.

The influence of historic and economic factors on participative management takes different forms: The Czech managers seem to be torn between the old autocratic way of thinking common during communist times and the recently introduced ways of Western management style. The Finnish appreciation of autonomy and individuality (leading to integration via participation) seems to be partly grounded in the centuries of foreign rule in the country's past. Germany introduced an economic system based on collectivist ideas with strong reliance on co-determination and works councils after the Second World War. This system is still in place today and leaves its marks on the participatory behaviour of managers. In Poland, the turbulent times after the initial introduction of market economy seem to have intensified the image of Polish managers as providers of stability, and the managers tend to do their image justice by exercising autocratic behaviour.

Table 11.24 Historic and Economic Factors

Country	History	Economic system	Chapters
Czech Republic	Foreign rule in the country's history and former communist system	Transition to market economy	6.2.7, 6.4.4, 6.5, 6.6.3
Finland	Foreign rule in the country's history	n.r.	7.6.3
Germany	Country's role in the Second World War	n.r.	8.6.3
Poland	Former communist system	Transition to market economy	9.2.2, 9.2.4, 9.5, 9.6.3
Sweden	n.r.	n.r.	

Notes: n.r. = no reference in the data. The country chapters do not contain separate sections for the presentation of historic and economic factors. Rather, references to history and economy are made whenever appropriate.

11.5.2 Power Distance

Power distance reflects the degree to which members of a society expect power to be unequally shared (Hofstede, 1980a; House et al., 2004). Table

11.25 shows that the view of power distance as portrayed by the interview partners largely overlaps with the quantitative results of the Hofstede and GLOBE studies (compare Chapter 4.1.3.2).

Table 11.25 Power Distance

Country	Summary findings	Chapter	Hofstede (2001)	House et al. (2004)
Czech Republic	Considered high in society and organisations, shared viewpoint that hierarchy is needed	6.5.1	High	-
Finland	Considered low in society and organisations	7.5.1	Low	Low
Germany	A certain level of power distance is considered necessary in society and organisations	8.5.1	Low	Medium
Poland	Considered high in society and organisations	9.5.1	High	Medium
Sweden	Considered very low in society and organisations, reflecting a high level of equality	10.5.1	Low	Low

Notes: The two right-hand columns show country positions relative to other nations (high = upper third, medium = middle third, low = lower third); compare Tables 4.4 and 4.13

The view of societal power distance as portrayed by the interview partners fits with the emerging country-specific models of participative management: The Swedish and German models are characterised by a strong reliance on participation. The Finnish version of democratic understanding stresses delegation in favour of participation, which is a different expression of low power distance. In contrast, the Czech and Polish models of participative management are characterised by placing stronger reliance on autocratic decision-making than is common in the other three countries.

Chapter 4.4 referred to the common assumption in the literature that low power distance fosters participative management. The current qualitative study's findings of an overlap between patterns of participative management and descriptions of power distance clearly support this assumption.

11.5.3 Individualism/Collectivism

Individualism/collectivism refers to the relationship between the individual and the level of collectivism that predominates in a society (Hofstede, 1980a; House et al., 2004). Individualism and collectivism emerged as factors related to participative management in three countries: Finland, Germany and Sweden (Table 11.26).

The qualitative data suggest that the dichotomy individualism vs. collectivism that is common in part of the cross-cultural literature may not hold true. The interviewees in Finland, Germany and Sweden differentiated between the individual level on the one hand and the societal/economic level on the other hand and they did not necessarily see absolute equivalence in the levels of individualism and collectivism between these two levels. Thus, the detailed findings of the current study can help explain why there is only little overlap with and between the results of earlier quantitative studies into the individualism/collectivism dimension. Additional explanations could stem from the observation that the scales might measure different aspects of individualism: For example, while Hofstede measured individualistic/collectivist value orientation in general terms, the GLOBE study differentiated between institutional collectivism (presented in Table 11.26) and in-group collectivism (compare Chapter 4.1.1.2). Additionally, Van Oudenhoven (2001) criticised the Hofstede individualism index for not measuring the actual level of collectivism in a society but rather the ideal level.

Table 11.26 Individualism/Collectivism

Country	Summary findings	Chapter	Hofstede (2001)	House et al. (2004)	Trompenaars (1993)
Finland	High individualism at the individual level, society is built upon collectivist principles	7.5.2	High individualism	High institutional collectivism	Low to medium individualism
Germany	The economic system is based on collectivist ideas (co-determination, works councils)	8.5.2	High individualism	Low institutional collectivism	Low to medium individualism
Sweden	Parallel importance of individualism and collectivism	10.5.2	High individualism	High institutional collectivism	Medium to high individualism

Notes: The three right-hand columns show country positions relative to other nations (high = upper third, medium = middle third, low = lower third); compare Tables 4.5 and 4.14. The results presented in the column furthest to the right are derived from Trompenaars (1993), who, for a large number of countries, presented the percentage of respondents believing in individual decisions, as well as respondents opting for individual responsibility.

The current findings echo the words of some researchers who have discussed the limitations of the individualism/collectivism concept. For example, Berry (1992) stressed that the cross-cultural management literature identified collectivism mainly with Asia, and individualism with the West, and failed to recognise "competing concepts of individualism within the West" (p. 9). Consequently, Berry defined different types of individualism, for example Finnish self-bossed/competent individualism, Swedish co-operative/committee individualism and German compartmentalised individualism. These types fit well with the findings of the current qualitative study. In particular Finnish self-bossed/competent individualism ties in with the autonomy and delegation findings and Swedish co-operative/committee individualism has its equivalent in the consultation tendencies emerging from the qualitative data.

Chapter 4.4 suggested that high collectivism and team-orientation foster participative management. This argument cannot be clearly supported, if one compares the quantitative and qualitative data at hand. However, there is no contradiction within the qualitative data themselves, particularly between the interviewees' evaluation of the level of individualism/collectivism in society and the emerging models of participative management. For example, the Finnish data stress the parallel importance of individualism and collectivism: Individualism shows in the preference for autonomous work of employees, and collectivism is represented in the awareness that autonomous work and ideas need to be integrated by way of using participation.

11.5.4 Uncertainty Avoidance

The third culture dimension explored in the qualitative interviews is that of uncertainty avoidance. It reflects the degree to which a society relies on social norms and procedures to alleviate the unpredictability of future events (Hofstede, 1980a; House et al., 2004). Uncertainty avoidance emerged as a factor related to participative management in four countries: the Czech Republic, Germany, Poland and Sweden (Table 11.27).

Table 11.27 Uncertainty Avoidance

Country	Summary findings	Chapter	Hofstede (2001)	House et al. (2004)	Boski (2003)
Czech Republic	Perceived chaos in society, yet enough flexibility to handle situation	6.5.2	-	High	-
Germany	Perception: too many regulations; but also: desire for structure and order	8.5.3	Medium	High	High
Poland	Considered too low, perceived chaos in society; longing for more stability	9.5.2	High	Low	Low
Sweden	Considered high	10.5.3	Low	High	-

Notes: The three right-hand columns show country positions relative to other nations (high = upper third, medium = middle third, low = lower third); compare Tables 4.6 and 4.15.

The qualitative data suggest a gap between the perceived and desired levels of uncertainty avoidance in Germany and Poland, similar to the quantitative results of the GLOBE study related to the "as is" and "should be" aspects of uncertainty avoidance (Figure 4.6). Similar to the dimension individualism/collectivism, there is neither a clear fit of the qualitative findings with the quantitative data, nor consistency among the results of the quantitative studies.

The preference for and usage of rules is typically considered an expression of uncertainty avoidance. There are many kinds of rules, but the differentiation between formal (official/written) and unwritten (informal/ verbal) was the most common emerging from the qualitative interviews (Table 11.28). When comparing the data of the five countries, unwritten rules seem to dominate over formal rules in Finland and the Czech Republic. As Table 11.28 also shows, there is a good fit of the qualitative data with the quantitative results of the Event Management study (Chapter 4.2.3.2), except for the Czech Republic.

Table 11.28 Rules

Country	Summary findings	Preference (Smith, 2003)
Czech Republic	Unwritten rules preferred over formal rules	Formal
Finland	Strong preference for unwritten rules, as compared to formal rules	Unwritten
Germany	Complaints about too many formal rules and regulations, despite desire for structure and order	Formal
Poland	(no data available)	Formal
Sweden	Preference for self-defined (formal) rules that ensure smooth interactions	Formal

Note: Detailed results from Smith (2003) are presented in Figure 4.8.

The qualitative interview data enrich and complement the quantitative data collected as part of the Event Management study: A higher usage of formal over unwritten rules does not necessarily imply that these rules are imposed from higher hierarchical levels, as the Swedish example shows. Furthermore, the quantitative scores do not provide evidence of whether these rules are liked or considered appropriate, whereas the qualitative data do include this dimension (German example).

The literature-guided assumption presented in Chapter 4.4 that high uncertainty avoidance leads to more formalisation of the participatory arrangements finds clear support in the qualitative data for Germany. Furthermore, the German findings suggest that Tett and Jackson's (1990) conclusion maintaining the fact that managers who dislike uncertainty and ambiguity use participation less frequently than other managers (Chapter 2.1.3), does not necessarily hold true in every country setting. Rather, the level of uncertainty avoidance seems to leave its marks on how and to what extent participative management is embedded in formal arrangements.

11.6 Interaction Among the Influence Factors

Although the main situational and society-related factors influencing the enactment of participation have been presented separately, it should be stressed that the manner in which a manager uses participation in a particular decision-making situation is usually defined by a combination of factors. Finding a strategy that suits the personal preferences of the manager, that takes into account the expectations of all parties involved, that does not contradict core values, guiding principles and other cultural norms, and that corresponds with the nature of the problem is no simple task. The following section of a Swedish interview transcript illustrates the complexity involved in finding the appropriate decision-making strategy. The example deals with limited parking space to be distributed among subordinates.

> Swedish manager: Well, the reason why I really wanted to discuss the problem in the group was that I couldn't come up with a solution myself, so I wanted to see their reactions. Well, kind of transfer the problem to them-
> Researcher: Yes, but wouldn't they start having a conflict?
> Swedish manager: Yeah, they would definitely. But I think the problem would probably be back to me anyway, to make a decision in the end, so at least I can see during that discussion, what their positions are.
> Researcher: But you might get the same information by talking to them one-on-one?
> Swedish manager: Yes, but I want to see how they interact with each other. [...] It's hopeless, it's a very difficult problem, because it's very hard to be rational about it. That's why it's so difficult. [...] I mean, small things like this are the most difficult ones to solve and they take a lot of time.

The transcript suggests that the interviewee had initially intended to solve the problem by himself. But he lacked rational arguments, which would have been the pre-requisite for Swedish subordinates to tolerate autocratic managerial decision-making. Thus, the manager initiated a group meeting and thereby risked a conflict, which is surprising in a Swedish setting. However, he assumed that the group would not be able to find a solution either, possibly because of their tendency to avoid conflict. Consequently, the manager would in the end have to solve the problem himself. However, the second time around the manager would act from a stronger position and his decision would be legitimate: He had conformed to the cultural assumptions of involving subordinates and listening to their arguments. Now, he could base his decision on a broader and likely more rational foundation.

The example shows that the manager's choice of decision-making process is not straight forward, but is rather embedded in a complex web of assumptions and considerations, explicitly or implicitly taking various factors into account.

11.7 Convergence vs. Divergence

The inter-country analysis presented in the above Sections 11.2 to 11.5 revealed areas of both convergence and divergence in the concepts relevant for an understanding of participative management (Table 11.29).

As Table 11.29 suggests, the areas of divergence are numerous. Regarding some of the aspects of participative management, the data reveal distinct findings for each of the five countries (e.g. values and guiding principles). Regarding other aspects, some countries tend to form clusters. For example, the Czech, Polish and Swedish interviewees share the assumption of conflict being a threat to a good decision-making process, which causes them to reduce participation, while Finnish and German managers view conflict as a natural ingredient of decision-making with no effect on the enactment of participation. A further example of both divergence and clustering lies in the understanding of participation. Among the Finnish, German and Swedish managers the perspective that participation means consultation prevails, whereas participation is limited to information provision in Poland and to consultation with only a subgroup of subordinates, namely experts, in the Czech Republic.

The examples show that there are no clear-cut clusters the five countries could be assigned to. Yet, the shared communist past and recent political and economic changes in the Czech Republic and Poland are still reflected in the data, at least to a certain degree. In both countries, participative management is a rather novel managerial concept and the findings seem to reflect the managers' struggles between the familiar and autocratic behavioural patterns of the past and the more recently introduced participatory ways of managing. On other aspects, the findings for the Czech Republic and Poland differ strongly. For example, individual-level values and guiding principles define the meaning of participative management in the Czech Republic, while organisational-level values and guiding principles prevail in the Polish context, leading to a disregard of subordinate commitment and motivation as possible participation outcomes.

Earlier attempts to cluster countries (compare Table 3.2) suggest that Finland and Sweden are similar on many managerial attributes and that Germany may not be very different from the two. The current findings indicate

Table 11.29 Areas of Convergence and Divergence

Aspects	Conclusions after country comparison
Meaning of pm in context	
Basic values	Divergence with regard to the values underlying participative management
Guiding principles	Divergence with regard to the guiding principles of participative management
Meaning of pm	Convergence among some countries with regard to participation being a tool
Responsible for dm	Mostly convergence with regard to the manager being responsible
Range of participants	Convergence with regard to subordinates, some convergence with regard to specialists
Role of the manager	Divergence with regard to the ascribed managerial role
Role of subordinates	Divergence with regard to the ascribed subordinate role
Other participants	Largely convergence with regard to the role of specialists
Enactment of pm	
Process	Convergence among some countries with regard to consultation
Setting	Convergence with regard to the differentiation between one-on-one and group meetings
Autocratic behaviour	Divergence with regard to expected subordinate acceptance of autocratic decision-making
Outcomes of pm	Convergence with regard to decision quality, convergence among some countries with regard to decision commitment and motivation, divergence with regard to additional outcomes
Situational influences	
Decision type	Divergence with regard to major vs. minor decisions, convergence among some countries with regard to HR decisions
Time-related issues	Convergence with regard to time pressure, some convergence with regard to decisions considered a waste of time
Potential conflict	Divergence with regard to conflict being threatening vs. natural
Open conflict	Divergence with regard to managerial involvement and reaction
Unit and org. type	Convergence among some countries with regard to unit/organisation size and service vs. production firms
Society-related influences	
Historic factors	Convergence among the two former communist countries with regard to communist influences
Economic factors	Convergence among the two former communist countries with regard to the current instability, yet country-specific reactions
Power distance	Divergence between low and high power distance countries with regard to the use of participation
Individualism/ collectivism	Divergence with regard to the dichotomy individualism vs. collectivism, yet fit with country-specific meaning of participative management
Uncertainty avoidance	Divergence between low and high uncertainty avoidance countries with regard to the formalisation of participatory arrangements

that although in many aspects the three countries are more similar to each other than to the Czech Republic and Poland, there are also many areas of divergence. For example, Finland and Sweden differ drastically in the meaning of participative management, which is considered a managerial tool for the integration of independent work and opinions among the Finnish managers and a "natural" ingredient of decision-making for the Swedes. Another example would be that the Swedish and German managers differ strongly on how they react to conflict in the decision-making process, namely by reducing participation (Swedes) vs. showing no specific reactions (Germans).

In summary, the current data suggest both convergence and divergence among the five country samples. No distinct clusters emerged, despite the fact that two country clusters found in earlier research are represented in the current sample. The main factors differentiating country samples within the same cluster are the preference for participation vs. delegation (Sweden vs. Finland), the attitude toward conflict (Sweden vs. Finland) and the focus on the individual vs. the organisation (Czech Republic vs. Poland).

Chapter 12

Final Theory Building,
Conclusions and Outlook

This final chapter concludes the current study into the meaning and enactment of participative management in five European countries. With regard to final theory building, the answers to the two research questions are expressed in propositions and a theoretical model. The chapter further includes concluding remarks about the way in which the study goals guiding the project have been dealt with. Finally, areas for future research are pointed out.

12.1 Research Questions: Conclusion

12.1.1 Overview

The current qualitative study represents an exploratory step into the meaning, enactment and context of participative management across countries. It is also a step toward the integration of various studies in the field of participative management. The outcomes of the current study are numerous and complex. *Research Question 1* concerns the country-specific meaning and enactment of participative management. As demonstrated in detail in Chapters 6 to 10 and summarised in the inter-country analysis in Chapter 11, there are fundamental differences and vast variation to be found among the five countries. Strongly related to this divergence is the role of contextual factors addressed in *Research Question 2*. Basic values and guiding principles as well as culturally-influenced role attributions for managers, subordinates and specialists alike influence the country-specific meaning of participative management, whereas situational factors determine the enactment of participative management in a partly country-specific manner. History, economy and societal culture factors influence both meaning and enactment of participative management.

12.1.2 Propositions and a Contingency Model of Participation

In this section, the main findings of the study are expressed in theoretical propositions, thus adhering to the recommendation of grounded theory to raise research findings to a higher theoretical level. It should be emphasised that, although the propositions may seem very general, they are grounded in the findings emerging from the interviews with middle managers in five European countries. The limitations of the study stated in Chapter 5.4.3 regarding sample size, generalisability, geographic focus, data type and concentration on managerial data apply and must be kept in mind. When the term "country" is used, it refers to the "culture-specific" country samples described in Chapter 5.1.4.

Proposition 1: The meaning, enactment and outcomes of participative management vary strongly between countries.

Proposition 2: Country-specific historic and economic factors may influence the meaning, enactment and outcomes of participative management.

Proposition 3: Societal culture influences such as power distance, individualism/collectivism and uncertainty avoidance shape the meaning, enactment and outcomes of participative management.

Proposition 4: The meaning of participative management is influenced by country-specific basic values, guiding principles and role attributions with regard to the manager, subordinates and specialists.

Proposition 5: Country-specific communication patterns may also influence the meaning of participative management.

Proposition 6: The various sources of influence on the meaning of participative management vary strongly between countries, except for the role of specialists.

Proposition 7: The meaning of participative management is an important, yet not sufficient determinant for the enactment of participative management. Four situational influences tend to play a further important role in shaping the enactment of participative management: decision type, time-related issues, conflict, and unit and organisation type.

Proposition 8: Decision type influences participatory decision-making, yet this aspect is country-specific in differing ways. A main distinction concerns the following dichotomy: "The more important a decision, the more participation" vs. "the more important a decision, the less participation".

Proposition 9: Time-related issues influence participatory decision-making in comparable ways across countries. Examples include: "The less time available, the less participation" and "decisions considered a waste of time lead to less participation".

Proposition 10: Conflict influences participatory decision-making, yet it is country-specific in differing ways. A main distinction exists between conflict viewed as threatening vs. natural: "Conflict perceived as a threat leads to a decrease in participation" vs. "conflict viewed as a natural organisational ingredient leads to no decrease in participation".

Proposition 11: Unit and organisation type may influence participatory decision-making in a country-specific way. Examples include: "Participative management is more common in service organisations than in traditional production firms" and "participative management is more common in small units and organisations than in large ones".

Proposition 12: The meaning and enactment of participative management influence the outcomes of participative management, specified through decision quality, decision commitment and additional outcomes.

Proposition 13: Decision quality is an outcome factor of participative management evaluated equally important and positive across countries.

Proposition 14: The acknowledgement of decision commitment varies between countries, ranging from "decision commitment is not perceived to be related to participative management" to "decision commitment is an important and positive outcome of participative management".

Proposition 15: In addition to decision quality and commitment, additional country-specific outcomes may be acknowledged, such as maintenance of good interpersonal relations or integration.

The propositions are summarised in the model depicted in Figure 12.1.

12.2 Study Goals: Conclusion

Table 12.1 summarises in which of the above chapters the study goals formulated in Chapter 3.1 are dealt with.

Study Goal 1 concerns the integration of the current qualitative findings with existing research. This issue is dealt with in the respective country chapters by focussing on the integration with the GLOBE, Vroom/Yetton

Figure 12.1 Contingency Model of Participative Management

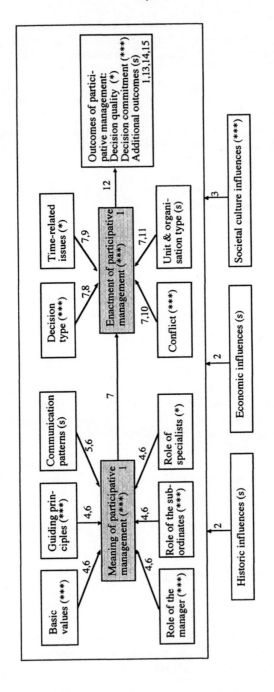

Notes: (***) = general concept or influence factor with major differences in country-specific meaning. (*) = general concept or influence factor with largely similar meaning across countries, (s) = specific influence factor only in some countries. Numbers correspond to propositions in the text.

and Event Management studies, with the industrial relations system prevailing in each country and with the existing literature on participative management and related concepts.

Table 12.1 Chapters Related to the Study Goals

Study goals	Relevant chapters
Study Goal 1: Integration	
1.1: Qualitative and quantitative results	Chapters 6.6.1, 7.6.1, 8.6.1, 9.6.1 and 10.6.1
1.2: Fit with the IR system	Chapters 6.6.2, 7.6.2, 8.6.2, 9.6.2 and 10.6.2
1.3: Fit with the literature	Chapters 6.6.3, 7.6.3, 8.6.3, 9.6.3 and 10.6.3
Study Goal 2: Theory building	Chapters 6 to 11 and 12.1
Study Goal 3: Practical relevance	Chapters 6 to 11
Study Goal 4: Convergence and divergence	Chapter 11.7

As for the integration with the three quantitative studies (*Study Goal 1.1*), the following conclusions can be drawn:

- The country indices originating from the Vroom/Yetton study (Chapter 4.3.3) are in large part in line with the qualitative findings. For example, the MLP (mean level of participation) score and additional quantitative indices such as reaction to conflict are mirrored in the country-specific models of participative management. The findings of the current study enrich the quantitative results by providing information about the meaning underlying participatory behaviour, the range of participants and the influence of the ascribed managerial, subordinate and specialist roles on the decision-making process.
- The Event Management study's index "guidance factor subordinates" (Chapter 4.2.3.2) tends to fit with the country-specific models of participation detected by the current study. The qualitative data add to this result by pointing out the factors that motivate managers to consult subordinates and by demonstrating that decision-making processes for "typical" events, as studied by the Event Management programme, need not necessarily follow the same patterns as strategic decisions.
- Participative leadership ideals (GLOBE study) show little variation among the five countries (Chapter 4.1.3.1) and are, therefore, rather incongruent with the findings of the current study. The GLOBE results also differ from the outcome of the other two quantitative studies. A likely explanation is that leadership ideals influence behaviour only indirectly and in combination with other intra-personal factors, such as habits, and exogenous factors, such as forces of the situation (Szabo et al., 2001).

With regard to the fit of the current findings with the country-specific industrial relations systems (*Study Goal 1.2*), the analysis revealed interesting links, which strengthen the assumption that the industrial relations system of a country parallels the level and models of participative management to be found in the country's business organisations. Whether one is the consequence of the other, i.e. practices of participative management directly follow the country's industrial relation system, can be debated. Yet there are indicators in some of the studied countries that the industrial relations system has indeed a guiding function for participative management, at least in the long run. In countries with a high level of industrial democracy, this system seems to provide individual organisation members (managers and subordinates alike) with a role model for the interaction between employees and employers/managers: At the company level, they experience how employee representatives (works council members or trade union representatives) negotiate with top management. At the sectoral or national levels, they see how unions deal with employer associations. The climate, in which these interactions take place, whether they are characterised by a generally consensual or a rather competitive spirit, seems to leave its marks on how managers and subordinates think and feel about participation and how they interact.

The comparison of the qualitative findings with the existing country-specific literature (*Study Goal 1.3*) showed a good fit. Some of the emerging concepts were also described in the management literature, although partly in a different context. Other findings were supported by the presence of equivalent descriptions in works of literary fiction suggesting that the detected patterns might not be restricted to a managerial context, but may, in fact, be quite deeply embedded in the country's culture. Overall, it was interesting to observe that a rather limited amount of data (six to eight interviews per country) on a highly specific topic (participative management) was able to bring to the surface many of the characteristics described in literature as being typical for the members of a particular country/culture.

Study Goal 2. Glaser and Strauss (1967) differentiated "substantive theory", applicable for a particular substantive area, from "formal theory" of a more general perspective. In the current study, the challenge of building theory in the area of participative management is met in three steps. Firstly, the emerging country-specific models of participative management (Chapters 6 to 10) represent "substantive theories" that are grounded in empirical data collected from middle managers in five countries and integrated with other sources (quantitative studies, industrial relation system, country-specific management literature). Secondly, the country findings are compared among each other and the conclusions resulting from this comparative analysis are confronted with the existing participation literature (Chapter 11), leading to a number of suggestions for modification and addition to existing theoretical positions about participative management. Thirdly, theory building toward a "formal theory" is continued in the formulation of theoretical propositions with regard to detected patterns. The propositions result in a general model of participative management in context (Section 12.1.2 above).

Study Goal 3. Practical relevance is an issue of all research conducted within the grounded theory approach. The country-specific Chapters 6 to 10 provide many examples of how middle managers think about and experience participative management in their respective countries. These examples, together with the more general country-specific descriptions, assist the reader in obtaining increased cultural sensitivity and knowledge, which is particularly important in a European context due to the economic integration. The recent developments in Europe imply that organisation members are increasingly interacting with managers, colleagues, subordinates and business partners from other countries and cultural backgrounds. In particular, cross-cultural encounters take place in such areas as joint ventures and other forms of international co-operation between firms (Adler, 2002), expatriation of individual managers (Fischlmayr, 2004) and cross-cultural face-to-face as well as virtual teams (Duarte & Snyder, 2001).

Study Goal 4. Gaining knowledge about convergence and divergence between countries and cultures, as described by the current study, has practical as well as theoretical relevance. With regard to business practice, similarities with and differences from the own cultural background can help better interpret the thinking and behaviour of managers, subordinates, colleagues and business partners with different cultural backgrounds. Particularly the awareness about and attention to areas of divergence can influence the success or failure of intercultural interactions. With regard to theoretical advancement, the current five-country study suggests that divergence prevails over convergence in many aspects of participative management. This finding echoes the conclusions of a number of other researchers:

"[O]rganisations worldwide are growing more similar, while the behaviour of people within them is maintaining its cultural uniqueness." (Adler, 2002, p. 66)

"In the globalised world, there will be a multitude of local villages with much interconnectedness, rather than a mere global village." (Usunier, 1998, p. 161)

12.3 Outlook

The current study and its complex findings suggest a number of different roads to follow with regard to future research:

Further exploring/testing the findings. The findings of the current study may serve as a basis for subsequent research, which may have quantitative as well as qualitative designs. With regard to a quantitative inquiry, the current study's theoretical outcomes, i.e. the propositions listed in Section 12.1.2

above, could serve as *a priori* hypotheses in theory-testing research. Such an approach would fit with Bryman and Bell's (2003) statement that qualitative research may facilitate quantitative research.

Country samples. The managers represented in the current study belong to a small number of European countries and cultures. Consequently, future research could concentrate on other countries in possibly other regions or expand the current five-country sample for a more inclusive view of participative management within Europe.

Managerial cohorts. As suggested in Chapter 5.4.3, the patterns detected from middle manager data likely apply to other managerial groups as well, because the issues emerging from the current study reflect deeply ingrained ways of thinking (e.g. with regard to the subordinate role or concepts such as conflict) which are likely to converge across hierarchical levels and organisational settings. However, only empirical research can reveal whether this assumption holds true. In some aspects, e.g. with regard to strategic decisions, the findings may well differ, when top managers are the focus of study. Moreover, front line managers may in some aspects reveal other specific patterns of behaviour than middle managers because of their increased closeness to operational work.

Subordinate cohorts. The current study builds exclusively on managerial data. However, managers represent a very specific cohort of each society and face similar challenges worldwide, which may well reflect upon their values, attitudes and behaviour. Future studies could explore participation from the perspective of other parties involved in managerial decision-making, most notably subordinates. Such a focus would add further complexity to the country-specific models of participative management emerging from the current study. It would be particularly interesting to explore to which degree and in which aspects managers and subordinates share similar perspectives. It might well be that models of participative management emerging from subordinate data look quite different from the current manager-based findings.

Data type. The current study employs interviews in the form of self-reports. As discussed in Chapter 5.4.3, there are limitations to this type of data, such as a certain level of uncertainty with regard to the congruence between interview statements and actual behaviour in naturally occurring situations. Future studies could for example combine self-reports with other qualitative methods, such as participant observation.

Cultures in direct interaction. The perspective taken by the current study is a comparative one. However, as pointed out in Chapter 5.4.3, behavioural patterns detected in intra-cultural settings may not fully overlap with those of inter-cultural settings. Consequently, future research could study participative management in the context of diverse decision-making groups, i.e. groups involving members of different cultural backgrounds. For example, what does participative management look like, when a manager from culture A is an expatriate in country B? In other words, what happens when the manager from culture A is faced with the question of whether and how to involve subordinates, who are members of culture B?

Wider use of grounded theory. With regard to methodology, the rich findings of the current study imply that grounded theory can be a useful analysis tool for several areas in management research, in particular when the aim is to address questions about the meaning and context of social phenomena. Furthermore, such projects need not be limited to single settings, but can also include a cross-cultural perspective, as has been demonstrated by the current study.

Bibliography

Aaltonen Mika & Berry Michael (1998). *From models of leadership in national epics to talk about leadership among Finnish students*. Manuscript. Turku: Turku School of Economics and Business Administration.

Adler Nancy J. (1983). A typology of management studies involving culture. *Journal of International Business Studies*, 14(2), 29-47.

Adler Nancy J. (1997). *International dimensions of organizational behavior* (3rd ed.). Cincinnati, OH: South-Western College Publishing.

Adler Nancy J. (2002). *International dimensions of organizational behavior* (4th ed.). Cincinnati, OH: South-Western College Publishing.

Adler Nancy J., Campbell Nigel & Laurent André (1989). In search of appropriate methodology: From outside the People's Republic of China looking in. *Journal of International Business Studies*, 20(1), 61-74.

Adler Nancy J. & Graham John L. (1989). Cross-cultural interaction: The international comparison fallacy? *Journal of International Business Studies*, 20(3), 515-537.

Agar Michael H. (1994). *Language shock: Understanding the culture of conversation*. New York: Willim Morrow.

Agar Michael H. (1996). *The professional stranger: An informal introduction to ethnography* (2nd ed.). San Diego: Academic Press.

Alvesson Mats & Berg Per Olaf (1992). *Corporate culture and organizational symbolism: An overview*. Berlin, New York: De Gruyter.

Ashkanasy Neal M., Trevor-Roberts Edwin & Earnshaw Louise (2002). The Anglo cluster: Legacy of the British empire. *Journal of World Business*, 37(1), 28-39.

Auer-Rizzi Werner & Berry Michael (2000). Business vs. cultural frames of reference in group decision making: Interactions among Austrian, Finnish, and Swedish business students. *Journal of Business Communication*, 37(3), 264-292.

Auer-Rizzi Werner, Reber Gerhard & Szabo Erna (2005). Governance-Strukturen und Führungsverhalten: Symptome von Entsolidarisierung in Deutschland und Österreich. *Industrielle Beziehungen*, 12(3), 231-251.

Avery Gayle, Donnenberg Otmar, Gick Wolfgang & Hilb Martin (1999). Challenges for management development in the German-speaking nations for the twenty-first century. *Journal of Management Development*, 18(1), 18-31.

Badawy Michael K. (1979, August). *Managerial attitudes and need orientations of Mid-Eastern executives: An empirical cross-cultural analysis.* Paper presented at the Annual Meeting of the Academy of Management, Atlanta.

Bakacsi Gyula, Takács Sándor, Karácsonyi András & Imrek Viktor (2002). Eastern European cluster: Tradition and transition. *Journal of World Business,* 37(1), 69-80.

Balawajder Krystyna & Popiolek Katarzyna (1996). Psychological aspects of the transformations in Poland: Changes in the sense of participation in the life of a plant. *European Journal of Work and Organizational Psychology,* 5(1), 125-135.

Bass Bernard M. (1985). *Leadership and performance beyond expectations.* New York: Free Press.

Berry John W. (1989). Imposed etics - emics - derived etics: The operationalisation of a compelling idea. *International Journal of Psychology,* 24, 721-735.

Berry Michael (1992). Know thyself and the other fellow too: Strategies for effective cross-cultural communication. In Berry Michael (Ed.), *Cross-cultural communication in Europe* (pp. 1-16). Turku: Eurooppa-Instituutin keskusteluaiheita (Institute for European Studies).

Berry Michael (1994a). Hidden barriers to managing multicultural business units. In Marsh David & Salo-Lee Liisa (Eds.), *Europe on the move: Fusion or fission?* (pp. 69-76). Jyväskylä: University of Jyväskylä Press.

Berry Michael (1994b, June). *Hidden barriers to communicating in multicultural business units.* Paper presented at the Colloquium of the Department of Communication, Arizona State University, Phoenix, AZ.

Berry Michael (1997). Speaking culturally about personhood, motherhood and career. *Hallinon Tutkimus (Administrative Studies),* 4, 304-325.

Berry Michael, Carbaugh Donal & Nurmikari-Berry Marjatta (2004). Communicating Finnish quietude: A pedagogical process for discovering implicit cultural meanings in languages. *Language and Intercultural Communication,* 4(4), 261-280.

Berry Michael, Lähteenmäki Satu & Reber Gerhard (1998, April). *Rational decision making depends of systems of meaning: Cultural dimensions of decision making by Austrian and Finnish managers.* Paper presented at the SIETARA Europe Congress, Bath.

Berry Michael & Nurmikari-Berry Marjatta (2005). Metaphors in developing intercultural communication competence. In Honka Jane & al. (Eds.), *The communication skills workshop. Celebrating the second 10 workshops* (pp. 81-91). Estonia: Communication Skills Workshop.

Berthoin Ariane, Dirkes Meinolf & Helmers Sabine (1993). Unternehmenskultur: Eine Forschungsagenda aus Sicht der Handlungsperspektive. In Dierkes Meinolf, von Rosenstiel Lutz & Steger Ulrich (Eds.), *Unternehmenskultur in Theorie und Praxis* (pp. 200-218). Frankfurt, New York: Campus Verlag.

Black J. Stewart & Gregersen Hal B. (1997). Participative decision-making: An integration of multiple dimensions. *Human Relations*, 50(7), 859-878.

Blum Karl (1994). Managing people in Germany. In Garrison Terry & Rees David (Eds.), *Managing people across Europe* (pp. 40-62). Oxford: Butterworth-Heinemann.

Böhnisch Wolf (1991). *Führung und Führungskräftetraining nach dem Vroom/ Yetton-Modell*. Stuttgart: Schäffer-Poeschel.

Böhnisch Wolf, Ragan Jim W., Reber Gerhard & Jago Arthur G. (1988). Predicting Austrian leader behavior from a measure of behavioral intent: A cross-cultural replication. In Dlugos Günter, Dorow Wolfgang & Weiermair Klaus (Eds.), *Management under differing labour market and employment systems* (pp. 313-322). Berlin, New York: De Gruyter.

Booth Simon, Maczynski Jerzy & Poniewierski Ziemowit (2002). Attributes of outstanding leadership: A comparison of British and Polish students. *Polish Journal of Applied Psychology*, 2(1), 7-27.

Boski Pawel (2003). Polen. In Thomas Alexander, Kammerhuber Stefan & Schroll-Machl Sylvia (Eds.), *Handbuch interkulturelle Kommunikation und Kooperation, Band 2: Länder, Kulturen und interkulturelle Berufstätigkeit* (pp. 120-134). Göttingen: Vandenhoeck & Ruprecht.

Brislin Richard W. (1986). The wording and translation of research instruments. In Lonner Walter J. & Berry John W. (Eds.), *Field methods in cross-cultural research*. Beverly Hills: Sage.

Brodbeck Felix C., Frese Michael & 44 co-authors (incl. Szabo Erna) (2000). Cultural variation of leadership prototypes across 22 European countries. *Journal of Occupational and Organizational Psychology*, 73(1), 1-29.

Brodbeck Felix C., Frese Michael & Javidan Mansour (2002). Leadership made in Germany: Low on compassion, high on performance. *Academy of Management Executive*, 16(1), 16-29.

Bryman Alan (1993). Charismatic leadership in business organizations: Some neglected issues. *Leadership Quarterly*, 4(3/4), 289-304.

Bryman Alan (2004). Qualitative research on leadership: A critical but appreciative review. *Leadership Quarterly*, 15(6), 729-769.

Bryman Alan & Bell Emma (2003). *Business research methods*. Oxford, New York: Oxford University Press.

Cabrera Elizabeth F., Ortega Jaime & Cabrera Ángel (2003). An exploration of the factors that influence employee participation in Europe. *Journal of World Business*, 38(1), 43-54.

Calori Roland, Steele Murray & Yoneyama Etsuo (1995). Management in Europe: Learning from different perspectives. *European Management Journal*, 13(1), 58-66.

Carl Dale, Gupta Vipin & Javidan Mansour (2004). Power distance. In House Robert J., Hanges Paul J., Javidan Mansour, Dorfman Peter W. & Gupta

Vipin (Eds.), *Culture, leadership, and organizations: The GLOBE study of 62 societies* (pp. 513-563). Thousand Oaks, CA: Sage.

Carley Mark (2002). *Industrial relations in the EU member states and candidate countries.* Dublin: European Foundation for the Improvement of Living and Working Conditions.

Chemers Martin M. (1993). An integrative theory of leadership. In Chemers Martin M. & Ayman Roya (Eds.), *Leadership theory and research: Perspectives and directions* (pp. 293-319). San Diego: Academic Press.

Chemers Martin M. (1997). *An integrative theory of leadership.* Mahwah, NJ: Lawrence Erlbaum.

Chhokar Jagdeep, Brodbeck Felix C. & House Robert J. (Eds.) (in press). *Culture and leadership across the world: The GLOBE book of in-depth studies of 25 societies.* Mahwah, NJ: Lawrence Erlbaum.

Child John & Kieser Alfred (1979). Organization and managerial roles in British and West German companies: An examination of the culture-free thesis. In Lammers Cornelius J. & Hickson David J. (Eds.), *Organizations alike and unalike* (pp. 428-449). London: Routledge.

Chisholm Rupert F. & Vansina Leopold S. (1993). Varieties of participation. *Public Administration Quarterly*, 17(3), 291-315.

Clark Ed & Soulsby Anna (1995). Transforming former state enterprises in the Czech Republic. *Organization Studies*, 16(2), 215-242.

Clark Ed & Soulsby Anna (1998). *Organisation, management and transformation: Institutional change in the Czech Republic.* London: Mansell.

Coch Lester & French John R. P. Jr. (1948). Overcoming resistance to change. *Human Relations*, 1(4), 512-532.

Cotton John L., Vollrath David A., Froggatt Kirk L., Lengnick-Hall Mark L. & Jennings Kenneth R. (1988). Employee participation: Diverse forms and different outcomes. *Academy of Management Review*, 13(1), 8-22.

Cotton John L., Vollrath David A., Lengnick-Hall Mark L. & Froggatt Kirk L. (1990). Fact: The form of participation does matter - A rebuttal to Leana, Locke & Schweiger. *Academy of Management Review*, 15(1), 147-153.

Cyert Richard M., Dill William R. & March James G. (1998). The role of expectations in business decision making. In Van Maanen John (Ed.), *Qualitative studies of organizations* (pp. 5-30). Thousand Oaks, CA: Sage. (Reprinted from Administrative Science Quarterly, 1958, 3(3), 307-340).

Czarniawska-Joerges Barbara (1993). Sweden: A modern project, a postmodern implementation. In Hickson David J. (Ed.), *Management in Western Europe: Society, culture and organization in twelve nations* (pp. 229-247). Berlin, New York: De Gruyter.

Dachler H. Peter & Wilpert Bernhard (1978). Conceptual dimensions and boundaries of participation in organizations: A critical evaluation. *Administrative Science Quarterly*, 23(1), 1-39.

Den Hartog Deanne N., House Robert J., Hanges Paul J., Ruiz-Quintanilla S. Antonio, Dorfman Peter W. & 169 co-authors (incl. Szabo Erna) (1999). Culture specific and cross culturally generalizable implicit leadership theories: Are attributes of charismatic/transformational leadership universally endorsed? *Leadership Quarterly,* 10(2), 219-256.

Den Hartog Deanne, Maczynski Jerzy, Motowidlo Stephan J., Jarmuz Slawomir, Koopman Paul, Thierry Henk & Wilderom Celeste (1997). Cross-cultural perceptions of leadership: A comparison of leadership and societal and organizational culture in the Netherlands and Poland. *Polish Psychological Bulletin,* 28(3), 255-267.

d'Iribarne Philippe (1998). Comment s'accorder: Une rencontre Franco-Suédoise. In d'Iribarne Philippe, Henry Alain, Segal Jean-Pierre, Chevrier Sylvie & Globokar Tatjana (Eds.), *Cultures et mondialisation: Gérer par-delà des frontières* (pp. 89-115). Paris: Le Seuil.

Dobbin Frank & Boychuk Terry (1999). National employment systems and job autonomy: Why job autonomy is high in the Nordic countries and low in the United States, Canada, and Australia. *Organization Studies,* 20(2), 257-291.

Donaldson L. (1993). *Anti-management theories of organization: A critique of paradigm proliferation.* Cambridge: Cambridge University Press.

Dorfman Peter W., Howell Jon P., Hibino Shozo, Lee Jin K., Tate Uday & Bautista Arnoldo (1997). Leadership in Western and Asian countries: Commonalities and differences in effective leadership processes across cultures. *Leadership Quarterly,* 8(3), 233-274.

Doucouliagos Chris (1995). Worker participation and productivity in labor-managed and participatory capitalist firms: A meta-analysis. *Industrial and Labor Relations Review,* 49(1), 58-77.

Duarte Deborah L. & Snyder Nancy Tennant (2001). *Mastering virtual teams.* San Francisco: Jossey-Bass.

Dvorakova Zuzana (2002, September). *Labour relations in the public services in the Czech Republic.* Paper presented at the Annual Conference of EGPA (European Group of Public Administration), Potsdam.

Dvorakova Zuzana (2003). Trade unions, works councils and staff involvement in the modernising Czech Republic. *The International Journal of Public Sector Management,* 16(6), 424-433.

Eberwein Wilhelm & Tholen Jochen (1993). *Euro-manager or splendid isolation? International management: An Anglo-German comparison.* Berlin, New York: De Gruyter.

Eironline (European Industrial Relations Observatory Online) (2001). *Annual review for Sweden.* Dublin: European Foundation for the Improvement of Living and Working Conditions. DL: www.eiro.eurofound.eu.int, Sept. 22, 2003.

Eironline (European Industrial Relations Observatory Online) (2002a). *Annual review for Finland*. Dublin: European Foundation for the Improvement of Living and Working Conditions. DL: www.eiro.eurofound.eu.int, Sept. 24, 2003.

Eironline (European Industrial Relations Observatory Online) (2002b). *Annual review for Germany*. Dublin: European Foundation for the Improvement of Living and Working Conditions. DL: www.eiro.eurofound.eu.int, Sept. 24, 2003.

Eironline (European Industrial Relations Observatory Online) (2002c). *Annual review for Poland*. Dublin: European Foundation for the Improvement of Living and Working Conditions. DL: www.eiro.eurofound.eu.int, Sept. 24, 2003.

Eironline (European Industrial Relations Observatory Online) (2002d). *Annual review for Sweden*. Dublin: European Foundation for the Improvement of Living and Working Conditions. DL: www.eiro.eurofound.eu.int, Sept. 24, 2003.

Eironline (European Industrial Relations Observatory Online) (2003). *Annual review for Poland*. Dublin: European Foundation for the Improvement of Living and Working Conditions. DL: www.eiro.eurofound.eu.int, Sept. 28, 2003.

Eisenhardt Kathleen M. (1989). Building theories from case study research. *Academy of Management Review*, 14(4), 532-550.

Eisenhardt Kathleen M. & Bourgeois L. J. III (1988). Politics of strategic decision making in high-velocity environments: Toward a midrange theory. *Academy of Management Journal*, 31(4), 737-770.

Emire (European Employment and Industrial Relations Glossaries) (2003). *Germany*. Dublin: European Foundation for the Improvement of Living and Working Conditions. DL: http://www.eurofound.eu.int/emire/emire.html, Oct. 30, 2003.

EPOC (1997). *New forms of work organisation: Can Europe realise its potential?* Dublin: European Foundation for the Improvement of Living and Working Conditions.

Evans Martin G. (1968). *The effects of supervisory behavior upon worker perceptions of their path-goal relationships*. Doctoral dissertation. New Haven, CT: Yale University.

Evans Martin G. (1970). The effects of supervisory behavior on the path-goal relationship. *Organizational Behavior and Human Performance*, 5, 277-298.

Festinger Leon (1957). *A theory of cognitive dissonance*. Stanford, CA: Stanford University Press.

Fichter Michael & Zeuner Bodo (2000, March). *The institutional framework of labor relations in the transformation countries of Central and Eastern Europe: Views on the research agenda*. Paper presented at the 12th International Conference of Europeanists, Chicago.

Fiedler Fred E. (1967). *A theory of leadership effectiveness.* New York: McGraw-Hill.

Field Richard H. G. (1979). A critique of the Vroom-Yetton contingency model of leadership behavior. *Academy of Management Review,* 4(2), 249-257.

Field Richard H. G. & House Robert J. (1990). A test of the Vroom-Yetton model using manager and subordinate reports. *Journal of Applied Psychology,* 75(3), 362-366.

Fischlmayr Iris C. (2004). *Expatriation: Ein Handbuch zur Entsendung von Mitarbeitern ins Ausland.* Linz: Trauner Verlag.

Flick Uwe (2002). Qualitative research: State of the art. *Social Science Information,* 41(1), 5-24.

Gales Lawrence M. (2003). Linguistic sensitivity in cross-cultural organisational research: Positivist/post-positivist and grounded theory approaches. *Language and Intercultural Communication,* 3(2), 131-140.

Gannon Martin J. & Associates (1994). *Understanding global cultures: Metaphorical journeys through 17 countries.* Thousand Oaks, CA: Sage.

Geertz Clifford (1973). Thick description: Toward an interpretive theory of culture. In Geertz Clifford (Ed.), *The interpretation of cultures* (pp. 3-30). New York: Basic Books.

Gelfand Michele J., Bhawuk Dharm P. S., Nishii Lisa Hisae & Bechtold David J. (2004). Individualism and collectivism. In House Robert J., Hanges Paul J., Javidan Mansour, Dorfman Peter W. & Gupta Vipin (Eds.), *Culture, leadership, and organizations: The GLOBE study of 62 societies* (pp. 437-512). Thousand Oaks, CA: Sage.

Gerstner Charlotte R. & Day David V. (1994). Cross-cultural comparison of leadership prototypes. *Leadership Quarterly,* 5(2), 121-134.

Gill Colin & Krieger Hubert (2000). Recent survey evidence on participation in Europe: Towards a European model? *European Journal of Industrial Relations,* 6(1), 109-132.

Glaser Barney G. (1978). *Theoretical sensitivity.* Mill Valley, CA: Sociology Press.

Glaser Barney G. (1992). *Basics of grounded theory analysis: Emergence versus forcing.* Mill Valley, CA: Sociology Press.

Glaser Barney G. (1998). *Doing grounded theory: Issues and discussions.* Mill Valley, CA: Sociology Press.

Glaser Barney G. & Strauss Anselm L. (1967). *The discovery of grounded theory: Strategies for qualitative research.* New York: Aldine.

Glew David J., O'Leary-Kelly Anne M., Griffin Ricky W. & Van Fleet David D. (1995). Participation in organizations: A preview of the issues and proposed framework for future analysis. *Journal of Management,* 21(3), 395-421.

GLOBE (2001). *GLOBE website*. DL: http://mgmt3.ucalgary.ca/web/globe. nsf/index, Sept. 28, 2001.

Glunk Ursula, Wilderom Celeste & Ogilvie Robert (1996). Finding the key to German-style management. *International Studies of Management & Organization*, 26(3), 93-108.

Goulding Christina (2000). Grounded theory methodology and consumer behaviour, procedures, practice and pitfalls. *Advances in Consumer Research*, 27, 261-266.

Goulding Christina (2002). *Grounded theory: A practical guide for management, business and market researchers*. Thousand Oaks, CA: Sage.

Grant Wyn (1996). Employers' associations. In Malcolm Warner (Ed.), *International encyclopedia of business and management* (pp. 1179-1187). London, New York: Routledge.

Greene Jennifer C., Caracelli Valerie J. & Graham Wendy F. (1989). Toward a conceptual framework for mixed-method evaluation designs. *Educational Evaluation and Policy Analysis*, 11(3), 255-274.

Griffeth Rodger W., Hom Peter W., DeNisi Angelo S. & Kirchner Wayne K. (1980, August). *A multivariate, multinational comparison of managerial attitudes*. Paper presented at the Annual Meeting of the Academy of Management, Detroit.

Guillet de Monthoux Pierre (1991). Modernism and the dominating firm: On the managerial mentality of the Swedish model. *Scandinavian Journal of Management*, 7(1), 27-40.

Gupta Vipin & Hanges Paul J. (2004). Regional and climate clustering of societal cultures. In House Robert J., Hanges Paul J., Javidan Mansour, Dorfman Peter W. & Gupta Vipin (Eds.), *Culture, leadership, and organizations: The GLOBE study of 62 societies* (pp. 178-218). Thousand Oaks, CA: Sage.

Gupta Vipin, Hanges Paul J. & Dorfman Peter (2002). Cultural clusters: Methodology and findings. *Journal of World Business*, 37(1), 11-15.

Gupta Vipin, Surie Gita, Javidan Mansour & Chhokar Jagdeep (2002). Southern Asia cluster: Where the old meets the new? *Journal of World Business*, 37(1), 16-27.

Haire Mason, Ghiselli Edwin E. & Porter Lyman W. (1966). *Managerial thinking: An international study*. New York: Wiley.

Hall Edward T. (1976). *Beyond culture*. New York: Doubleday.

Hall Edward T. & Hall Mildred Reed (1990). *Understanding cultural differences: Germans, French and Americans*. Yarmouth, MN: Intercultural Press.

Hammer Tove Helland (1996). Industrial democracy. In Warner Malcolm (Ed.), *International encyclopedia of business and management* (pp. 1921-1930). London, New York: Routledge.

Hammersley Martyn (1992). *What's wrong with ethnography?* London, New York: Routledge.

Hampden-Turner Charles & Trompenaars Alfons (1993). *The seven cultures of capitalism: Value systems for creating wealth in the United States, Japan, Germany, France, Britain, Sweden, and the Netherlands.* New York et al.: Currency Doubleday.

Hanges Paul J. (1997, August). *Results from the GLOBE project: Scale development and validation.* Paper presented at the 2nd International GLOBE Symposium, Wharton School of Management, University of Pennsylvania, Philadelphia.

Hanges Paul J., House Robert J., Ruiz-Quintanilla S. Antonio, Dickson Marcus & 169 co-authors (incl. Szabo Erna) (1998). *The development and validation of scales measuring societal culture and culturally-shared implicit theories of leadership.* Working paper. College Park, MD: University of Maryland.

Harris Stanley G. & Sutton Richard I. (1986). Functions of parting ceremonies in dying organizations. *Academy of Management Journal,* 29(1), 5-30.

Hasek Jaroslav (1960). *Die Abenteuer des braven Soldaten Schwejk.* Reinbeck bei Hamburg: Rowohlt.

Hegewisch Ariane, Brewster Chris & Koubek Josef (1996). Different roads: Changes in industrial and employee relations in the Czech Republic and East Germany since 1989. *Industrial Relations Journal,* 27(1), 50-64.

Heilman Madeline E., Hornstein Harvey A., Cage Jack H. & Herschlag Judith K. (1984). Reactions to prescribed leader behavior as a function of role-perspective: The case of the Vroom-Yetton model. *Journal of Applied Psychology,* 69(1), 50-60.

Heller Frank, Pusic Eugen, Strauss George & Wilpert Bernhard (1998). *Organizational participation: Myth and reality.* Oxford: Oxford University Press.

Heller Frank A. & Wilpert Bernhard (1997). Limits to participative leadership: Task, structure and skill as contingencies - A German-British comparison. In Warner Malcolm (Ed.), *Comparative management: Critical perspectives on business and management, Volume II: European management* (pp. 407-427). London, New York: Routledge.

Hetrick Susan (2002). Transferring HR ideas and practices: Globalization and convergence in Poland. *Human Resource Development International,* 5(3), 333-351.

Hickson David J., Hinings Christopher R., McMillan Charles J. & Schwitter John P. (1974). The culture-free context of organization structure: A trinational comparison. *Sociology,* 8, 59-80.

Hoffmann Jürgen, Hoffmann Reiner, Kirton-Darling Judith & Rampeltshammer Luitpold (2002). *The Europeanisation of industrial relations in a global perspective: A literature review.* Dublin: European Foundation for the Improvement of Living and Working Conditions.

Hofstede Geert (1976). Nationality and espoused values of managers. *Journal of Applied Psychology,* 61(2), 148-155.

Hofstede Geert (1980a). *Culture's consequences: International differences in work related values*. Beverly Hills, CA: Sage.

Hofstede Geert (1980b). Motivation, leadership and organizations: Do American theories apply abroad? *Organizational Dynamics*, 9(1), 42-63.

Hofstede Geert (1991). *Cultures and organizations: Software of the mind*. London: McGraw-Hill.

Hofstede Geert (1994). Management scientists are human. *Management Science*, 40(1), 4-13.

Hofstede Geert (2001). *Culture's consequences: Comparing values, behaviors, institutions, and organizations across nations* (2nd ed.). Thousand Oaks, CA: Sage.

Hofstede Geert & Bond Michael H. (1988). The Confucius connection: From cultural roots to economic growth. *Organizational Dynamics*, 16(4), 4-21.

Hofstede Geert & Hofstede Gert Jan (2005). *Cultures and organizations: Software of the mind* (2nd ed.). New York et al.: McGraw-Hill.

Holmberg Ingalill & Åkerblom Staffan (1998). "Primus inter pares" - Leadership and culture in Sweden. *Research Paper Series of the Centre for Advanced Studies in Leadership*, 1998/1. Stockholm: Stockholm School of Economics.

Hoppe Michael H. (1990). *A comparative study of country elites: International differences in work-related values and learning and their implications for management training and development*. Doctoral dissertation. Chapel Hill: University of North Carolina.

House Robert J. (1971). A path-goal theory of leadership. *Administrative Science Quarterly*, 16, 321-338.

House Robert J. (1977). A 1976 theory of charismatic leadership. In Hunt James G. & Larson Lars L. (Eds.), *Leadership: The cutting edge* (pp. 189-207). Carbondale, IL: Southern Illinois University Press.

House Robert J. & Aditya Ram N. (1997). The social scientific study of leadership: Quo vadis? *Journal of Management*, 23(3), 409-473.

House Robert J., Hanges Paul J., Javidan Mansour, Dorfman Peter W. & Gupta Vipin (Eds.) (2004). *Culture, leadership, and organizations: The GLOBE study of 62 societies*. Thousand Oaks, CA: Sage.

House Robert J., Hanges Paul J., Ruiz-Quintanilla S. Antonio, Dorfman Peter W., Javidan Mansour, Dickson Marcus, Gupta Vipin & 170 co-authors (incl. Szabo Erna) (1999). Cultural influences on leadership and organizations: Project GLOBE. In Mobley William H., Gessner M. Jocelyne & Arnold Val (Eds.), *Advances in global leadership* (Vol. 1, pp. 171-233). Stamford, CT: JAI Press.

House Robert J. & Javidan Mansour (2004). Overview of GLOBE. In House Robert J., Hanges Paul J., Javidan Mansour, Dorfman Peter W. & Gupta Vipin (Eds.), *Culture, leadership, and organizations: The GLOBE study of 62 societies* (pp. 9-28). Thousand Oaks, CA: Sage.

House Robert J., Javidan Mansour, Hanges Paul & Dorfman Peter (2002). Understanding cultures and implicit leadership theories around the globe: An introduction to project GLOBE. *Journal of World Business*, 37(1), 3-10.

House Robert J. & Mitchell Terence R. (1974). Path-goal theory of leadership. *Journal of Contemporary Business*, 3(4), 81-98.

Hunt James G. (2002). A comparative analysis of the management & leadership competency profiles reported by German, US and Australian managers. *International Journal of Organisational Behaviour*, 5(9), 263-281.

Hunt James G. & Ropo Arja (1995). Multi-level leadership: Grounded theory and mainstream theory applied to the case of General Motors. *Leadership Quarterly*, 6(3), 379-412.

IDE (Industrial Democracy in Europe International Research Group) (1981). *Industrial democracy in Europe*. Oxford: Clarendon Press.

IDE (Industrial Democracy in Europe International Research Group) (1993). *Industrial democracy in Europe revisited*. Oxford: Oxford University Press.

IIM (2003). Statistical analyses of the Vroom/Yetton database. Linz: Institute for International Management Studies, Johannes Kepler University.

Jacob B. M. & Ahn C. (1978, August). *Impetus for worker participation*. Paper presented at the 9th World Congress of Sociology, Uppsala.

Jacobi Otto, Keller Berndt & Müller-Jentsch Walther (1992). Germany: Co-determining the future. In Ferner Anthony & Hyman Richard (Eds.), *Industrial relations in the new Europe* (pp. 218-270). Oxford: Blackwell.

Jago Arthur G. (1980, November). *Organizational characteristics and participative decision making*. Paper presented at the 12th Annual Conference of the American Institute for Decision Sciences, Las Vegas.

Jago Arthur G. (1995). Führungsforschung/Führung in Nordamerika. In Kieser Alfred, Reber Gerhard & Wunderer Rolf (Eds.), *Handwörterbuch der Führung* (2nd ed., cols. 619-637). Stuttgart: Schäffer-Poeschel.

Jago Arthur G., Maczynski Jerzy & Reber Gerhard (1996). Evolving leadership styles? A comparison of Polish managers before and after market economy reforms. *Polish Psychological Bulletin*, 27(2), 107-115.

Jago Arthur G., Reber Gerhard, Böhnisch Wolf, Maczynski Jerzy, Zavrel Jan & Dudorkin Jiri (1993). Culture's consequence?: A seven nation study of participation. In Rogers D. F. & Raturi A. S. (Eds.), *Proceedings of the 24th Annual Meeting of the Decision Sciences Institute* (pp. 451-454). Washington, D.C.: Decision Sciences Institute.

Jago Arthur G., Reber Gerhard, Böhnisch Wolf, Maczynski Jerzy, Zavrel Jan & Dudorkin Jiri (1995). Interkulturelle Unterschiede im Führungsverhalten. In Kieser Alfred, Reber Gerhard & Wunderer Rolf (Eds.), *Handwörterbuch der Führung* (2nd ed., cols. 1226-1239). Stuttgart: Schäffer-Poeschel.

Jago Arthur G. & Vroom Victor H. (1978). Predicting leader behavior from a measure of behavioral intent. *Academy of Management Journal*, 21(4), 715-721.

Jago Arthur G. & Vroom Victor H. (1982). Sex differences in the incidence and evaluation of participative leader behavior. *Journal of Applied Psychology*, 67(6), 776-783.

Jahoda Gustav (1995). In pursuit of the emic-etic distinction: Can we ever capture it? In Goldberger Nancy Rule & Veroff Jody Bennet (Eds.), *The psychology and culture reader* (pp. 128-138). New York, London: New York University Press.

Jarvenpa Robert (1992). Finns. In Bennett Linda A. (Ed.), *Encyclopedia of world cultures (Volume IV): Europe (Central, Western, and Southeastern Europe)* (pp. 101-104). New York: G. K. Hall.

Javidan Mansour & House Robert J. (2001). Cultural acumen for the global manager: Lessons from project GLOBE. *Organizational Dynamics*, 29(4), 289-305.

Jesuino Jorge Correia (2002). Latin Europe cluster: From South to North. *Journal of World Business*, 37(1), 81-89.

Jick Todd D. (1979). Mixing qualitative and quantitative methods: Triangulation in action. In Van Maanen John (Ed.), *Qualitative methodology* (pp. 135-148). Newbury Park, CA: Sage.

Kabasakal Hayat & Bodur Muzaffer (2002). Arabic cluster: A bridge between East and West. *Journal of World Business*, 37(1), 40-54.

Kagitcibasi Cigdem (1994). A critical appraisal of individualism and collectivism: Toward a new formulation. In Kim Uichol, Triandis Harry C., Kagitcibasi Cigdem, Choi Sang-Chin & Yoon Gene (Eds.), *Individualism and collectivism: Theory, method, and applications* (pp. 52-65). Thousand Oaks, CA: Sage.

Kakabadse Andrew & Myers Andrew (1996). Boardroom skills for Europe. *European Management Journal*, 14(2), 189-200.

Kan Melanie M. & Parry Ken W. (2004). Identifying paradox: A grounded theory of leadership in overcoming resistance to change. *Leadership Quarterly*, 15(4), 467-491.

Keating Mary A., Martin Gillian S. & Szabo Erna (2002). Do managers and students share the same perceptions of societal culture? *International Journal of Intercultural Relations*, 26(6), 633-652.

Kennington Carolyn, Sitko-Lutek Agnieszka, Rakowska Anna & Griffiths Jane (1996). Matching training to the needs of Polish managers. *Management Learning*, 27(4), 465-483.

Kieser Alfred (1988). Von der Morgensprache zum »Gemeinsamen HP-Frühstück«: Zur Funktion von Werten, Mythen, Ritualen und Symbolen - »Organisationskulturen« - in der Zunft und im modernen Unternehmen.

In Dülfer Eberhard (Ed.), *Organisationskultur* (pp. 207-225). Stuttgart: Schäffer-Poeschel.

Kim Uichol, Triandis Harry C., Kagitcibasi Cigdem, Choi Sang-Chin & Yoon Gene (Eds.) (1994). *Individualism and collectivism: Theory, method, and applications.* Thousand Oaks, CA: Sage.

Kivi Aleksis (1954). *Die sieben Brüder.* Köln: Kiepenheuer.

Kluckhohn Florence R. & Strodtbeck Fred L. (1961). *Variations in value orientations.* New York: Harper & Row.

Knudsen Herman (1995). *Employee participation in Europe.* London: Sage.

Kohout Pavel (1987). *Wo der Hund begraben liegt (Kde je zakopán pes).* München: Albrecht Knaus Verlag.

Kondo Dorinne K. (1990). *Crafting selves: Power, gender, and discourses of identity in a Japanese workplace.* Chicago: University of Chicago Press.

Koopman P. L. & Wierdsma A. F. M. (1998). Participative management. In Drenth Pieter J. D., Thierry Henk & de Wolff Charles J. (Eds.), *Handbook of Work and Organizational Psychology, Volume 3: Personnel Psychology* (2nd ed., pp. 297-324). Hove, East Sussex: Psychology Press.

Kost Michael (1994). *Analyse der Industrieprivatisierung in Polen, Ungarn und der CSFR.* Frankfurt: Peter Lang.

Kotíková Jaroslava & Bittnerová Daniela (2003). *Industrial relations and corporate culture in the Czech Republic.* Prague: Forum Mitbestimmung und Unternehmen.

Koubek J. & Brewster C. (1995). Human resource management in turbulent times: HRM in the Czech Republic. *The International Journal of Human Resource Management, 6*(2), 223-247.

Kozminski Andrzej K. (1993). *Catching up? Organizational and management change in the ex-socialist block.* New York: State University of New York Press.

Laine-Sveiby Kati (1987). *Nationell kultur som strategi: En fallstudie Sverige-Finland.* Helsingfors: EVA (Näringslivets delegation).

Lane Christel (1997). Industrial reorganization in Europe: Patterns of convergence and divergence in Germany, France and Britain. In Warner Malcolm (Ed.), *Comparative management: Critical perspectives on business and management, Volume II: European Management* (pp. 517-540). London, New York: Routledge.

Lane Henry W., DiStefano Joseph J. & Maznevski Martha L. (1997). *International management behavior* (3rd ed.). Cambridge, MA: Blackwell.

Lang Rainhart (1998). Personalmanagement in Osteuropa. In Kumar Brij Nino & Wagner Dieter (Eds.), *Handbuch internationalen Personalmanagements* (pp. 313-353). München: Beck.

Laurent André (1983). The cultural diversity of Western conceptions of management. *International Studies of Management & Organization, 13*(1-2), 75-96.

Laurila Juha (2000). Management in Finland. In Warner Malcolm (Ed.), *The regional encyclopedia of business and management: Management in Europe* (pp. 211-217). London: Thomas Learning.

Lawrence Peter (1994). German management: At the interface between Eastern and Western Europe. In Calori Roland & de Wood Philippe (Eds.), *A European management model: Beyond diversity*. New York: Prentice Hall.

Lawrence Peter & Spybey Tony (1986). *Management and society in Sweden*. London: Routledge.

Leana Carrie R. (1986). Predictors and consequences of delegation. *Academy of Management Journal*, 29(4), 754-774.

Leana Carrie R. & Florkowski Gary W. (1992). Employee involvement programs: Integrating psychological theory and management practice. In Feris Gerald & Rowland Kendrith (Eds.), *Research in personnel and human resources management* (Vol. 10, pp. 233-270). Greenwich, CT: JAI Press.

Leana Carrie R., Locke Edwin A. & Schweiger David M. (1990). Fact and fiction in analyzing research on participative decision making: A critique of Cotton, Vollrath, Froggatt, Lengnick-Hall, and Jennings. *Academy of Management Review*, 15(1), 137-146.

Ledford Gerald E. Jr. & Lawler Edward E. III (1994). Research on employee participation: Beating a dead horse? *Academy of Management Review*, 19(4), 633-636.

Leichtfried Gerlinde (2004). *Diagnostik von Führungspotenzialen*. Doctoral dissertation. Linz: Johannes Kepler University.

Lewin Kurt, Lippitt Ronald & White Ralph K. (1939). Patterns of aggressive behavior in experimentally created social climates. *Journal of Social Psychology*, 10, 271-301.

Liberman Leonardo & Torbiörn Ingemar (2000). Variances in staff-related management practices at eight European country subsidiaries of a global firm. *International Journal of Human Resource Management*, 11(1), 37-59.

Liberman Yaconi Leonardo (2001). Cross-cultural role expectations in nine European country-units of a multinational enterprise. *Journal of Management Studies*, 38(8), 1187-1215.

Lindell Martin (2002). Finnish leadership and culture: More influenced by West or East? In Auer-Rizzi Werner, Szabo Erna & Innreiter-Moser Cäcilia (Eds.), *Management in einer Welt der Globalisierung und Diversität: Europäische und nordamerikanische Sichtweisen* (pp. 179-193). Stuttgart: Schäffer-Poeschel.

Lindell Martin & Arvonen Jouko (1997). The Nordic management style in a European context. *International Studies of Management & Organization*, 26(3), 73-91.

Linna Väinö (1971). *Der unbekannte Soldat*. Berlin: Verlag Volk und Welt.

Lippitt Ronald & White Ralph K. (1943). The social climate of children's groups. In Baker Roger G., Kounin Jacob S. & Wright Herbert F. (Eds.), *Child behavior and development*. New York: McGraw-Hill.

Locke Edwin A. & Schweiger David M. (1979). Participation in decision making: One more look, In Staw Barry M. (Ed.), *Research in organizational behavior* (pp. 265-329). Greenwich, CT: JAI Press.

Locke Edwin A., Schweiger David M. & Latham Gary P. (1986). Participation in decision making: When should it be used? *Organizational Dynamics*, 14(3), 65-79.

Locke Karen (2001). *Grounded theory in management research*. Thousand Oaks, CA: Sage.

Lord Robert G. & Maher Karen J. (1991). *Leadership and information processing: Linking perception to performance*. Boston: Unwin Hyman.

Lowe Sid (1994, January). *Hermes revisited*. Paper presented at the ISPAB Conference, Bangkok.

Maczynski Jerzy (1998). *Diagnozowanie partycypacji decyzyjnej*. Warszawa: Wydawnictwo IFiS PAN.

Maczynski Jerzy (2002). Cultural determinants of leadership style of Polish managers. In Auer-Rizzi Werner, Szabo Erna & Innreiter-Moser Cäcilia (Eds.), *Management in einer Welt der Globalisierung und Diversität: Europäische und nordamerikanische Sichtweisen* (pp. 195-216). Stuttgart: Schäffer-Poeschel.

Maczynski Jerzy, Jago Arthur G., Reber Gerhard & Böhnisch Wolf (1994). Culture and leadership styles: A comparison of Polish, Austrian, and U.S. managers. *Polish Psychological Bulletin*, 25(4), 303-315.

Maczynski Jerzy, Lindell Martin, Motowidlo Stephan J., Sigfrids Camilla & Jarmuz Slawomir (1997). A comparison of organizational and societal culture in Finland and Poland. *Polish Psychological Bulletin*, 28(3), 269-278.

Marr Rainer (2000). Management in Germany. In Warner Malcolm (Ed.), *The regional encyclopedia of business and management: Management in Europe* (pp. 229-245). London: Thomas Learning.

Marrow Alfred J., Bowers David G. & Seashore Stanley E. (1967). *Management by participation*. New York: Harper & Row.

Martin Gillian S. (2001). *German-Irish sales negotiation: Theory, practice and pedagogical implications*. Frankfurt: Peter Lang.

Maslow Abraham H. (1943). A theory of human motivation. *Psychology Review*, July 1943, 370-396.

McClelland David C. (1961). *The achieving society*. New York: Free Press.

McClelland David C. (1985). *Human motivation*. Glenview, IL: Scott, Foresman & Co.

McFarlin Dean B., Sweeney Paul D. & Cotton John L. (1992). Attitudes toward employee participation in decision-making: A comparison of European and American managers in a United States multinational company. *Human Resource Management*, 31(4), 363-383.

Meierewert Sylvia (2001). Tschechische Kulturstandards aus der Sicht österreichischer Manager. In Fink Gerhard & Meierewert Sylvia (Eds.), *Interkulturelles Management: Österreichische Perspektiven* (pp. 97-109). Vienna, New York: Springer.

Miles Matthew B. & Huberman A. Michael (1994). *Qualitative data analysis* (2nd ed.). Thousand Oaks, CA: Sage.

Miller Katherine I. & Monge Peter R. (1986). Participation, satisfaction, and productivity: A meta-analytic review. *Academy of Management Journal*, 29(4), 727-753.

Mills Anne (2000). Management in the Czech and Slovak Republics. In Warner Malcolm (Ed.), *The regional encyclopedia of business and management: Management in Europe* (pp. 193-202). London: Thomas Learning.

Mills Ted (1978). Europe's industrial democracy: An American response. *Harvard Business Review*, 56(6), 143-152.

Mintzberg Henry (1983a). An emerging strategy of "direct" research. In Van Maanen John (Ed.), *Qualitative methodology* (pp. 105-116). Newbury Park, CA: Sage.

Mintzberg Henry (1983b). *Structure in fives: Designing effective organizations*. Englewood Cliffs, NJ: Prentice Hall.

Müller-Jentsch Walther (1995). Germany: From collective voice to co-management. In Rogers Joel & Streeck Wolfgang (Eds.), *Works councils* (pp. 53-69). Chicago: University of Chicago Press.

Nasierowski Wojciech (1996). Emerging patterns of reformation in Central Europe: The Czech Republic, Hungary, and Poland. *Journal of East-West Business*, 2, 143-171.

Nasierowski Wojciech & Mikula Bogusz (1998). Culture dimensions of Polish managers: Hofstede's indices. *Organization Studies*, 19(3), 495-509.

Nasierowski Wojciech & Wright Philipp (1993). Perceptions of needs: How cross-cultural differences can affect market penetration into Central Europe. *The International Executive*, 35(2), 513-524.

Novy Ivan & Schroll-Machl Sylvia (2003). Tschechien. In Thomas Alexander, Kammerhuber Stefan & Schroll-Machl Sylvia (Eds.), *Handbuch interkulturelle Kommunikation und Kooperation, Band 2: Länder, Kulturen und interkulturelle Berufstätigkeit* (pp. 90-102). Göttingen: Vandenhoeck & Ruprecht.

Nurmi Raimo (1989). *Management in Finland*. Turku: Turku School of Economics and Business Administration.

Nurmikari-Berry Marjatta & Berry Michael R. (1999). Discovering cultural meaning as the first step towards developing intercultural communication competence. In Häkkinen Kirsti (Ed.), *Innovative approaches to intercultural education* (pp. 109-119). Jyväskylä: University of Jyväskylä, Continuing Education Centre.

Obloj Krzysztof (2000). Management in Poland. In Warner Malcolm (Ed.), *The regional encyclopedia of business and management: Management in Europe* (pp. 302-309). London: Thomas Learning.

Offermann Lynn R. & Hellmann Peta S. (1997). Culture's consequences for leadership behavior: National values in action. *Journal of Cross-Cultural Psychology*, 28(3), 342-351.

Parkum Kurt H. & Agersnap Flemming (1994). Managing people in Scandinavia. In Garrison Terry & Rees David (Eds.), *Managing people across Europe* (pp. 111-121). Oxford: Butterworth-Heinemann.

Parry Ken W. (1998). Grounded theory and social process: A new direction for leadership research. *Leadership Quarterly*, 9(1), 85-105.

Peng T. K., Peterson Mark F. & Shyi Yuh-Ping (1991). Quantitative methods in cross-national management research: Trends and equivalence issues. *Journal of Organizational Behavior*, 12(2), 87-107.

Peterson Mark F. & Smith Peter B. (1997). Does national culture or ambient temperature explain cross-national differences in role stress? No sweat! *Academy of Management Journal*, 40(4), 930-946.

Pettigrew Andrew M. (1979). On studying organizational cultures. *Administrative Science Quarterly*, 24(4), 570-581.

Pibilova Inka (2004). *Der Führungsstil österreichischer Manager in Tschechien: Eine explorative qualitative Studie auf Grundlage des Vroom/Yetton Modells.* Master thesis. Linz: Institute for International Management Studies, Johannes Kepler University.

Piske Reiner (2002). German acquisitions in Poland: An empirical study on integration management and integration success. *Human Resource Development International*, 5(3), 295-312.

Pusic Eugen (1998). Organization theory and participation. In Heller Frank, Pusic Eugen, Strauss George & Wilpert Bernhard (Eds.), *Organizational participation: Myth and reality* (pp. 65-96). Oxford: Oxford University Press.

Putnam Robert D. (1993). *Making democracy work.* Princeton, NJ: Princeton University Press.

Randlesome Collin (2000). Changes in management culture and competencies: The German experience. *Journal of Management Development*, 19(7), 629-642.

Reber Gerhard (2001). Is it a good idea to engage in a joint venture with a Finnish company? In Suominen Arto (Ed.), *Liikkeenjohdon ja kulttuurin rajoja etsimässä - Searching for the boundaries of business culture* (pp. 63-86). Turku: Turku School of Economics and Business Administration.

Reber Gerhard & Auer-Rizzi Werner (2003). The leadership behaviour of managers in Austria, the Czech Republic and Poland: An intercultural comparison based on the Vroom-Yetton model of leadership and decison making. In Stüting Heinz-Jürgen, Dorow Wolfgang, Claassen Frank & Blazejewski Susanne (Eds.), *Change management in transition economies: In-*

tegrating corporate strategy, structure and culture (pp. 203-221). New York: Palgrave Macmillan.

Reber Gerhard, Auer-Rizzi Werner & Maly Milan (2004). The behaviour of managers in Austria and the Czech Republic: An intercultural comparison based on the Vroom/Yetton model of leadership and decision making. *Journal of East European Management Studies*, 9(4), 411-429.

Reber Gerhard, Auer-Rizzi Werner & Szabo Erna (2004, July). *"Social ice-age" in the behavior of Austrian and German managers?* Paper presented at the Scandinavian Academy of Management (SAM)/International Federation of Scholarly Associations of Management (IFSAM) VIIth World Congress, Göteborg.

Reber Gerhard & Berry Michael (1999). A role for social and intercultural communication competence in international human resource development. In Lähteenmäki Satu, Holden Len & Roberts Ian (Eds.), *HRM and the learning organization* (pp. 313-333). Turku: Turku School of Economics and Business Administration.

Reber Gerhard & Jago Arthur G. (1997). Festgemauert in der Erde... Eine Studie zur Veränderung oder Stabilität des Führungsverhaltens von Managern in Deutschland, Frankreich, Österreich, Polen, Tschechien und der Schweiz zwischen 1989 und 1996. In Klimecki Rüdiger & Remer Andreas (Eds.), *Personal als Strategie: Mit flexiblen und lernbereiten Human-Ressourcen Kernkompetenzen aufbauen* (pp. 158-184). Bern: Haupt.

Reber Gerhard, Jago Arthur G., Auer-Rizzi Werner & Szabo Erna (2000). Führungsstile in sieben Ländern Europas - Ein interkultureller Vergleich. In Regnet Erika & Hofmann Laila Maija (Eds.), *Personalmanagement in Europa* (pp. 154-173). Göttingen: Verlag für Angewandte Psychologie.

Reber Gerhard, Jago Arthur G. & Böhnisch Wolf (1993). Interkulturelle Unterschiede im Führungsverhalten. In Haller Matthias, Bleicher Kurt, Brauchlin Emil, Pleitner Hans-Jobst, Wunderer Rolf & Zünd André (Eds.), *Globalisierung der Wirtschaft: Einwirkungen auf die Betriebswirtschaftslehre* (pp. 217-241). Bern: Haupt.

Reber Gerhard, Jago Arthur G. & Maly Milan (2002). Leadership styles of managers in the Czech Republic: Changes over time (1991-2001) and cross-cultural comparisons with two other countries. Manuscript. Linz: Institute for International Management Studies, Johannes Kepler University.

Redding Gordon (1976). Some perceptions of psychological needs among managers in South-East Asia. In Poortinga Ype H. (Ed.), *Basic problems in cross-cultural psychology* (pp. 338-343). Amsterdam: Swets & Zeitlinger.

Rieger Fritz & Wong-Rieger Durhane (1995). Model building in organizational/cross-cultural research: The need for multiple methods, indices and cultures. In Jackson Terence (Ed.), *Cross-cultural management* (pp. 50-60). Oxford: Butterworth-Heinemann.

Ronen Simcha (1986). *Comparative and multinational management*. New York: Wiley.

Ronen Simcha & Kraut Allen I. (1977). Similarities among countries based on employee work values and attitudes. *Columbia Journal of World Business*, 12(2), 89-96.

Ronen Simcha & Shenkar Oded (1985). Clustering countries on attitudinal dimensions: A review and synthesis. *Academy of Management Review*, 10(3), 435-454.

Rossman Gretchen B. & Wilson Bruce L. (1985). Numbers and words: Combining quantitative and qualitative methods in a single large-scale evaluation study. *Evaluation Review*, 9(5), 627-643.

Rossman Gretchen B. & Wilson Bruce L. (1994). Numbers and words revisited: Being "shamelessly eclectic". *Quality and Quantity*, 28, 315-327.

Sackmann Sonja A. (1997). Introduction. In Sackmann Sonja A. (Ed.), *Cultural complexity in organizations: Inherent contrasts and contradictions* (pp. 1-13). Thousand Oaks, CA: Sage.

Salzmann Zdenek (1992). Czechs. In Bennett Linda A. (Ed.), *Encyclopedia of world cultures (Volume IV): Europe (Central, Western, and Southeastern Europe)* (pp. 82-84). New York: G. K. Hall.

Sapir Edward (1929). The status of linguistics as a science. *Language*, 5(4), 207-214.

Sashkin Marshall (1984). Participative management is an ethical imperative. *Organizational Dynamics*, 12(4), 4-22.

Schaffer Bryan S. & Riordan Christine M. (2003). A review of cross-cultural methodologies for organizational research: A best practices approach. *Organizational Research Methods*, 6(2), 169-215.

Schneider Judith & Littrell Romie F. (2003). Leadership preferences of German and English managers. *Journal of Management Development*, 22(2), 130-148.

Schroll-Machl Sylvia & Novy Ivan (2000). *Perfekt geplant oder genial improvisiert? Kulturunterschiede in der deutsch-tschechischen Zusammenarbeit*. München: Rainer Hampp.

Schroll-Machl Sylvia & Wiskoski Katarzyna (2003). *Deutsche und Polen - Verstehen und verstanden werden. Interkulturelle Kommunikation im deutschpolnischen Geschäftsalltag*. Frankfurt: Deutsch-Polnische Wirtschaftsförderungsgesellschaft AG.

Schwartz Shalom H. (1990). Individualism-collectivism: Critique and proposed refinements. *Journal of Cross-Cultural Psychology*, 21(2), 139-157.

Schwartz Shalom H. (1994). Beyond individualism/collectivism: New cultural dimensions of values. In Kim Uichol, Triandis Harry C., Kagitcibasi Cigdem, Choi Sang-Chin & Yoon Gene (Eds.), *Individualism and collectivism: Theory, method, and applications* (pp. 85-119). Thousand Oaks, CA: Sage.

Schwartzman Helen (1993). *Ethnography in organizations*. Newbury Park, CA: Sage.

Silverman David (2001). *Interpreting qualitative data: Methods for analysing talk, text and interaction* (2nd ed.). London, Thousand Oaks, New Delhi: Sage.

Simon Harald, Bauer Brigitte & Kaivola Kalevi (1996). *Eurooppalainen johtajat - johtamiskultuurit ja menestystekijät*. Porvoo: WSOY.

Sirota David & Greenwood J. Michael (1971). Understand your overseas work force. *Harvard Business Review*, 49(1), 53-60.

Skreija Andris (1992). Poles. In Bennett Linda A. (Ed.), *Encyclopedia of world cultures (Volume IV): Europe (Central, Western, and Southeastern Europe)* (pp. 201-204). New York: G. K. Hall.

Smith Peter B. (1996). National cultures and the values of organizational employees: Time for another look. In Joynt Pat & Warner Malcolm (Eds.), *Managing across cultures: Issues and perspectives* (pp. 92-102). London: International Thomson Business Press.

Smith Peter B. (1997). Leadership in Europe: Euro-management or the footprint of history? *European Journal of Work and Organizational Psychology*, 6(4), 375-386.

Smith Peter B. (2003). Personal correspondence. Feb. 11, 2003.

Smith Peter B., Andersen Jon Aarum, Ekelund Bjørn, Graversen Gert & Ropo Arja (2003). In search of Nordic management styles. *Scandinavian Journal of Management*, 19(4), 491-507.

Smith Peter B., Dugan Shaun & Trompenaars Fons (1996). National culture and the values of employees: A dimensional analysis across 43 nations. *Journal of Cross-Cultural Psychology*, 27(2), 231-264.

Smith Peter B., Kruzela Pavla, Czegledi Reka, Tsvetanova Sevda, Pop Dana, Groblewska Beata & Halasova Daniela (1997). Managerial leadership in Eastern Europe: From uniformity to diversity. In Pepermans Roland, Buelens Anne, Vinkenburg Claartje J. & Jansen Paul G. W. (Eds.), *Managerial behaviour and practices: European research issues* (pp. 27-37). Leuven, Amersfoort: Acco.

Smith Peter B., Kruzela Pavla, Groblewska Beata, Halasova Daniela, Pop Dana, Czegledi Reka & Tsvetanova Sevda (2000). Effective ways of handling work events in Central and Eastern Europe. *Social Science Information*, 39(2), 317-333.

Smith Peter B. & Peterson Mark F. (1988). *Leadership, organizations and culture*. London, Newbury Park, CA: Sage.

Smith Peter B. & Peterson Mark F. (1994, July). *Leadership as event management: A cross-cultural survey based upon middle managers from 25 nations*. Paper presented at the 23rd International Congress of Applied Psychology, Madrid.

Smith Peter B., Peterson Mark F. & 13 co-authors (1994). Organizational event management in fourteen countries: A comparison with Hofstede´s dimensions. In Bouvy Anne-Marie, van de Vijver Fons J. R., Boski Paul & Schmitz Paul (Eds.), *Journeys into cross-cultural psychology* (pp. 364-373). Amsterdam: Swets and Zeitlinger.

Smith Peter B., Peterson Mark F. & 39 co-authors (incl. Szabo Erna) (2005). Demographic effects on the use of vertical sources of guidance by managers in widely differing cultural contexts. *International Journal of Cross Cultural Management*, 5(1), 5-26.

Smith Peter B., Peterson Mark F. & Misumi J. (1994). Event management and work team effectiveness in Japan, Britain and USA. *Journal of Occupational and Organizational Psychology*, 67, 33-43.

Smith Peter B., Peterson Mark F., Schwartz Shalom H. & 42 co-authors (incl. Szabo Erna) (2002). Cultural values, sources of guidance, and their relevance to managerial behavior: A 47-nation study. *Journal of Cross-Cultural Psychology*, 33(2), 188-208.

Smith Peter B., Peterson Mark F. & Wang Zhong Ming (1996). The manager as mediator of alternative meanings: A pilot study from China, the USA and U.K. *Journal of International Business Studies*, 27(1), 115-137.

Søndergaard Mikael (1994). Research note: Hofstede's consequences: A study of reviews, citations and replications. *Organization Studies*, 15(3), 447-456.

Sood James & Mroczkowski Tomasz (1994). Human resource management challenges in Polish private enterprise. *International Studies of Management & Organization*, 24(4), 48-63.

Sorge Arndt (1983). Book review: Culture's consequences: International differences in work-related values. *Administrative Science Quarterly*, 28(4), 625-629.

Soulsby Anna (2001). The construction of Czech managers' careers. *International Studies of Management & Organization*, 31(2), 48-64.

Soulsby Anna & Clark Ed (1998). Controlling personnel: Management and motive in the transformation of the Czech enterprise. *The International Journal of Human Resource Management*, 9(1), 79-98.

Spector Paul E. (1986). Perceived control by employees: A meta-analysis of studies concerning autonomy and participation at work. *Human Relations*, 39(11), 1005-1016.

Steers Richard M. (1977). Individual differences in participative decision-making. *Human Relations*, 30(9), 837-847.

Strauss Anselm & Corbin Juliet (1990). *Basics of qualitative research*. Thousand Oaks, CA: Sage.

Strauss Anselm & Corbin Juliet (1994). Grounded theory methodology: An overview. In Denzin Norman K. & Lincoln Yvonna S. (Eds.), *Handbook of qualitative research* (pp. 273-285). Thousand Oaks, CA: Sage.

Strauss Anselm & Corbin Juliet (1998). *Basics of qualitative research: Techniques and procedures for developing grounded theory* (2nd ed.). Thousand Oaks, CA: Sage.

Strauss George (1996). Collective bargaining. In Warner Malcolm (Ed.), *International encyclopedia of business and management* (pp. 647-658). London, New York: Routledge.

Strauss George (1998a). An overview. In Heller Frank, Pusic Eugen, Strauss George & Wilpert Bernhard (Eds.), *Organizational participation: Myth and reality* (pp. 8-39). Oxford: Oxford University Press.

Strauss George (1998b). Collective bargaining, unions, and participation. In Heller Frank, Pusic Eugen, Strauss George & Wilpert Bernhard (Eds.), *Organizational participation: Myth and reality* (pp. 97-143). Oxford: Oxford University Press.

Strauss George (1998c). Participation works - If conditions are appropriate. In Heller Frank, Pusic Eugen, Strauss George & Wilpert Bernhard (Eds.), *Organizational participation: Myth and reality* (pp. 190-219). Oxford: Oxford University Press.

Stymne Bengt (1995). Führungsforschung/Führung in Skandinavien. In Kieser Alfred, Reber Gerhard & Wunderer Rolf (Eds.), *Handwörterbuch der Führung* (2. ed., cols. 638-652). Stuttgart: Schäffer-Poeschel.

Suutari Vesa (1996a). Leadership ideologies among European managers: A comparative survey in a multinational company. *Scandinavian Journal of Management*, 12(4), 389-409.

Suutari Vesa (1996b). Variation in the average leadership behaviour of managers across countries: Finnish expatriates' experiences from Germany, Sweden, France and Great Britain. *The International Journal of Human Resource Management*, 7(3), 677-707.

Suutari Vesa & Riusala Kimmo (2000). Operating in "economics in transition": Adjustment and management issues faced by Finnish expatriate managers in CCE. *Liiketaloudellinen Aikakauskirja - The Finnish Journal of Business Economics*, 1/00, 87-107.

Suutari Vesa & Riusala Kimmo (2001). Leadership styles in Central Eastern Europe: Experiences of Finnish expatriates in the Czech Republic, Hungary and Poland. *Scandinavian Journal of Management*, 17, 249-280.

Symon Gillian & Cassell Catherine (1998). Reflections on the use of qualitative methods. In Symon Gillian & Cassell Catherine (Eds.), *Qualitative methods and analysis in organizational research* (pp. 1-9). Thousand Oaks, CA: Sage.

Szabo Erna (1998). *Organisationskultur und Ethnographie: Fallstudie in einem österreichischen Krankenhaus*. Wiesbaden: Deutscher Universitätsverlag.

Szabo Erna (2001). "Yes to participation, but..." A look beneath the surface of cultural stereotypes between Finnish and Swedish managers. In Suominen Arto (Ed.), *Liikkeenjohdon ja kulttuurin rajoja etsimässä - Searching for the boundaries of business culture* (pp. 87-100). Turku: Turku School of Economics and Business Administration.

Szabo Erna (2004). Participation in managerial decision making: Ireland and Germany in comparison. In Keating Mary & Martin Gillian S. (Eds.), *Managing cross-cultural business relations: The Irish-German case* (pp. 112-138). Dublin: Blackhall.

Szabo Erna, Brodbeck Felix C., Den Hartog Deanne, Reber Gerhard, Weibler Jürgen & Wunderer Rolf (2002). The Germanic Europe cluster: Where employees have a voice. *Journal of World Business*, 37(1), 55-68.

Szabo Erna, Jarmuz Slawomir, Maczynski Jerzy & Reber Gerhard (1997). Autocratic Polish versus participative Austrian leaders: More than a cliché? *Polish Psychological Bulletin*, 28(3), 279-291.

Szabo Erna, Reber Gerhard, Weibler Jürgen, Brodbeck Felix & Wunderer Rolf (2001). Values and behavior orientation in leadership studies: Reflections based on findings in three German-speaking countries. *Leadership Quarterly*, 12(2), 219-244.

Tannenbaum Arnold S., Kavcic Bogdan, Rosner Menachem, Vianello Mino & Wieser Georg (1974). *Hierarchy in organizations*. San Francisco: Jossey-Bass.

Tannenbaum Robert & Schmidt Warren H. (1958). How to choose a leadership pattern. *Harvard Business Review*, 36(2), 95-101.

Tayeb Monir (2001). Conducting research across cultures: Overcoming drawbacks and obstacles. *International Journal of Cross Cultural Management*, 1(1), 91-108.

Taylor Frederick W. (1911). *Principles of scientific management*. New York: Harper & Brothers.

Temple Bogusia & Young Alys (2004). Qualitative research and translation dilemmas. *Qualitative Research*, 4(2), 161-178.

Tett Robert P. & Jackson Douglas N. (1990). Organization and personality correlates of participative behaviors using an in-basket exercise. *Journal of Occupational Psychology*, 63, 175-188.

Thirkell John, Scase Richard & Vickerstaff Sarah (1997). Labour relations in transition in Eastern Europe. In Warner Malcolm (Ed.), *Comparative management: Critical perspectives on business and management, Volume II: European management* (pp. 737-753). London, New York: Routledge.

Traxler Franz (2000). Employers and employer organizations in Europe: Membership strength, density and representativeness. *Industrial Relations Journal*, 31(4), 308-316.

Triandis Harry C. (1988). Collectivism and individualism: A reconceptualization of a basic concept in cross-cultural psychology. In Verma Gajendra K. & Bagley Christopher (Eds.), *Personality, attitudes, and cognitions* (pp. 66-95). London: Macmillan.

Triandis Harry C. (1993). Collectivism and individualism as cultural syndromes. *Cross-Cultural Research*, 27(3&4), 155-180.

Triandis Harry C. (1995). *Individualism and collectivism*. Boulder, CO: Westview Press.

Trompenaars Fons (1993). *Riding the waves of culture: Understanding cultural diversity in business*. London: Economist Books.

Tung Rosalie L. & Havlovic Stephen J. (1997). Human resource management in transitional economies: The case of Poland and the Czech Republic. In Warner Malcolm (Ed.), *Comparative management: Critical perspectives on business and management, Volume II: European management* (pp. 754-773). London, New York: Routledge.

Usunier Jean-Claude (1998). *International and cross-cultural management research*. Thousand Oaks, CA: Sage.

Van Maanen John (1983). Reclaiming qualitative methods for organizational research: A preface. In Van Maanen John (Ed.), *Qualitative methodology* (pp. 9-18). Newbury Park, CA: Sage.

Van Maanen John & Barley Stephen R. (1984). Occupational communities: Culture and control in organizations. In Cummings Larry L. & Staw Barry M. (Eds.), *Research in Organizational Behavior* (Vol. 6, pp. 287-365). Greenwich, CT: JAI Press.

Van Oudenhoven Jan Pieter (2001). Do organizations reflect national cultures? A 10-nation study. *International Journal of Intercultural Relations*, 25(1), 89-107.

Vroom Victor H. (1993). Two decades of research on participation: Beyond buzz words and management fads. *Yale Management*, Spring 1993(5), 23-32.

Vroom Victor H. & Jago Arthur G. (1988). *The new leadership: Managing participation in organizations*. Englewood Cliffs, NJ: Prentice Hall.

Vroom Victor H. & Jago Arthur G. (1995). Situation effects and levels of analysis in the study of leader participation. *Leadership Quarterly*, 6(2), 169-181.

Vroom Victor H. & Yetton Philip W. (1973). *Leadership and decision-making*. Pittsburgh: University of Pittsburgh Press.

Vroom Victor H., Yetton Philip W. & Jago Arthur G. (1976). *Problem set no. 5*. Manuscript. New Haven: School of Organization and Management, Yale University.

Wächter Hartmut & Stengelhofen Theo (1992). Human resource management in a unified Germany. *Employee Relations*, 14(4), 21-37.

Wagner John A. III (1994). Participation's effects on performance and satisfaction: A reconsideration of research evidence. *Academy of Management Review*, 19(2), 312-330.

Wagner John A. III & Gooding Richard Z. (1987a). Effects of societal trends on participation research. *Administrative Science Quarterly*, 32(2), 241-262.

Wagner John A. III & Gooding Richard Z. (1987b). Shared influence and organizational behavior: A meta-analysis of situational variables expected to moderate participation-outcome relationships. *Academy of Management Journal*, 30(3), 524-541.

Warner Malcolm & Campbell Adrian (1993). Germany: German Management. In Hickson David J. (Ed.), *Management in Western Europe: Society, culture and organization in twelve nations* (pp. 89-108). Berlin, New York: De Gruyter.

Weibler Jürgen, Brodbeck Felix C., Szabo Erna, Reber Gerhard, Wunderer Rolf & Moosmann Oswald (2000). Führung in kulturverwandten Regionen: Gemeinsamkeiten und Unterschiede bei Führungsidealen in Deutschland, Österreich und der Schweiz. *Die Betriebswirtschaft*, 60(5), 588-606.

Wilpert Bernhard (1998). A view from psychology. In Heller Frank, Pusic Eugen, Strauss George & Wilpert Bernhard (Eds.), *Organizational participation: Myth and reality* (pp. 40-64). Oxford: Oxford University Press.

Wunderer Rolf & Grunwald Wolfgang (1980). *Führungslehre*. Berlin, New York: De Gruyter.

Yukl Gary (1998). *Leadership in organizations* (4th ed.). Upper Saddle River, NJ: Prentice-Hall.

Zander Lena (1997). *The licence to lead: An 18 country study of the relationship between employees' preferences regarding interpersonal leadership and national culture.* Stockholm: Stockholm School of Economics.

Zander Lena (2000). Management in Sweden. In Warner Malcolm (Ed.), *The regional encyclopedia of business and management: Management in Europe* (pp. 345-353). London: Thomas Learning.

Appendix A

Code Lists

Czech Data

adaptability
administratively competent
attitude toward participation
attitude toward subordinates
autocratic
autonomous
being able to influence
change decisions
charisma
communication skills
communist system
conflict
cooperation
critical
dealing with conflict
decision commitment
decision quality
decisive
delegation
differing opinions
difficult problem
diplomatic
economic efficiency
emergency situations

employees as specialists
employees directly concerned
expectation of autocratic leader
experience
experts (outside group)
extreme situations
face saver
fact-based decisions
female leaders
formal rules
group meeting
high risk situation
HRM decisions
individualism/collectivism
information
knowledge and expertise
level of participation
minor issues
non-participative
one-on-one meeting
operational work
outstanding manager/leader

own way (creative)
perspective on participation
power distance
procedural
professional manager
range of participation
rational decision
responsible for decision and outcome
sales decisions
social skills
strategic decisions
strategic view
superior
taking part in process and decision
team integrator
teamwork
technical decisions
time of decision-making
trust
organisation type
uncertainty avoidance
unwritten rules
wrong decision

Finnish Data

administratively competent

attitude toward participation

attitude toward subordinates

autocratic

autonomous

autonomy

change in attitude / opinion

clear responsibility

colleagues

common understanding

communication

conflict

consultation

control

cooperation

crisis situation

dealing with conflict

decision commitment

decision quality

decisive

delegation

differing opinions

difficult problems

diplomatic

discussion

employees as specialists

employees directly concerned

enactment of participation

experience

experts (outside group)

explain autocratic behaviour

facilitator

fairness

feedback

formal rules

group meeting

hands-off management

implementation

individualism

industrial relations

information

innovation

knowledge and expertise

learning (from mistakes)

level of participation

major implication

motivation

natural team

no-democracy area

non-participative

one-on-one meeting

personal issues

perspective on participation

planning and implementation

power distance

problems with uncertainties

range of participation

rational decisions

real problems

responsible for decision and outcome

role model

routine decisions

see the bigger picture

self confidence

solution ready

strategic decision

superior

taking part in process and decision

task-related problems

team as support system

team integrator

team orientation

teamwork

time is an issue

trust

uncertainty avoidance

unimportant/small issues

unknown soldier

unwritten rules

upward delegation

visionary

work based on thinking

work independently

work values

German Data

administrative decisions

administratively competent

aims manager vs. subordinates

apprentice system

attitude toward participation

attitude toward subordinates

autocratic

autonomous

colleagues

collectivism

communication

communism

complex decisions

compromise

conflict

consensus

consultation

contingency approach

coordination

dealing with conflict

dealing with emotions

decision commitment

decision quality

decisive

degree of participation

delegate

difficult decisions

diplomatic

discipline

economic success

employees as specialists

employees directly concerned

enactment of participation

equality and fairness

experience

experts (outside group)

explain autocratic behaviour

face saver

flexibility

formal rules

functioning team

goals / goal orientation

good relations with team

good solutions quickly

group meeting

honesty

HR decisions

HR development

industrial relations

influence by subordinates

information

know each other well

knowledge and expertise

learning opportunity

level of participation

long leash

motivation

necessity for participation (check earlier interviews for code)

negotiation

one-on-one meeting

organisational change

outstanding manager/leader

participation initiative

personality

perspective on participation

power distance

procedural

punctuality

range of participation

responsibility

responsible for decision and outcome

responsive

risk situations

role model

safety decisions

self-centred

social skills

stand up (for it)

status

strategic decisions

superior

take initiative

taking part in process and decision

task-related / rational

team building

team development

team integrator

teamwork

time management

time of decision-making

trivial problems

trust

uncertainty avoidance

unstructured problems

unwritten rules

work independently

work-related decisions

wrong decisions

Polish Data

administratively competent

aims manager vs. subordinates

attitude toward participation

attitude toward subordinates

autocratic

autonomous

chaos

collectivism

communication

communist system

consensus

consultation

control

controversial problems

cooperation

dealing with changes

dealing with conflict

dealing with emotions

decision acceptance

decision quality

decisive

dependency

diplomatic

economic success

efficiency/cost related

employees as specialists

enactment of participation

equality and fairness

experience

experts (outside group)

explain decision

face saver

female managers

formal rules

good relations with team

group meeting

group size

hard decision

high quality vs. trivial problems

HR decisions

humane orientation

industrial relations

information retrieval

innovative

knowledge and expertise

level of participation

moral rules

motivation

non-participative

one-on-one meeting

open discussion

outstanding manager/leader

personal issues

perspective on participation

potential conflict

power distance

procedural

pseudo participation

range of participation

rational reasons

respect

responsible for decision and outcome

risk situation

self-centred

small decisions

stability

status

strategic decisions

superior

team integrator

teamwork

technical problems

time of decision-making

trust

organisation type

uncertainty avoidance

unpopular decisions

valuing opinions of team

vision and charisma

work performance

work-related decisions

Swedish Data

administratively competent
approachable
attitude toward participation
autocratic
autonomous
collaborative team orientation
colleagues
collectivism
communication
communication skills
consensus
convincing
dealing with conflict
dealing with emotions
decision acceptance
decision quality
decisive
delegate
difficulties related to participation
difficulty to decide
diplomatic
easy decision
efficient
employees as specialists
employees directly concerned
empower
enactment of participation
equality and fairness
experience
experts (outside group)
explain decision

female managers
flexible
formal rules
gives an example
group meeting
handling performance problems
hard decision
help for the manager
high risk problem
honest
important problem
industrial relations
influence by subordinates
information
intra unit problems
know each other well
knowledge and expertise
known problem
lagom
larger than unit problems
level of participation
motivation
new cases
one-on-one meeting
open discussion
participation as a burden
participation as requirement
personal growth and development
personal issues
perspective on participation

potential conflict
power distance
prestige
procedural
rational reasons
respect
responsible for decision and outcome
routine decisions
self-centred
sensitive issue
small problem
smooth meetings/decisions
stand up (for own people, for it)
strategic decisions
superior
taking part in process and decision
talk on the side
team integrator
time of decision making
trial and error
trust
uncertainty avoidance
unimportant problem
unwritten rules
visible
vision and charisma
waste of time questions
win-win situation
work independently
work performance
work-related decisions

Appendix B

Key Categories of Participation and Related Concepts

Czech Data

Key categories of participation	Main codes	Remarks
Meaning of participation	Attitude toward participation, employees as specialists, responsible for decision and outcome	Positive attitude toward participation; manager responsible; employees serve as specialists who provide valid input; participation useful for operational work
Assumptions underlying participation	Being able to influence, trust	Decisions binding; participants should be able to exercise influence, otherwise participation useless
Enactment/form of participation	Group meeting, one-on-one meeting, autocratic, delegation, female leaders	
Social range of participation	Range of participation, experts (outside group)	Usually subordinates and other experts
Types of problems/decisions	Strategic decisions, operational work, employees directly concerned, sales decisions, technical decisions, wrong decisions, rational decision, emergency/extreme situations, HRM decisions	Operational matters: participative; strategic/change/emergency: autocratic
Time of decision-making	Time of decision-making	Time is a concern, time pressure: autocratic
Outcomes/effects of participation	Decision quality, decision commitment	Participation increases decision quaility

Related concepts	Main codes	Remarks
(Organisational) rules	Formal rules, unwritten rules	Unwritten rules preferred over formal rules
Collectivism	Individualism/collectivism	High individualism (egoism) vs. people don't think for themselves

Communist system	Communist system, procedural	Left its imprint on managerial & employee values and behaviour
Communication	Communication skills	Expected of an outstanding manager
Conflict	Differing opinions, conflict, dealing with conflict	Different approaches of dealing with potential conflict; open conflict: autocratic
Experts (outside)	Experts	Historically strong reliance on experts
Information	Information	Necessary basis for participation
Outstanding manager/leader	Professional manager, knowledge and expertise, decisive, autonomous, strategic view, social skills, critical, communication skills, attitude toward subordinates, charisma	Mainly required: communication skills; knowledge and expertise
Power distance	Power distance	Considered too high, too many privileges for the rich, misuse of power
Role of the manager	Superior, team integrator, autocratic, diplomatic	Autocratic behaviour expected
Role of the subordinates	Employees as specialists	Many have not learnt and do not expect participation -> some behave like children
Organisation type	Organisation type	Small organisations/units -> more participation
Uncertainty avoidance	Uncertainty avoidance	Misuse of new freedom, there should be more stability; rules in place but make little sense, not respected and executed, frequent changes in legislation
Work values	Own way (creative), diplomatic, adaptability	Bundle of values influences participation

Finnish Data

Key categories of participation	Main codes	Remarks
Meaning of participation	Attitude toward participation, delegation, discussion, level of participation, co-operation, autonomy, see the bigger picture, common understanding, differing opinions	Participation within the context of autonomy; participation equals discussion; helps to see the bigger picture; means finding a common understanding about a problem and integrating differing opinions
Assumptions underlying participation	Autonomy, differing opinions, planning and implementation, change in attitude	Participation requires that some participants change their attitude; participation reduces managerial autonomy; listening to differing opinions increases decision quality
Who/what decides about the use of participation		Typically the manager
Enactment/form of participation	Enactment of participation, taking part in process and decision, discussion, one-on-one meeting, group meeting, fairness, autocratic	Mainly discussions; informal, when differing opinions (I); one-on-one meeting: to get honest opinions, for personal issues; group meeting: fair to the participants, shows that nothing has been decided beforehand; autocratic: accepted when understood
Responsible for decision and outcome	Responsible for decision and outcome	Discussion, but manager decides
Social range of participation	Range of participation	Not limited to subordinates, may include all who know best or are concerned
Types of problems/decisions	Work based on thinking, innovation, implementation, time-related issues, no-democracy area, unimportant/small issues, difficult problems, major implications, real problems, rational decisions, strategic decisions, personal issues, task-related issues, problems with uncertainties, routine decisions, planning and implementation, crisis situation	Participation not good in non-democratic areas (e.g. army) and for unimportant issues, problems without rational solutions, personal issues, crisis (not much time); good for: difficult problems, problems with major implications, problems where rational solution is possible, real problems, strategic decisions, planning decisions
Outcomes/effects of participation	Decision commitment, decision quality, planning and implementation	Commitment expected after subordinates participated; quality increases through participation

Related concepts	Main codes	Remarks
Autonomy	Autonomy, autonomous, individualism, delegation, hands-off management, work independently, clear responsibility	Preference for autonomy, yet participation needed when impact on others; requires clear responsibilities
Communication	Communication, feedback, discussion	Communication directly related to participation
(Organisational) rules	Unwritten rules, formal rules	Unwritten participation rules, e.g. those directly concerned participate; attitude toward rules related to communication - words are binding!
Individualism	Individualism, unknown soldier	Finns individualistic, yet society based on collectivist principles
Conflict	Conflict, dealing with conflict	Conflict over substance issues is normal
Experts (outside)	Experts	Involved whenever adding value
Information	Information	Participation make sense only when same information available to all
Learning	Learning from mistakes	Fits with autonomy thinking
Outstanding manager/leader	Facilitator, information, see the bigger picture, hands-off management, visionary, discussion, dealing with conflict, self confidence, work values, knowledge and expertise, role model	Should act as a facilitator (enable others to work independently), e.g. provide information and give feedback; participation integral part of managerial role: synthesis
Power distance	Power distance	Co-operation of equals rather than hierarchy; Finland young as a society, no established hierarchy
Role of the manager	See the bigger picture, upward delegation, superior, information, team integrator, hands-off management	Clear managerial responsibility, no upward delegation to superior; integrates work and opinions, gets informed rather than involved
Role of the subordinates	Work independently, employees as specialists, knowledge and expertise	Given freedom to work rather independently
Team	Team orientation, teamwork, unknown soldier, team integrator, natural team, team as support system,	Teamwork ok when natural team exists; teams work when one or two individuals take the lead; active team development not role of the manager
Trust	Trust	Trust related to autonomy and delegation
Uncertainty avoidance	Uncertainty avoidance	Rules should not threaten freedom, yet stability and security valued
Work values	Work values	Such as honesty and openness

German Data

Key categories of participation	Main codes	Remarks
Meaning of participation	Attitude toward participation, level of participation, influence by subordinates, responsible for decision and output, degree of participation, necessity for participation	Attitude that manager alone is responsible belongs to the past; consensus orientation important, does not imply weakness; participation is considered necessary rather than preferred
Assumptions underlying participation	Knowledge and expertise, team development, time of decision-making	Knowledge and team development both necessary basis for participation; participation should not paralyse the organisation; instrumental view yet incl. decision commitment, participation success factor for an organisation
Who/what decides about the use of participation	Participation initiative	Manager and/or organisation
Enactment/form of participation	Enactment of participation, group meeting, one-on-one meeting, autocratic, consensus, consultation, degree of participation, taking part in process and decision, time of decision making, delegate, explain autocratic behaviour	Participative structures, e.g. workshops; degree depends on people, needs and requirements; autocratic possible if trust and a priori information or ex post explanation; one-on-one to get open opinions (not hide behind the group); when team participates, also responsible for outcome
Social range of participation	Colleagues, employees directly concerned, range of participation	Mainly subordinates, also experts; depends on problem and sector
Types of problems/decisions	Work-related decisions, risk situations, difficult decisions, HR decisions, unstructured problems, safety decisions, strategic decisions, trivial problems, administrative decisions, complex decisions	All kinds of work-related decisions qualify for participation; HR decisions problematic
Outcomes/effects of participation	Decision quality, good decisions quickly, economic success, decision commitment, consensus, compromise	High decision quality; participation leads to motivation and decision commitment

Related concepts	Main codes	Remarks
(Organisational) rules	Formal rules, unwritten rules	Formal rules important to follow

Collectivism	Collectivism, teamwork	Team orientation highly important; economic system based on collectivist ideas (e.g. Mitbestimmung)
Communication	Communication	Structured format typical (e.g. Personalgespräche, Vorgesetztenfeedback)
Conflict	Conflict, dealing with conflict, contingency approach	Necessary to differentiate when to get involved; conflict considered natural, in particular in group work
Experts (outside)	Experts (outside group)	Consultants should be used only for support, e.g. to keep conflict out of the organisation
Industrial relations	Industrial relations	Co-operative relations with works council -> collectivism
Information	Information	Important for motivation; information collection = first stage of participation
Learning	Learning opportunity, team building, apprentice system	Structured forms of learning, e.g. workshops and "KVP"; learning from wrong decisions and superior
Motivation	Motivation	Manager responsible for motivating subordinates; motivation through participation
Outstanding manager/leader	Trust, decisive, personality, role model, goal orientation, social skills, take initiative, communication, economic success, responsive, attitude toward subordinates, team integrator, trust, flexibility	Highly relevant: strong goal orientation - different goals may lead to a decrease in participation
Power distance	Power distance, status, communism	Lack of power distance associated with communism and seen negatively
Role of the manager	Functioning team, good relations with team, goals, work independently, HR development, superior, team integrator, know each other well, long leash	Team builder and team integrator; lets you work independently; sets goals, manager need not know everything, can utilise participation
Role of the subordinates	Attitude toward subordinates, employees as specialists	Human capital that should be utilised; highly specialised; some need more directives than others
Team	Teamwork, team development, functioning team	Considered crucial; manager responsible for functioning team = basis for effective participation
Uncertainty avoidance	Uncertainty avoidance, flexibility	There should be more flexibility; too many regulations (DIN)
Work values	Discipline, honesty, equality and fairness, punctuality, responsibility, trust	Basis for good co-operation

Polish Data

Key categories of participation	Main codes	Remarks
Meaning of participation	Attitude toward participation, level of participation, attitude toward subordinates, information retrieval, pseudo participation, organisation type	Main purpose is to collect information; subordinates expect superior to show a certain degree of autocratic behaviour
Assumptions underlying participation	Information retrieval	Instrumental view; participation only when there is a special reason for it
Enactment/form of participation	Group meeting, one-on-one meeting, autocratic, consensus	Group preferred for different reasons: valuing opinions of team, information retrieval
Social range of participation	Range of participation	Limited to subordinates; experts and superior when viewed as providers of information
Types of problems/decisions	Small decisions, strategic decisions, work-related decisions, HR decisions, unpopular decisions, technical problems, hard decisions, time of decision making, controversial problem	Problem type influences decision strategy; when information is required or controversial problem = participation; in trivial cases = participation (unless conflict or considered waste of time (efficiency related), then autocratic).
Outcomes/effects of participation	Decision quality, efficiency/cost related, decision acceptance	Participation ensures a maximum of information and efficient decisions; decision acceptance guaranteed no matter whether participation is used or not

Related concepts	Main codes	Remarks
Power distance	Power distance, dependency	Considered high in Poland, assumed to be left-over of former political system; "bosses are like gods"
Former political system	Communist system, procedural	Made responsible for autocratic and procedural managerial behaviour
Current political and economic situation	Chaos, stability	Perception of chaos, longing for more stability = more uncertainty avoidance
Uncertainty avoidance/rules	Uncertainty avoidance, formal rules	Longing for more stability

Conflict	Potential conflict, dealing with conflict, dealing with emotions, time of decision making	Different strategies: More autocratic in case of conflict; more participative to retrieve information as basis for autocratic decision. No conflict avoidance, but autocratic behaviour to speed up decision-making
Industrial relations	Industrial relations	Unions considered hindering by one interviewee
Information	Knowledge, information retrieval, valuing opinions of team	Collecting information is an important reason for the use of participation
Outstanding manager/leader	Outstanding manager/leader, vision and charisma, innovative, decisive, knowledge and expertise, dealing with changes	Representative of economic success; judged by the standing of the company; needs to have knowledge and expertise; provides stability in a changing world; can handle change
Role of the subordinates	Attitude toward subordinates, aims manager vs. subordinates	Assumed to expect somewhat autocratic leadership; assumed to have goals other than manager/organisation; instrumental view
Role of the manager/image of own superior	Superior, autocratic, team integrator, dependency, economic success, efficiency/cost related, knowledge and expertise	Boss needs to show a certain degree of autocratic behaviour, high dependency on superior; responsible for efficiency and cost control; needs to have knowledge and expertise

Swedish Data

Key categories of participation	Main codes	Remarks
Meaning of participation	Attitude toward participation, help for the manager, difficulties related to participation, level of participation, participation as requirement	Generally very positive attitude toward participation
Assumptions underlying participation	Equality and fairness, personal growth and development, trust	Humanistic view
Enactment/form of participation	One-on-one meeting, group meeting, autocratic, delegate, empower, taking part in process and decision, explain decision, influence by subordinates, responsible for decision and outcome, participation as a burden, consensus, smooth meetings/decisions	Predominantly group or one-on-one meeting, depending on type of problem; decision-making process characterised by intensive dialogue; manager often officially responsible for final decision and outcome
Social range of participation	Subordinates, colleagues, experts (outside group)	Includes subordinates as well as colleagues, own superior, experts
Types of problems/decisions	Waste of time problem, work-related decision, personal issue, employees directly concerned, hard decision, easy decision, (un)important problem, known problem, new case, larger than unit problem, intra-unit problem, strategic decision	Problem type influences which decision strategy is used
Outcomes/effects of participation	Decision quality, decision acceptance, smooth	Participation ensures efficient decisions and keeps interpersonal relations balanced

Related concepts	Main codes	Remarks
Interpersonal relations	Smooth meetings/decisions, dealing with emotions, potential conflict, equality and fairness, explain decision, lagom, formal rules, give an example, rational reasons, win-win situation	Ideally "smooth" interpersonal relations
Communication	Communication skills, one-on-one meeting, group meeting, open discussion, talk on the side, convincing, explain decision	Intensive dialogue, non-confrontational

Power distance	Power distance, equality and fairness	Considered very low in Sweden; low level reflected in high level of participation
Collectivism	Collectivism, equality and fairness, lagom	High level of collectivism reflected in preference for participation and dialogue
Uncertainty avoidance/rules	Uncertainty avoidance, formal rules, unwritten rules, fairness	High level reflected in formal rules (often defined by group), which help to secure smooth interpersonal relations
Conflict	Potential conflict, dealing with conflict, smooth	Avoidance of open conflict, non-confrontation interaction as part of smooth interpersonal relations; conflict impacts on decision strategy
Information	Knowledge, experience, information, experts (outside group), employees as specialists	Essential for effective participation
Outstanding manager/leader	Outstanding manager/leader, team integrator, collaborative team orientation, communication skills, approachable, decisive, autonomous, gives an example, prestige, stands up (for people), vision and charisma	Corresponds with image of own superior
Role of the manager/image of own superior	Superior, team integrator, autonomous, communication skills, approachable, lagom, handling performance problems, work independently	Manager as team integrator and responsible person for "smooth" decision-making and interpersonal relations in general; should not stick out too much, should give credit to the group; lets people work independently

Peter Lang · Europäischer Verlag der Wissenschaften

Jože Florjančič / Björn Paape (eds.)

Personnel and Management: Selected Topics

Frankfurt am Main, Berlin, Bern, Bruxelles, New York, Oxford, Wien, 2005.
492 pp., num. fig. and tab.
ISBN 3-631-53261-X / US-ISBN 0-8204-7390-1 · pb. € 74.50*

The book *Personnel and Management: Selected Topics* is a collection of various essays focusing on one the most topical problems in this field of research. The authors are well aware of the fact that this book presents only some individual topical chapters dealing with the issues of human resources and management. Nonetheless, they are convinced that this material can also have a significant impact on the deliberations about the development theory as well as its practical application in a given situation. The book has been published as the result of a long-term cooperation between the Faculty of Organizational Sciences of the University of Maribor, the Faculty of Economics of the University of Aachen and the European Centre of Integration Research (EZI) e.V., Aachen.

Contents: Management · Personnel

Frankfurt am Main · Berlin · Bern · Bruxelles · New York · Oxford · Wien
Distribution: Verlag Peter Lang AG
Moosstr. 1, CH-2542 Pieterlen
Telefax 00 41 (0) 32 / 376 17 27

*The €-price includes German tax rate
Prices are subject to change without notice
Homepage http://www.peterlang.de